The Goldsteins'
Wellness & Longevity
Program
Natural Care for Dogs and Cats

Robert S. Goldstein, V.M.D.

Susan J. Goldstein

"With the perfect balance of wisdom and compassion, Dr. Bob and Susan Goldstein lay before us the ultimate guide to wellness and longevity for our animal companions. In a world that often seems soulless, they stand as an example that faith, hope, love, and commitment are alive and well."

—*Sharon Callahan, author of* Healing Animals Naturally With Flower Essences *and* Intuitive Listening

"…this book is an incredible compilation of data, experience and knowledge. It will remain on and regularly be used from my bookshelf, as it should yours. Well done, Dr. Bob and Susan, for your work and dedication with this!"

—*Marty Goldstein, DVM, Director of the Smith Ridge Veterinary Center and author of* The Nature *of* Animal Healing

"From cancer to arthritis, cataracts to kidney stones, obesity to heart disease, this is the best guide available for your animal companion. Dr. Goldstein is the Dr. Spock for your pet; his advice is timely, scientifically based, and the best help that your pet can get."

—*Gary Null, PhD*

"Dr. Bob and Susan Goldstein have given us a text that opens the door to better health…by applying tools that raise the immune system's effectiveness, they have improved pets' chances for better vitality and longevity… Now the Goldsteins make their workable theories and practical tools widely known so veterinarians and their clients have a road map to health. Personally, I could not be more grateful."

—*Richard Palmquist, DVM, Chief of Medical Services at the Centinela Animal Hospital, Inglewood, CA*

"Susan and Robert Goldstein are pragmatic geniuses. This book offers such a wealth of useable information and guidance. The Goldstein Food Plan is a perfect example. The Goldsteins are extremely knowledgeable in the field of pet nutrition and clearly inform us about ideal nutrition. Yet, realizing the reality of pet owners' lives, they have presented a practical way of feeding pets for optimal health without running out of time and money."

—**Gerald M. Buchoff**, BVScAH, *President of the American Holistic Veterinary Medical Association*

⌀

"An excellent, informative, balanced collection of important veterinary issues concerning integrative medicine, this book is a 'must read' for any practicing veterinarian or animal companion owner. I have the greatest admiration for Dr. Goldstein and Susan. They have given us a wealth of knowledge long overdue."

—**Dan R. Kirby**, DVM, *owner of the Alamo Heights Pet Clinic, Inc., San Antonio, TX*

⌀

"*The Goldsteins' Wellness & Longevity Program* is a comprehensive foray into complementary strategies that should be implemented by owners and practitioners desiring to promote abundant living from birth until "letting go" of our beloved companions. The text chronicles the transition from the Western medicine trained mindset to a broader viewpoint encompassing a gamut of holistic approaches, including nutrition, Chinese medicine and herbs, homeopathy, homotoxicology, and supplements. It can be read cover to cover, and also serve as a quick reference text for useful adjunctive or first-line therapies. It is a 'must read' for those desiring a fuller spectrum of information for modalities now available to help us maintain our pets longer and with greater vitality."

—**Paula Jo Broadfoot**, DVM, *practitioner, national lecturer, and veterinary consultant for Heel, Inc.*

⌀

"The Goldsteins' book offers an informative, comprehensive, and easy-to-understand manual that teaches people how to evaluate their pets' diets, vaccination histories, and emotional states, so they can make better choices regarding their care—the best resource of its kind out there!"

—**Marc Morrone**, *host of the television series* Petkeeping with Marc Morrone

The Goldsteins' Wellness & Longevity Program

Project Team

Editors: Heather Russell-Revesz, Roberta Jo Liberman, Dominiqe De Vito

Copy Editor: Carl Schutt

Design: Cándida Moréira Tómassini

Cover photos courtesy of Isabelle Francais ; Back cover courtesy of Mary Bloom

T.F.H. Publications

President/CEO: Glen S. Axelrod

Executive Vice President: Mark E. Johnson

Publisher: Christopher T. Reggio

Production Manager: Kathy Bontz

T.F.H. Publications, Inc.
One TFH Plaza
Third and Union Avenues
Neptune City, NJ 07753

Library of Congress Cataloging-in-Publication Data

Goldstein, Robert S., 1942-
The Goldsteins' wellness & longevity program / Robert S. Goldstein and Susan Goldstein.
p. cm.
Includes index.
ISBN 0-7938-0545-7 (alk. paper)
  1. Dogs-Diseases-Alternative treatment. 2. Cats-Diseases-Alternative treatment. 3. Dogs-Health.
  4. Cats-Health. 5. Holistic veterinary medicine. I. Title: Goldsteins' guide to wellness and
  longevity for dogs and cats. II. Goldstein, Susan, 1947- III. Title.
SF991.G64 2005
636.7'08955--dc22
2005000109

This book has been published with the intent to provide accurate and authoritative information in regard to the subject matter within. While every precaution has been taken in preparation of this book, the author and publisher expressly disclaim responsibility for any errors, omissions, or adverse effects arising from the use or application of the information contained herein. The techniques and suggestions are used at the reader's discretion and are not to be considered a substitute for veterinary care. If you suspect a medical problem, consult your veterinarian.

www.tfhpublications.com

Dedication

To the One who created animals in the first place

To our daughters Abbey and Merritt who continue to share our lives as pioneers

To our family and friends

To the light beams at Earth Animal and Healing Center for Animals—past, present, and future

To Jack and Vivienne and Annie who watch over us from K9 Heaven

To Leigh, the K9 founder of our work and the other animals who touched our lives as family members: Emily, Christy, Sadie, Christopher, Penny, and Mogul

To MacMillan and Gershwin—"because if you keep love in your heart I am told there will come one day to stay a singing bird"

To Sharon Callahan, our mentor and the animals' true angel

To John Harricharan for *When You Can Walk on Water, Take the Boat*

To the late Dr. Lawrence Burton and Dr. Elizabeth Kubler Ross

To John Mancinelli for his dedicated support in the writing of the book

To our publisher and friend Dominique DeVito for her unconditional support and vision

To Heather Russell-Revesz and Roberta Jo Lieberman our editors—heartfelt thanks

To our late parents Ruth and Irving, Dottie and Dave

To Pookie and Jack-Harry

And to the fellow colleagues and healers who dare to swim against the tides for kinder and gentler ways of practicing veterinary medicine, especially our brother Dr. Marty Goldstein

To the thousands of patients that we've known and loved and their guardians

And finally to our loyal *Love of Animals* readers.

Table of Contents

Foreword

I have had the pleasure of working closely with the Goldsteins over the past several years. This book is a reflection of their true dedication and compassion for our most beloved friends. Being a Secular Franciscan, a follower of St. Francis of Assisi, I have a particular love for the animal kingdom and find great pleasure in helping animals with herbs and nutrition. I believe the love we give and receive from our pets is one of the most profound ways we can experience the love of God. Interestingly, animals naturally gravitate towards herbs when they are sick, as if they somehow know they need them. It also happens that they respond so well to them. Herbal and nutritional medicine should be foundational for animals for both prevention and treatment of disease, and the Goldsteins' book provides a comprehensive guide on selecting the best remedies.

Being a "wholistic" practitioner, the first and foremost objective in working with patients, human and animal alike, is to attain quality of life and longevity; thus, the title of this book is fitting. I believe and concur with the Goldsteins that by improving the ability to adapt and respond to life's changes in the healthiest way, using gentle, natural therapies, wellness and longevity can be attained. This is quite different from the Western allopathic medical model of diagnosis and treatment of symptoms with medications and vaccinations that are simply functional and suppress the innate ability to heal. The same is true of conventional veterinary practice. When it comes to the treatment, management, and prevention of a chronic illness, conventional medicine fails to consider some critical aspects of healing. Noninvasive traditional healing systems encompass a much greater understanding of chronic illness and are thus more therapeutic, utilizing such approaches as diet, acupuncture, and herbs. The underlying fundamental philosophy of traditional medicine utilizes herbs as a vital component for chronic illness, as well as acute illness, and is directed at promoting health and harmony by addressing and removing the cause along with enhancing the constitution and vitality of the animal.

You will find that in this book the Goldsteins' approach resonates with my own, which is to first create harmony and balance and to optimize the vital response, which to me is working in cooperation with the vital force. I build my protocols based on a philosophy of strengthening the whole person or in this case, the animal, from within. This is in alignment with the approach of Traditional Chinese Medicine and with what the western traditional healing medical systems (Eclectic and Physiomedical) referred to as the "vitalistic concept."

Within my practice, a constant theme amongst all the people I have worked with is stress, both obvious and hidden. The majority of people live in an artificial environment filled with a diversity of stresses; therefore, animals are also inadvertently exposed to a variety of toxic chemicals in our home and recreational environments throughout the day and night. Today, as a result of the coupling of our ego and advances in modern technology, we can change the natural environment virtually at will. Just think for a moment about what the average pet eats. Food is genetically modified and is grown using pesticides and herbicides. Then it is loaded with preservatives and rancid fats, refined, and heavily processed. Think about the synthetic materials in our homes and lawns. All this is mixed with enormous mental and emotional stress. We try to vaccinate against every possible pathogen, knowing quite well that this is impossible. And what are the consequences?

Prolonged stress leads to suppressed activity of antioxidant systems and reduced immune function. The combination of stress, routine use of vaccinations, and poor diet, overrides our adaptive capacity. This is the number one cause and effect of most conditions and diseases both humans and animals suffer from and can also be attributed to the increased cancer epidemic. It is astonishing to me how many pets are coming down with cancer at a young age. Being a specialist in integrative oncology utilizing herbal and nutritional medicine, I strongly encourage people to start their pets on a good program of healthy food, adaptogenic herbs, and specific nutritional compounds for the prevention of cancer and other diseases, and for the promotion of health that the Goldsteins so strongly recommend in this book.

By following the Goldsteins' Food Plan and suggestions, and providing adaptogenic herbs, adequate phytonutrients, essential fatty acids, amino acids, minerals, and living foods, you can help ensure a healthier, longer, and more vital life for your pets, free of disease and degenerative conditions that are so common. I cannot emphasize enough the importance of recognizing quality when making dietary and supplement choices in the marketplace. This without a doubt will determine the measurement of benefits and results you see. In this book, you will find a wealth of information to help you make informed decisions on what supplements to use and what brands to buy for a wide range of conditions. Our pets rely on us as caretakers, and this is the most essential resource to have in providing them with the best of health and loving care.

Bob and Susan's many years of successful practice have established them as true pioneers of natural veterinary medicine. They have made a commendable contribution to this field through both their clinical and literary work. This book is written with compassionate guidance in a way that is easy to understand and makes implementing a nutritious pet program convenient and simple, even for those with the busiest lifestyles. I consider it a tremendous gift and valuable resource for optimizing the health and happiness of our most beloved animals.

Donald Yance, master herbalist and author of *Herbal Medicine, Healing and Cancer: A Comprehensive Program for Prevention and Treatment*

Introduction

We have had a deep love of animals our entire lives. It's something that we share fundamentally with each other, our children, our friends, our veterinary clients, our newsletter subscribers, and now you, the readers of our book. Early in our careers, we assumed that Dr. Bob's veterinary training combined with Susan's experience in helping animal guardians were all we needed to make a difference in the lives of the animals we pledged to protect. Yet, instinctively, we knew there had to be more options available for keeping animals healthy.

We began our journey studying with mentors such as Dr. Lawrence Burton, founder of Immuno-Augmentative Therapy (IAT), Dr. Elisabeth Kübler-Ross, founder of the "Death and Dying" movement, and Dr. Bernard Jensen, an expert in alternative healing methods. We hungrily read books on alternative treatments for degenerative diseases and cancer written by pioneers such as Drs. Max Gerson, Josef Issels, Donald Kelly, and Hans Neiper. These true visionaries of alternative medicine opened our eyes to the possibility of treating animals outside of conventional methods. As a result, their work formed the basis for ours with animals.

To understand what we do, it's important to know the perceived similarities and differences in veterinary practice methods. The majority of veterinarians practicing today are allopathic—conventionally trained to use the diagnostic tools, vaccinations, and medical and surgical protocols learned in veterinary school. While the majority of conventional veterinarians are in private practice, the rise in degenerative diseases and the availability of sophisticated diagnostic equipment has necessitated the creation of veterinary specialty and referral centers. These centers house board certified doctors who focus on specialty areas such as surgery, oncology, internal medicine, and dermatology. Allopathic veterinarians are generally focused upon disease diagnosis and treatment, as well as the control of the associated symptoms and side effects.

When defining holistic veterinarians, things get confusing. Terms such as holistic, alternative, complementary, and homeopathic are used interchangeably by guardians and veterinarians, often leading to misunderstanding and a breakdown in communications. Alternative medicine is comprised of a diverse group of therapies typically not taught in medical schools (although several US veterinary colleges have begun offering classes in alternative treatments). Alternative therapies may augment or replace conventional medical therapy using modalities such as Western or Chinese herbal medicine, homeopathy, homotoxicology, acupuncture, chiropractic, therapeutic nutrition, and energy medicine.

The skeptics of holistic veterinary therapies cite the lack of scientific, evidence-based proof and the avoidance of a thorough medical history, physical examination, clinical diagnosis, and recommendation of the accepted medical therapies as the basis for their disbelief. A perfect example of an alternative treatment method that fuels skepticism is classical homeopathy. This form of alternative therapy has its own set of standards and remedies that do not rely upon nor work well with conventional diagnosis and medical treatments.

While debate rages in both holistic and allopathic circles, we believe there is really only one veterinary medicine—making available to animal patients many different treatment options based upon the experience of the doctor and the choices of the animal's guardian.

With this in mind we'd like to introduce you to Integrative Veterinary Medicine (IVM), which combines natural and alternative approaches with conventional diagnostic and treatment methods for the benefit of the patient. For example, an integrative veterinarian would advise the use of antibiotics for an animal with a serious bacterial infection. This same veterinarian may also administer herbs, nutritional supplements, and homeopathics to support the animal's natural defenses and minimize potential side effects of the drug. This is the veterinary medicine that we write about, embrace, and practice.

There are many factions in the veterinary community and divisions within each faction. It is our feeling that integrative veterinary medicine can help build a bridge between the "them versus us" mentality of conventional and holistic veterinarians. We ask, "Why not use the best of both worlds— take advantage of new medical discoveries and advanced diagnostic tools, while simultaneously utilizing the natural therapies that have worked for centuries?"

We ask these questions because today, the health of your companion is increasingly in jeopardy. Like thousands of veterinarians across the country, we're experiencing younger animals suffering from chronic diseases, that 15 years ago occurred exclusively in the very old. Cancer is nearly epidemic, and is the leading cause of death in dogs. Puppies and kittens as young as 6 months of age suffer from kidney, liver, and heart disease. And, as with humans, obesity and its related health complications are commonplace among our canine and feline companions.

We've dedicated ourselves to both healing companion animals and educating guardians. We've been privileged to witness miraculous healing powers at our Healing Center for Animals and our retail store Earth Animal, which provides many of the natural remedies discussed in this book.

Now we are thrilled to share our life's work with you and your friend. Concerned people walk into Earth Animal every day struggling to comprehend why their animals are experiencing chronic health disorders and emotional problems. They are confused by the number of drugs and vaccines prescribed by their veterinarians, and disheartened at how rapidly their animals are showing the degenerative signs of aging.

None of this is hopeless, however. With our easy-to-implement program, you can build a healthier, more wholesome and vibrant life for your dog or cat in just a few short weeks! It's our mission to help very sick animals, but it's our vision to show you how to prevent disease and restore superb health by focusing on wellness. Each step in our program is simple, proven, and practical. We'll tell you everything you need to know along the way. As you go through our book, keep a highlighter pen handy to make notes and circle important points.

Few things are more enjoyable than spending time with a dog or cat who is vital and has a glistening coat and bright eyes. We know that you want nothing less than a long, healthy, love-filled life for your animal, and we share your goals. Together, you and your dog or cat are about to embark upon an exciting journey of discovery. Join us with an open mind and heart, and get ready to watch your animal glow in good health.

Diet: Redesign the Blueprint for Your Animal's Health

We began our journey in the early 1970s, when little attention was paid to the importance of a nutritious diet and the role it plays in an animal's quality of life and longevity. In the early years of our veterinary practice, over 35 years ago, we were frustrated and disillusioned. Our office was a revolving door for ever-sick dogs and cats—young ones, old ones, different breeds—it didn't seem to matter. "There must be more to veterinary medicine than this," we told ourselves. "There must be a better way to return these animals to health than to wait for a sick animal to show up and then do little more than medicate their symptoms."

Our personal epiphany came as a result of an experience we had with our dog, Leigh. Leigh was a Golden Retriever trained by the Guiding Eyes for the Blind in Yorktown Heights, New York, where we lived and operated our first veterinary clinic. During the years between 1970 and 1977, Leigh became our dog "son," teacher, and founder of our work. Leigh had been diagnosed with hip dysplasia, a condition that often leads to crippling, degenerative arthritis and shortened life expectancy.

By seven years of age, Leigh was already beginning to lose mobility. He was no longer responding to conventional veterinary care of painkillers and anti-inflammatory medication; cortisone treatments were no longer keeping him comfortable. Faced with the painful dilemma of choosing invasive hip surgery—highly risky due to Leigh's advanced arthritis—or euthanasia, we sought another path.

Susan had been volunteering with the Foundation for Alternative Cancer Therapies (FACT), a group in New York City that helps people locate complementary cancer therapies. It was part of her

Getting Started: Tips for a Healthy Animal

- Toss out those plastic feed and water bowls and replace them with ceramic or stainless steel. Plastic bowls can leach petrochemicals into the water and can irritate the membranes around the mouth, causing irritation and depigmentation of the nose.
- Offer fresh, pure drinking water daily. A water filter is your best bet, but if you purchase bottled water, be sure to store it in glass containers and keep refrigerated. If you live within 100 miles of a nuclear power plant, consider a reverse osmosis water-processing unit. You should remove the water bowl 30 to 60 minutes before and after feeding to allow the stomach acids to do their work.

mission to honor her mother's request to help find a cure for this most-feared disease before her premature death at the age of 41. It didn't take us long to notice that all of the alternative dietary therapies for human cancer patients relied on enzyme-rich, nutrient-dense, uncooked foods and juices. If such a diet worked for people, we wondered, why not animals?

The light bulb snapped on and soon we were in the kitchen, preparing fresh meats and chicken, cooking up pots of whole grains, grating carrots, celery and parsley, extracting fresh carrot and celery juices, drizzling small amounts of olive and fish oil, and adding vitamins and minerals from our local health food store. We topped it all off with distilled water designed to flush inactive decaying minerals from the joints. Our beloved dog responded dramatically. Leigh's turnaround and healing led to his long life (to age 17)—and to our life's work.

Leigh and the other chronically ailing animals in our practice did so well that we began recommending better nutrition for other patients who had milder complaints, such as dull fur, frequent infections, itchy skin, or simply a lack of vitality. The results were stunning: sluggish dogs and cats moved with new ease, dander disappeared, eyes sparkled, energy returned. Along with our brother Marty Goldstein, veterinarian and author of *The Nature of Animal Healing*, and a handful of fellow veterinarians and health-care professionals, we began to challenge and change the way animals had been fed for the last 40 years.

Back then, you see, most people believed that their animal's nutritional needs could be met by opening up a bag, can, or cellophane bag of any brand of pet food sitting on their grocery store shelves. As part of this deeply rooted, marketing-driven belief system, folks were routinely chided to never give table scraps to their animals and were assured that any sort of vitamin and mineral supplementation was unnecessary because of a magical process called fortification.

Madison Avenue had folks eating out of their hand. They had been convinced that the "complete and balanced" ingredients in the bag met their animal's dietary needs. Although this "official" analysis revealed the levels of protein, fat, minerals, and moisture in a food, it paid no attention to the quality of the source. As far as food producers were concerned, a protein was a protein, whether it came from beef or shoe leather, from chicken or feathers.

Perpetuating an Illusion of Health

Pet food companies managed to perpetuate this illusion through the early 1970s while companion animal health steadily continued to degenerate. Cancer, kidney and liver disease, allergies, and arthritis became rampant among pets. What took so long for folks to recognize was that these and many other degenerative conditions are connected in a large way to diet. Other culprits, such as genetics, environmental and household toxins, overvaccination, medication, and emotional stress would also play out their roles in this drama.

Fifty years ago, most dogs and cats dined on farm-fresh meats, fertile raw eggs, dairy, and produce—all free of pesticides, hormones, and antibiotics. Grandma's wholesome communal soups and stews were the staple for both animals and humans. Then along came the commercial pet food industry. The "modern" companion animal diet would be based almost entirely on human food chain wastes and by-products, including those classified as "4-D"—animals that are dead, dying, diseased, or disabled and therefore not considered fit for human consumption.

"Guaranteed Analysis": What Does it Really Mean?

Pioneering veterinarian Dr. Mark Morris, founder of the Hills Pet Food Company, demonstrated that pet foods are assessed by their chemical content (the actual levels of fats, proteins, vitamins, and minerals), rather than their biological content (the ingredients used to achieve these nutrient levels). This is done by the Guaranteed Analysis, listed on the label of all pet foods. To qualify as a pet food, the following four categories must be listed on the label. A typical guaranteed analysis required to qualify as a canned pet food may look like this:

Crude Protein   10%
Crude Fat   6.5%
Crude Fiber   2.4%
Moisture   68%

But what constitutes those levels? As it happens, almost anything. Dr. Morris's blend, which qualifies for the above "guaranteed analysis," used these four ingredients:

- 1 pail crushed coal (carbohydrates)
- 1 gallon crankcase oil (fat)
- 4 pair old leather work shoes (protein)
- 68 lbs water (moisture)

His goal was to dramatize that what's important in pet food is not the chemical composition but the raw ingredients. The tag line on a popular brand of food reads: "The ingredient panel and chemical analysis on dog food labels are not guarantees of nutritional quality."

As manufacturing technology evolved, the pet food industry continued promoting highly cooked foods composed of rendered and rejected meat by-products; low-grade, milled bits of grains; synthetic vitamins and minerals; chemical additives, preservatives, artificial flavor enhancers, and dyes and coloring agents.

What we learned when we began delving into commercially prepared food surprised us:

- Most pet food is cooked at extremely high temperatures (actually sterilized—sometimes above 350°F), destroying most, if not all, of the living enzymes and most of the nutritional value that might have once been there. These high temperatures destroy bacterial contamination and extend the shelf life of the food (just like the pasteurization of milk extends its shelf life but destroys most of the benefits of the milk). Raw foods contain vital nutrients not present in cooked foods.

- What passes for protein is often unsavory by-products derived from animal sources that have been rejected for human consumption. These protein sources can also contain by-products such as feathers, beaks, cartilage, lungs and other highly indigestible materials, such as poultry fat made from rejected chicken parts.

- Pet foods also contain by-products of grains such as wheat and corn that have been grown with chemical fertilizers and sprayed with pesticides. Wheat middlings, brewers rice and soybean meal, which make up the bulk of many pet foods, are really the bits and pieces of stalks, bran layers, outer coverings, fines, and broken grains that cannot be sold for human consumption.

- Most pet foods use rendered (highly cooked) poultry or beef fat. These fats are also derived from 4-D sources and require (especially in dry foods) harsh preservatives such as ethoxyquin to prevent the fats from being oxidized and becoming rancid.

This long-running dietary debacle is one of the main sources of a great deal of disease and suffering in companion animals today. The then multi-million dollar, now multi-billion dollar contrived message to abandon feeding fresh foods to companion animals may have worked successfully to sell a lot of commercial pet foods and build a powerful industry, but tragically it also led to the downfall of our beloved animals' health and quality of life.

The truth about pet foods finally began to surface as more and more animals became sick. Immune systems were compromised and animals began to suffer from chronic, degenerative diseases including arthritis, diabetes, kidney failure, cancer, skin diseases, and allergies. Over the past 50 years, pet food companies somehow made it okay to source, manufacture, and sell meat and chicken rejected for human consumption. Those reaping the profits of this action did not make the connection that what's morally and ethically right for humans is also right for animals, and what's wrong for people is also wrong for animals.

Despite this unsavory history, the good news is that you can control your animal's diet, and once the light bulb clicks on, you will have choices and a clear path to follow.

Pottenger's Cats

The famous Pottenger Cat Study, done from 1932–1942 by Francis Pottenger, MD, clearly demonstrated the deleterious effects of feeding overcooked, life-force devoid foods—and then went on to convincingly prove the health-giving effects of a natural, raw diet.

Dr. Pottenger astutely noticed that his research cats were becoming weaker with each generation despite being fed what he and his colleagues believed to be the best possible diet: cooked meat scraps obtained from a sanitarium (including liver, beef, tripe, and sweetbreads—all fed to human patients), along with market-grade milk and cod liver oil. Pottenger became perplexed that his cats were poor surgical candidates and were beginning to show classical signs of nutritional deficiencies. The cats were producing fewer kittens, and the survivors were being born with skeletal deformities and organ malformations—in short, a degenerative state. Their lifespan also was dramatically shortened.

As his research program expanded and outgrew the supply of cooked sanitarium meats, Pottenger approached a local meat packing plant and secured a supply of raw meat scraps consisting of muscle, organs, and bone. This ration was fed to a segregated group of cats and, in a matter of months, these cats appeared in better health than the cats being fed the cooked ration. Also, their kittens appeared much healthier and did much better in surgery. The contrast between raw and cooked diets was so dramatic that Pottenger designed a formal protocol to study the cats. Over a ten year period, he observed the following:

- Cats fed the raw food diet looked and felt better, were never sick, and always produced strong, robust kittens.
- Cats fed the cooked diets were always sick, died younger, and gave birth to weak and deformed kittens.
- Over three generations of feeding cooked foods, the mother cats could no longer give birth. When cats were changed to the raw food diet, their health and reproductive ability was renewed. The only variables used in his clinical experiments were the food and its processing.

Dr. Pottenger's study says it all. Now, what does all of this mean for your animal? Let's fast-forward to modern times and translate Pottenger's findings into our own situation. Just like Pottenger, we are seeing chronic degenerative diseases earlier and earlier in the lives of our animals. The problems experienced by his cooked-food cats are remarkably similar to today's cats having heart, liver, kidney, thyroid, and bladder diseases as well as bone and central nervous system diseases. Cancer, arthritis, and chronic skin problems are all quite common and some are epidemic.

A New Landscape of Nutritional Choices

As a result of growing awareness, the landscape of nutritional choices for animals has changed dramatically over the past decade. Certain segments of the pet food industry finally began to improve the ingredients and expand into producing so-called "premium" foods, riding the wave into the natural-foods market. Whole wheat, brown rice, and whole turkey and chicken began showing up on labels, replacing wheat middlings, brewer's rice, and chicken by-product meal. "Naturally preserved" kibble began to replace foods laced with ethoxyquin and BHT, two controversial preservatives believed to be linked to cancer. Innovatively formulated supplements containing unheated, naturally derived vitamins, minerals, cofactors, essential fatty acids, and nutrients came onto the scene replacing cheap, inorganic minerals.

Thanks to consumer pressure and healthy competition, many of the players are cleaning up their acts, but most have a long way to go. We hope you will understand that our purpose has never been to "knock" a particular company. Our mission is to educate and enlighten in an effort to avoid more heartbreak. We also offer our help to open-minded pet food companies, and have been taken up on this offer several times.

A rapidly growing movement of concerned animal-people advocates feed balanced, raw diets to their dogs and cats. Broadly classified as BARF (Bones and Raw Foods), these diets attempt to mimic what wild cats (lions and tigers) and wild dogs (wolves) eat in the wild. The theory is that because of their diet, wild animals do not appear to suffer from cancer and other serious degenerating diseases.

The First Health Food Store —For Animals!

Back in 1979, Susan saw the need to open the first true health food store for animals. Inspired by a visualization of a vibrant cat licking his jowls, contented and full bellied, Susan called her shop "Lick Your Chops." Located in a 60-square-foot space, she blended healthy and raw individual ingredients. She then mixed up diets specific to each animal's needs. It was museum-like—folks could see, touch, and feel all the nutrient components in food, such as fresh whole grains and vegetables, and individual vitamins and minerals. It was a very visual experience, which led to quite a following. It has always been Susan's fantasy to open a pet food manufacturing plant that would be open to the public 24 hours a day. Imagine pawprints on a highway leading to the kind of place where the pet food company is so proud of its ingredients and results that all are welcome!

We were introduced to this concept over three decades ago by Juliette de Barclay Levy, a pioneer in the healing effects of feeding raw diets and herbs to domestic animals. Later in this chapter, we will spend a little more time with raw foods and direct you to the proper resources, so that if you are inclined, you can properly put together and balance a raw-food diet plan. In our experience, however, and at the request of thousands of clients and *Love of Animals* subscribers, we find that in this fast-paced world, many folks simply do not have the time or the motivation to embrace the raw food concept. Thirteen billion dollars per year are spent on processed (canned and dry) dog and cat food. This is why we developed the Goldstein Food Plan—an amazing, simple method of enhancing commercial dog and cat foods with essential nutrients and living foods.

Introducing the Goldstein Food Plan

We've seen our share of heartbreaking cases through our 35 years of practice. But over and over again, we see health restored once animals are switched to a high-quality diet and antioxidant-, vitamin-, and mineral-rich program. We'll never forget Brandy, an English Springer Spaniel with one of the worst cases of skin disease we'd ever seen. Within a few weeks on the Goldstein Food Plan, Brandy looked and felt like a new dog. Then there was Chica, an eight-year-old Pomeranian who rebounded from a liver crisis after she was introduced to natural foods, daily vitamins, and fresh vegetables...and these are just two of hundreds of success stories in our files.

Your dog or cat, regardless of age or health status, can also benefit. Just follow the Goldstein Food Plan and you'll see results in what seems like no time at all: more energy, healthier coat and skin, bright eyes, and most importantly, a strong immune system.

We've divided our Food Plan into three levels for convenience and simplicity. We'll take you step by step through the three levels and show you how each one will benefit your favorite four-footed friend. Ready to get started? Let's go!

The Goldstein Food Plan

Level I:
Switch your animal to a premium-quality, natural "base" food.

Level II:
Add a vitamin/mineral/antioxidant-rich supplement along with essential omega-3 and -6 fatty acids, and fresh vegetables.

Level III:
Incorporate healthy protein-rich "people food" and other healing recipes into your animal's daily meals.

Level I: Switch to a Natural Brand of Pet Food

Every year, we research and analyze the labels of leading brands of premium dog and cat foods, both canned and dry, then make a list of those that meet our approval. Learn how to rate your dog's or cat's base food starting on page 16.

Hopefully, after rating your animal's food, it falls in an acceptable range. If it does, that's great—stick with it. If your current choice is not rated high enough to be considered acceptable, do your research until you find a brand with all the nutrition your dog or cat needs.

Here are the standards we use for deciding what foods are in the top-notch category for optimal health:

- High-quality protein is the key. For dogs 18 months of age or older, we advise feeding as a base food a senior or "lite" formula that is made with chicken, beef, lamb, or turkey (listed on the label as one of the first four ingredients). Make sure the protein is not a by-product or a "meal," which often includes rejected meats and waste parts.

- Added vegetable or fish oil rather than highly processed saturated animal fats. Even though animals digest fats more efficiently than we humans can (which protects them from our higher risk of clogged arteries), highly saturated cooked animal fats like poultry fat and beef tallow can congest the skin, lungs, and liver, and deposit fat throughout the body. The addition of vegetable-derived oils, such as flax, sesame, and fish oils, add the required omega-3 and -6 acids that are almost totally devoid when the food contains only chicken or beef fat.

- Whole grains (preferably organic), with their fiber and nutrients intact. Stay away from sources that include grain by-products such as wheat middlings, bakery fines, brewer's rice, and white or wheat flour, which have had most of the nutrients processed right out of them and are loaded with simple sugars that stress many of the digestive organs.

- Fruits and vegetables for flavor and nutrition, instead of refined salt and sugars. Many premium foods now include blueberries, sweet potatoes, carrots, and other healthy ingredients that are far superior to artificial sweeteners. One word of caution: If you supplement with fresh fruit, it is always important to feed fruit alone. The sugar content in many fresh fruits mixed with the protein in the food can often ferment in an animal's intestines, causing gas and incomplete digestion.

- Natural preservatives, such as vitamins E and C, and the herb rosemary, rather than chemical additives such as ethoxyquin, BHA, BHT, propylene glycol, or propylene gallate. Despite a growing body of evidence that chemical preservatives are harmful, adding them to pet foods is still an industry standard. Chemical preservatives and additives can lead to skin allergies, regurgitation after meals, hyperactivity, mood swings, and aggressiveness. These conditions quickly disappear once the chemicals are removed from the diet. (By the way, tocopherol is the chemical name for vitamin E, one of the natural antioxidants and preservatives that are okay in your animal's dry base food.)

By switching to a natural, premium food and following the rest of our guidelines, you'll strengthen your animal's immune system and boost overall health. Within about 21 days, you should be able to sit back and admire how much better your dog or cat looks and feels.

Although switching to a better food makes a big difference, we highly recommend that you incorporate Level II into your animal's daily diet. This is especially important for those of you who have senior animals or one with any type of chronic condition like arthritis, chronic skin disease, or digestive upsets such as chronic diarrhea.

Level II: Supplement the Basic Diet for Powerful Protection

Although the new generation of premium natural foods is a vast improvement over the supermarket generics, here's the catch: All commercially available pet foods, even those brands formulated as "all-natural" or "organic" are cooked at high temperatures, destroying many of the naturally occurring vitamins, phytonutrients, antioxidants, and virtually all of the precious enzymes. These vital, "life-force" nutrients are found only in raw food. (For more about raw-food diets, see page 20.)

Adding a food-derived vitamin and mineral supplement is quite different from the poor quality highly cooked vitamins and minerals that are added to "enrich" most commercial pet foods. The Resources section has a recommened list of food-derived multiple vitamin and mineral combinations.

It's easy crossing the bridge from Level I to II. When you can't cook every day—and let's face it, not everyone has the time—you can rest assured that there will be no gaps in your dog's or cat's diet; achieve this by simply adding a food-derived, uncooked multiple vitamin/mineral combination, along with antioxidant- and phytonutrient-rich vegetables.

Don't Forget the Fresh Veggies!

Believe it or not, your dog (and even your finicky cat) will chow down on salad. You can improve your dog's health rapidly by offering grated organic carrots and some of your leftover chopped greens. (Some say a carrot a day keeps the veterinarian away!) An easy way to do this is to share some of your salad (minus the dressing) with your friend. Antioxidant-rich organic carrots are our favorites, but almost any vegetable will do—try spinach, celery, asparagus, or string beans. We also recommend watercress, parsley, and dandelion and beet greens. Feed one or more of these with meals or as snacks daily—if possible with each meal. Organic chopped apples or melons make handy training treats or snacks between meals. Be sure to chop them fine using a hand grater or food processor, which will help them to be totally digested. If you come to a dead end finding organic fruits and vegetables, at least wash the pesticides off using a specially formulated vegetable and fruit wash.

Raw or lightly steamed vegetables nourish your dog's and cat's immune and organ systems. Their abundant, living enzymes help to digest carbohydrates, proteins, and fats, reducing the incidence of gastrointestinal (GI) upsets and improving digestive efficiency.

Now we're ready to move on to Level III: The Enhanced Meal Plan. This level is for the pinnacle of health. It will give your animal the fastest results and is the best option for chronically ill or stressed canines and felines. Meals take only a little more time to prepare, and we'll show you plenty of shortcuts to make meal prep even easier. We have developed this alternative for those whose schedules do not allow the necessary time to totally home prepare.

Level III: Lift the Ban on Table Scraps!

Our Level III Enhanced Meal Plan incorporates all of the elements from Levels I and II—plus some "home preparing." This can be as simple as sharing portions of your own healthy meals with your friend or cooking up a big pot of meat, along with whole grains and vegetables, and serving them all week. Or, if you are so inclined, you can add to the natural base food a combination of raw or lightly steamed protein (chicken, turkey, beef, or lamb), along with high-quality fish or vegetable oil, fresh organic vegetables, and a moderate amount of organic grains like brown rice or oatmeal.

Here's how: Reduce the amount of natural commercial base food (canned or dry) by 35 to 40 percent. (Most people feed dry food to dogs and canned food to cats, and this method works well for both canned and dry foods.) Then add back to the base food a 35 to 40 percent portion consisting of your own mixture of protein, whole grains, and chopped or blended vegetables. You can find the ingredients on our Healthy Meals Shopping List on page 11. After you find your ingredients, mix them in the following proportions:

Protein: 65% for dogs, 75% for cats

Grains: 20% for dogs, 10% for cats

Vegetables: 15% for dogs, 15% for cats

To this mixture add flax or salmon oil for dogs (1 tsp per for every 25 lbs) and salmon oil for cats (1 to 2 tsp) per meal.

This mixture can be pre-prepared a few days in advance. In less that five minutes, you have enhanced your animal's natural base food (canned or dry) with healthy ingredients like raw or slightly cooked protein, carbohydrates, and fats. Certainly your animal is worth this effort!

Our Table Scrap Plan Is Easy on You

Mixing grated or chopped raw vegetables—particularly carrots—into the natural base food is the most important addition you can make if you want to do something easy. But if you're already cooking wholesome food for yourself, why not share some with your friend? And despite what you may have heard, feeding table scraps can be good for your animal, provided you follow our guidelines:

- Treat table scraps or leftovers as a supplement to your animal's base diet. Increase the amount of healthy "people" food gradually, especially if your animal has been dependent upon commercial pet food. In our household, we make sure there are leftovers from each meal. If we're cooking up a batch of oatmeal or baking potatoes, for example, we make a few extras to share with our dogs, Pookie and Jack Harry.

- Collect raw vegetables from your salad (oil-free please, unless you are using virgin olive oil alone) and any of the throwaway parts of vegetables (no moldy ones, of course) and leftover steamed veggies. Chop or grate what you gather and store in your refrigerator. Keep raw vegetables separate from steamed—raw foods will spoil faster because of naturally occurring enzymes and bacteria. Try to use up the veggies within four to five days of preparation.

- If you steam your vegetables, share the residue broth, which is mineral rich. You can add this broth to your animal's food or to the drinking water. For example, if you are steaming fresh asparagus, the residue water will be a rich green broth consisting of vitamins, minerals, and nutrients that will benefit the lower urinary tract and will be beneficial to the skin and coat.

- Add a teaspoon or tablespoon of plain, low-fat or nonfat, preferably organic, live-culture yogurt—for improved digestion.

- Drizzle on some cold-pressed extra virgin olive oil, fish, sesame or flaxseed oil—all good sources of highly beneficial omega-3, -6, or -9 essential fatty acids—to enhance skin and coat health and quell itching from the inside out. For cats you should add a nonpreserved fish oil, such as salmon oil, as cats need arachidonic acid (an essential fatty acid), which is only found in animal fats.

Healthy Meals Shopping List

You'll find that enhancing your animal's daily menu is much easier than you might have ever imagined. Here's a shopping list to get you started:

- Organic bulk carrots
- Organic eggs
- Green foods: broccoli, spinach, watercress, parsley, etc.
- Whole grains: brown rice, kamut, millet, whole oats, barley or quinoa
- Virgin olive, flaxseed, borage, or sunflower oil
- Shredded Parmesan, Romano, or mozzarella cheese
- Plain, low-fat, organic yogurt with live cultures
- Organic garlic cloves
- Source of supplemental protein, such as tofu, free-range chicken or turkey, or organic beef or lamb.

Tempting Finicky Eaters

We enjoy the challenge of working with finicky eaters and have several tricks up our sleeves to win over fussy dogs or cats to our food plan.

Sometimes, a very resistant animal needs to skip a meal before he or she can accept the new foods. A sugar addict is going to leave your loving efforts (morsels of raw veggies) behind. His or her taste buds are now accustomed to synthetic flavor enhancers. Think about it—if you were to raise a child on candy-coated cereals and donuts, this little person would stick up his or her nose at the introduction of a carrot! So, if you're not winning out of the gate, rethink, reposition, re-strategize. You may need a more subliminal approach. Try adding organic chicken broth and fewer veggies. Other flavor enhancers include low-fat plain yogurt, low-fat cottage cheese (feed organic dairy products if you can), grated cheese, and poached egg yolks.

- Offer organic egg yolks, raw or poached, soft-boiled or gently sautéed in a small amount of virgin olive oil—rich in sulfur and amino acids for cellular integrity.

More Favorites to Share

Here are some more nutritious "table foods" animals love. Yours will thoroughly enjoy daily taste-tests as you explore the list for new favorites:

- Brussels sprouts, green beans, watercress, broccoli, zucchini, cabbage, and beet greens—raw or lightly steamed, and chopped fine.
- Our animals adore baked potatoes, especially just below the skins, which are a rich source of potassium. Potatoes are one vegetable you should not serve raw. Organic is best, or scrub the skins well before cooking.
- Oats are great, as are all kinds of whole grains, such as brown rice, barley, and millet—your animal needs daily roughage and fiber, just like you do.
- Fruits are fine, combined with grains or as a snack. Organic apples and bananas are favorites with our animals.

- Add some extra protein if you selected a senior formula. Choose free-range or organic meat free of hormones and additives. Good choices include lean beef, or skinless, boneless chicken or turkey. If you can't buy organic meat, remove the skin, since that's where chemical residues are highest, and avoid any cuts that are preprepared, chemically preserved, salted, or sugared. Save an unseasoned portion, steam lightly and serve.
- Tofu is another great protein source, as are organic, free-range eggs, now readily available in supermarkets. Tofu is also touted as a cancer-fighting food.

Steer Clear of These Foods...

- Avoid foods made from refined wheat flour and white rice and any grain by-products, such as wheat middlings or bakery fines.

- Go sparingly on acidic foods like tomatoes and citrus. (While tomatoes are high in the beneficial nutrient lycopenes, their acidity will often upset the gastrointestinal tract.)
- Avoid foods that have been genetically modified; look for the "BST-free" label.

The Last Course: Food Program Wrap-Up

We know this program will improve the quality of your animal companion's life and simplify your own. Even if you can only manage Level I at first, take heart that you're doing your friend a lot of good. Don't feel guilty if you're not up to Level II or III right away—although we do encourage you to tempt your animal with fresh veggies and a home-cooked meal at least two to three times per week. Once you see the results, you may find that it's not that much trouble to go to the next level after all—and boy, is it worth it.

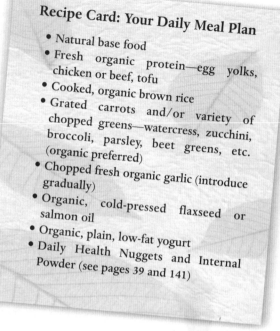

Recipe Card: Your Daily Meal Plan
- Natural base food
- Fresh organic protein—egg yolks, chicken or beef, tofu
- Cooked, organic brown rice
- Grated carrots and/or variety of chopped greens—watercress, zucchini, broccoli, parsley, beet greens, etc. (organic preferred)
- Chopped fresh organic garlic (introduce gradually)
- Organic, cold-pressed flaxseed or salmon oil
- Organic, plain, low-fat yogurt
- Daily Health Nuggets and Internal Powder (see pages 39 and 141)

Busy? Aren't we all! A good way to begin is simply to purchase your first bag of natural food and one of our recommended daily vitamin/mineral supplements (see Resources for recommended brands). Then, grate some organic carrots and add a dollop of low-fat, plain organic yogurt. Share your enthusiasm with your animal for this very important change in his or her diet. Visualize the "new dog or cat" you are about to bring to life!

On the day you start your program, mark your calendar with a big star. Then, 21 days later, take stock of how much healthier, happier, and more vibrant your dog or cat appears. You will be amazed at the difference even small steps will make in your pet's health and attitude, and you'll reap the benefits of knowing you've done a good thing for your friend.

Diet is the blueprint of health. It can help create a strong immune system that's naturally resistant to disease, and create a healthier life for your dog and cat—one that is free of the burden of constant veterinary visits and chronic use of potent medications. If your dog or cat is dealing with a chronic condition and you've been frustrated with the results, these simple dietary changes will help.

Fat Busters

What if you are dealing with an overweight animal? Now it's time to kick in one or more of our favorite "fat busters." Remember, it is much easier to take weight off an animal than a person. That's because your animal does not have the option of eating at will—he or she can eat only what you provide. These products are available at your local health food store.

Fat Buster Remedies

Try adding some organic **Apple Cider Vinegar** to your dog or cat's drinking water. (*Never substitute regular apple cider vinegar for organic. The apples in the non-organic form are sprayed with pesticides and could be harmful.*)

Organic Apple Cider Vinegar (in pure drinking water, daily)	
Cat/Small Dog (up to 14 lb)	1/2 tsp
Medium Dog (15-34 lb)	1 tsp
Large/Giant Dog (35-85+ lb)	1 1/2 tsp

Vitamin B6 is essential for proper formation of hormones and enzymes necessary for the metabolization of fats and proteins.

Vitamin B6 (daily)	
Cat/Small Dog (up to 14 lb)	25 mg
Medium Dog (15-34 lb)	50 mg
Large Dog (35-84 lb)	75 mg
Giant Dog (85+ lb)	100 mg

Lecithin helps emulsify fats, making it easier for the body to mobilize fats and burn them as fuel. As a bonus, it unclogs skin pores, allowing new hair to grow and helping the coat to become thicker and shinier. Add lecithin capsules or granules directly to the food.

Lecithin granules (daily, with meals)	
Cat/Small Dog (up to 14 lb)	1 tsp
Medium Dog (15-34 lb)	1 1/2 tsp
Large/Giant Dog (35-85+ lb)	2 tsp

L-carnitine is an amino acid with a powerful effect on the body's fat metabolism. Like a fatty-acid shuttle service, L-carnitine helps the body burn fat more efficiently at the cellular level. This leads to less accumulated fat in the body and less chance of fatty tumors. L-carnitine is also very beneficial to the heart muscles, improving the general circulation, and increasing your animal's energy level.

L-carnitine (daily, with meals)	
Cat/Small Dog (up to 14 lb)	250 mg
Medium/Large Dog (15-84 lb)	500 mg
Giant Dog (85+ lb)	750 mg

Weight-Off Drops is a homeopathic remedy that helps the body to support weight loss by helping to overcome addiction to food and moderating the appetite. Realize that many animals' problems come from the addiction to flavor enhancers and appetite stimulants added to commercial food. Weaning your animal off the "palatability ladder" and onto the Goldstein Food Plan will help to minimize addiction to unnatural chemical additives. Weight-Off Drops takes this to the next level if the personality of your animal is set up to eat all the time.

Weight-Off Drops (once or twice daily, apart from food)	
Cat/Small Dog (up to 14 lb)	5 drops
Medium Dog (15-34 lb)	7 drops
Large Dog (35-84 lb)	10 drops
Giant Dog (85+ lb)	12 drops

Mega-lipotropic is a digestive aid that will assist your animal's fat-burning ability with nutrients, minerals, and enzymes. It will help to lower triglyceride levels in the blood and will help the body metabolize fats (including lipomas). Mega-lipotropic contains L-carnitine, iodine (for healthy thyroid function), and lipase (a fat digestive enzyme). Follow the dosage directions on the package.

Rate Your Own Pet Food

A quick search for "natural pet foods" on the Internet yields an overwhelming number of raw and natural foods for dogs and cats, all claiming substantial health benefits. This list is growing every day, and we are pleased that the movement is toward better quality raw ingredients and improved animal nutrition.

The Goldstein Food Plan provides a complete, balanced food plan using a "natural base food" to meet the minimum daily requirements of dogs and cats. Although this base food is naturally preserved and contains a good amount of whole ingredients, it's only a starting point. The Food Plan then builds upon this natural base food with wholesome, unprocessed ingredients such as organic fresh flaxseed oil, fresh chopped organic vegetables, whole grains, organic yogurt, and meat (chicken, turkey, beef, or lamb). There is no all-in-one food (in bag or can) that can give your animal all he or she needs for optimal health, and many of us can't take the time to prepare a semi-raw diet from scratch utilizing all human-grade and organic ingredients.

Since we believe diet to be the cornerstone of your animal's health and longevity, we want to help you find the best natural base food to use as part of the Goldstein Food Plan. Think of your natural base food as the base paint that you purchase at a paint store. To make the paint more beautiful and to achieve the proper color, various pigments are added. These pigments *enhance* the base paint to help achieve the color you want in your living room. The same is true of your animal's natural base food—on the Goldstein Food Plan you will add various ingredients to *enhance* the health benefits of the natural food.

To that end, we present our "Rate Your Own Pet Food" chart, which will help determine if your current dog or cat food "makes the grade." If it does, you can use it as the natural base food for your animal's dietary program. We have prepared this chart for those of you who cannot put in the time to home prepare and who are looking for convenience and maximum nutritional health benefits for your animal.

First, you'll need to do a little research. We're pleased to see the proliferation of online information available on pet foods. Armed with our guidelines that follow and the knowledge of what makes a pet food healthy, you can go to a manufacturer's web site and evaluate any of their foods. After you've gotten the formula from the manufacturer's web site, rate it according to the key on pages 18 to 20. Each ingredient can achieve a score of 1 to 5. Fill in the chart we've provided, add up the score, and find out how your pet food rates.

Rate Your Own Pet Food

Fill out this chart using the key on pages 18-20.

Brand: _____

Ingredient	Type	Score
Proteins		
Carbohydrates		
Fats		
Chemical Additives and Preservatives		
Minerals		
Vitamins		
Phytonutrients and Antioxidants		
Beneficial Nutrients		
Nonbeneficial Materials		
		Total Score:

Key to Scoring Any Pet Food

Proteins

Score	Type
1	By-product meals (chicken, turkey, beef, lamb, corn gluten meal)
2	Chicken meal, turkey meal, beef meal, or lamb meal
3	Chicken, turkey, beef, or lamb
4	Human-grade chicken, turkey, beef, or lamb
5	Free-range or organic chicken, turkey, beef, lamb

Note: Minus 1 if canned food contains liver

Carbohydrates

Score	Type
1	By-products: wheat middlings, soybean hulls, husks, bakery fines
2	Processed grains: brewer's rice, wheat flour
3	Whole grains with wheat and/or corn
4	Whole grains: brown rice, barley, whole oats
5	Organic whole grains: brown rice, barley, whole oats

Note: Minus 1 from whole grains if food contains both whole and processed grain

Fats

Score	Type
1	Tallow, lard (highly saturated fat)
2	Poultry or animal fat (saturated fat)
3	Unsaturated vegetable oil: corn, sunflower
4	Omega fatty acid-rich oils: fish, flax, sesame
5	Organic fatty acid-rich oils: flax, sesame, sunflower

Note: In canned food with no added fat, scoring is based upon the quality of the animal protein source.

Chemical Additives and Preservatives

Score	Type
1	BHA, BHT, Ethoxyquin
5	Vitamin E, vitamin C, rosemary

Minerals

Score	Type
1	Inorganic sulfates, oxides (copper sulfate, iron oxide, zinc oxide)
3	Cooked amino acid chelates, proteinates (zinc proteinate, copper amino acid chelate)
5	Uncooked life-force amino acid chelates, proteinates (zinc proteinate, copper amino acid chelate)

Note: Minus 1 if food contains both inorganic and chelated minerals

Vitamins

Score	Type
1	None
3	Cooked vitamins
5	Uncooked vitamins

Phytonutrients and Antioxidants *(fruits, vegetables, grass, herbs)*

Score	Type
1	None
2	Cooked phytonutrients
5	Uncooked life-force phytonutrients

Beneficial Nutrients *(such as probiotics, prebiotics, lecithin)*

Score	Type
1	None
3	Cooked beneficial nutrients (such as acidophilus, inulin, chickory, glucosamine, lecithin)
5	Uncooked life-force nutrients (such as acidophilus, inulin, chickory, glucosamine, lecithin)

Nonbeneficial Materials *(those used to make the food artificially perform—i.e., help reduce gas, help to form stool, etc.)*

Score	Type
1	Yes (beet pulp, tomato pomace, cellulose, potato starch, animal digest, phosphoric acid)
5	None

Scoring

As you can see, the higher the score, the better quality the food. Combinations of ingredients should be looked at because they are often used to make the label look better while decreasing the overall nutritional value of the food. For example, a food that contains both chicken (score of 3) and chicken meal (score of 2) would receive a protein score of 2, the lower of the two ingredients. Foods that contain multiple ingredients that are essentially the same also should be reduced to the lower number. For example, if a food contains whole wheat (score of 3), but also contains wheat flour (score of 2) and wheat middlings (score of 1), that part would receive the lower score of 1.

Scoring:

45+: Ideal. No food you rate will score Ideal. The only method of getting an ideal food is to home prepare a complete and balanced organic diet that is either raw or slightly cooked, and contains all the required nutrients, antioxidants, and supplements.

26-44: Good. Foods that score in this range are acceptable as a natural base food for all stages of the Goldstein Food Plan.

20-25: Acceptable with Enhancement. You can use foods that score in this range as your natural base food, however, enhancement is necessary. It is important with these foods that you use either Level II or preferably Level III of our Food Plan.

19 and below: Unacceptable. Either this food contains too many unacceptable ingredients, or your animal is not getting the necessary nutrition from this food.

Should You "Go Raw"?

One of the most talked-about areas of dog and cat health is the question of whether or not to feed commercially prepared or the so-called Bones and Raw Food diet (BARF). Proponents of raw foods are often quite outspoken and say that the only method of offering your animal a healthy diet is by feeding a well-formulated, raw food program. Other animal health care professionals, including many holistic veterinarians, have concerns about the feeding of meat that could be contaminated with harmful bacteria such as salmonella, parasites, and perhaps even chemical contaminants (especially to a dog or cat that is immune compromised with a chronic degenerative disease).

Long before the first pet food was even thought of—and before Grandma's cauldron of stovetop meat and vegetable stew was shared by the whole family (including dogs and cats)—animals were expected to hunt for their daily ration of food. If your dog or cat were to exist in the wild, he or she would be tracking live prey (mostly rodents) and ingesting their total body components, including organ meats, bones, the intestinal tract, even the eyes. The carcass, consisting of bones and meat, would then be buried in the earth only to be dug up and once fermented, savored as a delicacy.

As unsavory as that may sound, there is something to be said for those instinctual flashbacks. In fact, your animal probably still recognizes and craves the nutritional value provided from eating raw meat: enzymes, essential fatty acids, pure fresh protein, B complex, and other key vitamins and minerals.

A Convenient Food Option

We would really be shortchanging your animal if we failed to mention the category of food premixes for dogs and cats. The one we most often recommend is Dr. Harvey's Canine Health and Feline Food Premix—a whole food offering 6 certified organic grains, 9 vegetables, 13 herbs and a multiple vitamin/mineral supplement. This premix is not cooked, and can replace your natural ("cooked") base food by simply adding warm water, fresh protein such as chicken or beef, and fat (fatty acids). This allows you to control the levels of fat and protein by simply adjusting the levels of the premix and increasing the amount of protein and fat. Dr. Harvey's Premix is on top of Susan's recommendations for those who do not feed an all-raw diet, but want the highest quality alternative. It's also on Dr. Bob's list of approved foods for animals with cancer who are being treated with a combination of nutrition and Chinese herbs that require a strict diet of no chicken, turkey, lamb, or fish. Another alternative to Dr. Harvey's is Soujourner Farms Premix, a food that was originally put together by the famed animal nutritionist Julliette deBarclay Levy. (By the way, it was Juliette's book, *The Complete Herbal Book for the Dog*, which helped start us on our journey toward the holistic approach to animal health.)

There are two practical issues to face when deciding on whether or not to feed raw or processed foods: time and money. Many people who live with animals lead active lives that are filled with all sorts of responsibilities from the raising of children to busy work schedules and lengthy business trips. The sourcing and preparing of organic and free-range meats, grains, and vegetables takes more time and costs more than processed foods. Any plan that does not first address these two basic issues will eventually fail.

After considering these more practical issues, it's time to look at the issues of health, disease, and the comparison of the lifestyles of wild animals versus the domesticated lifestyles of our dogs and cats. For simplicity, we have listed the opposing views on many of the main issues you should address when making the decision between feeding raw or processed food to your animal.

Contamination Concerns

Pro: We should feed our domesticated animal exactly what their ancestors and living counterparts eat in the wild. After all, our modern day canines' and felines' digestive tracts are well equipped and will not be affected by, nor become diseased with parasites or bacterial contamination such as salmonella.

Con: Our inbred domesticated animals really are not very similar to their ancestors. Years of inbreeding and feeding highly processed "dead" foods have led to domesticated dogs and cats who are much more prone to degenerative diseases, and caution should be followed when feeding raw food diets.

Raw Bones

Pro: Raw bones are softer and less likely to cause problems such as splinters.

Con: Raw bones do splinter occasionally, and again the intestinal tracts of our domesticated dogs and cats are not as strong and powerful as their ancestors. While many holistic veterinarians say that in most instances there are not problems feeding raw bones, there are many reports of impactions of bones in the mouth, throat, and in the large bowel, as well as perforation of the intestines.

Nutritional Balance

Pro: Raw food diets contain all the nutrients, food groups, vitamins, minerals, antioxidants, and phytonutrients that your animal needs for growth, health, and the maintenance of wellness.

Con: Nutritional balancing of the raw food diet is critical, particularly the preparation and addition of the proper amounts of protein, fat, carbohydrates, vitamins, minerals, and antioxidants. Small, undetected deficiencies in the meal preparation can show up as major deficiencies and even serious disease if the meal plan isn't balanced.

Why Raw Must Be Organic

We are invariably asked by subscribers of our *Love of Animals* newsletter and our clients for our opinion of feeding raw foods. Our take on raw meat is quite simple: "Go raw if it's pure." This means organically raised and grown. Here's why:

- We are staunchly opposed to the contemptible way livestock are factory farm raised and slaughtered these days, both from health and ethical perspectives. From a health standpoint, regular supermarket meat can be laced with hormones, antibiotics, and other toxic contaminants. In addition, "modern" methods of farming often precipitate depression and aggression, which has a definite biochemical effect on the animal's health and well-being and can translate into toxicity in the meat.

- If you cannot locate a source of raw protein in the pure state, we prefer that you seek out an alternative source such as raw, organic egg yolks which will provide your dog or cat similar protein and fat value as meat, plus extras such as lecithin, a nutrient that is good for the skin, brain, and nerves, and is also a good metabolizer of fats.
- You also should know that there is another acceptable option—protein sourced from range-fed animals. Although organic is by far the best way to go, range-fed protein sources are usually acceptable due to their producers' high environmental and nutritional quality standards. Range-fed animals are permitted to roam and graze freely as opposed to the complete lack of freedom imposed by traditional, crowded factory farming. If you've located range-fed food, it's a good option. You may want to lightly steam the meat, thereby reducing the potential for surface bacterial contamination.
- Never feed organ meat, especially liver, if the source is not certified organic. Organ meats are the detoxifying agents of the body and usually contain high levels of toxins and metabolic wastes, due to their inherent function. These body parts are the centers of waste for additional poisons due to hormones, antibiotics, steroids, vaccines, and pesticides. The chemical factor is dangerously high and should be avoided by your animal at all costs. It's a good idea to avoid feeding raw pork due to the potential for trichinosis. Pork is also difficult to digest.

We agree in principle with raw food diets, but like many of our colleagues are also greatly concerned with the potential for contamination from bacteria, handling, parasites, etc. In our position of dealing with many animals that are in a state of degeneration—often suffering from serious diseases such as cancer, liver or kidney failure, diabetes, Cushing's, and autoimmune diseases—we often recommend a middle-of-the-road approach.

Since there is no guarantee that your dog or cat won't contract food poisoning from eating raw food, we generally recommend slightly steaming all meats and poultry, and soft-boiling or poaching all eggs to reduce or eliminate surface contamination. When preparing meat, chicken, or turkey avoid the prepared grocery chopping which will often thoroughly mix the surface contamination. If you are going to go for the raw food approach, be sure to feed range-fed or organic meats from a farm that takes pride in the quality of life and honors the animals they raise. There are food labeling programs that help consumers select humanely processed meats, including "Certified Humane Raised and Handled," and labels that distinguish organic products as well. Please refer to the Resources section at the end of the book for a selection of books and companies that can assist in your decision to go raw.

Chapter 2

Nutritional Supplements: Spark Plugs of Health

Educating guardians that their dog or cat needs supplements is sometimes even more challenging than persuading them that they need vitamins and minerals themselves. This is because of the insistent messages by pet food companies that their foods contain all of the complete and balanced nutrition your dog or cat will ever need. Sure, clever advertisements told us that convenient canned and bagged foods were completely balanced and required no additional supplementation. Although the high heat of cooking destroyed, on average, 35 to 75 percent of the naturally occurring vitamins, the manufacturers solved this problem by "fortifying" the foods with 135 percent of the required nutrients. They were, of course, not fooling Mother Nature, as the nutrients were also cooked. And, more important, antioxidant vitamins (such as vitamin C) can be destroyed by almost 75 percent or completely inactivated from the cooking.

As discussed in Chapter 1, the "modern" pet diet was based almost entirely on human food chain wastes and by-products. The good news is that over the past decade, primarily because of consumer pressure, the pet food industry finally began to improve the ingredients and began producing what has come to be known as "super-premium" foods, followed by super-premium natural foods, and now even organic foods for animals.

Despite these advances, there is no question that your dog, cat, or other animal needs a little help from outside the bag to provide optimal nutrition to help prevent disease, create vitality, and encourage longevity. We call this Level II of the Goldstein Plan. We believe your animal's commercial food should be supplemented because:

The Myth of RDA

Recommended Dietary/Daily Allowances (RDAs) were not designed to promote optimal health and vitality but only to protect from severe nutritional deficiencies such as scurvy (vitamin C) or beriberi (vitamin B1). Hundreds of research studies now show that significantly higher levels of specific nutrients are required to prevent disease and support optimal health. To borrow an example from human medicine, for adult women the RDA for calcium is 800 mg per day, while research has shown that levels of 1,500 mg per day—nearly twice that level—are required to help prevent osteoporosis.

- Even high-quality pet foods must be cooked at high temperatures, thereby significantly diminishing the vitality and potency of the vitamins and enzymes within. As one of our *Love of Animals* newsletter subscribers wrote to us, "You wouldn't stir fry my vitamins, would you?" Imagine taking your daily supplements and throwing them into the frying pan with your morning eggs!

- Fresh fruits and vegetables today contain fewer nutrients due to the intensive farming and agribusiness practices of the last 60 years. Fertilization, pesticides, and the stripping away of topsoil have leached away many nutrients. Purchasing organic produce will go a long way toward sustainability—both of your animal's health and the planet's survival.

- Just as with humans, it may be difficult for your animal to ingest enough servings of fresh fruits and veggies each day to achieve optimal levels. Cats especially may be wary of unusual foods. Many dogs and cats have been hooked on the equivalent of canine and feline "junk food"—poor quality foods dressed up with palatability enhancers, which are little more than artificial additives intensifying the chemical load on the immune system.

- Feeding a high-quality nutritional supplement gives you the assurance that you are doing everything possible to protect your animal's health and well-being. For healthy animals not under stress or not living in an area with excessive radiation or air pollution, a daily vitamin based upon age, activity level, and life cycle should do the trick.

- An animal with a nagging ailment (e.g., chronically itchy skin, external or internal parasites, coughing, sneezing, diarrhea) or one that is battling a disease (e.g., arthritis, cancer or heart disease, liver or kidney problems) will need additional specific therapeutic nutrients to help with the condition.

Increasing numbers of veterinarians are seeing the benefits of nutritional approaches in their practice. According to biochemist Dr. Roger Kendall, "Although there are no officially established guidelines for implementing therapeutic nutrition in veterinary practice, many veterinarians are including the aforementioned approaches in their practices. Therapeutic nutrition is based on the idea that if the body is provided with a better nutritional environment, healing will occur at a higher level of efficacy. Over time, veterinarians should see improved results within their patients as a result of incorporating nutritional products in their practices….if properly incorporated into the veterinary practice, the use of therapeutic nutrition can bring about superior results."

First, let's take a look at some individual supplements that we believe have value above and beyond daily use.

Super Supplement I: Probiotics

Probiotics are composed of the friendly bacteria that normally live in the intestinal tract. Friendly means that their function is to improve digestion and intestinal health, as compared to unfriendly bacteria that invade and cause sicknesses such as *E. coli* and salmonella. These friendly bacteria, such as *Lactobacillus thermophilus* or *acidophilus*, *Enterococcus faecium*, and *Bifidobacterium bifidum*, will help to counteract the destructive side effects of antibiotics and will help to correct imbalances in the digestive tract itself. Unless there is a serious underlying disease, feeding probiotics (which can also be found in organic, live-culture yogurt) should help to alleviate all the side effects of the drugs and improper diet, which can cause bad breath, diarrhea, excessive gas, and foul-smelling stool.

When healthy, your animal's intestinal tract—which consists of the small and large intestines (the colon is part of the large intestines)—is usually filled with billions of beneficial bacterial flora. These "good guys," as they are often called, are essential to the process of digestion and absorption. They also produce B vitamins and prevent the overgrowth of harmful, often pathogenic bacteria and opportunistic fungi, which can lead to a disease state.

The normal flora of the intestines is required for proper assimilation of food and nourishment of the cells of the body. The flora balance can be upset or diminished by the following conditions:

- Trauma or injury
- Chronic disease (weak immune system)
- Toxins from food and/or the environment
- Artificial pet food ingredients—coloring agents, dyes, digests, chemical additives, or preservatives
- Stresses—emotional and physical
- Antibiotics and other medication such as chemotherapeutics

Friendly bacteria, the desirable tenant of your animal's intestines, will decrease in number as your animal ages. But they can also dwindle prematurely due to poor diet, stress, and medications, leaving your friend more vulnerable to disease. If your animal has been on antibiotics or is currently being treated, realize that these drugs will decimate all bacteria, including the beneficial type.

Probiotics, which contain ample amounts of *Lactobacillus acidophilus* and other friendly bacilli, may be purchased at your local health food store or high quality pet store. For best results, we recommend that you keep these products refrigerated.

Acidophilus (dosed in millions or billions of bacteria) come in capsules, liquid, or in live-culture yogurt. For daily use and to help prevent adverse intestinal effects of taking antibiotics, live-culture yogurt will be fine. If your animal has an intestinal disease such as chronic diarrhea or inflammatory bowel disease (see Chapter 8) then probiotic capsules containing millions of friendly bacteria are recommended.

Probiotics/Acidophilus (per meal)		
	Yogurt	In Millions
Cat/Small Dog (up to 15 lb)	1/2 tsp	200
Medium Dog (15-34 lb)	2 tsp	400
Large Dog (35-85 lbs)	1 Tbs	600
Giant Dogs (85+ lb)	1 1/2 Tbs	800

The addition of probiotics can reestablish the population of these beneficial organisms. Much research has demonstrated the beneficial impact that probiotics have on the immune system, the intestines, and in the treatment of cancer.

Super Supplement II: Phytonutrients

If you're living with a young dog or cat, consider incorporating phytonutrients into the daily diet now so your animal gets used to the taste and texture of some of these foods. Phytonutrients (also called phytochemicals or "life-force nutrients") refer to the hundreds of chemicals that plants synthesize for protective purposes against the formation of carcinogens. Phytonutreints are found in abundance in fruits, vegetables, herbs, and algae. These chemicals are produced by the plant to perform numerous biological and metabolic functions. Research is proving that these nonessential nutrients have a positive and often dramatic effect on wellness, health, and the prevention and treatment of disease and longevity. They fit into categories of compounds that are becoming more widely known, such as terpenes, amines, carotenoids, bioflavonoids, lignans, phytosterols, sterols, and sterolins, as well as names such as lutein, lycopens, tocotrienols, and chlorophyll, now associated with improved health and wellness. Phytonutrients are also free-radical scavengers and do humans and animals a huge service by helping the body detoxify toxic and cancer-causing agents. Besides slowing down the cancer process they can greatly reduce damage to cellular membranes. According to a 1991 *International Journal of Cancer* study and the National Cancer Institute, there is a relationship between reduced cancer risk and the frequency of the consumption of fruits and vegetables.

Longevity Enhancement: Phytonutrient Shopping List

- Beets (feed in limited quantities)
- Broccoli
- Brussels Sprouts
- Cabbage
- Carrots
- Cauliflower
- Cucumber
- Dandelion greens
- Garlic
- Kale
- Parsley
- Peas
- Spinach
- Watercress

Please buy organic whenever possible.

The "life-force" nutrients come from vegetables, herbs, and algae, such as broccoli, cabbage, watercress, spinach, garlic, parsely, and blue-green algae. For example, broccoli and blue-green algae contain naturally occurring quercetin, which inhibits tumor-promoting substances in the body by blocking inflammatory reactions. Others include fresh garlic, kale, cauliflower, carrots, Brussels sprouts, barley and wheat grass, and fresh fruit. Raw diets (BARF) that have fresh vegetables added are often loaded with phytonutrients.

For optimal protection, or if your animal suffers from a chronic condition, add more fresh fruits and vegetables into the food or as snacks. Your goal should always be to prevent cancer and other degenerative conditions, and these phytonutrient and enzyme-rich, vitamin- and mineral-laden foods are the best way we know of to accomplish it.

If you've been adding fresh garlic and shredded carrots to your animal's food, consider expanding your animal's taste and therapeutic horizons by adding some of the dark green phytos, such as watercress or broccoli. If you are really rushed, you can also add barley or wheat grass in powdered form. These are high in chlorophyll, a substance that purifies the system and is chemically quite similar to the life-giving and supporting hemoglobin found in all animals' blood. Keep in mind that despite your powerful nutritional intentions, these foods must be introduced slowly; otherwise, they'll go in one end and out the other. Rome wasn't built in a day—neither was your animal's current health condition. So *sois gentil*, as our grandmother would say in French, which means "go gently."

Super Supplement III: Essential Fatty Acids

In the last few years, much has been learned about the role of essential fatty acids (EFAs) in both animal and human health. "Essential" means that the body can't produce them and they must be part of the diet and consumed daily. We're relieved to see that essential fatty acids, nearly swept away in the low-fat diet craze, are finally earning the recognition they deserve.

Although EFAs are household words in human health these days, the animal health care community is still playing catch-up. Compounding the problem, fat metabolism is a tricky science filled with biochemical descriptions that can be daunting. There are omega-3, -6, and -9 fatty acids out there, each with its own virtues. To make matters worse, they can change their form in the body, and some bodies absorb some better than others.

When combined with specific enzymes, EFAs break down into tiny hormonal messengers called eicosanoids (including prostaglandins, thromboxanes, and leukotrienes), which control inflammatory and immune responses at the cellular level. In general, eicosanoids from omega-6 fatty acids produce inflammation, while those from omega-3s quiet the immune response. Omega-3s, in fact, can quiet your animal's skin outbreaks and itching episodes. One fatty acid that can wear two hats is linoleic acid (LA), an omega-6 that is generally considered a good guy, except for the fact that too much of a good thing can throw the system out of balance. And balance is what essential fatty acid metabolism is all about.

We feel that the most essential—and overlooked—fatty acid for dogs and cats is alpha-linolenic acid (ALA), known as an omega-3 fatty acid. Prime sources include flaxseed oil, soybeans, seeds and nuts, and deep-water cold fish such as salmon, sardines, and mackerel. Unfortunately, this fatty acid is one that is most deficient in both animal and human diets.

High levels of saturated fatty acids, along with heat processing, and chemical additives and preservatives (as are used in most commercial pet foods), can inhibit the body from properly utilizing fatty acids. As a result, the energy source from the EFAs runs out of "juice" when energy-blocking preservatives are present in cooked pet foods.

How can you be sure your dog or cat is getting enough EFAs in the diet? Many commercial dog and cat foods (even the natural brands) list chicken or poultry fat as the main source of fat and fatty acids. For example, chicken fat usually makes up 12 percent of the total volume of pet foods. And chicken (or poultry) fat contains about 20 percent linoleic acid (omega-6 fatty acids). This means that approximately 2 to 3 percent of the total food has essential omega-6 fatty acids. Chicken fat contains 30 times the amount of omega-6 as it does omega-3. Therefore, mathematically, chicken fat contains about 0.1 percent omega-3 fatty acids—all but nonexistent!

More importantly, pet foods are cooked at very high temperatures, which often destroy or inactivate the fragile omega fatty acids, especially the omega-3s. So while the good news is that many pet food manufacturers are adding more of the essential omega-3 and -6 fatty acids, and getting away from the trend of using only cheap, highly saturated chicken fat, they do not spend much time discussing the adverse effects that the high temperatures of processing have on these delicate fatty acids. It is our opinion that in order to achieve the proper balance between omega-6 and omega-3, you have to take it upon yourself to add omega-3 to the diet. One of the best ways to do this is with flaxseed and fish oils.

Felines Favor Fish Oil

Most cats do not like the taste of flaxseed oil, but they do love fish oil. Select high-quality fish oil from cold-water fish such as salmon, sardines, trout, or mackerel, and try squeezing a capsule into the food. Fish oil also contains adequate levels of arachidonic acid, an EFA required by cats and found only in animal fats.

Have you ever visited a health food store and looked for organic flaxseed oil? You will find it in the refrigerated section in black, opaque bottles. The manufactures of these delicate, nutrient, and fatty acid-rich oils state that you must keep the oil refrigerated in dark bottles to prevent rancidity, and to keep the health benefits of the omega-3 fatty acids active. Compare this to a bag of dog food that is sitting on the shelf for two months and has been cooked at 350°F. You don't have to be a rocket scientist to figure out that there is no nutritional comparison. We feel that your animal deserves the same nutritional benefits from such omega-3 rich oils as humans do. Keep the oil refrigerated in dark bottles to prevent rancidity. The brands we often recommend are Barleans or Spectrum oils.

Good fish oils contain about 40 percent polyunsaturated omega-3 fatty acids and high amounts of both Eicosapentaenoic Acids (EPAs)—usually 15 to 20 percent—and Docosahexaenoic Acids (DHAs)—10 to 15 percent. Clinical trials have shown that fish oils support lipid metabolism and cardiovascular function, and provide nutritional support for healthy skin and joints. The brand that we often recommend is Eskimo-3 Fish Oil.

Fish Oil or Flaxseed Oil maintenance and therapeutic doses are listed here:

Fish or Flaxseed Oil (per meal)		
	Maintenance	Therapeutic
Cat/Small Dog (up to14 lb)	1 tsp	2 tsp
Medium Dog (15-34 lb)	2 tsp	1 Tbsp
Large Dog (35-84 lb)	1 Tbsp	1 1/2 Tbsp
Giant Dog (85 lb+)	1 1/2 Tbsp	2 Tbsp

Beyond Essential Fats (Natura Products) is a unique fatty acid mixture that has been formulated by master herbalist and nutritionist Donnie Yance. It contains high-quality fish oil along with Siberian Sea Buckthorn Oil (a rich source of carotenoids) and Siberian Pine Seed Oil, which is 50 percent richer in Gamma Linoleic Acid (GLA) than evening primrose oil. Because of its concentration it contains the highest amounts of both EPA (25%)/DHA (20%)/GLA per serving of any other product we have seen. The unique fatty acid sources found in Sea Buckthorn Oil and Pine Seed Oils will help to improve the skin and coat (it's often fed to horses and eaten by mink in the wild). The Latin name for Sea Buckthorn is *Hippohae rhamnoides* which is translated to mean "shiny horse."

Beyond Essential Fats (daily)	
Cat/Small Dog (up to14 lb)	1/4 tsp
Medium Dog (15-34 lb)	1/2 tsp
Large Dog (35-84 lb)	3/4 tsp
Giant Dog (85 lb+)	1 tsp

Be wary of products in which the oil has been "stabilized," which means most of the omega-3s have been removed, typically by heating. And if you choose to go with regular flaxseed (available in whole-foods and health-food stores), feed the ground seed immediately; don't save it for the next meal, as it quickly will break down.

Recently there has been some debate regarding the ability of some dogs to efficiently convert flaxseed oil into beneficial fatty acid chains. The studies are all based on human subjects, and it is often difficult to directly translate results from people to animals and vice versa. We have been using flaxseed oil for our patients for years and are firm believers that there are benefits for dogs. We most often recommend fish oil for cats, with the exception of animals with cancer that are being treated with Chinese herbal remedies (see Chapter 9: Cancer). In our work with Dr. Jay Wen, we have found that animals with cancer respond better to the therapy when fish oil is removed from the diet and substituted with flaxseed oil.

You should see a marked improvement in your animal's skin and coat within two to three weeks. In addition, keeping your animal on Level II of the Goldstein Food Plan—with extras like chopped veggies, organic plain yogurt, and Daily Health Nuggets (see page 39)—will help you see results even faster.

Here is a quick and easy way to make sure your animal is getting a combination of beneficial fatty acids and protein, which will act as the energizers of the cells and promote wellness and healing at all levels. This elixir comes from the work of Joanna Budwig, who has been nominated many times for the Nobel Prize for her work in the treatment of human cancer (see Chapter 9 for more information).

This elixir can be fed to your dog or cat as a meal, snack, or topper. Here's our basic recipe:

1 Tbsp organic flaxseed oil

2 Tbsp organic plain yogurt or cottage cheese

Mix gently and thoroughly and feed two to three times per week. Keep refrigerated.

Dr. Budwig Elixir (with meals)	
Cat/Small Dog (up to 14 lb)	1 tsp
Medium Dog (15-34 lb)	2 tsp
Large Dog (35-84 lb)	1 Tbsp
Giant Dog (85 lb+)	1 1/2 Tbsp

Super Supplement IV: Vitamins, Minerals Amino Acids & Enzymes

Vitamins traditionally have been used as supplements when there appears to be a deficiency. But vitamins, like other nutrients, are required daily for the body's metabolic and physiologic process. Day-to-day stresses, modern cooking and processing techniques, and exposure to chemicals and infectious agents all deplete the body's vitamin reserves almost as quickly as they are taken in or manufactured. Therefore, adding vitamins in the proper amount, form, and type is critical for the maintenance or restoration of health.

- **Acid vitamins** function at the cellular level by acidifying cellular membranes, making them permeable for various nutrients. The following vitamins are classified as acid forming: Vitamin C (ascorbic acid); C-complex: Vitamin C plus bioflavonoids; B acid vitamins; Pantothenic acid; Para-aminobenzoic acid (PABA); Vitamin B6 (pyridoxine); and Folic acid.
- **Alkaline vitamins** raise the pH of the cell membranes, decreasing the permeability for nutrients to enter the cell. The following vitamins are classified as alkaline-forming: Vitamin B1 (thiamine); Vitamin B12; Vitamin B2 (riboflavin); Biotin; Vitamin B3 (niacin or niacinamide); Choline; and Inositol.
- **Fat-soluble vitamins** are bound to the nitrogen portion of foods and function to coat and protect cell membranes from oxidation and free-radical formation. Fat-soluble vitamins are also

involved in the manufacture of some hormones, enzymes, and antibodies. The following are fat-soluble vitamins: Vitamin A, D, E, F (fatty acids—linoleic, linolenic, arachidonic), and K.

- **Water-soluble vitamins** are involved in maintaining the pH balance of the body as it relates to the cell membranes. Additionally, they are either acid or alkaline in nature (see above for acid and alkaline vitamins). Functionally, they are involved in the passage of nutrients into the cells.

Vitamin A was discovered in 1930 when animal research proved that a diet deficient in vitamin A adversely affected growth and weakened the immune system. Vitamin A (retinol) and one of its many carotenoid cousins, beta-carotene (provitamin A), are two powerful fat-soluble vitamins. Among its scores of other functions, vitamin A is essential for proper immune system function, cell and tissue integrity, and health of the skin, eyes, gums, gut, intestines, and teeth.

Vitamin A is a powerful antioxidant in its role as free-radical scavenger. As a result, vitamin A can be beneficial in treating chronic degenerative diseases such as cancer, arthritis, and skin disease. In numerous studies, vitamin A and its derivatives have been shown to prevent primary tumor recurrences and have been shown to be particularly effective in cases of squamous cell carcinoma and malignant melanoma. Vitamin A also can help to mitigate damage from exposure to environmental pollutants.

Liver is rich in vitamin A, as is dandelion root, carrots, collard greens, kale, parsley, spinach, and broccoli. Colorful fruits and vegetables are teeming with vitamin A and its many carotenoid cousins.

Dogs can derive vitamin A from beta-carotene. Cats, however, cannot convert beta-carotene into vitamin A, so adequate amounts must be available in the diet. Deficiencies of vitamin A can depress the immune system and often lead to respiratory and eye diseases. Adequate levels of protein and zinc are necessary for its mobilization from storage in the liver. Vitamin A can be toxic at high levels, so care must be used to prevent overdosing.

Vitamin E, a fat-soluble vitamin, is one of the body's major antioxidants. Its role in preventing heart disease, healing tissue, and keeping the immune system in tip-top shape is well documented. It works in concert (synergistically) with selenium. Vitamin E has been shown to have anticancer properties and has been proven to enhance the effectiveness of specific chemotherapeutics.

Also, vitamin E has been shown to have "organ sparing" properties in conjunction with chemo or radiation therapy—that is, it protects the vital organs from the damaging effects of therapy designed to knock out cancer cells. When you supplement vitamin E, look for products containing mixed tocopherols, including alpha and gamma fractions, and choose natural vitamin E over synthetic.

Vitamin C. Numerous papers and books have been written about the effects of this vitamin as an antioxidant and general stimulant for the immune system. It has been reported that vitamin C has the following attributes:

- Stimulates the production of interferon.
- Activates natural killer cells (NK).
- Helps to neutralize cancer-producing chemicals and free radicals.
- Strengthens connective tissue.
- Increases levels of other antioxidant enzymes.
- Improves appetite.
- Improves day-to-day quality of life in terminal cancer patients.

Vitamin C is involved in many metabolic and physiological processes of the body. While animals do manufacture vitamin C, the body's reserves are quickly used up in high free-radical production situations such as the ingestion of chemical additives and preservatives, exposure to insecticides, herbicides, and environmental pollutants, and by certain medications, such as antibiotics and cortisone. Therefore, it's important to supplement with vitamin C, even though some literature and many pet food manufacturers say it's not necessary.

The two forms recommended are ascorbic acid and the pH-neutral Ester-C (a patented calcium polyascorbate). Numerous studies have been done using Ester-C for various conditions in animals. It has been shown to be effective in many situations, including degenerative joint disease, painful locomotion, regeneration of cartilage, and immune stimulation.

High doses of ascorbic acid can cause diarrhea. Therefore, in humans and animals the recommended upper-limit therapeutic dose of vitamin C is considered to occur at "bowel tolerance." This upper dose should only be used when vitamin C is being prescribed therapeutically for the treatment of a disease condition. Otherwise, use the suggested dosage guidelines that we recommend in specific conditions throughout the book. The dose is increased by 25 percent every four days until the stool loosens, then reduced to the next lowest level and maintained.

Amino acids are the building blocks of proteins. They are essential for healthy body tissue and for many metabolic and physiological processes. Amino acids are integral in the production of many hormones, enzymes, and immunoglobulins utilized by the organs to run bodily functions. The primary organ for amino acid metabolism is the liver. Supplementation is essential when weaknesses are present. In medical practice, several amino acids have been therapeutically linked to diseases and the maintenance of wellness. Two of the most important amino acids in animals are L-carnitine and taurine.

Taurine is an amino acid that is nonessential for dogs, but essential for cats. Low levels can lead to heart problems (cardiomyopathy) and retinal degeneration (blindness). Researchers identified a direct link between low levels of taurine and cardiac disease. In addition, they found that dietary supplementation with taurine led to clinical improvement in cats with dilated cardiomyopathy.

Veterinarians and cat lovers learned a very hard lesson about amino acid deficiencies in the early 1990s, when it was discovered that many well-known premium cat foods were deficient in taurine. This taurine deficiency led to numerous deaths of cats from a serious, often fatal heart condition known as cardiomyopathy. As a result, most cat foods and supplements are now supplemented with taurine to prevent deficiencies.

Carnitine, an amino acid, is a key player in the metabolism of fatty acids and the release of cellular energy. If coenzyme Q10 is like the flame inside the cell, carnitine is the shuttle, ferrying "good fats" into the heart cells to be burned as energy, and carting off spent, oxidized, toxic fats. L-carnitine supplements allow the heart muscle to utilize oxygen more efficiently. Supplementing with carnitine will help to lower triglyceride levels in the blood. Many dogs and cats have high levels of fat in the blood because they are eating cooked diets that contain excessive levels of cooked, highly saturated animal fats.

Human cardiologists have observed dramatic effects with carnitine and CoQ10 in their patients with cardiovascular disease and high cholesterol as well as kidney and liver failure. Carnitine has produced clinical improvement in dogs with cardiomyopathies as it helps the heart muscles to use lower levels of oxygen more efficiently.

We use carnitine in our "fat busters" program to help animals lose weight. (See Chapter 1.) Carnitine is a nonessential amino acid and can be produced by the body from other amino acids such as lysine and methionine. This further underscores the value of giving your animal a well-rounded dietary supplement, because simply supplementing with carnitine by itself may not be the answer. There may be other underlying deficiencies that can cause problems.

While carnitine is readily available in foods (such as meat and dairy products) and there is no specific dietary requirement, we have some precautions. Many dog and cat foods, while they contain the required amounts of protein, may contain inferior protein sources which are amino acid depleted, leading to low levels of carnitine. This is why it is important to follow our Food Plan and supplement your base food with pure, high-grade sources of meat.

Glutamine (technically called L-glutamine) is one of the most abundant of all amino acids. Glutamine takes on an essential role in seriously ill animals, because these weakened dogs and cats cannot synthesize amino acids any longer. They are often wasting and losing muscle mass, and as the muscles begin to break down they release glutamine into the system. The body uses these rapidly dwindling stores for energy and to produce cellular immune system fighters such as white blood cells.

In addition, research has proven that the cells of the gastrointestinal (GI) tract use glutamine as a source of energy to maintain proper function. For this reason, glutamine is often added to the diet by veterinary gastroenterologists and nutritionists to ensure adequate glutamine levels are available for the sickly animal. Studies have indicated clear improvement in patients with Crone's disease and inflammatory bowel disease (IBD) when glutamine is added to the diet.

If you are following the Goldstein Food Plan and adding fresh (lightly steamed) meat daily to your animal's diet, you are probably providing adequate amounts of glutamine. However, if your animal is suffering from a degenerative disease such as arthritis, diabetes, liver or kidney disease, inflammatory bowel disease, or cancer, then we recommend additional supplementation with glutamine.

Glutathione is made up of three amino acids (a tripeptide of glutamine, glycine, and cysteine). Glutathione is an extremely powerful antioxidant that fights off free radicals, and plays an important role for the body in the detoxification of environmental toxins, such as chemicals pollutants, and proven carcinogens. It also enhances the effectiveness of lymphocytes, the primary white blood cells that help prevent cancer. Glutathione can help fight off muscle weakness and fatigue that often occurs in chronically ill animals. In addition, glutathione improves the effectiveness and functioning of the macrophages, which are the white cells' first line of defense against invaders.

Coenzyme Q10 (ubiquinone or CoQ10) is found in every cell's "power plant," known as the mitochondria, and is therefore directly involved with energy production. As a powerful antioxidant, CoQ10 helps to neutralize and hold down the levels of age-related, inflammation-producing free radicals.

CoQ10 is essential in the manufacture of adenosine triphosphate (ATP), the fundamental energy source for all the body's cells and tissues. The ability to synthesize CoQ10 declines with age. Deficiencies generally affect the heart first, as the heart muscle requires the nutrient and is continually utilizing energy. In addition, it is a key antioxidant and has indications in many chronic diseases, including gingivitis, arthritis, and many types of cancer.

Research has shown that CoQ10 is beneficial in treating both congestive heart disease and cardiomyopathy and is gaining attention in the human field for its healing and antiaging properties. It is generally well tolerated with few side effects, other than increased energy.

Along with immune-system-boosting herbs such as echinacea, CoQ10 is particularly beneficial in the treatment and prevention of periodontal disease and gingivitis. It is important to note that many serious degenerative diseases such as feline leukemia in cats and lymphosarcoma in dogs simultaneously will have serious gingivitis and periodontal diseases. Being a potent antioxidant, CoQ10 is beneficial for both conditions.

There are no specific dietary requirements for dogs and cats as the body can manufacture it, and it is readily available in good-quality foods.

Enzymes are essential in the conversion of foods to meet the energy needs of the body. They are also involved as catalysts in the many biochemical processes. Enzyme deficiency is caused either by a specific organ functioning at a less-than-optimal level, or a deficiency or lack of availability of the proper nutrients required for enzyme production. Nutrients, such as minerals, amino acids, and fatty acids, are required for the synthesis of various enzymes.

Primary causes of deficiencies or inadequacy include allergies and chronic inflammation, chronic disease, excess free radicals (depleted antioxidants), mineral deficiency, and organ malfunction caused by the chronic use of antibiotics upsetting the intestinal environment.

Minerals and Their Benefits

Many of the raw ingredients found in pet foods are either mineral-deficient due to depleted soils or do not contain adequate levels of minerals. It is for this reason that pet food manufacturers add minerals to their products in order to meet AAFCO's Nutritional Profile requirements. Most minerals used in pet foods are inexpensive, inorganic mineral combinations such as copper sulfate and ferrous oxide (rust), which are not as well absorbed, assimilated, and utilized in the body.

Minerals carry out hundreds of metabolic functions in the body. For example, they move nutrients in and out of cells as well as throughout the systems. Important mineral ratios include sodium/potassium and calcium/phosphorus. The passage and control of mineral levels in the blood and body tissues are under the direct guidance of hormones. Copper can be toxic to the liver; however, the levels of copper in the body, as well as in the food, are important. Zinc, on the other hand, is a beneficial mineral, particularly for the metabolism and health of the skin. One of zinc's properties is that it will compete with copper for absorption into the blood. Therefore, it can indirectly lower the levels of copper by reducing its absorption.

The following is a short list of minerals and how they are required in the day-to-day metabolic processes.

Calcium: a catalyst of specific enzymes that are required by various vitamins and minerals to perform their physiological function. Calcium is required for proper contraction of the muscles of the heart, and also aids in the metabolism of fat by helping lipoproteins to be absorbed from the intestines. Calcium is the main constituent in teeth and bones.

Chloride: helps to regulate the quantity of carbohydrates and proteins that pass into the cell.

Chromium: assists in the release of sugar from the blood to the muscles and other tissues. It is also involved in helping fatty acids be properly absorbed from the intestines into the blood. Chromium in the form of chromium picolinate is indicated in the treatment of diabetes mellitus.

Copper: an integral part of protein metabolism and in the release of toxins from the body. In veterinary medicine, we are aware of the difficulties animals face when there are higher-than-normal levels of copper (especially in Bedlington Terriers). However, copper deficiencies also present specific problems. Deficiencies can lead to reduced immune functions, less resistance to disease, anemia, and overall physical weakness.

Iron: responsible for the uptake and use of oxygen by the cells. It is essential for life, as it is involved in the formation of hemoglobin and red blood cells. Metabolically, it is required for the proper balance of hydrogen and oxygen in the blood.

Magnesium: essential for the formation of amino acids, RNA and DNA, and in conjunction with calcium, for regulating the beating of the heart. It is also involved in the digestion and assimilation of proteins by the cells, by working in concert with and polarizing minerals for uptake through the cell membrane.

Manganese: an important catalyst and cofactor in many enzymatic and metabolic processes. Along with magnesium, it helps to get protein through the cell membrane. It is found in the joints, pancreas, pituitary, liver, and kidneys, and functions in lipid and cholesterol metabolism as well as the proper functioning of the pancreas in sugar metabolism.

Phosphorus: integral to the release of energy from the metabolism of proteins, fats, and carbohydrates. It assists in the process of absorption of sugar from the intestines and its storage in the liver.

Potassium: found in abundance in the extracellular fluid, and plays a critical role in the osmotic pressure. It is important in maintaining a regular heart rhythm, and is involved in carbohydrate metabolism and assimilation by the cells.

Selenium: an important antioxidant, functioning in this capacity along with the enzyme glutathione peroxidase. It is involved in the proper functioning of the pancreas and helping with the absorption of glucose into the cells. It is beneficial in animals with cancer.

Sodium: Responsible for the osmotic balance in the cells and extracellular fluid along with potassium. Sodium is involved in the absorption of proteins and sugars across the cell membrane.

Zinc: Involved with many metabolic and physiological processes, including digestion and the absorption of carbohydrates across cell membranes. Zinc is important in the metabolic processes of the skin.

Our Own Healthy Nuggets

In years past, dedicated animal people faithfully mixed up to a dozen different nutrients into their animal's base food. Many still do, and we applaud this approach. However, it eventually became clear to us that for one reason or another, people weren't able to get all of these nutrients into their dog's or cat's diet. The animals wouldn't eat all of the veggies or the supplements, or preparing the regimen proved too time consuming. About ten years ago, we began looking for a way to make it easier for people to feed their pets vital, health-enhancing enzymes along with a rich supply of key antioxidant vitamins and minerals.

We searched high and low for a daily supplement we could wholeheartedly endorse, but we never could find a product that met all of our requirements. That's when Dr. Bob decided to make one himself. It took years to get the formula just right—but it was well worth the effort.

We decided to call our supplement Daily Health Nuggets because all of the living enzymes, vitamins, and minerals are blended into a soft, bite-sized nugget that dogs and cats love. Their vitamins come straight from vegetables and fruits that are still teeming with live enzymes. Nuggets aren't cooked or exposed to high temperatures that would inactivate the vitamins. They contain vegetables and grasses such as kale, spinach, broccoli, and barley grass, all rich in phytonutrients and antioxidants that have been dehydrated at low temperatures and not subjected to the high heat of cooking. Every ingredient is of the same quality that you would choose for yourself—none are by-products or leftovers from the food industry. Here are some of the health benefits your dog or cat will receive from Daily Health Nuggets:

- Supports overall nutritional balance. This is the key to helping your animal overcome—or avoid—health problems that can result from a weakened immune system.
- Helps to cleanse the bloodstream and the body of toxins, thanks to green "superfoods" such as alfalfa, parsley, barley grass, kale, and broccoli—some of the most chlorophyll-rich, enzyme-packed foods around.
- Activated antioxidants that help prevent chronic inflammation and degenerative conditions ranging from cataracts to cancer. Carrots, blue-green algae, and turmeric offer a rich supply of antioxidants for this purpose. Powerful antioxidants, such as vitamins A, C, and E, are also added.
- Provides the antibacterial and antioxidant benefits of garlic, which also promotes healthy blood and a clean intestinal tract free of noxious waste accumulations, along with the probiotic *L. acidophilus*.
- Helps strengthen the immune system with Ester-C and selenium, which help ward off seasonal stress illnesses such as upper respiratory and urinary tract infections.
- Improves circulation and supports skin health, thanks to lecithin. Not only do dogs and cats love the rich taste of lecithin, it helps to reduce dandruff and adds shine to the coat. Because lecithin breaks down fat, it also improves metabolism, and there is proven evidence that

lecithin supports skin, liver, and brain function.

- Rich in omega-3 and -6 fatty acids, thanks to lignan-rich flax seed and pure salmon oil. The medical literature strongly suggests that low levels of omega-3 oils may be implicated in dozens of afflictions, from allergies and arthritis to eczema and immune disorders.

- Contains additional vitamins, fats, and amino acids to complement your dog's and cat's nutritional requirements.

- Highly palatable. No matter how excellent a supplement is nutritionally, it's no good if your animal won't eat it. Nuggets double as a treat, flavored with a pure, human-grade chicken coating that's top-shelf USDA inspected and approved. Daily Health Nuggets make it easy to give your dog or cat all of the health-enhancing nutrients needed to protect against disease and ensure optimal good health and longevity.

We encourage you to follow as many levels of the Goldstein Food Plan as you can. Our program, as outlined in Chapter 1, is the fulcrum of health and vitality for dogs and cats of all types at all stages of life. Add fresh, pure water, plenty of daily exercise, and top it all off with love for outstanding results.

Chapter 3

Cultivate Vaccination Wisdom

You just received a postcard from your family veterinarian—a "friendly reminder" that your dog or cat is due for his or her annual booster vaccine. Like most animal guardians, you dutifully make an appointment; after all, you want to do the best for your animal friend. When you take your animal in, he or she may receive quite a wallop—a combination of five or more vaccines packaged into a single injection.

Your animal's immune system may pay a high price for this annual ritual. There is increasing evidence that repeated vaccinations may contribute to a weakened or suppressed immune system, which can trigger disorders as varied as arthritis, skin disease, diabetes, epilepsy, and even cancer. The potential for a long-term reaction (vaccinosis) may be the underlying cause for many autoimmune diseases (lupus, anemia, seizures, allergic dermatitis, hypo- and hyperthyroid condition) leading to heart, liver, or kidney failure.

Reactions to vaccines can also be short term and transient and may include pain, swelling, or an allergic reaction, such as hives. Post-vaccine side effects also include lethargy, digestive upsets, eye discharge, and other negative reactions.

We stopped routine automatic vaccinations of our own animals well over 30 years ago due to a gnawing suspicion, derived from our clinical experience, that certain diseases in our patients were linked to vaccinations. It was not an easy decision, and a great deal of soul-searching had to be done before our conclusion was made. To make matters worse, at the beginning of our vaccine awareness

Do a Reality Check
Is your animal's veterinarian recommending esoteric vaccines? Make sure you ask just how likely it is your animal will come in contact with this virus. And if it is likely, how serious is the disease? For example, kennel cough (parainfluenza) is a disease that despite its annoyance does not last long and is not serious or life threatening.

transformation, we were relying on instinct and had zero clinical proof that these injectable drugs, representing nearly 60 percent of our veterinary practice income, were having long-term ill effects on our patients.

The Body Allows Disease to Happen

In 1977, we read an article published by two medical researchers, Archivides Kalokerinos, MD, and Glenn Dettman, PhD, in *The Journal of the International Academy of Preventive Medicine*, entitled "Second Thoughts About Disease: A Controversy and Bechamp Revisited." These two researchers brought out several academic and intellectual points that changed our approach to vaccinations forever.

We want to take you through the elegant arguments made by Kalokerinos and Dettman. To do that, we must turn back the clock to the 1860s and 70s to the days of the French chemist Louis Pasteur. French physician Antoine Bechamp, a contemporary of Pasteur who history has forgotten, conducted prolific scientific research from 1853 to 1905. In his book, *Blood and the Third Anatomical Element*, published in 1912, Bechamp accused Pasteur of plagiarizing and distorting Bechamp's theories. Bechamp believed that disease was endogenous or "born within."

Specific enzymes, which Bechamp named microzyma, evolved into bacteria and viruses and caused disease, but only under certain conditions and circumstances (such as when the body's systems are run down). Furthermore, he explained, this disease process can happen without having these microzyma seeded from the outside. So the story goes that Pasteur distorted Bechamp's work and claimed that "germs" invade the body to cause disease. As history would have it, Pasteur's Germ Theory of Disease became the guiding light for advances in medicine, including antibiotics to kill these "invading" germs and vaccines to protect the body from them. Interestingly enough, Pasteur later retracted his Germ Theory, publicly stating that the key to disease was the "internal environment," but by that time it was too late and his theories were widely accepted as fact.

Debunking the Germ Theory

The Germ Theory of Disease has endured into our modern era of medicine. Kalokerinos and Dettman wrote, "Perhaps one of the greatest dangers of Pasteur's Germ Theory is that it is a part truth. As a part truth, it has stolen the show and taken our attention away from the endogenous host factor's resistance against disease." We find it quite interesting that 140 years later, the holistic medical thinking is now exploring Bechamp's original theory that the medical basis for disease may have been built on a flawed theory, one that has overlooked the functioning of the immune system as a key part of health.

Kalokerinos and Dettman went on to report their work with Australian aborigines in the 1960s and 1970s. In that research, they demonstrated the immune-suppressing effects of vaccinations in aboriginal children, discovering that the infant mortality rate was markedly increased with the introduction of mass vaccinations to the population of children.

The last piece of startling information was their reporting on the work of Dr. Fred Klenner, who was involved with Linus Pauling in studying the immune-stimulating effects of vitamin C. In his research, Dr. Klenner proposed the theory that the rapid rise in infant leukemia was the direct result of the introduction of mass vaccination of children for polio (Jonas Salk, MD, developed the killed vaccine and Albert Sabine, MD, developed the live vaccine), and that the introduction into the population of the modified live virus polio vaccine had far-reaching, devastating effects. His work proposed a link between vaccinations and serious chronic degenerative disease, in this case leukemia.

Armed with this intriguing information, we began asking our referred clients who came to us seeking alternatives for their animals' serious diseases when their animals had received their last vaccination. In one survey, we questioned 35 people whose animals had cancer and found that 90 percent had received a vaccine within two months of developing the cancer. Anecdotal but convincing proof for us.

"Vaccinate Wisely" Protocol

You can imagine our confusion when we made the connection that a vaccine given at a well-intended office visit could potentially cause serious disease consequences for the animal in the future. So, in the painful silence that hovered over a period of a few years, the voice calling for us to try a different way became more insistent. Gradually, among certain clients we were able to hint that although we did not have sufficient proof, we strongly suspected that it was unwise to continue on an automatic vaccine regimen for the rest of their animals' lives. The problem became even more disturbing because we could not offer any alternatives or a program to replace our old ways.

Once we added common sense to the mixture of intuition and clinical experience, the basis of our "Vaccinate Wisely" protocol began to take shape. Our protocol separated the needs of a puppy and kitten from those of adult and senior animals. Our young clients were vaccinated only for those diseases that posed a risk. We then spread out the frequency of administering vaccines as much as possible. In addition, we recommended avoiding multi-disease combination shots, thereby minimizing the antigenic stress on a single visit. We never recommend a vaccine for any animal that is ill, degenerating, or immunologically compromised. Our physical examination, therefore, became very important before any vaccine was given. We also never administered a vaccine for convenience, such as when an animal was simultaneously undergoing anesthesia for a surgical procedure.

Pioneers, especially in the professional community, often walk on eggshells. We were already receiving criticism from our colleagues for our unorthodox recommendations regarding diet and the treatment of disease. Perhaps we stayed in the closet too long in the beginning for fear of being ostracized. But courage is a weird emotion and the more we came out and shared our suspicions with clients, the more agreement we got, until one day the first professional veterinary journal article came out announcing the link between the feline leukemia vaccine and vaccine-associated feline sarcoma (a soft-tissue cancer occurring at the injection site).

Folks, that was all it took and we went public, announcing our stand on vaccines and our recommended protocol. Today, if you fill out a client questionnaire at the Healing Center for Animals, you will note that on the bottom of the first sheet we state: Do Not Automatically Vaccinate Your Animal. We believe that once you understand the entire clinical picture surrounding vaccines, your animal's longevity and health will be greatly enhanced.

New Veterinary Guidelines Support Vaccination Caution

Few issues generate such passion as vaccinations; however, real progress is being made in the veterinary community. In 2001, the American Veterinary Medical Association (AVMA) took a giant step forward in easing their members' fierce dependency on automatic annual vaccines. The AVMA is the largest professional association of veterinary practitioners in the US with over 64,000 members—your veterinarian is probably one of them.

A position paper, generated in April 2001 by the AVMA's task force on vaccines, called the Council on Biologic and Therapeutic Agents (COBTA), placed the official stamp of approval on what we and our colleagues have been saying since the early 1970s: "There currently exists inadequate data to scientifically determine a single best protocol for vaccination or revaccination."

Here are a few highlights and "talking points" to share with your veterinarian on your next visit if he or she is not familiar with the AVMA published guidelines. You can find the entire report through their web site, www.avma.org.

- "The one-year revaccination frequency recommendation found on many vaccine labels is based on historical precedent and United States Department of Agriculture regulation, not on scientific data. Even in those cases where scientific data was submitted to qualify the label claim, the data generated does not resolve the question about average or maximum duration of immunity."
- "There is evidence that some vaccines provide immunity beyond one year." In fact, according to researchers, "There is no proof that many of the yearly vaccines are necessary and that protection in many instances may be lifelong."

One of the leading reference manuals for the practicing veterinarian, *Kirk's Current Veterinary Therapy XI*, a practicing veterinarian's "bible," states that annual revaccination of dogs and cats "lacks scientific validity and verification." In addition, the text continues, "Almost without exception, there is no immunological requirement for revaccination."

At long last, the mainstream veterinary community has begun to question the advisability of automatic annual vaccinations, and the potential link to immune suppression and chronic degenerative diseases such as arthritis, autoimmune disease, skin disease, diabetes, heart disease, epilepsy, and cancer.

More Support From the Medical Community

Some may criticize the AVMA guidelines as somewhat politically oriented, because this organization is really lobbying for the veterinary profession. In 2003, the task force from the American Animal Hospital Association (AAHA), the association that is more practically oriented for the practitioner, published "Important Vaccination "Do's and Don'ts," summarized as follows:

- Do Not Vaccinate Needlessly. Don't revaccinate more often than is needed, and only with the vaccines that prevent diseases for which that animal is at risk.
- Do Not Vaccinate Anesthetized Patients. Should an anesthetized animal develop a hypersensitivity reaction, they may vomit and are at increased risk of aspirating.
- Do Not Vaccinate Pregnant Dogs. The dog may abort or fetuses may get infected.
- Do Not Vaccinate Animals on Immunosuppressive Therapy. These animals may not develop

an adequate immune response, but even worse, they could develop disease (e.g., postvaccinal distemper, clinical canine parvovirus).

- Do Make Sure the Last Dose of a Puppy Immunization Series Is Administered at 12 Weeks of Age. At 12 weeks of age, interference by maternal antibody is less of a concern, and the puppy's immune system is more mature; thus, there is a greater opportunity for a robust immune response to the vaccine.

- Do Not Assume That Vaccines Cannot Harm a Patient. Vaccines are potent, medically-active agents and have the very real potential of producing adverse events.

- Do Not Revaccinate a Dog With Vaccines Previously Known To Induce Anaphylaxis in That Dog. Test the animal's serum for antibodies to determine if the animal is immune. The risk from vaccine-induced anaphylaxis may be much greater than the risk of infection.

What Does This Mean for Your Dog or Cat?

As the political and scientific battles over vaccinations rage on, the question remains: What should you do for your puppy, kitten, adult, or senior animal who shares your home, right now?

Our general advice is to vaccinate only for high-risk infectious diseases (called core diseases), depending upon the likelihood of your dog or cat being exposed to other animals and the area of the country in which you live. For example, leptospirosis has been a part of most vaccination programs for 40 years, but if you live in an area that is not heavily populated with rats or deer (which transmit leptospirosis), you can safely eliminate this vaccine from your program. The same goes for Lyme disease and canine parainfluenza (kennel cough), which is a self-limiting disease.

Core Vaccines or Diseases	
DOG	CAT
Distemper	Feline Distemper
Adenovirus	Herpesvirus
Parvovirus	Calicivirus
Rabies	Rabies

We also suggest that you:

- Minimize the number of diseases per injection. Vaccinations, most commonly given as modified live vaccines (MLVs), often contain several diseases combined into one injection. Dogs are often vaccinated as puppies and annually thereafter for distemper, adenovirus, leptospirosis, parainfluenza, and parvo. You'll hear these combination vaccines referred to as DA2LP+PV or as a "5-in-1" or "7-in-1." Vaccine manufacturers still make individual disease (monovalent) vaccines, although they are now more and more difficult to find. Ask your veterinarian to request them from his or her suppliers with the minimum amount of core diseases present.

- Your animal should not receive more than one vaccine type per visit. It is important to give the least number of vaccines to achieve optimal immunity.

- Request that your veterinarian give each vaccine in a different location (i.e., shoulder, neck, hindquarters) and keep a record of where each injection is given. This is especially important in cats who are susceptible to vaccine-induced feline sarcoma.

- Know the signs of an adverse vaccine reaction. These range from redness, pain, and swelling at the injection site to systemic allergic reactions (anaphylaxis) in which the face swells rapidly and breathing is compromised within minutes of receiving the shot. This is an emergency situation, and the animal must quickly receive injectable medication in order to reverse the effects.

- Ask your veterinarian to use an inactivated or killed vaccine with no adjuvant when that choice is available, especially for kittens and cats. Spread each vaccine out at a minimum of three- to four-week intervals.

- Do not vaccinate dogs or cats that have had adverse reactions to any vaccine or who currently have an immune-compromising disease such as cancer.

- Do not vaccinate elderly, weak, or debilitated dogs or cats, and never allow your veterinarian to vaccinate at the same time as any surgical or medical procedure that requires anesthesia.

- Do not start a vaccine program too early. The antibodies found in mother's milk will protect the youngster and her offspring will have natural immunity. As a general rule, never vaccinate before nine weeks of age. When considering a new puppy or kitten, ask the breeder about prior vaccinations—too many too soon can set up the youngster for future health issues.

- With cats, never allow a vaccination to be given in the scruff of the neck or between the shoulder blades! Insist that vaccinations be given in the hindquarters (right and left rear legs). In the event a vaccine-induced sarcoma develops, the affected limb can be amputated if there is no other choice to save the cat's life.

- Keep accurate records for all of your animal's vaccinations and medical history, including the type of vaccination given, the location of the injection, the manufacturer of the vaccine, and the lot/serial number or sticker from the vaccine vial.

- Continue to schedule an annual veterinary examination with bloodwork to ensure continued health, and simply "hold the vaccines" for most animals (based upon titer test results).
- Monitor serum antibody levels annually. Revaccinate every three years or as determined by the blood levels of serum antibody.
- Do not vaccinate animals currently battling any chronic or acute disease, including epilepsy or a systemic infection.
- Ask your breeder whether reactions to vaccines are in the bloodline. Breeds such as Akitas, Weimaraners, and those with dilute coat color such as Shetland Sheepdogs and Harlequin Great Danes, are more susceptible to adverse reactions.
- Feed an immune-boosting diet rich in antioxidants to strengthen your animal's defenses against disease, enhance longevity, and improve quality of life.
- Detoxify after the vaccine with a homeopathic remedy (see page 55).

The Titer Testing Option

The next time your animal is on the table and your veterinarian is about to reach for the needle, look him or her straight in the eye and say, "Doctor, I'd like to run a serum antibody titer test on Oliver this year before revaccinating." If your veterinarian has been paying attention to the literature or is currently evolving toward the holistic veterinary community, he or she will cheerfully agree to draw blood for a titer test.

After your puppy or kitten has received the initial series and a single series of boosters one year later, do not give future vaccinations automatically. (Most areas of the country legally require rabies so, of course, you must follow local regulations.) If you live in an area with a high occurrence of a specific disease or need proof of immunity for kenneling or the groomer's, ask your veterinarian to test your dog's immunity level with a simple blood test called a serum antibody (titer) test.

If the level of antibodies is adequate, don't revaccinate. Here you may run into resistance from your veterinarian. He or she may tell you there is no definitive scientific proof that titers are 100 percent accurate. In response, quote from the AVMA guidelines: "Vaccination does not protect every individual patient even when they are properly vaccinated."

According to Antech Diagnostics, one of the country's leading diagnostic blood laboratories, "In the intervening years between booster vaccinations, and in the case of geriatric pets, circulating humoral immunity against the clinically important infectious agents can be evaluated by measuring serum vaccine antibody titers as an indication of the presence of immune memory. Titers do not distinguish between immunity generated by vaccination and/or exposure to disease agents, although the magnitude of immunity produced just by vaccination is usually lower."

Sample Core Vaccination Programs for Puppies and Kittens

Discuss this type of gentle, noninvasive approach with your veterinarian. Ask your veterinarian to use an inactivated or killed vaccine when that choice is available. And request whenever possible to vaccinate for one disease (called a monovalent vaccine) at a time, spreading them out at three-week intervals, as follows:

Sample Vaccine Program for Puppies (Review with your family veterinarian)

9 weeks	Canine distemper and Canine Adenovirus 2
12 weeks	Parvovirus (killed)
15 weeks	Canine distemper and Canine Adenovirus 2
18 weeks	Parvovirus (killed)
6 months	Rabies (one-year, usually required by state law)
16 months	Canine distemper and Canine Adenovirus 2 (Check titer—vaccinate only if antibody level is low)
20 months	Rabies booster (usually required by state law)
24 months	Parvovirus (Check titer—vaccinate only if antibody level is low)
Year 4	Rabies (three year)
Year 5	Canine distemper and Canine Adenovirus 2, followed by Parvovirus (killed) in one to two months (see note below)

Sample Vaccine Program for Kittens (Review with your family veterinarian)

9 weeks	Feline distemper (Panleukopenia)
12 weeks	Rhinotracheitis/Calici
15 weeks	Feline distemper (Panleukopenia)
18 weeks	Rhinotracheitis/Calici
6 months	Rabies (one-year)
16 months	Feline distemper (Panleukopenia) (Check titer—vaccinate only if antibody level is low)
20 months	Rhinotracheitis/Calici (Check titer—vaccinate only if antibody level is low)
24 months	Rabies booster (three-year)
Year 4	Feline distemper (Panleukopenia) and Rhinotracheitis/Calici (give 4 to 5 weeks apart) (see note below)
Year 5	Rabies booster

Note: For dogs and cats, starting in year 4, check titers yearly for distemper, adenovirus 2, parvo or feline distemper, rhinotracheitis/calici. Hold off on vaccinating if titer proves immunity.

Except where vaccination is required by law, all animals, but especially those that previously experienced an adverse reaction to vaccination, can have serum antibody titers measured annually instead of revaccination. If adequate titers are found, the animal should not need revaccination until some future date. Rechecking antibody titers can be performed annually thereafter, or can be offered as an alternative to pet owners who prefer not to follow the conventional practice of annual boosters.

How Well Do Titers Assess Immunity?

Now we arrive at the heart of the issue—the validity of antibody testing. As the subject of adverse effects of vaccines and vaccinosis is still debated, so is the subject of measuring antibody titers as a definitive check for immunity in your animal. Many veterinarians are questioning why, where, and how to correctly interpret the results of titer testing as a measure of the level of immunity to a specific disease.

There are actually two parts to immunity. The first—the more tangible aspect—is the level of serum antibodies, which can be measured with a blood test. The second, cellular memory, represents the body's inherent ability to fight disease when challenged. When your animal's immune system is operating at a high level, cellular memory is more powerful than any vaccine. Prof. Richard Halliwell showed that animals can be protected by cellular memory even when serum antibodies are below acceptable levels or are seemingly inadequate to fight off the disease. This explains why animals who have never had a certain vaccination can fight off a disease without succumbing to it.

Since it is virtually impossible to test for cellular memory other than by challenging the animal's immune system with disease, we are left with two options: vaccinate or test for levels of serum antibodies. Since frequent vaccinations carry now proven inherent risks, many veterinarians are recommending annual titer testing and vaccinating only as necessary to maintain titers at protective levels.

If your veterinarian is unfamiliar with the procedure, offer the references cited on page 53 and names and phone numbers of the main laboratories that do testing. There are variations in interpretation among laboratories as well as variations based on the type of tests the lab does; therefore, work closely with your veterinarian and laboratory to ensure you will receive a proper interpretation.

Other factors might influence your vaccination program. For example, show dogs or cats might need twice-a-year titer tests to make sure they are maintaining sufficient immunity. Outdoor cats and cats living in multi-cat households may also have an increased risk of exposure to certain diseases. Remember, the ultimate immune-system booster is good nutrition, proper supplementation, pure water, and exercise.

In the Face of Resistance

Resistance to titer testing often comes in the form of "I don't know of a lab that will run this test" or "It costs more for the titer test than for the vaccine, so why not just get the vaccine?" While this may be correct in the short run, over the long run it is neither economically sound nor, more importantly, good for your animal's health.

The use of blood tests to check antibody levels is even more important if your animal is geriatric or immune compromised, has a chronic degenerative disease, or a long history of annual revaccination, since these animals are most at risk for problems stemming from vaccinations.

One of the leading proponents of serum antibody testing as an alternative to automatic revaccination is Jean Dodds, DVM. Based in Santa Monica, California, Dr. Dodds is founder and president of Hemopet/Pet Life Line, a nonprofit blood bank program for animals incorporating an adoption program for canine donors. Her knowledge has widely influenced both holistic and traditional thinking on the subject of vaccines. In addition, a new option called TiterChek checks immune status for distemper and parvovirus antibody status in dogs in 15 minutes at your veterinarian's office. The test is available through veterinarians from Synbiotics, Inc.

Titer Testing Comes of Age

These laboratories all perform titer testing:
- Cornell Diagnostic Laboratory (607) 253-3900
- Antech Diagnostics (800) 872-1001
- IDEXX Veterinary Services: Eastern Region (888) 433-9987 Western Region (800) 444-4210
- Kansas Veterinary Diagnostic Laboratory (785) 532-5650

Some of the tests available include canine distemper and canine parvovirus in dogs; and feline herpesvirus, rhinotracheitis, feline panleukopenia (feline parvo), feline leukemia, and feline calicivirus in cats. The tests correspond to core vaccines for each species.

Show your veterinarian the following references if he or she is not familiar with titer testing:

"There is less risk associated with taking a blood sample for a titer test than giving an unnecessary vaccination."—"Titer Testing and Vaccination: A New Look at Traditional Practices," participants Ronald Schultz, Richard B. Ford, Jory Olsen, and Fred Scott, *Veterinary Medicine*, March 2002.

"While difficult to prove, risks associated with overvaccination are an increasing concern among veterinarians. These experts say antibody titer testing may prove to be a valuable tool in determining your patients' vaccination needs."—*Veterinary Medicine*, March 2002.

"Research shows that once an animal's titer stabilizes, it is likely to remain constant for many years."—*Veterinary Medicine*, March 2002.

The Real Issue: Are Vaccines Dangerous?

The heart of the controversy is whether or not vaccines can cause serious degenerative disease. The most common side effects discussed by conventional veterinarians and animal health care professionals are the physical side effects. After a vaccine is given, the animal may experience pain, swelling, soreness, loss of appetite, stiffness of joints, and fever. In some instances, there can be an allergic reaction with major redness, itching, and hives. In rare instances, anaphylaxis occurs—a severe reaction resulting in major swelling (usually in the face), generalized hives, difficulty breathing, and in some cases, shock, and/or death.

It is easy to determine these physical side effects because they usually occur within minutes after the injection. However, what are the long-term, hidden effects of vaccines?

Vaccine-Induced Sarcomas in Cats

Recently, the veterinary research literature has made doctors and people aware of a disease called Vaccine-Induced Feline Sarcoma. The research literature states that 1 in every 1,000 to 10,000 cats will develop this aggressive form of cancer. There are approximately 70 million cats in the US, which equates to nearly 20,000 cats developing this deadly disease secondary to receiving a vaccine. The first question is, How would you feel if one of these cats that developed this deadly cancer lived with you?

The proposed theory of vaccine-induced sarcomas is that post vaccine, an uncontrolled inflammation is set up that eventually worsens and leads to cancer. Most veterinarians comment that since the incidence of vaccine-induced sarcomas is so low (compared with the number of cats that are vaccinated), then vaccines are quite safe. In the cats that do develop the sarcomas, they explain that immune suppression and/or genetic predisposition is involved and therefore really not relevant in the overall picture. That opinion is totally missing the boat!

Holistic veterinarians are quite familiar with a real reaction secondary to the vaccines, which can have debilitating and devastating effects on the organs of the immune system. When the immune system becomes compromised, all sorts of serious degenerative diseases can occur—cancer is just one example. Other common diseases that have been linked to vaccines in dogs and cats include:

- Hypothyroidism in dogs
- Hyperthyroidism in cats
- Epilepsy
- Liver and kidney disease
- Autoimmune disease, such as anemia
- Diabetes
- Cushing's or Addison's disease (dysfunction of the adrenal glands)
- Degenerative joint disease and arthritis
- Chronic skin disease

- Heart disease such as cardiomyopathy
- Cancer—all forms

We often think about those initial 35 animals in the early 1970s that had received a vaccine within two to three months of their diagnosis. They started our questioning process about the safety of vaccines. While not clinically proven, certainly it is not clinically disproven and therefore should be taken into consideration when all vaccines are given, especially in geriatric, debilitated, and immune-compromised animals.

The Spectre of Vaccinosis

Vaccinosis is a homeopathic term that describes symptoms of a disease resulting from giving a vaccine. These include low-grade fever, weakness, loss of appetite, itchy skin, and even more serious conditions such as epilepsy. British physician Compton Burnett gave the condition its name. It was also Burnett, using his vast knowledge of homeopathic remedies, who discovered that by using the homeopathic remedy *Thuja occidentalis*, he was able to reverse many of the symptoms of these diseases.

The homeopathic literature (both for people and for animals) has reported many times that in suspected post-vaccination diseases where homeopathic remedies have been used to control a disease, the symptoms of that disease immediately return after another vaccine is given.

Homeopathic Detoxification: The Right Thing to Do

While there are few definitive studies linking vaccines directly to degenerative diseases (except, of course, for vaccine-induced feline sarcomas), it has been repeatedly observed by many holistic veterinarians and health care practitioners that vaccines will compromise the immune system, leading to all sorts of serious diseases.

Therefore, if you live in a state where vaccines are required by law or if you have made the decision to vaccinate because of the fear of your animal developing a serious disease, we urge you to consider homeopathic detoxification with *Thuja occidentalis* 30C (available in small shaker vials at your whole-foods market). This will help to remove the side effects of the vaccine and prevent vaccinosis.

These remedies will be most effective if they are given immediately after the vaccine is administered; they will not interfere with the immunity that the vaccine is intended to promote. Homeopathic remedies can even counteract the effects of vaccines given many years ago.

Homeopathic remedies may loose their potency if handled. To administer, fold a small index card in half and shake out the Thuja pellets into the fold. Without touching the remedies, gently crush the pellets from the outside. Place the powdered remedy directly onto the membranes of your animal's mouth or onto the tongue. Give the remedy for three, five, or seven days—depending on how many diseases are in the vaccine.

Thuja occidentalis	
Cat/Small Dog (up to 14 lb)	1 pellet
Medium Dog (15-34 lb)	2 pellets
Large/Giant Dog (35+ lb)	3 pellets

A New Vaccine Attempts to Minimize Risk

At a recent veterinary conference we were exposed to expensive advertising and video presentations by pet food companies and companies that make vaccines. One video, produced by Merial Company (one of the largest suppliers of vaccines to the veterinary profession), brought home how far the awareness about vaccines has progressed. It was about a newly introduced Feline Leukemia vaccine: "New Non-Adjuvanted PureVax Recombant Leukemia Vaccine, and the Vet Jet transdermal vaccination system provide enhanced immune response through targeted antigen presentation." What Merial has done is remove the adjuvant (the chemical additive that is in the vaccine injection that is designed to cause local inflammation and increase the body's response to the vaccine). It is the adjuvant that is suspected in causing the vaccine induced fibrosarcomas that occur in cats. Through "targeted antigen presentation," only the genetic material of the leukemia virus which produces the immune response is given, meaning it does not multiply in the cat's body (it's not alive) and potentially contaminate or infect the environment. (A concern with giving modified live vaccines (MLV) is that the virus of that particular disease can be shed from the body and contaminate the environment. These MLVs actually multiply inside the body, which is the method that they use to stimulate the immune response.) Lastly, transdermal means that the vaccine is forced into the layers of the skin using pressure instead of needles. These layers of skin contain the cells that start the immune response. Since there is no needle, there is no pain, and a smaller volume of the vaccine can be delivered to achieve maximum protection. This also means the skin will be exposed first to the virus particles and start the immune reaction. In injection vaccines, the skin is bypassed—a much less natural type of exposure.

Certainly congratulations should be offered to Merial for taking the bold step of attempting to minimize the inherent risks associated with vaccines. Pressure from guardians, veterinarians, and researchers is finally making a difference. Still, this new vaccination should never be given to pregnant cats, and side effects such as fever or inflammation can occur.

Alternatives to Vaccines: Homeopathic Nosodes

Nosodes are actually homeopathic remedies. Simply, a nosode is the actual disease-causing agent, such as the bacteria or virus that is homeopathically potentiated and diluted. (See Chapter 4: Natural Healing Modalities.) The theory is that by giving the diluted form of the disease orally—one of the body's natural routes of exposure—the immune system has the opportunity to develop antibodies and natural immunity without the potentially devastating effects of vaccines.

Nosodes have been used and are accepted in Europe. They are not currently in favor in the United States because there have been no clinical studies proving they are effective in preventing disease. We believe nosodes are a promising alternative to vaccines and warrant further research.

What You Can Do

According to the AVMA paper, "There is a critical need for more fully developed, scientifically based, and statistically valid evaluation of vaccine products to provide practitioners with a basis for developing vaccination programs that maximize benefits and minimize associated risks for the patients under their care."

Discuss the AVMA guidelines or find a doctor who is open to the new thinking on vaccines. Take your dog or cat to the doctor for an annual physical along with titer tests for the most prevalent diseases and a general blood screening that should be reviewed medically and nutritionally.

At the same time, we also encourage you to make every effort to reduce your dog or cat's overall exposure to chemicals, including antibiotics, steroids, heartworm medication, and flea and tick medication. While high-tech veterinary medicine can be a lifesaver, the routine reliance on multiple drugs and chemicals will gradually wear down your animal's liver, kidneys, and other organs of detoxification. It's far better to support the immune system with healthy foods, targeted supplements, fresh pure water, and plenty of exercise and affection daily.

Additional Vaccination Information

For those of you with human children who are battling the vaccine dilemma, you may be interested in joining the National Vaccine Information Center (www.909shot.com) or reading *A Shot in the Dark: Why the P in the DPT Vaccination May Be Hazardous to Your Child's Health* by Harris L. Coulter and Barbara Loe Fisher. This is valuable information for young and growing children and their parents.

Chapter 4

Natural Healing Modalities

For the last several years, medical and veterinary practitioners have been expanding their horizons to satisfy their clients' desire for gentler, yet effective, remedies for themselves and their animal friends. Today, acupuncture, homeopathy, flower essences, and herbal medicine are just a few of the healing modalities readily available to animals throughout the country.

It is only natural that the human alternative health movement would filter down to our companion animals. As a culture, we are becoming acutely aware of the role of a preventive, proactive approach to living and longevity. In addition, people are questioning the side effects and risks inherent in the Western "allopathic" model of drugs and surgery, which often ignores the root cause of disease. Symptom suppression is no longer automatically seen as "the cure" to society's epidemic of chronic degenerative disease.

In this chapter, we present several of our favorite complementary healing modalities. We use most of them in our practice and know they can help you and your animal friends achieve lasting heath and wellness. Most have professional standards of training and certification which are strongly advised when selecting a practitioner. In addition, when choosing any healer or health care professional, we encourage you to also follow your intuition, which is usually right on target.

Tap Into Acupuncture

When Dr. Bob first began practicing holistic veterinary medicine in the early 1970s, there was a wide gulf in philosophy between it and conventional practice. Back then, it seemed utterly impossible that the two would ever find common ground. Now, nearly three decades later, much has changed.

In 1998, the FDA gave its stamp of approval to acupuncture, an age-old practice of healing and a cornerstone of alternative therapy. Holistic medicine and therapies are rapidly becoming accepted, even mainstream.

> "It does not matter whether medicine is old or new, so long as it brings about a cure. It matters not whether theories be eastern or western, so long as they prove to be True." —Jen Hsou Lin, DVM, PhD

Many veterinary practices now routinely ask their clients whether their animals have been under any "emotional stress" as part of the medical workup. Many hospitals, while remaining committed to conventional medicine, have added an "alternative practitioner" under their shingle, often one who is certified in acupuncture.

We have been using acupuncture since the 1970s. Dr. Bob's brother, Martin Goldstein, DVM, was one of the first veterinarians to become a certified veterinary acupuncturist. Since then, acupuncture has been one of the "door opening" alternative therapies for conventional practitioners. It gained rapid acceptance in the animal field because when performed skillfully, acupuncture can quickly alleviate pain and discomfort for a variety of conditions. We know of many animals who were carried into the office yet walked out on their own feet.

The art and science of acupuncture is over 3,000 years old. Over the centuries, practitioners mapped out locations of specific acupuncture points, which are strung together like Christmas lights to form pathways called meridians. The animal's life-force energy, called chi (pronounced "chee"), flows along these meridians. A blockage at any point along the way can upset the balance and lead to a diseased state.

The insertion of very fine, filament-like needles in specific areas releases opiate-like compounds called endorphins, which help reduce pain and provide a sense of well-being. The needles stimulate the acupoints, which act on several systems at once (neurologic, immunologic, and endocrine) to release and redirect blocked energy. Veterinarians may insert needles alone or add warmed herbs (moxibustion), vitamin B12, or a low electrical current (electro-acupuncture) to enhance the effects.

Acupuncture is especially effective in older and aging animals suffering from inflammatory conditions such as spinal problems, hip and elbow dysplasia, and other forms of arthritis. In addition, it can help relieve gastrointestinal conditions such as colitis and inflammatory bowel disease, and help with the prevention of chronic stomach problems such as gastritis and bloat; neurological problems such as loss of control of the hind legs (degenerative myelopathy) and epilepsy; and inflammatory lung problems such as asthma, to name a few. It can also ease postsurgical pain.

Acupuncture is not a panacea—you must be prudent when dealing with serious diseases. The treatment of cancer, for example, requires careful and precise balancing of the body's energy, and if approached improperly, could cause the cancer to grow even faster.

Fitting Acupuncture Into Your Program

You'll find that acupuncture ties in nicely with both conventional therapies as well as other holistic modalities, such as homeopathic, herbal, glandular, and nutritional supplements. Your goal is to select whatever therapy is necessary to stabilize your animal's condition, as well as the most supportive, noninvasive natural therapies to rebuild the immune system.

A course of acupuncture may require multiple treatments. Certainly you are likely to see subtle results within the first session or two, but more often a weekly or biweekly series of treatments for six to ten sessions may be necessary to obtain optimal results. Afterwards, your animal may benefit from periodic "tune up" visits to maintain health.

How to Choose a Veterinary Acupuncturist

How do you find a qualified veterinary acupuncturist? First, it is recommended that the individual be certified through the International Veterinary Acupuncture Society, a non-profit organization dedicated to the worldwide promotion of acupuncture as an integral part of veterinary care. The Society establishes high standards of veterinary acupuncture through responsible research, educational programs, and accreditation examination.

In 1998, a group of veterinarians formed the American Academy of Veterinary Acupuncture (AAVA) to further serve the needs of American veterinary acupuncturists. The society was formed to promote both veterinary acupuncture and Traditional Chinese Medicine (TCM) through education and leadership. The AAVA offers a directory of qualified veterinarians as well as educational and informational materials about the art of acupuncture in animals. See the resources section for the the contact information for these organizations.

To help you connect with a veterinarian who is right for your animal, seek out referrals from people you trust. When you and your animal meet the veterinarian, look for a practitioner who is gentle, caring, and compassionate. With acupuncture, technical proficiency alone may not be enough to produce lasting results. Acupuncture is a very intuitive field and remains as much an art as a science.

One of our clients, Beth Errichett, has a dog suffering from a degeneration of the spine. Along with a nutraceutical program, Dr. Bob recommended acupuncture. Beth was resistant, confessing that she "went that route and it did not work. I really didn't care for the practitioner." Bob explained to Beth that those feelings could actually block positive results, and he recommended another certified acupuncturist whose "vibes" worked better with her and her animal. Now they are getting positive results.

Be forewarned that acupuncture may not be appropriate as a healing modality for animals with cancer. Seek the guidance of a certified veterinary acupuncturist and discuss the pros and cons before starting acupuncture as part of your therapy program.

Aromatherapy/Essential Oils: An Ancient Healing Modality Rediscovered

You know the old expression, "You can lead a horse to water, but you can't make him drink"? Well, that really rings true when it comes to essential oils. Over the years, we've had plenty of introductions to essential oil companies; however, it wasn't until a painful personal experience that we made the connection and saw the benefits of this unusual healing modality.

For years, Susan has suffered from a painful inflammation associated with an old lower back injury. These flareups, which often handicap her for days, were treated with bed rest, homeopathics, Chinese herbs, and chiropractic adjustments. If you have ever had your back "go out," you know how debilitating it can be. As a result, Susan is constantly seeking better solutions and is particularly sensitive to others (be they human or animal) who share the same problem.

Early last year, Dr. Jim Martin, her chiropractor, introduced her to the essential oil Valor, a blend of rosewood, birch, helic ivy, blue tansy, frankincense, and spruce oils. During an intense episode, she applied a dab directly to her feet and spine. The pain spontaneously reduced. Coupled with the use of a magnetic back brace, her mobility continued to improve. Was it for real? We didn't know until we began to use the oils on our own animals.

Our late Boxer, Vivienne, had a rocky beginning in life. She was the runt of the litter and had her ears cropped, a practice we find reprehensible. She was antisocial, full of tension, often cowering and prone to stomach and intestinal upsets. It's very important, when introducing essential oils to animals, to first ask permission. So, Susan offered Vivienne a light sniff of the essential oil Valor and observed her response. Vivienne came over and sniffed with enthusiasm—the classic sign that this was the "right" remedy. Encouraged by this affirmation, Susan placed a dab on the palm of her hand and gently rubbed the oil into Vivienne's spine with her fingers and palm. The results were as immediate as they were remarkable: Vivienne, our problem child, mellowed out and relaxed on the spot. In the process, we could see her spine softening and straightening.

Over the next ten days Susan continued to alternate Valor and another oil blend, Release. Vivienne was visibly enthusiastic after each application. We could almost see the memories surfacing and releasing.

How Do Essential Oils Work?

The oils are absorbed through the skin or from the mucous membranes of the nose and enter the bloodstream and cross the blood-brain barrier very quickly—within five to six seconds they can penetrate cellular membranes and increase their oxygenation. As a result, they are natural chelators, binding to metals and chemicals and helping detoxify the body. In the brain, they reach the area called the limbic system, which is the emotional center where memories of fear and trauma are held, and can help balance the animals' emotions and reduce the adverse effects of stress. The amygdale, which is a small structure found in this part of the brain, is important in both the sorting and releasing of emotional trauma and fear.

Recently, we tried an oil on our sun conure, MacMillan. For the last 12 years, we have been "smuggling" him into the seaside inn where we go on vacation. When the seagulls fly by, he begins to squawk and becomes agitated. Not only do we fear being "found out," but we also want him to experience joy while on holiday. So, Susan selected Abundant Health's essential oil Joy, which is a blend of rose, bergamot, mandarin, Ylang ylang, lemon, and geranium, placed a tiny amount in the palm of her hand, and allowed the vapors to diffuse near him. He became totally peaceful—the squawking simply stopped. We were now more convinced than ever that we were onto a genuine healing modality.

Caution!

It is important to note that these oils are potent and even toxic if they are taken orally. Only use them topically on dogs, and with the diffuser method for cats or dogs.

Digging deeper, we learned that essential oils raise the vibrational frequency of the cells—the higher the frequency, the greater the health of any organism. Essential oils have been used for 6,500 years, originating in what is now Pakistan. They are considered the "first medicine" and are mentioned frequently throughout the Bible and in Egyptian hieroglyphs. Much research has been done worldwide on the oils since the 1920s, beginning with French scientist Rene-Maurice Gattefosse, PhD, who did his research on essential oils for humans.

You now can tap into a wealth of knowledge and experience in essential oils and their use in animals. One great reference is *Holistic Aromatherapy for Animals: A Comprehensive Guide to Their Use of Essential Oils and Hydrosols With Animals* by Leigh Bell, who says, "Just as aromatherapy has become a scientifically validated medical practice for people, it has become an increasingly popular health treatment for animals." *Veterinary Aromatherapy* by Nelly Grosjean and *Reference Guide for Essential Oils* by Connie and Alan Higley, are two other good resources.

Essential oils can stimulate and boost the immune system, and are antiviral, antibacterial, and antifungal. However, there is an art to their processing, and a code of ethics and integrity needs to be present for these healing agents to be potent and productive. Herbs intended for healing should be grown organically in an uncontaminated environment free of fertilizers and pesticides and, once harvested, distilled fresh. Failure to adhere to rigorous standards may compromise the oil's purpose and effectiveness.

How to Get Started Using Essential Oils

We've selected a few of our favorite blended oils, which will tackle the most frequent conditions your dog or cat may encounter (see the box on page 65). They may be used in aromatic form by inhalation or diffusion (good for both cats and dogs), or topically for dogs. *They are never to be given orally*. If you are using an oil for the first time, dilute it by combining three to four drops of the essential oil with one-half teaspoon olive, sesame, or almond oil. Also, it's best not to combine essential oils—use just one at a time. If you want to try a second oil, wait at least four hours to allow the body to respond without overloading.

It's extremely important that your animal's first experience with essential oils be a positive one. When introducing your animal to an oil, allow your dog or cat to come to the oil by sniffing it, and use your intuition to guide you. A few drops rubbed into your cupped hands is a good way to offer it to them, or spritz the environment with a diffuser. You may work with the oils topically on dogs by applying them to the paws, along the spine, at the tips of the ears or on the back of the neck. (Keep the oil away from your animal's eyes.) Remember that your animal's nose is much more sensitive than your own, and the oils are very concentrated, so be sparing in their application.

Blended Formulas		
Formula	Condition	Benefits
Valor	Arthritis, tension	Helps to realign the spine, relieve pain (aspirin-like), soothes swelling and inflammation
Lavender	Allergies	Natural anti-histamine, anti-inflammatory, antiseptic. Promotes general sense of well-being. Known as the "universal" oil
Frankincense	Tumors	Long considered a holy oil; anti-infectious, immune-stimulating, anti-tumoral, antidepressant
Lemongrass	Infections	Assists with tissue regeneration, restorative tonic, anti-inflammatory, analgesic, vasodilator
Peace & Calming	Stress, Hyperactivity	Promotes relaxation and grants a sense of peace, calms overexuberant youngsters
Release	Emotional trauma	Helps to release emotional holding patterns, overcome grief
Di-Tone	Parasites	Digestive aid, antiparasitic

Note: Essential oils are not intended as a substitute for medical diagnosis and treatment. Contact your veterinarian if symptoms persist.

Essential Oil Safety Guidelines

- Diffuser method dosage for a dog: dilute the oil to one-half the recommended adult human dose before diffusing. For a cat, dilute the dog dosage by half again (equivalent to one-quarter of a human dose). Remember, less is more when it comes to essential oils.
- For dogs only: Apply oils to an area of the body where they cannot be ingested, such as the back of the neck.
- Do not apply essential oils topically to cats. Cats are very sensitive, and skin irritation might result. Instead, use a diffuser and place it in a room where kitty loves to hang out.
- If you desire to use more than one type of oil daily, dispense the oils at least four hours apart.
- Never administer essential oils to any companion animal orally.
- Never force an oil—respect your animal's reaction. Always offer a "test sniff" first to gauge your animal's reaction.

Chiropractic Can Take the Kinks Out

Chiropractic focuses on realigning the spine and redirecting the energy to all parts of the body. The purpose of redirecting the energy flow is to assist in restoring well-being and harmony. According to the American Veterinary Chiropractic Association (AVCA), which certifies animal chiropractors, 683 veterinarians worldwide are certified to perform chiropractic work on animals, 571 in the United States. Many animal clinics now offer both acupuncture and chiropractic treatments as a part of their services.

The chiropractic approach to healing can be useful in the treatment of joint disease, neurological disorders, behavior issues, and for overall wellness. It can even help an animal overcome self-inflicted wounds such as hot spots and lick granulomas. High-performance dogs benefit from regular adjustments, as do dogs who have suffered an injury.

This specialty, like acupuncture or any other alternative therapy, requires considerable technical expertise and knowledge. Before embarking on a relationship with a chiropractor, we suggest conferring with several references whose animals have been successfully treated. A good practitioner will always take into consideration the overall sensitivity of the animal: nutritional needs, emotions, spirit, and the environment even before treatment.

When you are comfortable with your choice of doctor, it is important to check out your animal after the first adjustment. Was there an improvement, was there a worsening, or was there no change? And, more importantly, how did your animal react to the treatment? Sometimes when using energy medicine, the condition may worsen before it gets better (because the body heals in the opposite way that it gets sick). Be sure to communicate with your doctor. And if in doubt, observe your animal for signs of whether the treatment was helpful. See Resourses for more information.

Flower Essences: Rebalance the Emotions

Through our many years of practicing holistic veterinary medicine, we have become keenly aware of how emotional issues are often at the root of physical disease. It is now our conviction that no matter how well we treat the physical condition, if we ignore its emotional aspects, true and complete healing will not occur.

Flower essences—made from the blossoms of flowering plants—have the capacity to shift the emotional "imprint" of animals and people in a powerful way. Beginning with the well-known Bach Remedies developed in Great Britain in the 1930s by Dr. Edward Bach, there are now a number of companies offering a vast array of products dedicated to animals, and custom-blended formulas developed for the specific needs and emotional requirements of individual animals.

In our practice, we've been using flower essences for several years with outstanding results. They complement holistic veterinary medicine, are inexpensive, completely harmless, and without side effects. (You cannot say that about too many modalities in veterinary pharmacology!) And, as more is learned and applied in the emerging field of energy or vibrational medicine, we expect that specific flower remedies will be increasingly prescribed to address a myriad of emotionally based disorders, such as grief, loneliness, jealousy, and anxiety, to name a few. Thanks to the groundbreaking research of Candace Pert, PhD, author of *Molecules of Emotion: Why You Feel the Way You Feel*, we now understand the powerful, intimate influence of emotions on the immune system and their role in either creating disease or healing it.

> ### Good News
> The good news about flower essences is that they are completely compatible with conventional or allopathic drugs. Flower essences also address our basic philosophy that illness has an emotional component.

Consider anxiety, for example. Anxiety comes in many forms, produces many symptoms, and can be precipitated in animals by events like adoption, relocation, the introduction of a new human or animal into your home, or the absorption of human negativity.

You may be wondering how a few drops of liquid plant extract could facilitate emotional rebalancing. As flower essence formulator and Anaflora founder Sharon Callahan points out, "From the beginning of history, it has been known that within Nature is placed all the means to heal all forms of illness and suffering." She believes that flower essences are especially effective at releasing past and present suffering and abuse in our animals, repairing the damage done to our relationships, and enabling new levels of trust. Flower essences work on physical, mental, and/or emotional planes, Callahan explains. "As the essence enters the physical body, usually orally, it gives off a pure, harmonious frequency. The aspect that is 'out of harmony' is drawn to this healthy frequency and begins to vibrate in harmony with it."

Several years ago, we had the privilege of administering a specially prepared Anaflora remedy to our beloved Corgi, Annie, while she was making her transition from the physical world to the spiritual one. Despite the fact that it was Annie's time to leave her physical body, she was having a difficult time leaving us. Sharon's remedies, which were flown to us overnight, helped us all let go. To this day, we don't know what we would have done without them.

While our ability to understand our world through principles of scientific discovery have developed incredibly during the recent past, there is no current scientific explanation of how flower essences actually work. While this may be unsettling to some, consider that scientific knowledge cannot understand many aspects of healing. For example, homeopathic medicine (to which flower essence therapy is closely related) and acupuncture are and continue to be respected healing modalities despite the lack of a scientific explanation of how they assist the body in its healing process.

Healing With Flower Essences

There are two flower remedies we find ourselves returning to again and again: Return to Joy and Rescue Remedy.

Anaflora's Return to Joy, a combination flower essence containing bleeding heart, sweet chestnut, gorse, echinacea, shooting star, flannel flower, and lady's slipper, sets the stage for healing by relieving stress and helping to rebuild trust, facilitating the reopening of the heart.

Many of the animals with a chronic degenerative disease or a behavior problem who consult with our Healing Center are immediately given a prescription for Return to Joy along with remedies to help heal their physical condition. As a starter remedy, we recommend Return to Joy if your animal:

- is exhibiting emotional problems of any kind
- is having a behavioral problem
- seems to have difficulty trusting other animals or people
- has difficulty receiving or giving affection
- is withdrawn or hyperactive
- has been recently adopted from a shelter, weaned, or relocated
- has suffered from or if you suspect abuse
- is living in a home with emotional uncertainty or unrest

For dogs and cats, add 5 drops of Return to Joy to fresh water daily for one month or until improvement is noted emotionally and physically.

Another of our favorite flower essences is Bach's Rescue Remedy—a preparation made from the essences of 38 flowers. Rescue Remedy is particularly beneficial when you are dealing with an animal going into or is in shock. Clinical signs of shock include increased heart rate, weak pulse, pale mucous membranes, increased respiration rate, decreased body temperature, and low blood pressure.

Your veterinarian will take emergency steps to resuscitate an animal in shock using fluids, oxygen, positive-pressure ventilation, steroids, and other medications as needed. However, the first minutes following traumatic injury, fright, or blood loss will be critical, and this is where Rescue Remedy steps in—not as a replacement for medical therapy, but to start the body in a positive direction, on your way to the emergency veterinarian.

Use Rescue Remedy for the treatment of the following emergencies:

- Shock/trauma
- Heat prostration
- Snake bites
- Bee stings
- Spider bites

- Fireworks trauma
- Prior to emergency surgery
- Wasp stings
- Sports injuries

For dogs and cats, put two or more drops on your animal's tongue or rub it directly into the gums. It can also be diluted and sprayed from a spray bottle—spray it directly into the living quarters of your home, and particularly in the most commonly used areas.

Our respect for Rescue Remedy took on a powerful new meaning during a blizzard one cold winter. At the time, we were living on five secluded acres, enjoying a great deal of wildlife activity. One morning, we were awakened by shrill screams coming from the woods. A hawk was entangled with a blue jay, stuck together by their talons, while the predator bird attempted to take its prey. The screams were so unnerving that Dr. Bob, clad only in his flannel pajamas, took to the snow drifts armed with a broom.

He used it to pry the birds free, leaving a badly wounded blue jay on its side in the cold snow. Dr. Bob picked the poor thing up and examined him—the bird's chest was ripped open and he was going into shock. The clock was ticking and death was near, but so was Susan—anxiously awaiting with a bottle of Rescue Remedy. The blue jay was immediately given the flower essence remedy, and over the next several days the Rescue Remedy continued to help him. "Blue" lived on and spent two and a half months resting and relaxing in our office, until one Sunday morning when Dr. Bob, Susan, and their daughters Abbey and Merritt witnessed Blue's ascension back into the wild. As we opened his cage to set him free into the great outdoors, Blue flew high into the clear blue sky. We stood with tears streaming down our faces—letting go is often

> ## Take Rescue Remedy Wherever You Go
>
> Bach's Rescue Remedy (or Anaflora's Recovery) is a miraculous emergency support elixir that should be in every purse, home pharmacy, briefcase, or glove compartment. You never know when you will come across an emergency and benefit from it.

so bittersweet and emotional. Just as Blue was almost out of sight, we witnessed what we all still regard as a miracle. The little bird stopped dead in his flight, cocked his head around looking down at all of us, and gave a shrill screech good-bye. That picture of Blue remains a mystical photo in our minds—truly an aeronautical impossibility to stop dead in a flight path!

As our awareness of the emotional and spiritual needs of our patients increases, we have witnessed firsthand how flower essences address these needs. We encourage you to keep an open mind concerning energy and vibrational medicine and continue to be aware of your own emotions and stresses as well as those of your animals.

Glandular Therapy

Glandular therapy, also called cellular or organ therapy, is broadly defined as the use of raw glands and organ concentrates to achieve therapeutic results in the body. Historically, references to gland therapy appear in ancient times, and the use of animal parts in the treatment of diseases of people has been thoroughly documented. Early physicians such as Aristotle and Pliny the Elder discussed their use, and the 1600s theories discussed the workings of gland therapy based upon the principle that "like organs will help cure the same organ." Simply interpreted, the eating of an organ or a specific tissue will heal the same organ in the body. For example, a person suffering from liver disease would eat liver to help cure the disease, or the eating of raw heart tissue would help heal a weakened heart.

There were arguments for and against this unproven theory. Skeptics questioned why the consumption of a particular tissue type in the treatment of corresponding tissues would have any validity at all. Critics stated that any tissue that is eaten is then digested into its building-block components of proteins, fats, and carbohydrates, which in turn would be exposed to the body's digestive enzymes, and therefore completely inactivated. Scientists who supported the theory proposed that the raw glandular tissue, besides being composed of the basic food parts, also contained other factors that were responsible for their activity.

Documenting the Theory

It wasn't until the late 1800s and the early 1900s that gland and cellular therapies began to acquire some scientific basis. First came the understanding that the body is composed of many organs, including specific glands that produce or secrete various chemical compounds (hormones) that have a powerful effect on the functioning of the body and its systems. The use of crude organ extracts began in the early 1900s, and was included in day-to-day medical practice. It was also at this time that scientific literature was rapidly expanding with new reports and "miracle cures" from these glandular substances.

The first documented proof of the efficacy of organ therapy came in 1912 when injections of thyroid extract were able to help children suffering from myxedema and cretinism. In 1924, the *Journal of the American Medical Association* reported, "In Addison's disease, there is a definite adrenal deficiency. In some cases, dried adrenal gland produces improvement." In 1931, Dr. Paul Niehans, considered the father of gland therapy, administered raw parathyroid gland to a patient suffering from serious muscular spasms after a thyroidectomy and accidental destruction of the parathyroid glands. The response was immediate and dramatic, and the patient was cured. And Henry R. Harrower, MD, a pioneering endocrinologist/organotherapist and founder of the famed Harrower Laboratory, reported on the numerous uses and applications of gland therapies in the *Endocrine Handbook* in 1939.

An Organ Therapy Pioneer

One of the pioneers of the organ therapy movement was Dr. Royal Lee, who in the 1940s looked at the use of gland therapy from a different angle. Lee theorized that as an organ becomes weakened and diseased, the cells are broken, releasing their contents into general circulation of the body. The body's healing system, comprised of various organs and chemicals, finds this cellular breakdown debris and immediately reacts by forming an antibody, the body's mechanism to destroy invaders. He further theorized that these antibodies not only attack the cellular debris, they also attack the entire organ that is being broken down—an autoimmune response. The result is an inflammatory process in which the body inflames its own tissue. The organ weakens and begins to function at less-than-optimum levels, setting the stage for degenerative disease. If, for example, this autoimmune response occurs in the thyroid glands, causing them to function at less-than-optimum levels, the end result could be hypothyroidism.

Lee stated that gland extracts work not by "like healing like" but rather in a more straightforward way. The cellular debris contains intrinsic factors that are organ-specific and attracted to the same organ of the body. These factors stimulate production of antibodies that the body perceives as a foreign invader. Gland extracts help to defend the organ by neutralizing the antigen-antibody response and thereby minimizing the autoimmune and inflammatory processes. Then the organ— finally freed from internal attack—would be able to rest and heal.

This would mean that when a person, or animal, took the raw cellular material of, for example, bovine liver, it would be absorbed into the bloodstream and directed to this person's own liver. Similarly, raw adrenal tissue would be attracted to the adrenal glands. These organ-specific "intrinsic" factors would support and protect the liver and adrenal from further self-inflammation and serve to improve their function in the patient.

Synthetic Forms

The discovery of chemical compounds and hormones isolated from these gland concentrates changed the direction of glandular therapy. Modern technology then gave birth to synthetic forms of the naturally occurring substances, such as cortisone and thyroid hormones. While these synthetic compounds were labeled "wonder drugs" because of their quick, clinically proven action, we learned the hard lesson that they also caused numerous side effects, such as immune suppression following the administration of cortisone. More importantly, when you isolate a single compound from a gland, you lose the potential benefits of other related compounds that exist and have equal or synergistic effect. The whole gland keeps intact these interrelated compounds.

Glandular therapies can be valuable for all organs of the body. The most common glands available are pituitary, thyroid, pancreas, heart, brain, liver, kidney, prostate, ovary, bone marrow, pineal, hypothalamus, lung, stomach, intestine, bone, and adrenal glands. They can be purchased at human health food stores, from chiropractors, and from holistic veterinarians—especially those that perform Nutritional Blood Tests (see page 85).

Hair Analysis

One of the most controversial alternative modalities is hair analysis. Dr. Bob and his brother Marty utilized hair analysis in their practice in the '70s and '80s. However, based upon inconsistencies in results and the air of "hocus pocus" around the efficacy and accuracy of the testing, they stopped its use as part of their diagnostic protocols.

Bob Smith, founder of Pet Test, recently helped to change our minds about the efficacy of hair analysis. Smith spent many hours convincing Dr. Bob of the value and benefits of offering the hair analysis test in his practice. Pet Test is a health screening device that indicates the levels of toxic exposure and heavy metal buildup in the body. Hair analysis can be of benefit for your animal if you suspect that he or she has been exposed to environmental toxins such as lead or aluminum. Symptoms of these types of toxicity include general signs such as irritability, weakness, depression, and vomiting, which can also be the result of many other conditions.

We recently tested a group of alpacas that were suffering from an undiagnosed disease that was causing liver complications. Dr. Bob suggested a hair analysis to rule out excessive amounts of heavy metal contamination. When the results indicated extremely high levels of aluminum, Dr. Bob suggested that the food be analyzed as well, and sure enough, the results came back with very high levels of aluminum. An interesting side note that came out of this process is that the food-testing laboratory indicated to Bob that high levels of aluminum in pet food is quite common and usually secondary to the ground-up aluminum leg bands that are often found on chickens. Chicken meal is a predominant ingredient in most dog and cat foods.

Another hair analysis patient of ours is Precious Derose, who lives in urban northern New Jersey. Her guardian Liz was concerned about lead contamination from paint in her area and decided to have hair analysis done. The testing confirmed high lead levels that Precious was not detoxifying properly. We placed Precious on a detoxification program consisting of two homeopathic remedies (vaccine and chemical drops), and she is now doing quite well physically and as confirmed by follow-up blood and hair analysis.

Bob Smith states the following with regards to his extensive experience with hair analysis, "For years I have helped physicians treat their own pets and helped veterinarians treat zoo animals. Sometimes the physician wanted to find the cause of their pet's health problem to treat the cause of the illness rather than just treat the symptom(s), so they used the hair test to find the cause. Sometimes the physician practiced preventative medicine and wanted to reduce potential health problems for their own pet, so they used the hair test to find weaknesses and used preventative measures to ensure their pet did not develop some health problem like cancer, diabetes, cardiovascular disease, etc. I have found toxins in pet's food and other sources to be 5 to 10 times that found in humans, and found many pets with genetic errors, some due to breeding and some due to the usual mutations that occur. Since pets look different, varying in size, color, genetics, etc., their nutritional needs are also different."

How Does Hair Analysis Work?

The analysis of hair is a reflection of the "toxic burden and mineral imbalances" that are found in the body. These toxins and imbalances are present long before a disease rears its ugly head. If you or your veterinarian are aware that these burdens do exist and take the necessary measures to reduce or balance their levels, you have taken a major step toward disease prevention.

How Can You Use the Information Derived From Hair Analysis?

Throughout this book we repeatedly discuss the accumulation of toxins and metabolic wastes without appropriate elimination as the cause of many diseases. The common day-to-day conditions that we routinely see in dogs and cats such as vomiting, diarrhea, discharge from the eyes and ears, strong smelling urine and greasy, smelly skin are all related to the body attempting to eliminate toxins. When you couple this toxic load with a compromised immune system, you are setting the stage for chronic disease to set in.

Hair analysis then is another healing modality that can give you and your veterinarian another piece of valuable information with regards to your animal's overall health. Knowing that your animal is carrying excessive toxins or mineral imbalances gives you the basis to institute corrections such as improving the diet (see Chapter 1), adding active antioxidants and phytonutrients, and adding toxin-reducing herbs, nutraceuticals, and homeopathics that also function in balancing the immune system.

In addition, Bob Smith's statements echo the feelings and beliefs of many holistic veterinarians with regards to the potential toxicity of commercially available pet foods and the shift in focus from treatment symptoms with drugs to using preventive measures to stave off future conditions and diseases. See Resources for more information on hair analysis.

Herbal Medicine: The Healing Power of Plants

Herbal medicine is broadly defined as the use of various botanicals to achieve specific therapeutic and healing results. The medicinal use of herbs dates back over 5,000 years to ancient Chinese cultures. From references in the Bible, to the ancient Greek physician Hippocrates, to the Native Americans whose level of knowledge concerning herbs amazed European settlers, historically herbs have been used to heal both the body and mind.

Recently, there has been a resurgence of interest from both the lay and medical communities in more natural types of therapies. This resurgence initially was confined to Europe, but it has worked its way into the United States. This resurgence in interest is based upon three issues:

- Many drugs (both old and new) and therapeutics often have serious side effects and contraindications.
- People are searching for more natural, gentler approaches to chronic degenerative diseases.
- A desire to expand the approach to disease from suppressing symptoms to also looking for the cause of the condition and methods of prevention.

Today, the World Health Organization (WHO) estimates that 4 billion people, or 80 percent of the world's population, use herbal medicine for some aspect of their primary health care. Herbal medicine is a major component in nearly all traditional medicine systems worldwide. Of over 100 plant-derived pharmaceutical medicines, nearly three-quarters are used in pharmaceutical products in ways that directly correlate with their traditional uses as plant medicines by native cultures. Pharmaceutical companies who once eschewed the commercial value of herbs are now plying the rain forests in search of herbs with potential medicinal value.

Perhaps the biggest deterrent to acceptance of herbal medicine in the United States is the Food and Drug Administration (FDA). There is a tremendous body of literature describing which herbs work for specific clinical conditions and the methods of administration of these herbs. Yet specific proof and actual pharmacology are lacking. As a result, herbs are categorized by the FDA as food substances, and because they have not been through the extensive clinical trials required by medications, specific claims about the use of herbs are strictly prohibited.

As a result, both the lay and medical communities have been kept in the dark about the use, efficacy, and benefits of medicinal herbs. Veterinarians and herbal practitioners turn to recent publications on the use of herbs, as well as relying on experts (master herbalists) and the wealth of information available on the Internet to become educated in the use of medicinal herbs.

As with glandular therapy, the methods of the FDA and medical research tend to drive the use of the modality away from its original intent. Research and business are isolating what they believe to be the "bioactive" ingredient in the plant, extracting it, making a synthetic version, and converting it into a medication. The problem is that many whole herbs contain numerous other active ingredients that often work synergistically to give efficacy to the herbal preparation. As an example, allicin is the active antibacterial agent isolated from garlic. Modern technology has now isolated more than 20 additional antibacterial phytonutrients and antioxidant ingredients in garlic that are believed to work along with allicin to produce beneficial results. Master herbalists prefer to use the entire herb for this reason. A great deal of evidence points to the fact that the extract of the entire plant works more efficaciously than isolated parts.

The Herbs

If you shop in a human health-food store, you may be overwhelmed by the varieties of herbal preparations available to the consumer. We encourage you to invest in a good book about herbal healing and animals. Check the Resource section at the end of the book for recommended educational materials. Be sure to stick with herbs from reputable sources and look for standardized formulas, which guarantee purity and potency.

As with any remedy derived from natural sources, the purity of the individual ingredients will directly affect the efficacy of the product. The methods used in growing and harvesting the plants, the mix of soil, whether it has been commercially harvested or wildcrafted, and the storage of the herbs all can affect their potency. The critical issue is the method used for processing the herbs. Factors such as how the plants are picked and stored, and which part of the plant is used also will impact their efficacy.

Safety is another critical issue when using herbs, as some herbs may be toxic or potentially dangerous for the health of an animal. This can be especially true if the selected herb suddenly becomes "in vogue" through attention by the media or the Internet. Garlic is a good example of an incredible herb whose potential for healing has become mainstream, but many remain in the dark about potential problems with it. Garlic has potent antibacterial, antiviral, and antiseptic properties that can be greatly beneficial; however, prolonged usage at higher doses can cause anemia, especially in cats.

> ### Forms of Herbal Remedies
> Herbal remedies are generally available in the following forms:
> - Liquids: teas, decoctions, infusions
> - Extracts and elixirs
> - Ointments, salves, or creams
> - Bulk herbs (usually dried)
> - Oils
> - Tinctures (hydroalcohol, glycerin)
> - Capsules or tablets

It is important to speak to your veterinarian before embarking on any herbal remedies for your cat or dog. For example, when we were students learning about holistic medicine, a cat named Tiger was referred to our clinic for difficultly breathing. Physical examination and radiographs of the chest were all normal, and Tiger acted and appeared totally normal, except for these periodic bouts of breathing difficulties. As part of our physical examination we ran a fecal analysis, which turned up an egg of a lungworm called Strongyloides. In the past, Tiger had been subjected to all sorts of medications including antibiotics, cortisone, and potent worming medications, all to no avail, so we decided to treat Tiger with garlic. We used the aged garlic preparation called Kyolic for 30 days, after which his breathing problem was cured and his fecal examination was negative for lungworms.

Common Herbs

Here is a brief description of the more popular herbs and their intended use:

- Aloe vera: Skin healer
- Black walnut: Anthelmintic (heartworms)
- Echinacea: General immune system stimulator, natural antibiotic
- Garlic: Lowers blood pressure, natural antibiotic, antioxidant
- Ginkgo biloba: Cognitive dysfunction, Alzheimer's disease
- Goldenseal: Intestinal antibacterial
- Hawthorn berry: Tones heart, improves cardiac output
- Licorice: Natural anti-inflammatory, skin problems
- Milk thistle: Liver detoxification, anti-inflammatory, antioxidant
- Mullein: Upper respiratory infection and inflammation
- Saw palmetto: Prostate health
- Skullcap: Seizures
- Slippery elm: Enteritis, gastrointestinal upsets
- Tea tree: Antiseptic, antifungal
- Valerian: Natural calming and tranquilizer
- Wormwood: Intestinal parasites
- Yucca: Arthritis

Our Approach to Herbal Medicine

An experienced herbal practitioner is truly a healer who can match the herb, the patient, and the condition together to maximize healing. In our practice, we tend to lean away from the selection of one herb for one condition, and lean toward combining individual herbs to enhance the synergistic healing experience. We worked with Master Herbalist Jane Smolnick to create the Earth Animal blended herbal products, which come from wildcrafted Vermont herbs, each meant to achieve a specific result. For example, Earth Animal's Pee Pee formula is a blended product of uva ursi, marshmallow root, dandelion deaf, horsetail, gravel root, and yarrow that work together to soothe inflammation and control infections in the urinary bladder. Many herbal preparations have been standardized for potency and dosage. Look for remedies that have been extracted from organic, wildcrafted herbs, and extracted and blended using minimal amounts of alcohol for preservation (check the label for percentages). Their strength and dosage are standardized by weight and animal species. This is often a better method for the animal than selecting a more potent product designed for human usage, and adjusting the dosage downward accordingly.

For a list of herbal resources and reputable herbal suppliers, please see the Resources section at the end of this book. Check with a holistic veterinarian who has experience with herbs and their inter-reaction with other natural remedies and medications before you administer them.

The Science and Art of Homeopathy

We have had great success through the years using homeopathy, a healing modality that's been around for over 200 years. Although it's one of the least understood of all holistic modalities, it can be amazingly effective. Animals respond quickly to the right remedy, and homeopathic remedies don't cause undesirable side effects like traditional medications. There are over a thousand individual homeopathic remedies available.

Homeopathy is based on the experiments and study of eighteenth century physician Dr. Samuel Hahnemann, who articulated the principle of *similia similibus curentur*, or "like cures like." This means that if a large amount of a substance causes certain symptoms, then a tiny amount of the same substance could treat those symptoms. Homeopathic treatment is designed to stimulate the innate healing power of the body so that all systems will again function at optimum levels.

Homeopathy uses naturally occurring substances to gently promote the healing of the body. Minute amounts of a substance that would otherwise provoke the symptoms instead mobilize the body's own resources to restore health. For example, *Apis mellifica*, a homeopathic remedy made from honeybee venom, can be used to treat bee stings or other conditions with stinging pains, redness, and swelling.

Rhus toxicodrendron, from poison ivy plants, can be used to take the itch out of the skin or quiet many types of joint inflammation.

Homeopathic Medicines and the Principle of Dilution

Homeopathic remedies are highly diluted plants (such as poison ivy), herbs (such as alfalfa), inorganic materials (such as salts or metals), animal parts (such as venom), physiological secretions (such as squid ink), and even diseased tissue itself. The substances are grown or collected under controlled conditions and diluted and vigorously shaken (succussed) in order to potentiate or release the energy of the resulting remedy.

Paradoxically, the greater the dilution, the more potent the remedy. For example, the strength 1X means that 1 part of the substance has been mixed with 9 parts of water. If it is 3X, this process has been done three times. If a substance has been diluted 1 part in 99 parts of water three times it is labeled 3C. Other common dilutions include 12X, 30C, and 200C.

How can a substance, highly diluted to the point where it is barely detectable, have any effect on the body at all? While the answer continues to confound conventional scientists, thousands of homeopathic physicians and veterinarians have experienced firsthand the often miraculous effects these simple remedies have. Keep in mind, the mode of action of many conventional drugs is not clearly understood either.

In general, the effects of taking the remedies are gentle and gradual. There are times, however, that a more rapid response will be experienced. Aggravations of symptoms or recurrences of previously experienced illnesses and symptoms can occur. In many instances, the symptoms become more intense just before they release. It is as if the body is bringing the symptom to a head and then releasing it. Once released, the body is healthier (or healed) from that particular symptom.

We remember the little Cocker Spaniel, Ginger, who was suffering from a chronic skin condition (pyoderma). Ginger was on antibiotics and cortisone for years and still would have severe outbreaks of itching and skin infections several times per year. While the antibiotics and cortisone would help for a while, it was not long before the pyoderma would rear its ugly head again. We started Ginger on the Goldstein Food Plan and treated her with several combination homeopathics (BHI mixture of Skin (for skin) + Infection (for infection) + Sulfur (for itching)) to help her through the rough times. While Ginger initially responded well to this therapy, the episodes then began to worsen. We urged Ginger's guardian not to reach for antibiotics, but to nurse Ginger through the episode with a soothing herbal shampoo, which she did. Later, Ginger broke out with pustules (boils) all over her body and was miserable. We all stayed the course and let the toxins work their way out of the skin, medicating only if Ginger broke her skin in her attempt to relieve the itch. It worked! Ginger went through the healing crisis and came out the other side with a much improved coat. For the next few years, Ginger only had one skin episode per year (when the pollen hit in March), but otherwise she maintained a beautiful coat and skin. The continued use of antibiotics or cortisone would have just continued the cycle, because they stop the detoxification process through the skin, keeping the toxins and metabolic wastes inside. Ginger's guardian's trust in us, and her ability to stay focused, allowed Ginger to heal once and for all and stop this chronic cycle.

The controversy about homeopathy exists because conventional learning has taught us that symptoms are bad and should be suppressed. For example, we all have been instructed that with a fever, we should take an aspirin to "knock down" the temperature, because it's dangerous. In reality, the opposite is true! The body's normal immune response is to mobilize white blood cells and elevate body temperature in an attempt to fight off the invader. Stopping this process with aspirin or antibiotics is not necessarily the smartest thing to do. Interfering with this normal mechanism of raising the temperature because of discomfort and fear that high fevers can cause brain damage is actually counter-productive to the healing process.

In homeopathy, bringing the symptom to a more intense level before it is released is good, especially compared to the cover up achieved when using medications. Aggravations, as they are called, are not truly side effects of the remedy but an indication that the body is responding to the medicinal stimulus.

Healing Crisis

See if you can remember when you were a youngster and had a high fever. You felt warm, inflamed, and really uncomfortable. Your Mom instructed you to stay bundled under several blankets and "sweat it out." Remember the specific moment that the fever broke? The relief from the heat and the feeling of well-being was actually the end result of the "healing crisis" that the body experienced.

Classical (Single) or Combination Remedies: Which Is Best?

Combination homeopathics differ from single remedies in their user's approach to a condition. Combination homeopathics mix several low-dilution remedies together as the best way to address a symptom, support an organ or tissue, or help set the stage for regeneration and healing. For example, a combination homeopathic for arthritis may contain several ingredients. Some may address inflammation, others pain, while still others may support the body in the elimination of excess minerals and toxins. The overall result is that the remedy works with the body's metabolic processes to reduce the symptoms at their origin and to promote healing.

In contrast, classical homeopaths follow a more rigid set of rules, viewing an animal as having one disease that is showing several or many symptoms. Based upon their training, they select the single homeopathic remedy that most closely mimics the profile of symptoms, and then wait for a period of time, ranging from hours to days, to observe the result or symptom produced. Classical homeopaths contend that adding other medications or even natural remedies might produce a "false read" and interfere with the treatment. The classical homeopath is not focused on the name of the disease but strictly on the symptom, with the idea if he or she can evoke that symptom with a remedy, the process will lead to a healing.

While we support the classical approach and have found it to be remarkably successful in many instances, we lean away from this type of treatment when it comes to serious diseases. Consider a critically ill animal with cancer. Evoking or bringing symptoms to a head—allowing the process to get worse before it gets better—may not be in the best interest of the animal. In addition, there may not be time to go with a single homeopathic remedy and wait patiently for the results. When faced with this situation, we will recommend a combination homeopathic that may contain six to ten different remedies along with other nutritional and medical approaches. We will also prescribe vitamins, minerals, enzymes, nutraceuticals and Chinese herbs. (For more information about treating cancer in animals, see Chapter 9.)

You Can Use Homeopathy at Home

Homeopathy, whether in the form of a single or combination remedy, can be used at home for relatively superficial, non-life-threatening conditions such as itchy skin, sneezing, coughing, bruises, and limping. The actual amount of a homeopathic remedy given is not as critical as the frequency of administration, which can be based upon the severity of symptoms. In the acute stage, your veterinarian may advise you to give the remedy as often as every 5 to 15 minutes, decreasing to hourly upon improvement.

For most common symptoms and routine usage, however, you'll give most remedies one to three times daily. And for maintenance, when the condition is either totally under control, you can give it anywhere from once daily, twice weekly, or just keeping the remedy around in case symptoms flare up.

How to Administer Homeopathic Remedies

Homeopathic remedies come in two common forms—liquid and small white pills, or pellets. In our experience, predissolved remedies placed into your animal's mouth work best. Unlike other supplements or medications, homeopathic remedies do not have to be (and should in fact not be) swallowed. They are most effective when given either an hour before or after eating.

To give the liquid or pills dissolved in distilled water, pull your dog or cat's lower lip away from the teeth and use an eyedropper to place the drops in the space between the cheek and gum. To prepare the pills as a powder, first tip them out of their container (try not to touch them—it may lessen their effectiveness) onto a folded white piece of stiff paper or into a 3" x 5" index card. Crush the pills into a fine powder with the back of a spoon.

Next, pour the powder into your animal's mouth as described above. The remedy is absorbed from these tissues, so there is no need to open the mouth and force the remedy down the throat. You can place the powder directly on the tongue or in the pouch between the gums and cheek. Again, try not to touch the pills as you pour them out onto the paper.

Arnica montana is perhaps the best-known and widely used homeopathic remedy for acute pain from traumatic injury or bruising, and in the event of surgery, it will help minimize tissue damage. Readily available in most health food stores, *arnica* can be given as often as every 15 minutes until relief is achieved, at the following dosages:

Arnica montana	
Cat/Small Dog (up to 14 lb)	1 pellet
Medium Dog (15-34 lb)	2 pellets
Large Dog (35-84 lb)	3 pellets
Giant Dog (85+ lb)	4 pellets

Many homeopathics are in a form that can be used topically. The most common ones are arnica gel and calendula (extract of marigold). Used topically, calendula will soothe inflamed, burned, or weepy skin, and even inflamed gums. Keep these in your holistic first-aid kit.

General Dosage Chart	
In the event you need to give a remedy and aren't sure of the dosage, follow this dosage chart. Give twice daily. Consult your veterinarian if symptoms do not abate promptly.	
Cat/Small Dog (up to 14 lb)	1 pellet
Medium Dog (15-34 lb)	2 pellets
Large/Giant Dog (35-85 lb)	3 pellets

Homotoxicology: A Modern Approach to Homeopathy and Healing

In the 1930s, after physician Dr. Hans-Heinrich Reckeweg witnessed his father's kidney disease cured through homeopathy, he set out on a mission to bring together the then-popular medical disciplines of allopathic (Western-type) medicine and homeopathy. Thoroughly versed in homeopathy, Dr. Reckeweg began to compile certain disease and therapy patterns, along with frequently used symptom-oriented remedies, and developed an extensive formulary, geared toward the Western/allopathic methods and diagnoses.

Drs. P.J. Broadfoot and Rick Palmquist, two leading experts in alternative veterinary medicine and contemporaries of Dr. Bob, define Homotoxicology as "the branch of medicine which seeks to identify the toxins in the body, helps to mobilize the natural defense mechanisms, and frees the body from toxic debris. The working principles of this form of biological medicine uses the body's own self-regulating mechanisms to bring about a true healing."

Dr. Reckweg created the "Phase Table of Homotoxicology" which describes how the body gets sick. Knowing how illness develops sets the stage for a support program to help the body heal.

> **Phase 1: The Excretion (Fluid) Phase**—occurs when the body attempts to rid itself of toxins. Signs include vomiting, diarrhea, and nasal discharge.
>
> **Phase 2: The Inflammation Phase**—occurs when Phase I is by-passed, or when the body generates a "fever" to help promote healing. Any illness that ends in "-itis" will fit into this category (i.e., arthritis, sinusitis, colitis, gastritis).
>
> **Phase 3: The Deposition Phase**—the "gel between the cells" is affected by toxins that have not been eliminated, and are therefore stored as metabolic "junk." In this stage toxin damage continues, the cells become diseased, and this is the point of no return (at this point the focus is shifted from healing the disease to controlling the disease).
>
> **Phase 4: The Impregnation Phase**—the early stages of cellular disease, in which the toxins have entered the cell, and the immune system attempts to surround and wall off the toxins by storing them inside the cell.
>
> **Phase 5: The Degeneration Phase**—damage occurs to cellular defense and energy production mechanisms. This is a severe state of illness.
>
> **Phase 6: The Dedifferentiation Phase**—the state in which the biological and genetic control mechanisms have been damaged, leading to cancer—loss of the growth regulation of tissues and uncontrollable cell growth, which will eventually kill the body.

Dr. Broadfoot expands on these phases by saying, "It is critical to our understanding that we see these phases as the natural progression of illness. As veterinarians recognize the ebb and flow of body defense mechanisms, they can begin to support these systems by providing guidance to the body's regulatory mechanisms and by using natural, biological therapeutics such as herbs, nutrients, nutraceuticals, and homotoxicological compounds."

Dr. Bob and his brother Dr. Marty Goldstein started using this type of combination homeopathics in the early 1970s. Products made by the BHI/Heel companies (which were developed by Dr. Reckweg) became a regular part of their therapy. These preparations are available in human health food stores. They often come in pills made of many low-potency homeopathic remedies, as a solution to a single condition. For example, the BHI remedy Arthritis is one pill that is made up of 13 individual low-potency homeopathic remedies: *Bryonia, Rhus toxicodendron, Colocynthis, Arnica montana, Colchicum autumale, Dulcamara, Ledum palustre, Ranunculus bulbosus, Berberis vulgaris, Causticum, Rhododendron chrysanthtium, Lycopodium clavatum,* and *Ferrum phosphoricum.*

Often Dr. Bob mixes the remedies together to achieve specific end results. For example, for arthritis he may recommend a combination of BHI Arthritis (for joints) + Pain (for pain) + Traumeel (for inflammation); or for diarrhea a combination of BHI Intestines + Diarrhea + Inflammation mixed together with distilled water, and given to a dog or cat via an eyedropper 2 to 3 times daily. These remedies work incredibly well to alleviate the symptoms, while at the same time helping (and not suppressing) the body to go through a natural healing of the condition.

Music Is a "Nutrient," Too

We have always intuitively known that animals appreciate and respond to fine music. For as long as we can remember, our classical music station remains on whenever we're off to a long day at the office, with the intent of keeping our animals company and nipping boredom or separation anxiety in the bud.

MacMillan, our 15-year-old sun conure, and his buddy, Gershwin, a 10-year-old zebra finch, spend their days tuned in to classical music while we are away at work. Over the years we've watched MacMillan bebop, sway, and head bob to those tunes that strike a chord with him. Even our dogs came alive as the day faithfully began with music.

Over and above the aspects of pure enjoyment, we've long suspected that music as part of a daily diet offers many other health benefits, having a positive influence on the immune system in general. We've known that beautiful music is not only uplifting but acts as a natural tranquilizer during times of stress. In addition, it serves as a companion during times of solitude. But we didn't make the connection that music can also be therapeutic and healing until we came across the work of Susan Raimond, a harpist and pioneer in the field of harp therapy for animals.

Soothe Your Friend With Harp Sounds

If your dog or cat is feeling under the weather or is dealing with a stressful condition resulting from age, disease, or an emotional problem such as separation anxiety, we suggest that you consider adding Sue's harp music to your collection. "Just take a portable boom box, pop a tape or CD in, and in three minutes you'll begin to see a change. In 10 to 20 minutes, the animal comes into a resting state," she advises.

Raimond, of Mt. Laguna, California, coined the term "cytocymatics," which indicates how sound—specifically vibrations of harp music—affects cells. The harp is a vibrational instrument boasting 4,000 years of documented use as a healing modality. It's been touted by some as the most powerful form of medication and is at the forefront of a great deal of clinical research in an attempt to prove its healing benefits in the modern age.

Raimond is the founder of Pet Pause, a company that produces music to calm and heal animals and people. Sue began researching harp therapy by working with mobile groomers. She'd play a compact disc of her own music while dogs, cats, and horses were being groomed and proved that her idea could effectively calm animals during the process.

She then sought a medical environment at the Pine Valley Veterinary Clinic, using harp music to soothe patients awaiting sedation before surgery. The vibrations and sound waves produced a therapeutic response of lowered heart rates, blood pressure, and respiration.

Clearly, the harp music was affecting the autonomic nervous system, which operates below the level of consciousness to protect animals and people during stressful situations, at a cellular level. Her therapy purports to increase oxygenation of the tissues, improve digestion, lower respiration rates, and ease birthing.

In addition to dogs, cats, wolves, and birds, she's worked her harp music magic on gorillas, horses, donkeys, cows, rabbits, monkeys, guinea pigs, fish, snakes, frogs, lizards, zebras, giraffes, rats, raccoons, opossums, goats, sheep, and dolphins.

Music's Healing Vibrations

We are always on the lookout for ways to eliminate or reduce stress in animals. That's why we were delighted to come across an inquisitive high school student, Dayna Barnett, daughter of veterinarian Dr. Mike Barnett, who shares our mission. Dayna won first place in Zoology at the Reading Berks County Science Fair in Reading, Pennsylvania, when she and Dr. (Dad) Barnett, acting as the project's medical advisor, delivered a scientific paper dealing with the effects of classical music on the stress levels of dogs. Her report was taken from an experiment with ten kenneled dogs (all healthy and between the ages of two and seven) by assessing bloodwork and other laboratory physical characteristics and observing body language via remote video camera.

The Research Protocol

The canine participants were broken into a control group of five dogs, who would be kenneled without music, and an experimental group of five dogs with music. Over a period of five days, each animal was closely observed at regular intervals by veterinarians, who assessed variations in behavior, heart, and respiratory rates as well as appetite. In addition, free-catch urine samples were collected and sent to a commercial lab for urine cortisol-to-creatinine ratio studies. Cortisol is a major "fight or flight" stress hormone and marker, released in large quantities from the adrenal glands during anxious situations.

The lab results indicated that the calming effect of the music in the experimental group was a factor in a significant decrease of corsitol/creatinine versus those in the control group whose values were significantly higher. Other clinical observations recorded by veterinarians included panting and pacing versus standing, sitting, or lying down, and decreased heart and respiratory rates. The veterinarians concurred that the dogs subjected to classical music appeared calmer based on objective behavioral data, and had a slower respiratory rate.

I asked Dayna—who intends to become a musical psychologist—what the end result of her experiment has proved from a more altruistic perspective. She now longs to demonstrate the effect of such music on different species in order to prove her hypothesis that "Every animal benefits from classical music." Dayna is already seeing results as music is now pumped into her dad's veterinary practice. She envisions a world filled with classical music in all kennels and veterinary practices.

We hope that you will take notice of Dayna's hard work and efforts by providing your animal with a daily dose of classical music, especially if your dog, cat, bird, or other animal spends long periods of solo time, exhibits emotional imbalances or anxiety, or is suffering from a chronic debilitating disease.

The Nutritional Blood Test (NBT)

Blood tests are one of the main diagnostic tools utilized by veterinarians and medical doctors. The chemical analysis of blood identifies levels of enzymes, minerals (electrolytes), proteins, as well as the metabolites—the chemical breakdown products of the cells' metabolism. Blood values are then evaluated along with other diagnostic results (such as ultrasound and radiographs) and serve as the basis for the doctor to make a diagnosis and recommend the proper and appropriate medical therapy.

The metabolic process begins in the mouth with the ingestion of food, which is swallowed and passes through the esophagus and into the stomach. There the food is mixed with various acids and digestive juices, and enters the small intestines where the absorption of nutrients into the blood stream occurs. The bulk, fiber, and indigestible parts of the food continue through the large intestine, and are eventually excreted as waste bowel movements. The nutrients that have entered the blood are shipped to the cells of the body, where, through very complex biochemical processes they are converted to energy required by the cells to function. The metabolic cellular wastes are then excreted by the cells and carried by the blood to the liver (the body's filter), inactivated, neutralized, and sent to the kidneys to be expelled from the body. Some metabolic wastes also find their avenue out of the body via the lungs and the skin.

Blood analysis measures the levels of these celluar wastes circulating in the blood. It is from this routine blood analysis that a veterinarian can determine the health of a particular organ. For example, alanine transferase (ALT) is abundantly found in the cells of the liver. When a dog or cat has liver disease, the levels of ALT in the blood can dramatically increase, helping your veterinarian make the diagnosis of liver disease.

The Nutritional Blood Test (NBT) is an expanded version of traditional blood testing. Instead of looking at abnormally high or low levels of chemicals found in the blood, it focuses on the biochemical processes in the cells that actually produce the abnormal levels of chemicals to begin with. Think of the sophisticated equipment used by your auto mechanic to diagnose car problems. By testing the exhaust, your mechanic can get a sense of how the various parts of your automobile are working, and can replace certain parts, making your auto run better. The NBT analysis, by testing for the metabolic wastes present in the blood, serves the same function as testing the exhaust from your car.

Another important factor is that the NBT analysis, when viewing these levels of blood chemicals, does not stop at a specific diagnosis or diseased organ. The NBT looks deeper into the actual chemical processes that occur within the cell. When chemical values in the blood are elevated or depressed, the NBT traces these results back to a specific type of cell and determines the nutrients, vitamins, minerals, antioxidants, and cofactors that are needed to allow a cell to function at optimum health. Once determined, these nutrients can be added to the diet to insure their availability when called upon by the cells that make up that weakend or diseased organ.

How Does the NBT Expand Conventional Blood Testing?

Conventional blood testing measures organ and tissue health against what is called the "normal reference range." This normal range is determined by averaging the blood results of thousands of healthy animals and calculating the normal values. Values that fall outside this normal reference range are used to indicate the health of a particular organ. For example, the blood urea nitrogen (BUN) is a chemical waste found in the blood. It is produced by the metabolic process, routed through the liver, sent to the kidneys, and excreted in the urine. BUN levels measure the nitrogen wastes produced by the body. When these levels in the blood are elevated (above the normal reference range), this is a signal to your veterinarian that the kidneys are not functioning properly, and a diagnosis of kidney disease is made. Based upon this diagnosis your veterinarian then may prescribe a treatment program that includes a low-protein diet to reduce the level of nitrogen wastes in the blood. In addition, antibiotics, cortisone, and fluid therapy may be prescribed based upon the clinical condition of your animal.

What is not addressed in this equation is the fact that the kidneys are the receptacle for the high levels of BUN in the blood. The kidneys did not produce these chemicals—their function is to get rid of these chemicals. When you look at the body as a whole, you must take into consideration not only the weakened kidneys, but also the organs that oversee protein metabolism and are actually producing the elevated BUN levels in the blood. Let's go back to our automobile analogy: If you are adding sand to the gas tank and you visit your mechanic for repairs, the solution is not found in replacing the sand-clogged carburetor. The solution is stopping the addition of sand to the gas tank. The same is true for the body. Weakened kidneys require a global approach—not only looking at the overloaded kidneys, but also looking at how much protein is in the diet, and simultaneously looking at the organs that oversee protein metabolism in the body (such as the thyroid, adrenal glands, and the liver). Making these organs function more efficiently will contribute to lowering the metabolic waste load to an already burdened kidney. By reducing protein input and strengthening the efficiency of the liver, adrenal, and thyroid you take the "pressure" off the overloaded kidneys and allow them to rest and work more efficiently.

The NBT Process

Instead of utilizing the normal reference range set by the blood laboratory, the NBT assessment relies on an optimum range (a narrower range than the traditional one), which helps identify which organs and metabolic processes are functioning at peak efficiency and which are beginning to weaken. The NBT testing is based upon the principle that changes occur in the blood and can be identified before symptoms of disease appear. Therefore, results that are within the optimum range indicate cells, tissues, and organs that are generally of good health. When results are outside the optimum range, it does not necessarily indicate disease. However, it may indicate that a particular organ system is weakening or not functioning at optimal efficiency. Just as the interpretation outside the normal range in traditional blood testing forms the basis for the diagnosis of a specific disease, the optimum range interpretation forms the basis for determining optimal organ function and health.

After the blood is analyzed via the NBT, a list of vitamins, minerals, enzymes, glands, medicinals, and nutrients, along with recommended natural remedies (such as herbs or combination homeopathics) are recommended based upon the physical status of your animal. It is at this point that your veterinarian can recommend a custom-blended nutritional powder or combination-fixed formula remedy, along with the herbs or homeopathics that most closely match your animal's condition. Often, especially with seriously ill animals, the NBT is repeated every two to three months, and the program is updated to more closely match how your animal is doing in response to the nutritional program.

The Development of the NBT

Early in our professional lives, along with Dr. Bob's brother, Dr. Marty Goldstein, we became aware of the metabolic testing of blood through the work of Dr. Kenneth Brockman, a chiropractor and naturopath who was hounded by the medical establishment for his unorthodox practices. We analyzed Dr. Brockman's work and began adapting his principles to the blood of dogs and cats. At the same time, another brilliant medical practitioner, Dr. James Cima, organized and professionalized Brockman's work and published an updated version, which was also quite helpful for our work. Over the next 10 years (from the mid-1970s to the mid-1980s) we worked on what would later develop into the NBT's Optimum Ranges. It was also during this time that we began to see the effect of diet changes and the addition of vitamins, minerals, enzymes, antioxidants, and glands on the health and wellness of our patients.

Early on in the development of the NBT, we discovered some interesting concepts that have laid the groundwork for how we use the NBT today. We found that many sick animals with degenerative diseases had medically normal blood results, while the blood of perfectly normal animals was often riddled with abnormalities. Clients would say things like "I know my animal is not well, but my veterinarian cannot find anything wrong, and her blood results are all normal!" This got us thinking, perhaps the interpretation of "normal values" that we were taught to use as the basis for our diagnoses did not really paint a complete picture for the early identification of a disease process.

Take the adrenal glands as an example. When you read about the adrenal glands in Chapter 8, and their pivotal role in the overall immune function of the body, you quickly understand their importance for wellness. There are specific blood tests that will evaluate diseased adrenal glands, such as diagnostic tests for Cushing's disease. These tests for Cushing's disease (like ACTH stimulation or Dexamethasone suppression tests) are "black or white" in their results—either your animal tests positive for Cushing's disease and requires medical therapy, or your animal does not. However, in the "or not" category, there is a gray zone—called Cushinoid. Your animal may test negative for Cushing's disease, but have symptoms that resemble Cushing's, such as an increase in thirst and urination, along with hair loss and a potbellied appearance.

The shortcomings of this traditional "black and white" approach are that there are no medical indicators to evaluate a compromised adrenal gland that is still functioning within normal medical parameters; however, the compromised gland will often become Cushing's positive. The conventional medical approach in this instance is to "wait and see," and if your animals does become positive for Cushing's, then initiate therapy. The NBT analysis can detect indicators for early Cushing's disease. For example, the alkaline phosphatase level (ALP) is a metabolic indicator of adrenal function, and elevated ALP indicates an overactive gland that should receive nutritional or remedy support. If this overproductive adrenal gland is caught early and properly supported, you can actually prevent disease from forming down the road—true preventive care.

One last point while we are discussing the NBT and the adrenal gland. In the above example for Cushing's disease, we are focusing on a gland that is hyperactive and overworking. Similarly, the NBT analysis can determine a weakening gland, which could lead to an overall weakening of the immune system, or more seriously an exhausted adrenal system (an Addison's disease crisis). The typical normal range for ALP is 5-131. Readings within this range are deemed normal. Readings above 131 are called elevated, and become suspicious for potentially early Cushing's disease. What about readings below 5, like 2 or 3? These are also deemed normal; however, these low readings are often an early metabolic warning of a sluggish and weakening gland, and should be the focus of nutritional support.

Your animal doesn't close his eyes at night with a healthy gland and wake up with a serious crisis! There are early weaknesses or stresses that affect the adrenal glands along the way that can be determined through the NBT analysis. If corrected nutrtionally, the development of disease may be prevented.

Tellington TTouch: A New Way to Connect With Your Animal

Tellington TTouch, also known as TTouch, can make a world of difference in your animal by changing behavior and attitude, releasing tension, reducing stress, encouraging relaxation, improving performance in working and show dogs, and easing pain. You'll find it to be a focused method of bodywork that teaches your animal to learn while increasing awareness, self-confidence, and concentration. At the same time, it will deepen your relationship with your friend.

TTEAM founder Linda Tellington-Jones travels the globe as she teaches TTouch and demonstrates its wonders on all species, from dogs, cats, and horses to snakes, tigers, bears, birds, dolphins, and even an octopus. TTEAM is truly global: it is practiced and taught in over 30 countries.

TTouch is a nonverbal language consisting of circles, lifts, and strokes that deepen understanding and communication between a guardian and an animal. The work is cumulative, and you can make a difference by doing only two or three minutes of the circular TTouches at a time. You can work on any part of the body, and you don't have to understand anatomy to be successful.

"To bring a new feeling of awareness to the body—which will make your animal more confident and actually more intelligent—simply curve your hand lightly in the shape of a big paw, and softly push the skin in one and a quarter circles, usually in a clockwise direction," Tellington-Jones explains. To make the work fun and the various TTouches easy to identify and remember, she calls that hand form the Lying Leopard. In fact, all of the TTouches have animal names.

TTouch can be used on virtually any species, including cats, dogs, horses, llamas, and humans. Dramatic shifts in behavior have been reported with dogs who are timid, shy, hyperactive, aggressive, afraid of loud noises or thunder, bark excessively, fear-biters, leash-pullers, and those who are sensitive on the paws or hindquarters, resistant to grooming or nail clipping or prone to carsickness. For socializing and prevention of chewing, TTouch can seem like a miracle. TTouch also supports allopathic and holistic veterinary care for many conditions, from arthritis and allergies to aging.

TTouch has helped many "fraidy cats" who don't like to be held or only accept one person in their lives. Often as little as two sessions of five to ten minutes can make a turnaround in behavior. The TTouches can also help ease digestive sensitivities and improve general health in an aging feline friend.

Ear TTouches can be used for all animals (and people, too!) for general improvement of health; and, in the event of injury or illness, you can use them to keep or bring an animal out of shock while on the way to your veterinarian. See the Resource section for more information about TTouch.

Traditional Chinese Medicine (TCM)

Traditional Chinese Medicine is a body of science that uses a combination of herbs (Chinese Herbal Medicine or CHM), physical medicine (acupuncture), mental medicine (meditation techniques), and other methods that assess the energy patterns of the body, called Chi. The understanding of the theories and practice of TCM often require that the practitioner or medical doctor spend years of training to become proficient. For busy veterinarians, this often makes TCM difficult to include in the currently acceptable approaches to medical treatments that exist in most veterinary hospitals and specialty or referral clinics.

Dr. Bob has been working with Jiu Jia (Jay) Wen, DVM, a veterinary Chinese herbalist who received his training in Veterinary Acupuncture and Herbal Medicine at Beijing Agricultural University in China. Dr. Wen is the first veterinarian to be licensed to practice in the US from the People's Republic of China. While Dr. Wen endorses TCM, he is more modern and practical when treating his own patients, especially those with cancer. Dr. Wen has said the following: "The time has come for traditional Chinese herbalists to modernize their approach. TCM is over 5,000 years old and things have changed. One has to change their traditional approach (which includes acupuncture, Chi, and opposites such as Yin and Yang) to the more modern approach of matching the Chinese herbal remedy to the clinical condition of the animal."

Traditional Chinese Medicine, as written by the ancient masters, depends almost solely upon the physical examination of the body, as opposed to Western medicine, which rests almost solely upon diagnosis for the basis of its medical recommendations. In TCM, the practitioner would recommend different supplements at different stages of the disease, because these ancient doctors thought that the different symptoms of one disease were actually several diseases. Dr. Wen explains, "During the initial stage of influenza, a person felt chilled. Later on he or she would be feverish and painful. In the end, there may be a lingering cough. An ancient physician would use three separate formulas for this one illness. As modern doctors, we now recognize that a virus causes all these symptoms. We can use one formula throughout the entire course of the disease."

It takes years to be proficient at diagnostics. Modern diagnostic equipment and techniques have given doctors the ability to find the causes of disease and its effect upon the body. We have found that it is possible to use herbal supplements based upon modern diagnostics, allowing a veterinarian with little training in herbal therapies to use familiar diagnostic tools (such as blood analysis, x-rays, ultrasounds, biopsies and diagnostic imaging) to establish a diagnosis.

Dr. Bob and Dr. Wen often work together utilizing this modern approach to TCM, especially when it comes to the treatment of cancer (see Chapter 9 for more information). Dr. Wen has created a line of Chinese herbal products called White Crane, which is sold only through veterinarians (see Resources for more information). These are some of Dr. Wen's products:

- **Adrenosol**: for Cushing's disease (a disease of the adrenal glands)
- **BackRelief**: for back pain and spasms and slipped discs
- **ColonGuard**: for inflammatory bowel disease
- **DermGuard**: for allergic and itchy skin
- **Epitrol**: for epilepsy
- **HeartAssist**: for heart conditions
- **HipGuard**: for arthritis of the hip and knees
- **Immunoderm**: for immune skin disease such as lupus
- **Incontinence Support**: for urinary incontinence
- **JointGuard**: for arthritis
- **KidneyGuard**: for kidney conditions and failure
- **LiverGuard**: for liver conditions and disease
- **Relaxol**: for depression and cognitive dysfunction.

Chapter 5

Treating Common Conditions

When it comes to our animal's well-being, most of us would rather be safe than sorry. We don't hesitate to bring our cat or dog to the veterinarian's office when there is a health concern. In the event of a "red alert" episode—such as a serious eye injury, uncontrolled bleeding, or severe trauma or injury—an immediate trip to your nearest animal clinic is clearly in order. However, in many nonacute, nonemergency situations, you may feel comfortable treating your animal at home. Doing so may even help you avoid the use of veterinarian-prescribed, potent, immune-suppressing medications and other chemical agents when a gentle approach might do the trick.

Here we have compiled an alphabetical listing of three dozen of the day-to-day, sometimes nagging conditions that may occasionally afflict your animal. In some instances, a visit to your family veterinarian may be prudent to rule out any underlying serious medical condition or to get the initial problem under control. Consult our Holistic First-Aid Kit on page 132 so that you can handle minor occurences without running to the store repeatedly. You can then follow up with effective home remedies to continue healing and prevent recurrences (check out the Resources at the end of the book for a full listing of where to find the products we recommend). Many of these and other health issues can be prevented simply by upgrading your animal's diet, as we describe in detail in Chapter 1. Doing so will make you a more confident animal guardian, one who is able to observe and support your friend's health without panic or uncertainty.

Abscesses

Outdoor cats, especially males (even neutered ones), often develop swollen areas on the skin from the bites and scratches they receive during territorial encounters with their peers (a good reason to keep your feline friend indoors). If they engage in the fight, the swollen areas will be on the face or front legs. If they are retreating, the abscesses will often be on the back end or hind legs.

A biting tooth punctures the skin, delivering bacteria, hair, and debris into your cat's deeper tissues. The puncture wound quickly scabs over, sealing everything in, and an abscess begins to fester. While cats win the prize for the most abscesses, dogs and cats are equally prone to "boils" (a collection of waste materials working their way through the skin in normal detoxification).

Topical Treatments

If the abscess is still open and draining pus, you can apply aloe vera liquid or gel inside and around the affected area. If the abscess is closed, it will be swollen, hot, and painful, and you'll need to establish a drain hole. Before you pull off the scab to open the abscess, or the abscess opens up on its own, soak it in a mixture of warm water and baking soda, or apply a compress with water and baking soda to the area. This will bring the infection to the surface and cause it to "pop." Find the crusted-over bite wound and remove the scab by grabbing it with your fingers (between the nails) and pulling quickly and firmly, so pus can drain out. If you can't find the bite wound, seek help from your veterinarian, as this festering can lead to a toxic reaction. This is important, because without adequate drainage, the infection can travel deeper into the body, resulting in a condition called septicemia (blood poisoning).

With dogs, be sure to keep the open wound clean; cats will do most of the cleaning themselves. You can clean the wound with plain water and hydrogen peroxide. You can also apply a small amount of a liquid garlic extract, such as **Kyolic**, to help keep the infection down. It usually takes only a couple of days for the infection to start healing.

Once the abscess has closed and there are no signs of infection, apply aloe vera and calendula topically (to the surface of the body). Be sure to wait until it's completely closed to apply the calendula because this remedy can instigate premature healing, and an abscess needs to have sufficient time to drain completely before closing up again.

Oral Treatments

Once the condition is stable, or if you caught it early enough before the toxic reactions begin, you can orally administer either bee propolis or aged garlic supplements (**Kyolic** or **Garlicin**). These natural antibiotics effectively improve the body's immune system and fight infection. For best results, divide into two doses with meals.

Bee propolis and a garlic supplement can help fight infection.

Bee propolis (daily, divided doses)	
Cat/Small Dog (up to 14 lb)	250 mg
Medium Dog (15-34 lb)	500 mg
Large/Giant Dog (35+ lb)	750 mg

Garlic (daily, divided doses)	
Cat/Small Dog (up to 14 lb)	1 tablet
Medium Dog (15-34 lb)	2 tablets
Large/Giant Dog (35+ lb)	3 tablets

Acne (Feline)

Feline acne, also known as "stud chin," is a fairly common condition that causes blackheads, pimples, or scabs on the underside of your cat's chin, which will feel rough to the touch. In extreme cases, the entire chin becomes infected and lymph glands in the neck begin to swell. An acute case such as this requires treatment by your veterinarian, who will usually prescribe antibiotics for the infection. But this level of infection is rare, particularly if you apply natural remedies before the acne becomes a problem.

Getting Started

First, identify and remove the source of the bacteria. Plastic food and water bowls are the most common culprits, because they harbor bacteria in their pores. When your cat eats or drinks, his chin repeatedly comes in contact with the bacteria. Stainless steel, porcelain, or glass bowls are a better choice. No matter what sort of bowl you use, it should be washed after every meal, just as you wash your own dishes.

Topical Treatments

To treat established acne, remove any blackheads, pimples, or pustules by squeezing each one gently to remove the accumulated oils and/or pus inside. Do not rub the area, as this will make the inflammation worse. Pat the spot with warm water and a natural soap to clean it. A gentle brand is **Dr. Bronner's Castile Soap** (lemon or almond is fine). Castile soap is a vegetable-based shampoo containing no harsh detergents, chemical additives, or preservatives. Then dab vitamin E oil or fresh aloe vera juice onto each blemish (fresh gel from a household aloe vera plant works the best; purchased aloe vera gel is also effective). Apply two to three times daily until the skin is clear and healthy.

Anal Glands

The anal glands of dogs and cats are related to the scent glands of skunks, which are used to deter predators. They contain a smelly type of material, which is usually expressed along with a bowel movement that contains a sufficient amount of fiber. Frightened dogs will often involuntarily let go of this material, and it's a smell that you will not soon forget. Anal glands can cause problems when they become impacted and/or blocked. This often happens with improper diet that contains little in the way of beneficial fiber, which helps these glands excrete. Since many commercially prepared diets are highly processed and devoid of beneficial fiber, blockage occurs all too often. Continued blockage of the glands will often lead to a painful abscess (see *Abscess*, above), which if left untreated will often open into the surrounding skin. This is often a painful and malodorous situation.

The first sign of brewing anal sac problems will be "scooting" (your animal will drag his or her backside on the ground) and excessive licking, which are attempts to alleviate the discomfort. If you see this, it is time to bring your dog or cat to the veterinarian (or groomer) and have the anal sacs expressed before they progress to the infectious stage. It is also the time to switch to a beneficial fiber-rich diet that contains lots of vegetables. This will help in long-term prevention.

If the condition has progressed to a blockage and abscess, your veterinarian will most likely lance open the abscess and treat it with antibiotics both systemically and topically.

Appetite

A change in appetite, while not indicative of a specific condition, is one of the best barometers of the start or progression of a condition. It's not the appetite, per se, but rather any change in your dog or cat's eating habits. For example, be aware if your cat who is normally a good eater is suddenly quite picky; or if your dog who is normally low key about eating is now ravenous.

If a change in your animal's eating habits has occurred, that is the signal to visit your veterinarian, have a complete physical and blood examination, and get a diagnosis. Awareness is the key, so if something is brewing you'll have time for corrective measures, and won't be forced into a potent medical or life-saving treatment plan.

For picky and finicky animals who are not sickly or developing an illness, see Chapter 1 for suggestions for flavor enhancers that will be helpful for your animals.

Bad Breath

First, make sure that the source of bad breath is not infected teeth or periodontal disease. This can be determined by looking at the teeth and gums for redness or swelling. You may also observe an accumulation of hard brown tartar on the side of the teeth that is pushing the gums up and setting up a local inflammation. If this appears to be the source of the odor, it would be wise to visit your veterinarian (see *Gingivitis*). Professional teeth cleaning under sedation may be needed to remove the tartar.

The second source of odor comes from the stomach as a result of digestive difficulties. Switching to a diet that is rich in whole foods, antioxidants, and phytonutrients will go a long way in the elimination of odor from faulty digestion.

Oral Treatments

Simple bad breath can be helped with chlorophyll. One of the best sources is chopped fresh parsley mixed into the food daily. Add from 1 teaspoon per meal for small dogs and cats, and up to 2 tablespoons per meal for large and giant dogs. The herbal product **Clean Breath** from Earth Animal can help fight bad breath. Access to chew toys that assist in maintaining oral health is also critical. There are many such products on the market today, including a full range from Nylabone that is rated for different types and sizes of dogs.

Bee Sting

The incidence of bee stings increases during summer and autumn, and your animal may be vulnerable when he or she is outdoors. You must seek veterinary help if you notice swelling either locally or on the face. Be prepared by keeping a supply of the Bach flower essence called **Rescue Remedy** on hand at all times, along with a bottle of **Benadryl** (an over-the-counter antihistamine), available at any drugstore. The recommended dose for Benadryl is 2 milligrams for each kilogram (kg) of body weight (1 kg = 2.2 pounds).

We approve of a one-time "hit" of Benadryl if your animal has been stung and is showing signs of a reaction (the swelling described above), regardless of how mild. The flower essence formula Rescue Remedy (available at most health food stores) will help divert your animal's attention away from the pain and swelling from the bite. Do this on the way to your veterinarian or the emergency clinic.

Oral Treatments

Administer homeopathic **Arnica montana**, which is also an excellent remedy for the side effects of stings and bites of all types. Arnica can be purchased in small vials containing pellets. Fold a 3 x 5 inch index card lengthwise and shake out the *Arnica* pellets into the fold. With your fingers or the back of a spoon, gently crush the pellets from the outside of the index card without touching them. Slide the powder directly onto the membranes of your animal's mouth or onto the tongue.

Arnica Montana (twice daily)	
Cat/Small Dog (up to 14 lb)	1 pellet
Medium Dog (15-34 lb)	2 pellets
Large Dog (35-84 lb)	3 pellets
Giant Dog (85 lb+)	3 pellets

Bee and wasp stings and nonpoisonous spider bites also respond to **Apis mellifica**, a homeopathic remedy extracted from bees. Give the crushed pellets immediately, again in 30 minutes, then at 1 and 2 hours, and then 3 to 4 times daily for the next 3 to 4 days, or until relief is accomplished. *Apis* is also effective for a variety of allergic reactions as well as rashes and generalized inflammatory conditions.

Once your animal has experienced a reaction to a bee sting, he or she may be "sensitized" to the allergen and if stung again, may be at risk of more intensive reactions during future episodes. This sensitization is called anaphylaxis, and in addition to insect bites and bee stings, other causes include vaccines, medications, pollens, and molds.

Caution: Anaphylaxis (an acute reaction to an insect or spider bite or bee sting) may cause rapid swelling, labored breathing, intense itching around the face, incoordination, choking, or shock in your animal. In this case, you must seek emergency veterinary treatment with epinephrine immediately.

Sting Relievers

You never know when you'll need Rescue Remedy for an insect bite. It is also a good idea to have a supply of Benadryl. We recall the time when our beloved Boxer, Jack, was bitten on the eye by a venomous spider, causing an anaphylactic reaction—extremely swollen lips and eyelids and labored breathing. We administered Rescue Remedy and one dose of Benadryl on the way to the veterinary hospital. By the time we arrived for the injection, Jack's eyes were beginning to open and his breathing was stable.

Bladder Problems

Bladder problems can be just as difficult for animals as they are for humans. Like us, animals may experience excruciating pain when trying to pass urine. Many become irritable and may even cry out when attempting to urinate.

Clinical signs are frequent but unproductive efforts to urinate. Even if well trained, most animals fail to hold the urine in and are more prone to indoor accidents, to everyone's distress. Just as frustrating is the inability to "go" at all. This is not only exasperating but dangerous, especially in cats. Anytime you observe your animal unproductively straining to urinate, or if you see blood in the urine, visit your family veterinarian and, if need be, use medication to prevent an emergency situation.

Bladder conditions can be secondary to bacterial infection, stones (urolithiasis), powerful medications, and conditions such as cystitis and cancer. *Important note: If the bladder condition is secondary to calcium oxalate stones, as diagnosed by your veterinarian, see the section in Chapter 8 on bladder diseases.* Improper diet and the resulting high levels of metabolic wastes and toxic breakdown products can directly irritate the bladder and set the stage for problems. Therefore, the goal of treatment is to minimize metabolic wastes and toxins by improving the diet.

Oral Treatments

The most important supplemental remedy for treating bladder problems is **vitamin C** (ascorbic acid). Not only is it effective in acidifying urine, its ability to boost the immune system helps to prevent future episodes.

Vitamin C (twice daily)	
Cat/Small Dog (up to 14 lb)	250 mg
Medium Dog (15-34 lb)	500 mg
Large Dog (35-84 lb)	750 mg
Giant Dog (85 lb+)	1000 mg

Bladder problems are so common that we worked with master herbalist Jane Smolnick to develop Earth Animal's **Pee Pee** formula as a simple herbal treatment for bladder conditions.

Pee Pee (twice daily)	
Cat/Small Dog (up to 14 lb)	7 drops
Medium Dog (15-34 lb)	10 drops
Large Dog (35-84 lb)	15 drops
Giant Dog (85 lb+)	18 drops

Calluses

Calluses commonly occur on the elbows and other bony protrusions. They are firm, hairless, growth-like masses that cover an area of the skin on the joint. They are usually black and scaly. They protect the bony joint the way nature intended. Occasionally, though, they may become swollen, hot, or inflamed. The usual sign of inflammation is excessive licking or limping on that limb or extremity. A comfortable bed is important to keep tender calluses off a hard floor and to give your animal some relief. Besides protective bedding, vitamin E or aloe vera gel applied directly to the area will reduce discomfort, swelling, and inflammation.

Cataracts

Cataracts are defined as an opacity of the lens of the eye. This opacity should not be confused with the cloudy, bluish lens that occurs with normal aging. The latter is termed a senile cataract or nuclear sclerosis and does not interfere with sight. A true cataract is a white opacity that either partially covers the lens (immature) or fully covers the lens (mature). The mature cataract often will result in blindness.

Cataracts can be genetic in origin, secondary to nutritional imbalances or deficiencies, or the result of a disease such as uveitis or diabetes. They are quite common in dogs and less common in cats. Poodles, Schnauzers, and Cocker Spaniels lead the list for dogs at risk of genetically induced cataracts. In cats, more susceptible breeds include Persians, Himalayans, and Birmans.

There is no medical therapy. Surgery (either removal or emulsifying the lens) is the treatment of choice. If surgery is elected then it should be done sooner rather than later to avoid any secondary complications from the cataract.

Cataracts follow a path similar to other developing degenerative conditions. In an attempt to heal itself, the body sets up a local inflammatory process. If the body is depleted of antioxidants, the inflammatory process will continue. This chronic situation leads to a deposit of metabolic wastes in the lens, resulting in the cataract.

An improved diet rich in antioxidants and phytonutrients will set the stage for a healthy eye and lens and help it to heal before cataract formation begins. In addition, one or more of the following alternatives, if used early enough, may save your animal from surgery before sight is affected.

Oral Treatments

Earth Animal's **Vision**, a combination of eyebright, chamomile, and bayberry, will support circulation to the eye.

Vision (twice daily, orally)	
Cat/Small Dog (up to 14 lb)	7 drops
Medium Dog (15-34 lb)	10 drops
Large Dog (35-84 lb)	14 drops
Giant Dog (85+ lb)	20 drops

Alpha-lipoic acid, a potent antioxidant available from your health food store, can help prevent cataracts from forming and progressing.

Alpha-lipoic acid (daily)	
Cat/Small Dog (up to 14 lb)	50 mg
Medium Dog (15-34 lb)	100 mg
Large or Giant Dog (35+ lb)	200 mg

We have been working with a new product called **Cataract Glandular Drops**. These natural drops are added directly to the eye and usually will show dissolution of the cataract in 30 to 50 days. The principal components of Cataract Glandular Drops are Cataract Reductor A USP and Cataract Reductor B USP, which are normal components of the lens. These natural cataract reductors function as a lubricant and relieve dryness of the eyes. In addition, they improve the transparency of the eye lens by reducing the opacifying materials. One drop directly in the eye twice daily for 30 days should show an improvement in the opacity of the cataract. If improvement is shown, finish the bottle of drops; if there has been no improvement, discontinue the drops.

In addition, you can use **Cataract Drops**, which are an oral combination homeopathic available as part of the Nutritional Blood Test (NBT) program (see Chapter 4 for more information). At home, at night, examine your animal's eyes under artificial light to see how much grayness there is. Use this as a reference point. Begin using the drops (add directly in the mouth or add to the food, *not the eyes!*) twice a day for two months. At that point, reexamine the eyes under the same type of light. If there has been improvement continue the drops orally twice weekly.

Cataract Drops (twice daily with food)	
Cat/Small Dog (up to 14 lb)	5 drops
Medium Dog (15-34 lb)	7 drops
Large Dog (35-84 lb)	12 drops
Giant Dog (85+ lb)	15 drops

Constipation

Sometimes what guardians think is constipation in their animals is often something else, such as serious diarrhea where the animal strains excessively but can only get out a small amount of liquid. If your animal strains excessively to move his bowels, you need to get a proper diagnosis from your veterinarian. Conditions such as megacolon (a stretched, nonfunctioning colon), a fractured pelvis that has healed improperly and is constricting the colon, and foreign bodies all have to be ruled out before you institute preventive measures.

Oral Treatments

If your veterinarian has not diagnosed a disease causing the constipation, there are preventative measures that you can take with your animal's diet. Many dog and cat foods are devoid of beneficial fiber and can lead to constipation. Add finely chopped fibrous vegetables such as kale or cabbage to the diet, or natural fiber sources such as rice polish or psyllium husks, to help prevent and control constipation.

Mix **psyllium husks** or **rice polish** with some warm water (50/50) and add directly to the food.

Psyllium Husks/Rice Polish (with meals)	
Cat/Small Dog (up to 14 lb)	1 tsp
Medium Dog (15-34 lb)	2 tsp
Large Dog (35-84 lb)	1 Tbsp
Giant Dog (85+ lb)	1 1/2 Tbsp

Another beneficial vegetable is pumpkin—mashed and combined with mashed or ground-up pumpkin seeds. Follow the above doses for psyllium.

Dandruff

Most people think dandruff is just dry, flaking skin. This is only partly true. Dandruff is dead skin cells that are being replaced by new cells (this process is called skin turnover, and it's normal unless it accelerates, leading to dandruff formation). Animals who stay in dry, heated rooms will have drier, scalier skin, but dandruff (especially excessive) is the result of irritating metabolic wastes and toxins that are being eliminated through the skin. The toxins accumulate in sebum (oil that is discharged from the glands of the skin).

Animals should be regularly combed and brushed, which helps to remove dead hair and debris. Periodic bathing (every 3 to 4 weeks, with a natural shampoo that doesn't contain any chemicals) will also be helpful in reducing the dandruff.

Oral Treatments

Add organic **flaxseed oil** or **fish oil** to the food. These two oils are high in the beneficial omega-3 and omega-6 fatty acids.

Flaxseed oil or Fish oil (with meals)	
Cat/Small Dog (up to 14 lb)	1 tsp
Medium Dog (15-34 lb)	2 tsp
Large Dog (35-84 lb)	1 Tbsp
Giant Dog (85+ lb)	1 1/2 Tbsp

Lecithin helps keep the elimination process active and effective. It works by dissolving the sebum and oils in the skin pores so they'll be less likely to accumulate and clog pores. As a bonus, cleaned skin pores will allow new hair to grow, so the coat will become lusher. Add lecithin capsules or granules directly to the food.

Lecithin (with meals)	
Cat/Small Dog (up to 14 lb)	1/2 tsp
Medium Dog (15-34 lb)	1 tsp
Large Dog (35-84 lb)	2 tsp
Giant Dog (85+ lb)	1 Tbsp

Topical Treatments

A mixture of organic apple cider vinegar and water (about 2 tsp cider to one pint of water) applied to the skin as a dip, especially on any hairless areas, will help reduce irritation and remove grease, thereby opening the pores and hair follicles.

Shampoo your animal with a product that includes lecithin as one of the main ingredients. Once the skin has been cleaned and the pores are open and functioning well, you can turn to products between shampoos that will help win the battle against dander and odors. We like **Tropiclean**, which prides itself on being environmentally safe, cruelty free, and uses real foods such as kiwi and papaya to get the job done.

Diarrhea

Diarrhea, one of the most common problems of cats and dogs, is most often transient. If the stool is loose but your animal is acting as though he or she feels fine and is eating and drinking normally, you probably can handle the problem at home. If you see any worsening of symptoms or see no improvement within 24 hours, seek veterinary assistance as dehydration can rapidly occur.

Sometimes diarrhea can be a sign of a more serious condition such as colitis, inflammatory bowel disease, or hemorrhagic gastroenteritis (inflamed bowel with blood—see section in Chapter 8 on gastrointestinal diseases). As a general rule, any vomiting or diarrhea with blood should be treated as an emergency.

To determine whether your animal is dehydrated, do a "skin pinch" test to evaluate the elasticity of the skin. Grab a fold of skin on the neck or side of the chest. If it doesn't snap right back to its normal position, but instead remains peaked, your pet is dehydrated. In some cases, your veterinarian may elect to administer fluids and electrolytes intravenously.

Getting Started at Home

Begin home treatment with a 12- to 24-hour meal skip to rest your animal's digestive tract. Then give your animal this bland, home-cooked diet for a few days: Combine 1 pound lean, chopped meat, 1 cup uncooked white rice, and 1 quart water. Cook until the rice is soft and the meat is fully cooked. The fat from the meat will be floating on top: skim it off, then pour off the extra water into a separate bowl.

Start with just a spoonful or two. As long as no diarrhea recurs, continue offering small amounts at two-hour intervals, gradually increasing the amount of food until it's about half your animal's usual meal size. At alternate hours between solid food feedings, offer your animal a small amount of the reserved cooking water. If he or she drinks it all, continue rationing the broth in small amounts offered every two hours until the thirst seems to be satisfied—at that point, water can be made available as free choice. (It's wise to limit water intake at first because the highly irritated gut tends to move too quickly, eliminating larger volumes of liquid before they can be absorbed. This not only fails to help prevent dehydration, it also perpetuates the inflammation in the bowel.)

Continue this special diet for up to three days, depending on how your animal seems to be doing. When he or she is well again, gradually reintroduce the regular diet over a two- to three-day period.

Oral Treatments

Slippery elm syrup or **Kaopectate** will place a protective coating on your animal's intestines so they can heal. Give every four hours for 24 hours or until diarrhea stops, whichever happens first. (If, after 24 hours, your animal's diarrhea is continuing or any other signs have developed, contact your veterinarian.)

Slippery elm syrup/Kaopectate (every four hours)	
Cat/Small Dog (up to 14 lb)	1 tsp
Medium Dog (15-34 lb)	2 tsp
Large or Giant Dog (35+ lb)	1 Tbsp

For diarrhea that is accompanied by lots of straining and gas (but no blood) we recommend **goldenseal** tincture, three times daily.

Goldenseal (three times daily)	
Cat/Small Dog (up to 14 lb)	5 drops
Medium Dog (15-34 lb)	10 drops
Large Dog (35-84 lb)	12 drops
Giant Dog (85+ lb)	15 drops

Another one of our favorite remedies is **Dia-Relief** from Dr. Goodpet. This homeopathic remedy is absorbed through the tongue.

Dia-Relief (twice daily, orally apart from meals)	
Cat/Small Dog (up to 14 lb)	5 drops
Medium Dog (15-34 lb)	7 drops
Large Dog (35-84 lb)	10 drops
Giant Dog (85+ lb)	12 drops

Earth Animal's **The Runs** is a medicinal herbal combination that contains chamomile, slippery elm, and white oak bark, and is quite effective in settling down irritated intestines and helping to control simple diarrhea.

Remember, when diarrhea persists, it can lead to dehydration. Keep in touch with your veterinarian, and be sure to report whether your animal is able to drink liquids without losing them in continued diarrhea.

Drooling (excessive), see *Gingivitis*.

Ear Infections

Both dogs and cats have their share of ear problems. Dogs with floppy ears (like Basset Hounds and Cocker Spaniels) are more prone to infections and trapped burrs; however, all dogs, especially Golden Retrievers, can get these infections. Cats seem more susceptible to ear mites. The ear may be filled with brown or black wax-like material. A more severe inflammation or infection may emit a smelly brown or pink pus or even blood from the ear.

If any of these conditions describes your animal's ears, please consult your veterinarian first. After treatment, you can use a variety of home remedies to keep the ears clean and healthy and prevent recurrences. When working at home, never put a cotton swab—or anything smaller than your elbow—in your animal's ear. Also, don't pull out any hair, even if it looks matted or loose. If the ear requires medical attention, your veterinarian will remove the hair.

Topical Treatments

To soothe an irritated ear, place several drops of room-temperature chamomile tea into the ear. This herb will help your animal feel better, regardless of the severity of the infection.

Ears dirty with wax can be cleaned with slightly warmed olive oil (no warmer than your own body temperature—otherwise, you could accidentally burn the ear canal). Add up to 10 drops of oil to the affected ear, gently massage the ear canal alongside the face, and then let your animal shake out the dissolved wax and oil (stand clear!). Then add vitamin E oil from a capsule—a 200 iu size is fine—and massage it into the ear canal to further promote healing.

Highly diluted apple cider vinegar can also be used as an ear cleaner because the acid medium kills yeast and fungi. One-quarter of a teaspoon of the apple cider vinegar can be diluted into a cup of water and carefully applied in the ear with an eyedropper.

Once you've initiated cleansing from the inside out, you can maintain the ear with a natural brand of ear wash. The one we recommend is **Clean Ears** available from Earth Animal. Simply place the drops in the ear weekly with gentle massage.

Oral Treatments

You may also want to consider a change in diet, especially if your friend has been ingesting the same protein source day after day, even year after year, or if she's been eating a store-bought food containing chemicals or by-products. If your animal companion suffers from chronic ear infections, consider adding **Lactobacillus acidophilus** (probiotics or "friendly flora") to the diet, either in capsule form or from plain, low-fat, live-culture yogurt.

Ear Mites

These nasty little microscopic bugs live in the ear canal of both cats and dogs, especially young animals that have immature immune systems. The mites cause chronic irritation, excessive wax production and accumulation; left untreated, they can progress to secondary ear infections and inflammation, which can cause hearing loss. A severe infestation should be treated by your veterinarian. (You can tell it's severe by the strong smell and if your animal's ears are sore, making him or her resentful of your efforts to treat the problem.)

Topical Treatments

In a less severe or early infestation, a gentle, effective home remedy can be made from equal parts of rosemary, lemon, and eucalyptus oils (about 10 drops of each) mixed in 4 ounces of warm olive oil. Place about 10 drops of the mixture into the affected ear, gently massage the canal alongside your animal's face, and let him or her shake out the wax and dead mites. You can buy all the essential oils you need at your local health food store. A ready-to-use formula is **Natural Herbal Ear Wash** from Halo, Purely for Pets, or Earth Animal's **Clean Ears**.

Be sure to hold the earflap tightly while you are putting in the oil and massaging the canal, otherwise the remedy will be flung everywhere before it's had a chance to do its job. Also, don't pull out any hair, even if it looks matted or loose. Apply this treatment twice daily for four days, then daily for one week. Do it again after one week and two weeks to kill any new mites that have hatched from eggs inside the ear since the earlier treatments. Once you have finished, your animal's ear should be clean and a healthy pink color. If you begin to see a waxy accumulation again, reapply the treatment twice more in the next week.

If your animal grabs its ear and scratches furiously, herbal preparations may not be strong enough to deal with the problem. This would be one of those times when conventional medicine might be indicated. You might have to just bite the bullet and use medication for seven to ten days to get rid of the problem, and then keep the ear healthy with natural remedies.

Eye Problems

Healthy vision is important to your companion's quality of life, although many animals get along just fine as they age with diminished eyesight. Major enemies to the eyes include genetic weaknesses, improper diet, and a lack of vitamins and minerals (particularly vitamins A and D). Cataracts and glaucoma are two common age-related eye diseases in dogs and cats. (See the information on cataracts in this chapter.)

Oral Treatments

Eyebright, abundant in the Pacific Northwest, will strengthen your animal's eyes, helping to decrease inflammation and improve vision. Contact your local health food store for eyebright in capsule or elixir form. Herbal combination products, such as Earth Animal's **Vision** (a combination of eyebright, golden seal, and Ginkgo biloba), have proven to be beneficial to animals losing their sight due to cataracts or degeneration of the cornea.

If your animal has eye problems, give a natural form of **vitamin** A. The most natural source is from preservative-free fish oil, which can be found in human health food stores. The unit of measurement is international units (IU). Give vitamin A for two months at the following dosage, then cut in half for maintenance:

Vitamin A (once daily)	
Cat/Small Dog (up to 14 lb)	2,500 iu
Medium Dog (15–34 lb)	5,000 iu
Large Dog (35–84 lb)	7,500 iu
Giant Dog (85+ lb)	7,500 iu

Eye Strengthener Juice

This eye strengthener juice is high in naturally occurring vitamin A, vitamin C, and phytonutrients, all essential for good eyesight.

Cat/Small Dog: 1/2 carrot, 1/2 apple
Medium Dog: 1 carrot, 1 apple
Large/Giant Dog: 2 carrots, 1 large or 2 small apples

Juice and mix in drinking water or offer straight.

If juicing is not an option, be sure to grate fresh carrots and mix with food daily and offer fresh chunks of apples as a snack. Please use organic produce.

Fatty Tumors

One of the most common reasons that people visit their veterinarian is to examine a mass that occurs below the skin of their animal. These soft, free-moving bumps are called lipomas or fatty tumors. They often occur on the underbelly or back, directly below the skin or on the extremities. When you feel them, they are usually not inflamed or painful. They often come up very slowly and continue to grow steadily. Generally, a fatty tumor the size of an olive can double in size over a six- to eight-month period.

While fatty tumors are generally nonmalignant, noninvasive, and most often harmless (unless they get in the way of an extremity or block a vital area such as the throat), it's still important to address them. Their origin is quite straightforward. The body uses fats (lipids) as an energy source. In the cells, fat is burned to release energy which the body uses to function. Excess lipids are stored in "fat depots," most commonly around the waist and midsection; however, there is fat below the skin throughout the system. This fat is constantly being used in metabolism and replaced from the turnover of fats.

Problems related to fat metabolism occur for many reasons. In people, rich desserts loaded with whipped cream and foods loaded with butter and mayonnaise are often the underlying cause of benign fatty tumors. In animals, it's even simpler. Excluding the people-oriented type of snacks, there are two basic culprits underlying the formation of fatty tumors in animals:

- Feeding your animal a diet that contains too much saturated fat.
- Feeding your animal a diet that contains the wrong type of fat.

Many commercial dog and cat foods (especially those formulated for puppies, kittens, and working animals) contain high levels of fat. Fat levels of 18 to 20 percent in commercial dog foods are not uncommon; dry cat foods can run as high as 24 to 25 percent. Such formulas are often advertised as "energy-packed" and good for your animal's daily needs. Unfortunately, they really can overload the system with fat.

The second and more important culprit is the type of fat. In most commercial pet foods, the most common source of fat is rendered from "rejected" poultry parts—animals deemed unfit for human consumption. While younger, growing, or more active animals do require more fat in their diet, fat is also an appetite stimulant. The more fat added, the tastier the food. Rendered poultry fat is made up predominantly of saturated fats—the most difficult to digest and the most likely to be stored away in fat depots rather than burned as fuel. In addition, the fats in pet foods require preservatives, and many still contain chemical preservatives and antioxidants such as ethoxyquin, which will further stress the body's metabolism.

Getting Started at Home

If your animal is prone to benign fatty tumors, follow the Goldstein Food Plan, starting with a base of naturally preserved senior dog or cat food. A senior food has the lowest amount of added fat—often half what you will find in regular formulas. Add chopped vegetables, organic low-fat yogurt, and flaxseed oil (an excellent source of "healthy fats"—omega-3 fatty acids). These dietary changes will lessen the fat burden on your dog or cat's body. This type of diet will also increase the level of beneficial fiber, which will help cleanse the intestines and improve the absorption of fats and proteins. You should see a gradual reduction in your animal's fat stores or fatty tumors over a period of six to eight weeks. **Mega LipoTropic** is a digestive enzyme combination from Best For Your Pet, which is effective in helping to dissolve lipomas. Also, check out the "fat busters" section in Chapter 1 for more ideas on how to reduce the fat in your animal's diet.

Fleas, *See Chapter 6*

Gas (Flatulence)

All mammals have "friendly" bacteria residing in the intestines to help the digestive breakdown process. If they are not present in proper amounts, "unfriendly" bacteria pick up the slack and can actually be the cause of a disease. The result: diarrhea and/or flatulence. These symptoms also can result when the bacterial balance is normal but meals are too large, overwhelming the digestive bacteria and enzymes. Inefficient digestion and, again, excessive fluid and gas are the result.

Oral Treatments

If your animal has a deficiency of digestive enzymes, it's a simple matter to replace them. Here's our home remedy for intestinal bacteria imbalance. Give your animal plain, organic, low-fat or nonfat live-culture yogurt, which contains the friendly bacteria acidophilus.

Low-fat plain yogurt (with meals)	
Cat/Small Dog (up to 14 lb)	2 tsp
Medium Dog (15-34 lb)	1 Tbsp
Large Dog (35-84 lb)	1 1/2 Tbsp
Giant Dog (85+ lb)	2 Tbsp

Give the appropriate amount with each meal. A main cause of low levels of friendly bacteria is antibiotic use, so always feed yogurt when your animal is on antibiotics.

Also, putting one or two cloves of freshly chopped garlic in the food helps purify the intestinal tract and remove the mucus buildup from poor diets. Add a sprinkle of parsley to counteract garlic breath. (*Caution: Feeding high amounts of garlic can cause anemia, especially in cats. For this reason do not feed garlic to animals that are prone to or have anemia, or in advance of a surgical procedure.*) The average dose for garlic is one full clove for every 25 lbs of weight to a maximum of 3 cloves. With aged garlic supplements (such as Kyolic) we recommend half the recommended human dose.

You can also use aloe vera juice: 1 tsp for every 25 pounds.

Another option is **Lactobacillus acidophilus**. Give with each meal.

Lactobacillus acidophilus (with meals)		
	Capsules	Liquid
Cat/Small Dog (up to 14 lb)	1	1/2 tsp
Medium Dog (15-34 lb)	2	1 tsp
Large/Giant Dog (35+ lb)	3	2 tsp

If your animal's gas is due to indigestion from too-large meals, cut the meals into smaller portions and feed them at intervals throughout the day. If the gas is severe, you'll get faster results if you start with a fasting period.

An abrupt change in your animal's diet also can cause gas. Believe it or not, even if you bought the same brand of pet food that you always buy, you may have changed your animal's diet without realizing it. Some of the larger commercial pet food producers shop around for the cheapest ingredients whenever they make a new batch of food. The overall nutritional analysis of the food may stay the same, but some of the ingredients may have changed. We recommend that you choose a brand that is free of chemical preservatives and colors, with consistent ingredients.

Food allergies can be another cause of excess gas. If you suspect your animal is having an allergic reaction to commercial pet food, consider switching to another brand or formula.

Gingivitis (Gum Disease)

Gum problems can range from mild irritation at the gum line to major periodontal disease with tooth and bone infection. In all cases, be sure to get a proper veterinary examination and diagnosis first. If it's severe, veterinary treatment will be necessary. Treatment usually consists of cleaning the teeth and the periodontal space between the teeth and gums with an ultrasonic tooth scaler, followed by a course of antibiotics and often cortisone to remove the inflammation. In severe instances tooth extraction of loose and infected teeth may be necessary.

It is enormously important that you pay close attention to the condition of your dog's or cat's teeth and gums, not just from the perspective of comfort during chewing and eating but because there is a definite link between oral hygiene, your animal's immune system, and the long-term health of organs such as the heart, kidneys, and liver.

In both people and animals, the heart is vulnerable to the constant seeding of infectious agents, one result of which may be endocarditis, an infection within the heart chambers. The liver and kidneys are also at risk due to their burden of detoxification.

The best way to ensure long-term dental health in your dog or cat is to provide appropriate chew toys, brush his or her teeth—ideally weekly—and follow the Goldstein Food Plan by feeding plaque-defying foods like whole grains and fresh vegetables. Make these simple changes, and your animal will be far ahead of the game.

Be alert to the signs of gum disease, which may include one or more the following:

- tartar buildup
- bleeding gums
- inflammation (redness, swelling) at the gum line
- foul odor
- loose teeth
- difficulty eating (due to pain)

Avoid giving your animal foods containing refined sugar, white flour, or other harmful ingredients. These plaque-builders are the chief culprits of gum diseases, causing inflammation and swelling. Contrary to popular belief, chewing most brands of biscuits is *not* an effective means of keeping the teeth clean. The problem starts at the periodontal area between the tooth and the gum line. While chewing biscuits may exercise the jaw muscles, it does little for periodontal disease or the buildup of tartar; at best, it causes intermittent, inconsistent stimulation of the gums in the locations where pieces of biscuit might brush against them. A chew toy with stimulating knobs or ridges is a much healthier option.

Oral Treatments

Add **Ester-C** to strengthen your animal's immune system, facilitating the destruction of the germs and microorganisms that can enhance gum disease. Mix with plain, organic yogurt for palatability.

Ester-C *(twice daily)*	
Cat/Small Dog (up to 14 lb)	250 mg
Medium Dog (15-34 lb)	500 mg
Large Dog (35-84 lb)	750 mg
Giant Dog (85+ lb)	1,000 mg

Use **echinacea** alternating for two weeks on and two weeks off to help stimulate immune-cell function in your animal, slowing the progress of bacteriological invaders.

Echinacea (twice daily)	
Cat/Small Dog (up to 14 lb)	7 drops
Medium Dog (15-34 lb)	10 drops
Large Dog (35-84 lb)	12 drops
Giant Dog (85+ lb)	15 drops

Coenzyme Q10 is a powerful antioxidant that can help reduce inflammation in the gums. Give this dose daily.

Coenzyme Q10 (once daily)	
Cat/Small Dog (up to 14 lb)	20 mg
Medium Dog (15-34 lb)	30 mg
Large Dog (35-84 lb)	50 mg
Giant Dog (85+ lb)	60 mg

Topical Treatment

Fresh aloe vera from the plant works well to reduce inflammation and redness. Rub it gently onto the gums with your fingers.

Ultrasonic Cleansing

Should your veterinarian find advanced tooth and gum disease, he or she may recommend a complete dental procedure using an ultrasonic cleaner. While this will effectively reduce tartar and plaque and stimulate the periodontal space, this type of cleaning is usually performed under general anesthesia, which is not without risk, especially for elderly animals or those already battling chronic illness. Even with a presurgical blood test, there is no guarantee of success, as the animal can be allergic to the anesthesia and other complications can occur during surgery. If one is available in your area, consider using a trained animal dental hygienist who will perform thorough, anesthesia-free teeth cleaning for dogs and cats. Ask your veterinarian for a referral.

Anesthesia-Free Teeth Cleaning

Kathy Klein of Escondido, California, gazes into the mouths of dogs and cats for a living, and what she sees often isn't pretty. It's estimated that 80 percent of dogs and 70 percent of cats have gum disease by the time they are three years old. But the animals that come into contact with Klein are lucky indeed, for her unique specialty service also spares many animals the risks of anesthesia.

Working in holistic and traditional veterinary offices, Klein performs anesthesia-free teeth cleaning for dogs and cats through her business, SmilePet. She also trains vet techs and veterinarians in her technique, which uses hand scalers similar to those used in human dental hygiene, as well as a pumice powder and antimicrobial oral rinse.

The process takes about an hour, and the animal often literally goes home with a smile on his or her face. Her next step is to persuade the animal's guardian of the importance of regular brushing.

"Many people shy away from brushing their dog or cat's teeth because they simply don't know how to humanely restrain their animal," Kathy explains. "Or perhaps they tried it one time and gave up. The key is to place your dog or cat in a position where they can't escape, then use your voice and hands (massage) to soothe and relax the animal."

Klein recommends this technique: "Sit on the floor, on a large towel or cushion. Place your animal very carefully in an upside-down position, so as not to hurt their back, and cradle the animal with your legs, with the back of the head in your lap. This works for most small to medium-sized dogs. Cats—and dogs that try to paw you—can be wrapped in a beach towel. Large dogs can be taught to lay on their side."

"Then take a hold of their face with your left hand, pull the lip out and get back there and brush. You don't have to look at the teeth to brush them, really, your main goal is to keep the gums healthy by stimulating them. Just like our teeth, you want to push the gums back."

Tartar buildup is the biggest culprit. Of her clients that do maintain regular brushing, their animals' gums are most likely to remain pink and healthy.

"Prevention is the key—if you start young with regular care, you're much less likely to run into problems later. You don't want to be facing anesthesia when your animal is 11 or 12 years old and needs six teeth pulled out, which is a common scenario."

Klein says that finger brushes are fine for a cat or very small dog but for most dogs, she recommends a real dog toothbrush with bristles designed not to be too harsh on their gums and enamel. It's also important to use pet-appropriate toothpaste.

Hairballs

The dreaded hairball is one of the most common conditions in cats. Hairballs are hair that is ingested in the self-grooming process, mixed with saliva and mucus from the mouth and intestinal tract. Shaped like a normal fecal roll, hairballs can become large enough to cause gagging and vomiting, or a blockage in the intestinal tract.

Over-the-counter hairball remedies are petroleum jelly-based pastes that "grease" the hairball so it can move more freely through the intestinal tract. We don't recommend these products. Even though they are effective, they do not cleanse the intestinal tract; rather, they tend to coat it with a greasy film, which can interfere with normal gut functioning and impair the absorption of vital nutrients.

Consider hairballs from an "as it happens in nature" point of view. Wild cats eat their prey whole—hair, nails, bones, everything. These ground-up pieces of undigested material act as an "intestinal broom" to help sweep the cat's intestinal tract clean of any residues, including the excess mucus that may line the tract. This is good! It's a chance to "wipe the slate clean" once in a while. You've probably seen cats go outside and eat grass and then regurgitate—the fibrous material in grass helps purge and clean the esophagus and stomach.

So, what to do for hairballs? For starters, regularly groom your cat to remove excess fur that your friend might otherwise ingest. Then, don't fight them—help them do their job. How? Add fiber to the diet. Soak a bit of psyllium or rice polish (both available in your local health food store) in warm water for five minutes and add to the food. This supplies not only fiber but also essential vitamins and minerals. Dosage is 1 teaspoon with each meal as a preventive. For cats that are prone to hairballs, you can double the dose.

Hair Loss (Alopecia)

Hair loss, or alopecia, is one of the most common conditions seen by veterinarians and, as with many skin conditions, the causes can be numerous. Besides allergic reactions and flea infestations, there are other causes such as gland and hormonal imbalances and mineral deficiencies (particularly zinc deficiency). It is important when hair loss occurs to visit your veterinarian and get the proper diagnosis. For more information on serious and chronic skin conditions see Chapter 8.

For simple hair loss you may be dealing with a fatty acid deficiency. Simply adding essential fatty acids to the diet may do the trick. We recommend a combination of **organic flaxseed oil** and **salmon oil** for omega-3 and -6 fatty acids.

Fish and Flax Oil (with meals)	
Cat/Small Dog (up to 14 lb)	1/2 tsp
Medium Dog (15-34 lb)	1 tsp
Large Dog (35-84 lb)	2 tsp
Giant Dog (85+ lb)	1 Tbsp

For itchy conditions we also recommend **evening primrose oil**.

Evening Primrose Oil (daily)	
Cat/Small Dog (up to 14 lb)	500 mg
Medium Dog (15-34 lb)	750 mg
Large Dog (35-84 lb)	1,000 mg
Giant Dog (85+ lb)	1,500 mg

In addition, the combination of **lecithin, innositol**, and **choline** has been found beneficial for the regrowth of hair, or you can use **Earth Animal's Daily Health Nuggets**.

Lecithin, Innositol, and Choline (daily)	
Cat/Small Dog (up to 14 lb)	125 mg
Medium Dog (15-34 lb)	250 mg
Large Dog (35-84 lb)	500 mg
Giant Dog (85+ lb)	750-1,000 mg

Hot Spots

The saliva from a single flea can trigger a round of frenzied biting, licking, and scratching in an allergic animal. This type of dermatitis is the most common cause of hot spots, although allergic reactions to food and environmental substances, other parasites, or fungal infections can also contribute.

As a result of the unrelenting itch, your animal may furiously scratch or bite at his or her skin, actually creating tissue damage in the process. You'll see a wet spot on the coat; if you lift the wet hair you will often find an irritated, infected, and sometimes bleeding wound covered by the hair. Severe hot spots will require veterinary treatment and possibly a round of cortisone to stop the destructive cycle.

Topical Treatments

For less severe hot spots, home treatment is usually effective. If necessary, clip any thick hair from the spot so your treatment will make good contact with the inflamed skin. Remove any crust or sticky debris with a cooled, strong black tea bag. Black tea contains tannins that are antiseptic for the skin. (Don't use herbal tea for this treatment.)

Now it's time to apply your home remedy: a preparation made from the plantain plant. This common lawn weed has large, green, paddle-like leaves and a few long stems like green shoots in the middle that are covered by green seeds. Chop the leaves finely in a food processor, then apply the resultant green slurry directly onto the hot spot. Hold your animal's head for several minutes to keep him or her from scratching or licking off the botanical medicine, thereby giving its healing and soothing properties time to take effect. (Plantain is dark green and will stain carpets, so apply this remedy outside or on an easily cleanable surface.)

Baking soda, mixed with a little water to make a paste, is another soothing remedy. Apply it just as you would the plantain. Another option is to soothe the inflamed area with fresh aloe vera juice. Once the hot spot is cooled down, make sure the underlying cause is treated. For further information, see also *Itchy Skin* and *Lick Sores* in this chapter.

Earth Animal's **Itchy Skin** contains medicinal herbs such as nettles, echinacea, and licorice (a natural cortisone) to help calm simple itchy skin. Also, bathe with a soothing, therapeutic shampoo such as Veterinarian's Best **Hot Spot Shampoo** or **Leciderm**.

Itchy Eyes

Itchy eyes are often a symptom of an allergy, either to an insect bite or to airborne irritants such as pollen. Insect bites can cause such serious itching and swelling that your animal injures himself by excessive rubbing at the eye. Veterinary care is essential to prevent eye damage.

Topical Treatments

If your dog or cat is pawing at the eye, or rubbing it on furniture or carpets, try the following remedies to soothe the itch:

Quercetin is a powerful antioxidant and eye protectant. Give the following dosage daily in two doses.

Quercetin (daily, in divided doses)	
Cat/Small Dog (up to 14 lb)	100 mg
Medium Dog (15-34 lb)	200 mg
Large Dog (35-84 lb)	300 mg
Giant Dog (85+ lb)	400 mg

Ready-made products are also available, including our own Earth Animal's **Clean Eyes**, Anitra's **Herbal Eyewash Kit**, containing eyebright and goldenseal, and **Similasan** (homeopathic eye drops), which is available at most health food stores. Use the **Similasan II** formula for itching eyes.

Itchy Skin (Pruritus)

If itchy skin is driving your animal up a wall, first look for the underlying cause and resolve it. Keep in mind that your animal may have an internal condition rather than something external like fleas. An itchy rash can also be a good sign, as it is one of the first signs of detoxification when internal toxins move outward. See Chapter 8 for more information on skin conditions.

Topical Treatments

For temporary relief of itchy symptoms, you can try:

Plantain—Chop leaves into a wet paste and apply directly to the skin. Caution: Do not do this over a carpet. The juice will stain.

Aloe vera—Cut open a leaf and apply the gel directly to the area.

Tea bags—Apply a wet, cool tea bag directly on the irritated skin (not herbal tea).

Baking soda—Make into a wet paste and apply it to the skin.

Lemon tonic—Cut a fresh whole lemon into quarters and put into a bowl. Pour distilled water over it and let it sit for one to two days in the refrigerator. Give your animal a sponge bath with the liquid.

Sulfur solution—Make a solution of 2 teaspoons elemental sulfur (available at your pharmacy) in 1 pint distilled water. Bathe your pet in this liquid. It will also help keep fleas, ticks, and mites away.

Scratch Free—from Dr. Goodpet, a combination homeopathic remedy. Follow label directions.

Itchy Skin—a combination herbal remedy available from Earth Animal. Follow directions on the label.

Kennel Cough

If your dog has ever suffered from canine infectious tracheobronchitis, commonly called kennel cough, you'd know it. The dry, harsh, "honking" cough along with the gagging and retching are hard to miss. In the early stages of the disease, your dog may also produce varying amounts of mucus. While it's a terrible-sounding disease (and in some cases the coughing can drag on for several weeks), it usually runs its course without lasting damage. From a holistic perspective, it's a perfect example of how a healthy immune system can protect your animal—or set him up for a disease condition.

Kennel cough typically crops up in dogs who have been in close proximity with other dogs at boarding kennels, grooming parlors, shows, field trials, shelters, or pet stores. Stress may also be a factor. What's happening is a severe inflammation and infection in the upper respiratory tract overwhelms the body's natural defenses. A number of upper respiratory tract invaders have been linked to the disease, most notably *Bordetella bronchiseptica* and canine parainfluenza viruses. Other bacteria and fungi may play the role of opportunists, riding the coattails of the primary viral invaders into a weakened respiratory tract.

This disease sounds much worse than it is. Generally, the signs clear up with or without treatment within 7 to 14 days. If your veterinarian suspects a secondary bacterial infection, he or she may prescribe an antibiotic such as tetracycline or amoxicillin along with short-term anti-inflammatory medication. A cough suppressant can help interrupt the cough-and-gag cycle. Because the primary cause of kennel cough is viral, antibiotics will have little effect other than to help minimize your dog's symptoms.

If your animal has a strong immune system, she will more likely be naturally resistant to the disease. However, even animals with strong immunity can be affected, although their symptoms may be much milder and of shorter duration. Keeping your animal on a high level of our Food Plan (see Chapter 1) will put you well on your way to true prevention.

The conventional approach to prevention is through vaccination. The veterinary literature recommends the use of Bordetella and Parainfluenza as well as adenovirus and distemper vaccines, since they have been isolated from dogs with kennel cough. However, according to *Kirk Veterinary Therapy* even the use of intranasal or injectable Bordetella and Parainfluenza vaccines "will not completely prevent the respiratory infections." A vaccinated animal can still get an upper respiratory infection, although the clinical signs will usually be milder.

The Boarding Kennel Dilemma

You may have been faced with this dilemma: You need to board your dog while you travel, but the kennel will not accept your animal without proof of vaccinations to "prevent" kennel cough. As we discussed in Chapter 3 on Vaccines, research and clinical observations over the last 20 years have repeatedly linked annual vaccinations to a host of chronic degenerative diseases. At the same time, there is no scientific proof supporting the practice of annual revaccinations—and much emerging evidence that they may in fact do harm.

The best way around this potentially sticky situation is to arrange for the services of a pet sitter who visits or stays at your home while you are away. If you must board your animals, you may have no choice but to vaccinate. If this is the case, select the intranasal vaccine that contains only Bordetella and Parainfluenza. Do not go the route of the combination injectable vaccine, which also includes distemper and hepatitis (adenovirus). This way you avoid overloading the immune system with five to seven different vaccines at the same time.

Vaccinate about seven days before boarding. Beginning 24 hours after the vaccine, administer the homeopathic remedy *Thuja occidentalis* (12X or 30C) for five to seven days. Or use 1 teaspoon **Viratox**, a detoxifying homeopathic tincture available from Homeovetix, daily for seven days.

Thuja occidentalis (once daily)	
Cat/Small Dog (up to 14 lb)	1 pellet
Medium Dog (15-34 lb)	2 pellets
Large/Giant Dog (35+ lb)	3 pellets

Oral Treatments

Should your dog come down with kennel cough, we recommend the following: For milder bouts of coughing and gagging, start with a fast for 24 to 36 hours using Susan's recipe for Potato Peeling Broth (see page 298). This will alkalinize the body and set the stage for healing. The liquids also have a flushing and cleansing effect and will combat dehydration. The broth also helps push accumulated mucus from the throat.

If coughing, gagging, and spitting up are severe and causing your dog to lose sleep, you may want to visit your veterinarian for a course of medication to help minimize the symptoms and give partial relief.

We like the combination homeopathic remedy **Cough** by Homeopet. It contains homeopathic *Drosera rotundifolia*, which provides excellent symptomatic relief for kennel cough. Give directly in the mouth twice daily or add daily to the drinking water.

Cough (twice daily)	
Cat/Small Dog (up to 14 lb)	7 drops
Medium Dog (15-34 lb)	10 drops
Large Dog (35-84 lb)	12 drops
Giant Dog (85+ lb)	15 drops

Cough and Wheeze, available through Earth Animal, contains mullein, coltsfoot, and lobelia—all upper respiratory friendly herbs.

Cough and Wheeze (twice daily)	
Cat/Small Dog (up to 14 lb)	7 drops
Medium Dog (15-34 lb)	10 drops
Large Dog (35-84 lb)	12-15 drops
Giant Dog (85+ lb)	15-20 drops

Vitamin C has been clinically proven to help boost the immune system and help the body fight off viral and bacterial infections. Cut the dose in half after two weeks.

Vitamin C (twice daily)	
Cat/Small Dog (up to 14 lb)	750 mg
Medium Dog (15-34 lb)	1,000 mg
Large Dog (35-84 lb)	1,250 mg
Giant Dog (85+ lb)	1,500 mg

Finally, add garlic (regular strength) such as **Kyolic** or **Garlicin**. Continue for 3 to 4 weeks after symptoms begin. (See page 110 for important information on garlic and anemia.)

Garlic (twice daily)	
Cat/Small Dog (up to 14 lb)	1 tablet
Medium Dog (15-34 lb)	2 tablets
Large/Giant Dog (35+ lb)	3 tablets

Lick Sores (Granulomas)

Dogs and cats will occasionally lick at an irritated spot in an effort to satisfy the itch. Excessive licking, however, can lead to a "hot spot" and then to a nonhealing raw spot. Your animal can actually lick off all the fur and create a raw spot on the skin. If you see your animal continuously working on a spot, the first step is to stop the licking.

Your veterinarian may place your animal on a short course of cortisone to put a halt to the self-trauma. An Elizabethan collar will also keep your animal from doing further damage (ask your veterinarian about this). Now you can take care of the skin irritation directly. Be sure to follow up with these treatments, as the Elizabethan collar alone will not stop the itching, just prevent your animal from accessing the spot.

Oral Treatments

Lick sores can also be an emotional habit, one that your animal may revisit when there is a stressful situation. For this reason, flower essences may be extremely beneficial (see the section on flower essences in Chapter 4). We always recommend Anaflora's flower essence **Lick Granuloma**, which is a remedy made specifically for the emotional and habitual aspects of a lick granuloma.

Itchy Skin, available from Earth Animal, contains medicinal herbs such as nettles, echinacea, and licorice to help prevent the allergic aspect of lick sores.

Itchy Skin (twice daily)	
Cat/Small Dog (up to 14 lb)	7 drops
Medium Dog (15-34 lb)	10 drops
Large Dog (35-84 lb)	12 drops
Giant Dog (85+ lb)	15 drops

Topical Treatments

Try one of these natural skin soothers:

- Aloe vera gel
- Baking soda paste
- Cool, wet tea bag (black tea)
- Plantain leaf

Mange, Demodectic

Demodectic mange is a disease of the skin causing inflammation and loss of hair in domestic animals. Demodectic mange (or Demodex) is a noncontagious form of mange of dogs (and, rarely, of cats) that brings home the importance of maintaining a healthy immune system. The mange mites are normal inhabitants of the body. Normally they cause no problems, but when your animal's immune system is compromised from stress, poor-quality diet, chronic use of medications, or overvaccination, the mites find their way to the skin and lodge in the pores, causing hair loss, scabbing, swollen skin, and often secondary bacterial infection which looks and smells terrible.

Demodex is caused by the parasites *Demodex canis* and *cati*. Clinical studies have shown that Demodex is associated with a decrease in certain lymphocytes of the cellular immune system. It usually starts with several nonirritated, patchy hairless areas and may stay confined to these areas or it can involve the entire animal. Conventional treatment often involves use of a potent insecticide such as ivermectin or amitraz (Mitaban) to kill the mites, along with antibiotics to quell secondary pyoderma (bacterial dermatitis). While this approach may be necessary to knock down the infection, it does little to correct underlying imbalances in the immune system, which allowed the mites to flourish in the first place. While there are potential side effects from these potent medications, in many cases it is important to choose them because of the devastating effect that this mite has on the skin and health in general.

Caution: Ivermectin should not be used in Collies, Shelties, or Old English Sheepdogs. Stop using these medications on any dog if at any time you observe vomiting, diarrhea, or convulsions. Gloves should be worn when applying these treatments.

Topical Treatments

Bathe your dog twice weekly with a naturally medicated shampoo. Shampoos that contain neem oil or tea tree oil can really help. Good brands are **Tropiclean** and **Veterinarian's Best**.

Oral Treatments

If you and your veterinarian have chosen to use medical insecticides, it will be important to help the body detoxify the chemical residues. We recommend a specific Chinese herbal remedy called **H7 Immune Stimulator**. Your veterinarian can secure H7 Immune Stimulator and **Chemical Drops**—a prescription homeopathic detoxisode that will assist the body in gently riding itself of chemical residues—through the Nutritional Blood Test (NBT) program.

Another Chinese herbal remedy, **Viola 13**, has been found to be effective in assisting the immune system in battling demodectic mange. The brand that we recommend is ITM's Seven Forests.

Whether or not your animal goes on mange medication, support the immune system with Level II or higher of the Goldstein Food Plan (see Chapter 1).

You can also bolster the immune system with the following supplements for four weeks or until all signs of mange are gone. When under control, reduce the dose in half for maintenance.

Ester-C (twice daily)	
Small Dog (up to 14 lb)	250 mg
Medium Dog (15-34 lb)	500 mg
Large Dog (35-84 lb)	750 mg
Giant Dog (85+ lb)	1,000 mg

Vitamin A (once daily)	
Small Dog (up to 14 lb)	2,500 iu
Medium Dog (15-34 lb)	5,000 iu
Large Dog (35-84 lb)	7,500 iu
Giant Dog (85+ lb)	7,500-10,000 iu

Vitamin E (once daily)	
Small Dog (up to 14 lb)	200 iu
Medium Dog (15-34 lb)	400 iu
Large Dog (35-84 lb)	600 iu
Giant Dog (85+ lb)	800 iu

Selenium (once daily)	
Small Dog (up to 14 lb)	25 mcg
Medium Dog (15-34 lb)	50 mcg
Large Dog (35-84 lb)	75 mcg
Giant Dog (85+ lb)	100 mcg

Earth Animal's Immune Boost (twice daily)	
Small Dog (up to 14 lb)	7 drops
Medium Dog (15-34 lb)	10 drops
Large Dog (35-84 lb)	15 drops
Giant Dog (85+ lb)	20 drops

Motion Sickness

Whether it's from fear or dizziness, some cats and dogs invariably get sick when traveling in a car. The symptoms can include quivering, drooling, or outright vomiting. It's not only unpleasant for the others in the car, but the poor animal is miserable, too. To add insult to injury, a travel-phobic animal may constantly meow, whine, cry, or yowl from the start of the trip to the finish. Many veterinarians recommend a tranquilizer (like acepromazine) for your animal. We're reluctant to endorse this approach for several reasons.

Tranquilizers will often last three to four times longer than the trip and will cause lethargy. Some animals become unsteady on their feet, and sometimes the tranquilizer releases inhibitions, making them act aggressive or even schizophrenic. Also, tranquilizers are potent drugs, and their repeated use can harm your animal's health, especially the potential effect of blocking nervous control of the heart (thereby lowering blood pressure). This drug should never be used on Boxers, who are particularly susceptible to these adverse effects on the heart and circulation.

In our opinion, tranquilizers, with only rare exception, are just not necessary. Instead, try our natural approach. Begin by withholding all food and water for a few hours before you travel. Then choose from the following remedies.

Oral Treatments

We strongly recommend starting one of the "rescue" formulas before and during travel or any stressful activity. **Rescue Remedy** is probably the best known and easiest to find in health food stores. We have seen outstanding results with **Recovery Formula**, one of a line of animal-specific flower essences from Anaflora.

Ginger can help calm the stomach. You can use capsules (from the health food store) or crystallized ginger (from your grocery store spice section).

Ginger (given before traveling)
Cat/Small Dog (up to 14 lb): 1/2 capsule or 1 peppercorn-size piece of crystallized ginger
Medium/Large Dog (15–84 lb): 1 capsule or 1 pinky-fingernail-size piece crystallized ginger
Giant Dog (85+ lb): 1–2 capsules or 1 lima-bean-size piece of crystallized ginger

Calm Stress, a liquid homeopathic from Dr. Goodpet, can also help your animal when traveling.

Calm Down, available from Earth Animal, contains calming herbs such as chamomile and peppermint, which can gently calm and help to balance your animal's anxiety about traveling.

Calm Down (given before traveling)	
Cat/Small Dog (up to 14 lb)	7 drops
Medium Dog (15-34 lb)	10 drops
Large Dog (35-84 lb)	12 drops
Giant Dog (85+ lb)	15 drops

To help prevent vomiting due to car sickness, add peppermint, ginger, or chamomile tea to drinking water. You might have to experiment until you discover the remedy that works for your animal. Of course none of this is a magic bullet that will instantly solve the problem. You should combine these therapies with a training protocol that lessens the stress of travel, such as starting with short rides that are as pleasant as possible, and progressing to longer rides. Consult a trainer for more information.

Overweight/Obesity

Animals gain weight for any number of reasons. As with people, the wrong food and not enough exercise will add pounds seemingly overnight. Taking your animal for a walk every morning and evening is a good start at reversing the trend, and it will be good for both of you!

Many commercial pet foods are extremely high in fat, and the type of fat used has been based upon cost and economics rather than nutrition or health. Once ingested, highly saturated fats are stored rather than burned for energy. The result: your animal gains weight.

At-Home Treatment

Switch to a senior or "lite" formulated, naturally preserved food. See Chapter 1 for the "skinny" on a healthy diet for your dog and cat.

Give **vitamin B6**, available at health food stores, to improve the metabolism of fats.

Vitamin B6 (daily)	
Cat/Small Dog (up to 14 lb)	25 mg
Medium Dog (15-34 lb)	50 mg
Large Dog (35-84 lb)	75 mg
Giant Dog (85+ lb)	100 mg

To improve the digestion of fats, offer **organic apple cider vinegar** in a separate bowl of drinking water.

Apple Cider Vinegar (daily)	
Cat/Small Dog (up to 14 lb)	1/2 tsp daily
Medium Dog (15-34 lb)	1 tsp daily
Large/Giant Dog (35+ lb)	1 1/2 tsp daily

Check out the "fat busters" section in Chapter 1 for more information on how to help control your animal's weight.

Parasites, Internal

Many types of internal parasites can affect your dog or cat. The most common in dogs are roundworms, hookworms, whipworms, and tapeworms. The most common in cats are roundworms, hookworms, and tapeworms. Common protozoan parasites are coccidia and giardia. Coccidia occurs in both dogs (*Isospora canis)* and cats (*Isospora felis*), while giardia occurs mostly in dogs and rarely in cats. Internal parasites are easily detected by eye or through microscopic examination.

Roundworms (ascarids—*Toxicaris canis* and *cati*) usually do not cause clinical symptoms in healthy, well-cared-for animals, except for diarrhea and occasional vomiting and coughing (as the larvae of the worm migrate). They can be transmitted to puppies and kittens from their mothers (*in utero*) or from exposure to the stool of an infested animal. Unless the animals are debilitated, they do not cause problems, and may even outgrow these worms by six months of age. If your new puppy or kitten appears potbellied or unthrifty, or has diarrhea, you may wish to have the youngster tested and treated with conventional medications such as piperazine, milbemycin oxime (Interceptor), or fenbendazole (Panacur).

Hookworms (*ancylostomiasis*) and whipworms (*tricuriasis*) are more serious internal parasites and can cause bloody stool, diarrhea, weight loss, and lower bowel problems such as colitis. Tapeworms (*cestodiasis*), which are transmitted by the bites of fleas, usually cause no symptoms, but they can cause weight loss. Since tapeworms are long, segmented worms, the segments can break off and actually crawl out the rectum (they look like white or beige grains of flattened rice). This causes itching, which you'll see as licking and rubbing of the hindquarters.

Because tapeworms are transmitted by fleas, you must resolve any flea infestation of your pet and his or her environment. (For more on how to be rid of fleas, see Chapter 6.)

Oral Treatments

Natural treatment and prevention of intestinal parasites in dogs and cats can be supported by the old home remedy of garlic. Don't be put off by the studies that have concluded that garlic doesn't work. Of course it doesn't! Garlic is not fatal to all worms like potent medications, and likewise, no deworming medication should be seen as a "cure" for worms. The scientific community is looking at it from the wrong point of view.

Worms thrive in a kitten or puppy who has an immature immune system or in adult animals in a compromised or run-down condition. The intestinal tract of an infested animal is usually clogged with mucous and breakdown products from improper diets and toxic overload. The worms simply take advantage of the animal's impaired state. Worms thrive in mucous and wastes.

Garlic acts as an intestinal purifier to dissolve excess mucous accumulations in the intestinal tract.

Mucous gives the worms a place to flourish, and when it is removed by the garlic, the worms become vulnerable. Rather than killing them, the garlic simply makes your animal an unattractive place for the worms to live. If your pet is heavily infested with internal parasites, his or her intestines may need a double dose of garlic to help restore a clean intestinal lining. Again, if infested and clinically sick, see your veterinarian for conventional therapy. *Caution:* *Excessive amounts of garlic can cause anemia.* Follow the recommended doses. See your veterinarian if your animal is clinically ill with worms.

Garlic cloves or Aged Garlic tablets (Kyolic or Garlicin)
Cat/Small Dog (up to 14 lb) 1/2 clove fresh garlic per meal, or 1/2 capsule aged garlic supplement two times per day
Medium Dog (15–34 lb): 1 clove fresh garlic per meal, or 1 capsule aged garlic supplement three times per day
Large/Giant Dogs (35–85+ lb): 2 cloves fresh garlic per meal, or 2 capsule garlic supplement two times per day

No More Worms and Fungi, available from Earth Animal, uses natural ingredients like black walnut, wormwood, cloves, and garlic to help prevent and treat parasites.

No More Worms and Fungi (twice daily)	
Cat/Small Dog (up to 14 lb)	7 drops
Medium Dog (15-34 lb)	10 drops
Large Dog (35-84 lb)	15 drops
Giant Dog (85+ lb)	20 drops

Diatomaceous Earth is a nontoxic, safe substance made from crushed fossils of freshwater organisms and marine life. You can find it in gardening stores, pet stores, or over the Internet.

Diatomaceous Earth (daily)	
Cat/Small Dog (up to 14 lb)	1 tsp with food
Medium Dog (15-34 lb)	2 tsp with food
Large Dog (35-84 lb)	1 Tbs with food
Giant Dog (85+ lb)	1 1/2 Tbs with food

Feeding a diet that is high in soluble and insoluble fiber will further speed parasites' exit from your animal. During the period you are treating the worms, avoid feeding your animal any mucous-producing foods such as milk, cheese, or even yogurt.

Ringworm

Ringworm (*Dermatophytosis*) is contagious and may be transmitted from animal to human and vice versa. In order to identify ringworm so you can properly treat it, it is important to know that the physical symptoms may differ greatly in dogs and cats, and that ringworm spores may be carried without visible signs. If your veterinarian confirms that your dog tested positive for ringworm, he or she may exhibit a hairless and irritated thick, scabby surface, usually an inch or so in diameter. This is usually a round or irregularly shaped circular area on the skin, and is often hairless. A positive cat, however, may only exhibit hair loss along with a gray skin tone, without scabbing or thickening. As for you, if you notice any circular, scabby, inflamed areas on your body, chances are you have ringworm as well.

Ringworm is often treated conventionally with an over-the-counter antifungal medication such as Tinactin, along with a potent prescription medication called Griseofulvin designed to destroy the fungus. Healing time is usually several weeks as the hair grows back; however, the animal can remain contagious during this period. If you go natural with supplements, topical and medicinal herbs, you can expect a similar healing time, but with the added advantage of strengthening the body to prevent future recurrences. Drugs do treat the surface problem but they do not get at the source (a compromised immune system).

Oral Treatments

If you are dealing with an active case of ringworm, first review and upgrade the Goldstein Food Plan detailed in Chapter 1. Giving your animal a natural diet, raw foods, and daily doses of vitamins and minerals, while avoiding chronic use of drugs and vaccines, should give your dog or cat the ammunition to fight off any exposure. If your animal falls in the weakened immune system category or is diagnosed with ringworm, we think it is a good idea to add some extra fatty acid supplements, antioxidants, and skin-enhancing vitamins and minerals to his or her diet for the next several weeks. These include **zinc**, **flaxseed oil**, and **Coenzyme Q10** along with **Daily Health Nuggets**, available from Earth Animal.

Coenzyme Q10 (daily)	
Cat/Small Dog (up to 14 lb)	15 mg
Medium Dog (15-34 lb)	25 mg
Large Dog (35-84 lb)	50 mg
Giant Dog (85+ lb)	75 mg

Flaxseed Oil (with meals, daily)	
Cat/Small Dog (up to 14 lb)	1 tsp
Medium Dog (15-34 lb)	2 tsp
Large Dog (35-84 lb)	3 tsp
Giant Dog (85+ lb)	5 tsp

Zinc (amino acid chelate form, daily)	
Cat/Small Dog (up to 14 lb)	10 mg
Medium Dog (15-34 lb)	15 mg
Large Dog (35-84 lb)	20 mg
Giant Dog (85+ lb)	30 mg

We also recommend Earth Animal's **No More Worms and Fungi,** a medicinal herbal remedy. Its main ingredients are black walnut, wormwood, cloves, quassia, and garlic plus flower essences to balance the emotions, as we believe there is a connection between your animal's emotions and the skin.

No More Worms and Fungi (twice daily)	
Cat/Small Dog (up to 14 lb)	7 drops
Medium Dog (15-34 lb)	10 drops
Large Dog (35-84 lb)	15 drops
Giant Dog (85+ lb)	20 drops

Topical Treatments

Your animal is also going to need a topical treatment along with a targeted herbal or homeopathic fungal remedy. First, wearing a pair of disposable latex gloves, clip away the hair in the affected area. Be extremely careful to dispose of the hair in a highly sanitary manner. Vacuum the area, scrub with a disinfectant, wear gloves, and discard all of your animal's bedding. Then remove the vacuum cleaner bag and dispose of it as well.

Next, shampoo your animal with **Leciderm** or another mild, chemically free shampoo to which you have added the juice from a fresh lemon and a few drops of tea tree oil. You may reinforce with a topical treatment by mixing 5 percent tea tree oil and 1 teaspoon fresh lemon juice to 2 cups strongly brewed Goldenseal or green tea. Add this mixture to a washcloth or cotton pad and treat the infected area four times daily. Dab on some neem oil or cream, which will soothe and enhance healing.

Be sure to give your animal plenty of fresh air, exposing the ringworm area to natural sunlight as well. Nature has a way of expediting healing.

Scars

Scars are a common result of damage to the skin. Besides being unsightly, scars can be tender, and no hair will grow at the site. To keep scars from forming after an accident, or to reduce the size of scars already present, rub vitamin E oil or aloe vera gel into the unbroken skin at the site, three times daily.

Sexual Problems (Mounting and Spraying)

Dogs

Male dogs can exhibit the socially embarrassing behavior of mounting people's legs and other objects. To address this emotional behavior, which we have found to be more a symptom of hyperexcitability than sexuality, use the flower essence **Good Dog!** from Anaflora.

Cats

Male cats, and occasionally females too, will spray strong-smelling urine onto vertical surfaces (such as walls, doorways, bushes, etc.). In males, this can be a normal expression of dominance and territory marking, usually reserved for intact tom cats (the behavior usually fades away after neutering).

Sometimes, however, neutered males and even females will spray, usually because of emotional stress. For example, one kitty we know who never exhibited problem behaviors suddenly started spraying when her guardian's marriage fell apart. Another common trigger is a new animal entering the household—this can upset a cat's feeling of security, leading to unacceptable behavior such as spraying.

We prefer to treat the problem rather than try to suppress the symptoms. First, resist the temptation to scold or punish your cat for spraying—discipline may upset him or her even more, making the problem worse. Instead, take an objective look at your home environment. Odds are, it won't be difficult to identify one or more changes that may have upset your cat's sense of security. Three flower essence formulas available from Anaflora may help: Try **Spraying Cat** or **Calm Kitty** to calm and soothe everyday nervousness in your cat, or **Special Stress** to provide relief when an animal is exposed to stressful situations.

Then, do whatever you can to reassure your cat that he or she is cherished, no matter what is going on in the household. It may be a simple matter of inviting your friend into your lap more often, or more frequent brushing or combing sessions. Of course, addressing the underlying problem in the home is paramount, such as resolving any human-to-human conflicts.

At the same time, it is important to thoroughly clean the places that were sprayed to erase any lingering odors, which can act as a "bull's-eye" for repeated sprayings by every cat in the house, not just the original sprayer. For this, we suggest using an enzymatic cleaner that will neutralize stains and odors. These are available at pet stores.

Stool Eating (Coprophagia)

This unsavory habit in dogs, technically called coprophagia, may be due to low production of digestive enzymes and/or a dietary deficiency of trace minerals.

You may not want to accept this, but in some cases coprophagia is considered normal, due to the fact that your dog's wild ancestors probably did exhibit scavenger-like behavior, including "recycling" of fecal material—their own or someone else's. It may start as an instinctive act and, depending on your dog's personal taste preferences, become a natural (albeit nasty) habit. Many dogs even raid kitty litter boxes.

If there's an underlying medical problem associated with your dog's coprophagia, the behavior will stop when the problem is resolved. If it's just a socially unacceptable expression of your dog's ancestry, your only

Holistic First-Aid Kit

Keep these on hand:

Bach Flower Rescue Remedy: great in times of emotional or physical trauma.

Calendula ointment and Arnica ointment: herbal salves for any bruise or bump that isn't bleeding.

Aloe vera gel: apply to any skin problem, from wound to rash.

Vitamin E capsules: also good for skin problems.

Gauze, cotton pads, and surgical tape: to bind and protect injured areas.

Styptic pencil: to stop bleeding from small wounds.

Activated charcoal and milk of magnesia: part of the universal antidote for poisoning.

Pepto Bismol: for stomach upsets.

Benadryl: for insect stings.

recourse will be to limit his opportunity to do it. Keep the yard picked up, keep the litter box out of reach, and when in public places keep him on a leash. (And don't let him kiss you on the lips!) Keep in mind that scolding or yelling at your dog for this behavior probably won't work, and can be detrimental to your relationship.

Oral Treatments

To resolve a trace-mineral nutritional deficiency, give powdered kelp (2 tsp mixed with food). You can find kelp in health food stores—look for kelp that comes from deep, cold Norwegian sources. **Solid Gold Sea Meal**, available from Earth Animal, is a good brand.

To resolve a deficiency of digestive enzymes, add them to your animal's food. Two brands we like are both called **Enzymes**—one available from Dr. Goodpet, and the other from PetGuard. Follow label directions.

Teething

Teething can be just as annoying in puppies and kittens as it is in children. Your animal may become irritable and begin chewing household items. This type of behavior produces that "hurts-and-feels-good" sensation we all remember from our days of losing our baby teeth. Gently rubbing aloe vera gel onto the teeth and gums will work wonders.

Rawhide chews may help reduce inflammation and give your puppy an acceptable item to chew. Be sure to give only a high-quality chew, made of chopped, compressed rawhide, and not processed with bleach, peroxide, arsenic, chromium, or artificial colorings.

Stick with products made in the US and Canada, where pesticides and other toxic chemicals are less likely to be in the hide material—pesticides and other toxins that are banned in this country are used in Mexico and other countries and have been found to be present in alarming amounts in some rawhide chews. Chunks of raw carrot also make healthy chews.

Urinary Incontinence

If your animal has been leaving urine around the house, ask your veterinarian to rule out a medical condition such as an infection, nerve damage, or a behavioral problem. The most likely culprit is urethral sphincter hypotonus or urinary incontinence, which occurs when your dog or cat loses control of the muscles that control urination. This is most often seen in spayed females.

Commonly prescribed drugs for this condition do have side effects. In November 2000, the FDA asked firms to recall drug products containing phenylpropanolamine—for years the drug of choice prescribed by veterinarians for the treatment of urinary incontinence. The action came after the FDA reviewed results of a study conducted by scientists at Yale University School of Medicine that showed an increased risk of hemorrhagic stroke (bleeding into the brain tissue) in people who were taking the drug, which is commonly found in over-the-counter cough and cold medications as well as weight loss products and decongestants.

Oral Treatments

Urinary Incontinence Drops from HomeoPet is a homeopathic product. Dosage is 10 drops for dogs, 3 drops for cats, three times daily for oral application, in food or water. This product has no side effects.

Urinary Incontinence Drops (3 times daily)	
Cat/Small Dog (up to 14 lb)	3 drops
Medium/Large/Giant Dog (15+ lb)	10 drops

Spay and Neuter, a flower essence available from Anaflora, helps to restore the balance of energy disturbed by the spaying process.

Pee Pee Drops from Earth Animal is a medicinal herbal preparation that soothes and tones the tissues of the lower urinary tract.

Other Treatments

Exercise can make a difference; in fact, anything that improves circulation is good—playing Frisbee, jumping, agility training, etc. If your animal is older, though, don't overdo this.

Acupuncture, acupressure, and chiropractic treatments can be very effective in improving the general energy flow of the body and removing energy blockages. They can help tone the bladder muscle. Contact a certified veterinary acupuncturist to learn more.

Vomiting

Vomiting in animals can be a symptom of a very serious condition. Unchecked, it can lead to dehydration and even death. There are many causes of vomiting, from simple stomach upsets to violent vomiting due to serious disease or poisoning. If your animal is vomiting violently, or for more than one day, call your veterinarian right away.

Oral Treatments

In simple instances of gastrointestinal upset, withhold food and water for two hours to allow the stomach to quiet down. You can administer a soothing remedy such as **slippery elm bark** syrup and/or **aloe vera** (available at health food stores) during this period of fasting—both are slippery and can soothe the irritated lining of the stomach and upper intestinal tract.

Slippery Elm Bark or Aloe Vera (every 4 hours)	
Cat/Small Dog (up to 14 lb)	1 tsp
Medium Dog (15-34 lb)	2 tsp
Large Dog (35-84 lb)	1 Tbsp
Giant Dog (85+ lb)	1 Tbsp

When no vomiting has occurred for two hours, offer a small amount (one or two tablespoonfuls) of water or broth to drink, then gradually increase the frequency and amount of liquid offered until your animal's thirst is slaked. If vomiting recurs, start over with the two-hour rest period.

A problem with vomiting, of course, is that your animal can vomit the treatment right back out. If this is happening, try the homeopathic remedy **Ipecac**, 1 pellet in the mouth two times daily.

You can also try **Pepto Bismol** for your cat or dog, administered through a oral syringe.

Pepto Bismol	
Cat/Small Dog (up to 14 lb)	1 tsp
Medium Dog (15-34 lb)	2 tsp
Large Dog (35-84 lb)	1 Tbsp
Giant Dog (85+ lb)	1 Tbsp

Other tummy-soothing choices include peppermint, ginger, or chamomile tea in drinking water. These work well for preventing vomiting due to carsickness (see *Motion Sickness*).

Wounds

For open wounds like scrapes or cuts, first clean the wound with hydrogen peroxide, then soak the area in wheat grass or barley juice (rehydrating the powder form is fine), for the beneficial chlorophyll they contain. This will help keep the exposed tissues clean and free of toxins. For closed wounds, such as a puncture or a bite, use a warm solution of mineral salts from the ocean (available in health food stores). Sea salts work well to help pull out toxins; mix according to package directions. Deep wounds should be treated by a veterinarian as soon as possible.

Chapter 6

Flea-Free
Forever—Naturally

As little as ten years ago, despite an average of a billion dollars a year spent on flea remedies in this country, misery reigned—animals were suffering, fleas were thriving, homes reeked of toxic pesticides, and the liver, kidneys, lungs, and nervous systems of every exposed animal (not to mention his or her human family members) struggled to survive under the weight of those toxins. Nobody benefited but the chemical companies and, frankly, the fleas, which were only too happy to engage in a war they were preprogrammed to win.

On the one hand, the so-called "cure" for the problem was weakening the animals' immune systems, undermining their ability to fight off the infestation themselves. At the same time, this gave the bugs the opportunity to become resistant to the chemicals—which they did—in spades. As stronger chemicals were used, a vicious, destructive cycle was started which picked up speed and gave birth to the "superflea," a mutated, resistant form that could survive this chemical onslaught.

Dogs, cats, carpets, and yards were marinated in poisons on a regular basis. In the name of killing fleas, people were literally putting their animals at risk—it wasn't a question of whether their health would suffer; it was a question of *when*. Yet who could blame them for resorting to these chemicals? The bugs were driving them buggy. In the anxious heat of battle, nobody wanted to believe the pesticides were the problem. But it was true. This was truly the dark ages in the war against fleas.

Over the past 30 years, we have researched, tested, and developed natural, nontoxic ways to protect companion animals from the misery and disease wrought by fleas. We've had great success. With our gentle yet effective methods, you can reset the balance of power so your dog or cat wins the war against fleas. And wins it fair and square—without spraying, dipping, or fogging with chemicals that are as hard on "the good guys" as they are on the bad.

What follows is our full-circle program that attacks the problem in three specific, no-nonsense steps. Get ready to say good-bye to fleas—forever! Our time-tested program works, it's easy and, best of all, it's safe.

Three Steps to Freedom

Step 1. First, we'll tell you how to boost your animal's own flea-fighting immune strength with a dietary program of basic nutrients, supplements, and "superfoods" to fight these pests from the inside out.

Step 2. Next, we'll outline a whole range of natural, toxin-free options to rid your animal, home, and yard of fleas once and for all.

Step 3. Emergency! This step is the 911 call for animals that already have a flea problem and need emergency help *now*! Follow our sensible guidelines and you'll have the problem under control in no time, without resorting to harsh chemicals.

Before we delve into specific solutions, bear with us for a little bit of insight into the historical use of pesticides. In the past 30 years, the flea pesticide industry mushroomed, offering an ever-increasing array of immune-suppressing, expensive, and ineffective pest poisons to dog and cat lovers. Until fairly recently, many flea prevention and control products were made from a derivative of nerve gas that destroys the pest's nervous system so that it dies. (Have you ever watched a fly or wasp buzz and spin crazily after being sprayed? That's the nerve gas doing its job.)

These are basically the same poisons that were used in World War II—toxic agents that were long ago banned worldwide in unanimous international agreements against "chemical warfare." Until recently, it was considered perfectly okay to use these substances (in much smaller amounts) on animals. Unfortunately, the negative effects are cumulative, and these lethal products slowly but surely take their toll on us, on our animals, and on the planet.

We have personally witnessed the true cost of using these products.. We will never forget a young family's adorable puppy who had to be euthanized after extensive medical efforts to reverse chemical poisoning caused by an over-the-counter flea and tick collar. This poor little puppy was playing in a yard of apple trees being sprayed with pesticides. The combination of the spray and the chemical flea collar worked synergistically to permanently damage the dog's nervous system.

Imagine the chills that run down our spines when we see a young child cuddling an animal wearing one of these things. To us, the dangers are so obvious that it makes us want to scream. But people are busy, and they need a quick fix, and aggressive advertising campaigns tell them these products are safe and effective.

Creating the "Super Flea"

Heavy use of insecticides and pesticides has been largely responsible for the production of the "super flea," which has adapted to withstand progressively stronger poisons. As a result, fleas (and ticks, too) have longer life cycles today than they did 50 years ago. They are no longer just seasonal pests. They breed quickly and can sustain themselves and their eggs in cold weather. It used to be that one good zap of a veterinary fogger would effectively wipe them out. Now they bounce back and require higher doses of more potent poisons. If we continue to use these chemicals, we are likely to eradicate our animals—and ourselves—long before we get rid of the far more adaptable pests.

When we were first married, Dr. Bob was a captain in the US Army stationed at a major Army chemical center. As a military veterinarian, he had the task of vetting research animals on post and witnessing firsthand the testing and development of chemical pesticides. The two of us were young and naive about a lot of things, including the downside of these poisons. Neither of us was aware of their harmful effects, particularly with regard to animals and the environment, nor were we in tune with how morally wrong it is to invasively test on animals. But out of all adversity some good must come, and we often recall that early experience with those animals and chemicals as an important reminder of the needless suffering that goes on in laboratories and in homes, with our own precious animals.

Life Cycle of the Flea

A flea survives by biting your animal and drawing blood. Then it lays large numbers of eggs—one female flea can lay from 15 to 25 eggs per day. The eggs fall off the animal and hatch into larvae in 2 to 3 days. The larvae then become pupae, building a tough cocoon to protect themselves and staying on the ground, in your house, in your car, or in your animal's bed, where they mature into adult fleas in anywhere from one week to six months, depending on the environment. It is during this inactive period that fleas can "winter over." Fleas and ticks breed in temperatures of 50°F and above. When weather conditions are right they will mature and become the pesky adult fleas we dislike so much.

The chemical industry is responsible for the production of these poisons, but consumers buy them and keep the industry alive because they do not know there are other choices. As more people choose nonchemical alternatives, and as more researchers climb onto the nontoxic bandwagon, the poisonous flea products will finally fall by the wayside.

What You Can't See *Can* Hurt You

Part of the reason it's been so difficult to convince people of the dangers of poisonous flea products is because their toxic effects are delayed and cumulative. Their poisonous vapors may be invisible, but they come into contact with every part of your animal's body, beginning with the eyes, and the nose—the gateway to the lungs. Through the lungs they enter the blood and then the heart, where they are pumped through the body to the liver, the body's toxic waste dump. There they must be detoxified before they go to the kidneys to be eliminated through the urine.

The vapors are also readily absorbed through the skin, causing rashes and itching in many animals. If your dog or cat is healthy enough, his or her immune system will tolerate this offense. We wish there was a special immune system "scanning machine" which could predict which animals will survive the physical stresses of these poisons, and which will eventually develop cancer or die from kidney failure—all because of our lack of awareness.

In the 1970s, as we began to fully grasp the damage that was being done by pesticides, we pledged to search for a better, healthier way to manage fleas. It became our mission. Over the course of many years, we developed a special blend of food supplements, herbs, vitamins, and minerals that really stops fleas in their tracks. We are proud to share our healthy, gentle but highly effective solution to the problem.

Step 1: Boost Your Animal's Immunity for a Flea-Free Life

If you have more than one animal in your home, you may have noticed that the one who is sicker or older has more fleas than the younger, healthier animal. By the same token, have you ever wondered why some dogs and cats seem to pick up ticks just about anywhere, whereas other animals don't have a tick on them their entire life?

Now, think back to your own experiences at family picnics, lingering in the rosy glow of sunset over the last bits of conversation and watermelon. I'll bet you can name the friends and relatives who can enjoy a summer evening without ever being bothered by mosquitoes. And I'll bet you can name the ones who are constantly swatting, finally saying in frustration, "I have to go inside, I'm being eaten alive!"

There's a reason for this. When the immune system of the target victim is strong and vital, pests find him or her to be much less appetizing, and they move on to tastier prey. Animals with a weaker immune system give off a particular odor that's like a neon sign over a roadside diner—it announces to the parasite world that this potential host, with its weakened immune system, will have tasty blood. This, dear friends, is the key to having a happy, itch-free animal!

Even when there is a bite, the optimally healthy, immune-strengthened animal doesn't react to it as much—this may seem backwards, but animals with balanced immune systems display very little outward reaction to the bite of a flea, because their immune system is organized and "knows what to do" when faced with this kind of intruder. A weakened immune system, on the other hand, is instantly overwhelmed. It overreacts to a fleabite, launching an out-of-control, allergic response, which results in extreme itching and discomfort.

If your cat or dog suffers from a chronic flea infestation, consider it an indication that things on the inside are not as healthy as they could be. You might even want to thank the fleas for being a "smoke detector" for your animal's health. If you're astute enough to hear the alarm, you've been given a free warning—a chance to build up your animal's health before more serious disease is manifested.

The Secret to Boosting Immunity

After years of exploring and testing natural flea programs, we've found that the addition of specific foods and supplements to the diet not only boosts immunity and promotes radiant health, but also makes the blood and smell of animals "distasteful" to fleas and ticks.

One of our first clues in the search for a natural pest repellent came when we read an article in a local health food store suggesting that adding brewer's yeast to an animal's food would ward off fleas. The first types of yeast we tried were commercial and highly processed (debittered to make them more palatable), and they didn't work the way we needed them to.

We then located a type of imported, unprocessed yeast. We tried it and got a better response. We knew we were on the right track, but we still were not satisfied. We used our intuition and spent countless hours researching and reading, learning from ancient teachers and other cultures as well as from the latest scientific studies. Like vintage wine, our formula kept improving until we were able to develop Earth Animal **Internal Powder**.

Here are the results, in a nutshell:

- Start by feeding your animal a natural base food (described in Chapter 1).
- Add living foods rich in phytonutrients and antioxidants, such as grated carrots, parsley, and plain yogurt (detailed in Level II of our Food Plan).
- Mix Earth Animal's Internal Powder into your animal's food and add plain, low-fat, organic yogurt each day. The following dosage schedule is for preventive maintenance; you may safely double the dosage during flea season or if fleas begin to get the upper hand.

Internal Powder (with meds)	
Kitten/Puppy	1 tsp
Cat/Toy Dog (up to 9 lb)	1 1/2 tsp
Small Dog (10-20 lb)	2 tsp
Medium Dog (21-50 lb)	1 Tbsp
Large Dog (51-85 lb)	1 1/2 Tbsp
Giant Dog (86+ lb)	2 Tbsp

Or you can find your own sources for the key ingredients (listed on pages 142 to 144) and put them together yourself.

Tap into Flea-Fighting Foods

If you're a "make your own" type of person, you can buy all these flea-fighting ingredients separately and mix them together. Or, you can purchase one of the ready-made formulas that include some or all of these ingredients (Internal Powder has them all). In our experience, the more complete your formula, the better your results.

Brewer's Yeast. High-grade, unprocessed brewer's yeast supports and boosts the immune system, which then secondarily repels the parasites. Brewer's yeast is high in B vitamins, particularly B1 (thiamine) and B6 (pyridoxine, a natural anti-histamine) and sulfur-containing amino acids. In addition, B vitamins will help calm a stressed-out nervous system.

For years, many folks tried brewer's yeast without success. This may be because they weren't using the right type of yeast combined with enhanced ingredients. It took us years to figure this out, and we are delighted to be able to share our success with you now.

That's also why we were not the least bit disturbed when the use of yeast as a pest repellent was disparaged in the prestigious *Journal of the American Veterinary Medical Association* (JAVMA). Like most mainstream researchers, they

Not All Brewer's Yeasts Are Created Equal

Make sure you find a strong-smelling brewer's yeast—not one that is so debittered that it looks like a white powder and has no smell. You can enhance the effectiveness of brewer's yeast by adding fresh, raw garlic or herbal products such as Earth Animal's Herbal Internal Powder or No More Fleas.

were looking for a "magic bullet" that would instantly rid the animal of all fleas. In truth, brewer's yeast is a key part of a *total* plan for good health.

Garlic has been used for thousands of years for medicinal purposes in many cultures. Native Americans used it to repel parasites. Garlic works against fleas by helping the body cleanse and detoxify, resulting in a stronger immune system. Garlic also imparts a taste to the blood that is offensive to pests, and produces what to some is an unpleasant odor through the skin. The good news is that it does not linger on your animal's breath.

Garlic is also an effective internal parasite remedy. Many types of worms live and breed on or in the mucosal lining of the intestines. When too much mucus accumulates, parasites thrive by hunkering down within the protective coating of the mucus. Garlic helps the body rid itself of mucus accumulation in the bowels, providing a less hospitable environment for the worms. (See Chapter 5 for more information about ridding your animal of internal parasites.)

For flea and general immune-system protection, use 1 garlic clove per day for small dogs and cats, 2 cloves for medium, large, and giant breeds. If you prefer to give a daily garlic supplement, you can give small animals 1 tablet, medium animals 2 tablets, large animals 3 tablets, and giant animals 3 to 4 tablets. *Caution: Research has shown that garlic can thin the blood, so it is recommended not to use garlic before surgery or if your animal is anemic.*

B Vitamins. As mentioned above, vitamins B1 (thiamine) and B6 (pyridoxine) are known for their flea- and tick-repelling qualities as well as their beneficial effects on the skin. Brewer's yeast and rice bran contain high levels of all the B-vitamins, including B1 and B6. To give your animal even more of these flea-fighting benefits add a B-complex supplement. As with all supplements, some dogs and cats may turn their noses up to anything strange in their food, so introduce slowly and mix with a bit of plain organic yogurt first.

B-complex (daily)	
Cat/Small Dog (up to 14 lb)	50 mg
Medium Dog (15-34 lb)	100 mg
Large/Giant Dog (35+ lb)	150 mg

Minerals are also essential for the healthy metabolism and functioning of the skin. The most important minerals for optimal skin health are calcium, phosphorus, and zinc. Internal Powder contains ample supplies of these minerals, including naturally occurring sulfur, which has flea-repelling characteristics. If you are making your own "brew," mix together the following minerals:

Calcium (daily)	
Cat/Small Dog (up to 14 lb)	50 mg
Medium Dog (15-34 lb)	75 mg
Large Dog (35-84 lb)	100 mg
Giant Dog (85+ lb)	150 mg

Phosphorus (daily)	
Cat/Small Dog (up to14 lb)	25 mg
Medium Dog (15-34 lb)	50 mg
Large Dog (35-84 lb)	75 mg
Giant Dog (85+ lb)	100 mg

Zinc (daily)	
Cat/Small Dog (up to 14 lb)	15 mg
Medium Dog (15-34 lb)	25 mg
Large Dog (35-84 lb)	35 mg
Giant Dog (85+ lb)	50 mg

Herbal Internal Powder

One of the potential side effects of brewer's yeast is that some animals are allergic to yeast. To this end we developed our Herbal Internal Powder, a yeast-free concoction that includes a mineral-rich combination of alfalfa, garlic, blue-green algae (spirulina), kelp, papaya leaf, nettle leaf, and hawthorne berry powder. This concentrated herbal powder is now being used by thousands of animals that are allergic to yeast.

We will never forget how encouraged we were by our dear friends Steve and Joan Margolies when we first developed our natural program for fleas. Steve and Joan, along with their seven dogs, decided to leave their small farm in Bedford, New York and move to Florida. While living in New York their dogs were on our program and were flea-free. They moved to a swampy area in Florida, and were warned by their neighbors about the serious flea infestation they would have to deal with. Joan defiantly said "my dogs don't get fleas." As it turned out, our program held up in these conditions, and their dogs remained flea-free—even throughout Florida's summer and peak flea season.

Allergies—Taking It Up a Notch

A few summers ago, for the first time in years, we found ticks on our Boxers, Jack and Vivienne. This fact, coupled with the call volume we'd been receiving, was just the boost we needed to search for an additional formula for keeping fleas *and* ticks away without resorting to drugs.

For animals that do not have yeast allergies, but are plagued with resistant flea infestation, as Jack and Vivienne were, we recommend combining the herbal and yeast Internal Powders. Mix 4 ounces Herbal Internal Powder with 8 ounces of your regular Internal Powder into a clean, empty container. It will turn the mixture an interesting shade of green, but should work effectively on your animal (and your nerves).

This small act of common sense worked like a charm and, in less than 48 hours, our guys were flea- and tick free. Soon after, we reported the combination to subscribers to our newsletter, *Love of Animals*. The results were spectacular! The herbal powder is very concentrated and therefore intensifies the yeast.

Add one or more of these super-immune foods to give your formula extra power (most are available at your health food store or through private distributors):

- Super Blue-Green Algae for Animals—add one-third teaspoon per pound of normal food.
- Spirulina—sprinkle on food (1/4 tsp for a 10 lb cat, 1 tsp for a 70 lb dog).
- Wheat grass—sprinkle on food (1/4 tsp for a 10 lb cat, 1 Tbsp for a 70 lb dog).
- Alfalfa—one tablet for smaller animals, two to three for larger animals. Some animals will just eat the tablets, or you can mix them with food or grind them up and mix with food.
- There are some excellent prepared products available in specialty human health food stores and fine animal supply stores that mix brewer's yeast and garlic with B vitamins, herbs, vitamins, minerals, and other food supplements. We enjoy introducing friends to these wonderful companies that offer products of integrity—see the Resources section for more information.

Dr. Bob's "Kick It Up a Notch" Flea and Tick Prevention Program

You will need:

1 lb jar of Dr. Bob's Internal Powder

8 oz jar of Earth Animal Herbal Internal Powder

1 empty jar of Internal Powder or other lidded container for mixing

Mix 4 oz Herbal Internal Powder with 8 oz Internal Powder. Shake well. Dose your animal the same as referenced on the jar of regular Internal Powder. To use Internal Powder straight, double the dosage during peak flea and tick season. It is not necessary to increase the level when blending the two.

Step 2: Premises Control: The Safe, Easy Way to Deflea Your House and Yard

Believe it or not, there is a safe and effective way to get rid of fleas living in your home. The **borates**, derivatives of boric acid, come in a very fine powder that is generally mixed with an inert carrier. Sprinkle the powder on your carpet and upholstered furniture, work it into the nap with a broom and vacuum any excess. The powder is so fine that enough will still be there for many months to come, and through many vacuumings, to keep the fleas at bay.

The borates are harmless to humans and animals, but they are particularly effective at killing fleas in the larval stage. They will also kill adult fleas, but it takes longer and does not work like an insecticide; rather, it happens slowly as the flea ingests the borate. Because the borates are most effective on flea larvae and newly hatched fleas, if applied properly and at the correct time, they can be a very effective part of your flea prevention program. Borates are available in safe, nontoxic formulas, which you can find in local stores or by calling the manufacturers (see Resources section).

Step 3: If Your Animal Is Already Infested

In the bad old days, this was the time when most folks went for the "heavy artillery." We are relieved to tell you that you can permanently forget about the dips, bombs, and foggers. There is simply no excuse any longer for using those toxic, dangerous products. Here's what we recommend to wipe out fleas…forever.

Immediate steps:

- Bathe your animal with a natural herbal shampoo.
- Begin the Goldstein Food Plan at Level II or higher (see Chapter 1).
- Add freshly chopped garlic to every meal.
- Start your animal on B-complex vitamins as described above.
- Mix Earth Animal **Internal Powder** with Earth Animal **Herbal Internal Powder** and add to meals at double the label dose. (Mixing with a little warm water or broth makes the dry powder super-palatable.)
- Use a topical spray such as **100% Natural Flea and Tick Repellent** by Quantum Herbal Products or Earth Animal's **Bug Off**. These sprays contain potent herbs such as erigeron (also known as fleabane) as well as organic extracts of cajeput oil, rose geranium oil, St. Johns Wort, wormwood, black walnut, neem, and rue. Spray the product onto your animal and "rake" your fingers through the fur to distribute well. Be sure to reach all the areas fleas and

ticks hide in, such as the armpits, between the toes, behind and inside the ears, the base of the tail, the groin area, and the belly.

- Use **Rescue Remedy**, a Bach Flower remedy, to help ease an extreme stress reaction. Give 3 to 5 drops in the mouth or in fresh water.

- We've had great success with remedies developed by Dr. Jay Wen, a veterinary expert in Chinese herbal medicine. One of his products, **DermGuard** from Natural Solutions, Inc., is an excellent choice for dogs and cats who may be suffering from fleabite dermatitis and its attendant itching, scratching, biting, and skin inflammation. The formula includes the herbs schizonepeta, silver root, bupleurum, bitter orange, mountain root, platycodon, ligusticum, dahurican angelica root, poria, mint, honeysuckle, scutellaria, cicada, silkworm, licorice root, and zaocys. Follow the label's directions. If you are treating secondary bacterial or fungal infections along with the flea-fighting program, this supplement is safe to use with antibiotics, shampoos, or antifungal medications.

- Apply aloe vera to any "hot spots," to help soothe and heal the area. Use a gel or apply directly from the plant. Calendula, available in your health food store in gel or spray, is another excellent skin soother.

- Use an herbal flea collar after allowing it to "air out" overnight when you first remove it from its package. Watch your animal's neck for signs of a reaction; certain herbs, such as pennyroyal and citronella, can be quite concentrated and strong.

- Use a boric acid carpet product as mentioned in Step 2, then vacuum thoroughly and throw away the bag or contents of the canister into a plastic garbage bag and seal it securely then discard.

Follow-Up Steps:

- Repeat the shampoo every week for four weeks.
- Continue to use the external spray as often as needed.
- Use a fine-tooth flea comb to check for fleas or "flea dirt."
- Vacuum the house at least once a week (and, again, discard the bag or canister contents in a sealed plastic bag).

Comb Away Fleas

One of the most effective ways to reduce and monitor flea infestations is with a flea comb. Its teeth are finely spaced and, as you comb, the fleas are trapped along with the hair. Fleas move and jump very fast. Grab the wad of hair with the flea and quickly immerse in a bowl of soapy water or the toilet. This is really the only method of mechanically removing and killing the fleas from your animal. The wooden-handled combs are the most user-friendly

The Allergic Reaction—a 911 Call to Action

Having your beloved animal desperately biting and scratching night and day can be a distressing experience. After a discouraging cycle of chemical warfare and cortisone, followed by a brief respite, you're hit with reinfestation and an itching response that's even worse than the one before. This is truly a vicious cycle.

When your animal is constantly scratching and biting, he or she has a fleabite allergy or dermatitis. This is an allergic reaction to the saliva of fleas. Your animal can react by producing a variety of symptoms. The mildest is minor itching, scratching, and redness of skin. The most severe is an emergency condition where your animal may chew through the skin in a desperate effort to relieve the itch. This self-inflicted wound is often called a "hot spot" and seeking professional advice at this stage is absolutely necessary. See your veterinarian at once if your animal is scratching or biting so badly it has caused baldness, considerable redness, and/or bleeding. (See Chapter 5 for more information on hot spots.)

Your veterinarian may prescribe a brief course of an anti-inflammatory drug, such as cortisone, which will offer relief instantly, ending the suffering and self-trauma. Be sure to discuss having your animal bathed and dipped with a nontoxic product under the close supervision of the hospital staff, to be thoroughly rid of fleas that are present. A flea- and tick-free body is essential at this point.

Using cortisone to overcome an acute medical situation is a valid use of conventional veterinary therapy, but do not use the cortisone repeatedly as a crutch. Cortisone and many other drugs are immune-system suppressants. Long-term use may help set the stage for other health problems down the road, such as cancer, kidney failure, or another degenerative disease. If your animal has been given a cortisone injection, be sure you offer him or her plenty of water and give antioxidant detoxifying vitamins as described below for at least a month after discontinuing the medication. You can circumvent the need for chemical dips and other harsh methods of flea control by using the natural steps described above.

We advise avoiding any of the in-vogue flea medications, which have caused dozens of reported side effects and multiple deaths of cats and dogs, unless you discuss their appropriateness to your animal with your veterinarian. Once your dog or cat is over the acute flea crisis, help him or her to never again experience a fleabite reaction. Also, help your animal clear out toxins from his or her body and work to boost the immune system by giving the detoxification antioxidants listed below for at least four weeks. Better yet, start the antioxidants a couple of days before and continue at a higher dose for two to three weeks after application. Continue your regular flea-fighting supplement program to maintain immunity to fleas. Generations of Goldstein animals, as well as those of our family and friends, have known the same freedom.

The Detox Antioxidants

Vitamin C (3 times daily)	
Cat/Small/Medium Dog (up to 34 lb)	250 mg
Large Dog (35-84 lb)	500 mg
Giant Dog (85+ lb)	750 mg

Vitamin A (daily)	
Cat/Small/Medium Dog (up to 34 lb)	2,500 iu
Large Dog (35-84 lb)	5,000 iu
Giant Dog (85+ lb)	7,500 iu

Vitamin E (mixed tocopherols, daily)	
Cat/Small/Medium Dog (up to 34 lb)	200 iu
Large Dog (35-84 lb)	400 iu
Giant Dog (85+ lb)	600 iu

In some instances, you and your veterinarian may want to bring immediate death to all fleas living on your animal. In these cases, we recommend Bayer's Advantage (Imidacloprid) applied to the skin. While this is still a chemical, it is far superior to the old generation of sprays, dips, bombs, and collars, and is preferable to any of the toxic, chemical-based flea control methods. There is absolutely no rationale for "bombing" the house!

When administering, we recommend that you stay with your animal for at least two hours after applying the small amount of liquid directly onto the skin at the nape of the your animal's neck. Wearing cotton gloves that you should later discard, gently stroke your animal before and after you give the product, and keep an eye on your friend to make sure that he or she does not have a reaction or attempt to lick off the product. Within a few minutes, it penetrates into the deeper layers of the skin, where it will be effective for about a month. If you follow the steps of our program, you can stretch that interval to six to eight weeks or use it on a contingency basis.

We advise avoiding any other of the in-vogue flea medications, which have caused dozens of reported side effects and been linked to multiple deaths of cats and dogs. Also, do not use any of these products on kittens or puppies under four months of age, or on animals with compromised immune systems. Once your dog or cat is over the acute flea crisis, help him or her to clear out toxins from the body and work to rebuild the immune system by giving the antioxidants listed above for at least four weeks. Better yet, start the antioxidants a couple days before and continue at a higher dose for two to three weeks after application.

Chapter 7

The Immune System:
The Key to Health and Wellness

Cancer and other serious degenerative and immune-mediated diseases are at unprecedented—some would say epidemic—levels. "Epidemic" sounds scary, but what it means is that the incidence of the disease is growing more quickly and more extensively among a particular population of people or animals than would normally be expected. Given the broad array of innovative diagnostic and therapy choices of modern medicine and the millions of dollars spent annually on research and development, it seems that we should be making progress against these types of diseases, not losing ground.

It is true that we have come a long way in the development of better pet foods, many of which now use human-grade, raw, and organic ingredients. Vaccination protocols have been examined and amended along with the automatic, chronic use of drugs such as antibiotics and cortisone. However, we still need to do a better job of getting out the message about the importance of the immune system in the overall health of animals. Later in this chapter we will discuss the theory of "immune surveillance." This controversial theory, which acknowledges the immune system's innate ability to heal the body, was put forth decades ago by orthodox scientists (including a Nobel laureate).

At the time of the introduction of such miracle drugs like penicillin, with its rapid action and ability to alleviate serious symptoms and cure diseases, the importance of the immune system was dropped out of the equation by skeptics and business people motivated by the promise of a "quick cure" and its attendant economic rewards. The Western medical paradigm became a model obsessed with diagnosis along with treatment protocols that suppress symptoms rather than support the immune system in the healing process.

Despite growing public interest in alternative therapies, conventional medicine remains largely focused on the signs, diagnosis, and treatment of diseases. In our view, the largely unrecognized role of the immune system in healing has contributed to the rising incidence of chronic diseases. For example, if an animal (or person) is treated with antibiotics for a respiratory infection, coughing and wheezing are controlled; however, there is a corresponding immune suppression and cessation of the normal process of eliminating metabolic wastes and toxins associated with the disease. If this treatment is repeated year after year without the simultaneous support of the immune system and the body's organs of detoxification, eventually this pattern will lead to further degeneration and weakening of the immune system, often resulting in a non-healing, terminal disease, and in this example may lead to lung cancer.

Integrative health care is based on supporting the immune system and protecting it when potent drugs are required. You can't fool Mother Nature! While you will often achieve temporary relief of symptoms using drugs, eventually the body's underlying healing mechanism will cave in and leave the patient even more vulnerable to disease.

The Domesticated "Lifestyle" and the Immune System

Wild wolves and tigers—the ancestors of our companion animals who are dependent upon us for all of their needs—had finely tuned immune systems in order to survive. That being said, we'd like to point out a few important differences in the immune systems of wild and domesticated animals:

- Wild animals eat totally uncooked and unprocessed meals that are rich in antioxidants (naturally occurring compounds that neutralize free radicals) and phytonutrients (nutrients found in fresh fruit, herbs, grasses, and vegetables) which are void of harsh chemical additives and preservatives. (See Chapter 2 for more on the importance of antioxidants and phytonutrients.) In addition, wild animals eat their entire prey and therefore get the total complement of required nutrients. In contrast, most domesticated animals eat cooked, by-product-filled, nutrient-devoid foods.

- Wild animals propagate and breed naturally—selection and survival are dependent upon survival of the fittest with sickly, genetically weaker animals weeded out by nature. Domesticated animals often are prone to genetic defects and weakness from the mass breeding of puppies and kittens who are bred by opportunistic individuals rather than dedicated hobby breeders. Mass breeding usually means that the puppies and kittens are bred without proper screening, health testing, or knowledge of genetics.

- Most wild animals still live in environments relatively free of pollution and modern civilization, although that is rapidly changing as development increasingly encroaches upon wild-animal habitats. Domestication has engendered a whole new lifestyle of stressors for "modern" dogs and cats.

Stressors on the Immune System

The immune system is an integrated, efficient, highly organized network of glands, proteins, cells, enzymes, and other biological chemicals that oversee, coordinate, and control the body's healing mechanism. There are many factors and stressors that can weaken the immune system and lead to disease. In our opinion, they include:

> Genetics: 30% of the pie
>
> Overuse of Vaccines and Medications: 20% of the pie
>
> Poor Nutrition: 20% of the pie
>
> Emotional Stress: 15% of the pie
>
> Environmental Toxins: 15% of the pie

Some holistic practitioners might disagree with this breakdown, believing that diet is the only important stressor to concentrate on. While diet is very important to your animal's health, diet alone is only one slice of the pie. There are other equally import areas to focus on in the holistic approach. While these percentages may be debatable, what is clear is that there are many ways you can take control of your animal's heath.

Genetics. The terms "puppy mill" and "kitten farm" describe the commercial breeding of dogs and cats for the eventual purchase by animal-loving people. Commercial breeders are usually motivated by monetary gain, as opposed to nonprofessional, or "hobby" breeders. While the idea of placing cute puppies and kittens in devoted homes is appealing, the method of getting there is filled with pitfalls such as:

- Using female dogs and cats as breeding machines, often breeding twice yearly (breeding every other year is often the recommended schedule).
- Keeping dogs and cats in crowded cages and unhygienic living conditions.
- Being fed the cheapest food available, because these are businesses run by the economic bottom line.
- Inbreeding related animals, which can lead to the propagation of weaker, more disease-prone dogs and cats susceptible to diseases such as arthritis, diabetes, autoimmune disorders, and cancer.

Overuse of medications and vaccines. While national advertising and your family veterinarian may be persuasive, too many chemicals can overwhelm your animal's immune system, leading to chronic autoimmune disorders—even cancer. Stop and consider the risks (see Chapter 3: Vaccination Wisdom) before you automatically revaccinate your animal every year, and request that your veterinarian use only those vaccines that are absolutely necessary.

Poor nutrition. Typical commercial pet food diets are loaded with by-products, food fragments, and human food-chain waste products, as well as laced with chemical additives, preservatives, artificial colors and flavor enhancers. These enzyme-devoid foods have undermined the health of domestic dogs and cats for years. While the number of healthy and even organic pet foods is growing rapidly, dogs and cats still need "real" food to thrive. Our Goldstein Food Plan (described in Chapter 1) lists the kinds of "real" food you should be feeding your cat or dog, and gives you a simple way to enhance your animal's diet.

Emotional stress. Extended periods of separation, lack of stimulation, and an abusive or unsettled home life are a few of the negative emotional scenarios that companion animals are often subjected to. Animals often carry past trauma into new environments, which must be released for the animal to be at peace. While animals are often much more intuitive than people, unlike humans, animals do not have a highly developed reasoning ability and typically absorb all emotions around them—both positive and negative. The buildup of negative emotions without a corresponding mechanism to reason them away or let them go will eventually lead to immune suppression and increased risk of disease.

Environmental toxins. Chronic exposure to pesticides, herbicides, air and water pollution, and other toxins suppresses the immune system and dramatically increases the level of free radicals, which wipe out the body's reserves of neutralizing antioxidants, leading to premature aging, chronic inflammation, and increased risk of disease.

So, if you're interested in doing everything you can to help your animal live a long, healthy life—and stay out of the veterinarian's office for other than routine annual checkups—the perfect place to get started is with an understanding of the importance of the immune system. While the complexity of this multi-organ system takes it well beyond the scope of this brief introduction, we'd like you to understand a few basic concepts, some of which have been controversial until quite recently.

An Immune System Primer

The immune system is a collective term that broadly defines the body parts that mount a defense against foreign invaders, be they environmental toxins or pathogens such as viruses or bacteria. The body's first line of defense is the armor shield composed of the skin, the membranes that line exposed body cavities (such as the mouth), and an invisible barrier located in the blood that protects the brain, aptly called the blood-brain barrier. These are physical barriers used by the body to thwart foreign invaders.

The second line of defense is a more specific system of blood cells called cell-mediated immunity. Circulating white blood cells spring into action to engulf and destroy foreign invaders through the familiar process of inflammation.

A deeper level of the immune system, the humoral immune system, is composed of specific cells and antibodies designed to destroy foreign cells or foreign material. The most well-known cells in this category are T- and B-lymphocytes. Lymphocytes are the basic cells of the immune system, produced in the bone marrow as well as the thymus, spleen, and lymphatic systems. Stem cells originate in the bone marrow and give rise to both T- and B-lymphocytes. The B cells produce the circulating antibodies known as immunoglobulins, which are proteins that have a variety of jobs, such as helping to protect the body against infection and exposure to specific toxins.

A common cause of inflammation for all cells, tissues, and organs is the formation of free radicals—reactive oxygen molecules (unpaired electrons) that bond to tissue, start an oxidation process and evoke an inflammatory response. Free radicals are generated during normal metabolic processes. However, excessive free radicals form when the body is exposed to high levels of drugs, chemical preservatives, pesticides, herbicides, and environmental chemicals. These foreign substances deplete the body's reserves of antioxidants (such as vitamins E, A, and C), which normally control and help to neutralize the level of free radicals. The resulting inflammatory response, if left unchecked, will lead to degradation of tissue and less-than-optimal functioning of the organs.

Your goal is to keep these molecular marauders in line by supplementing your dog or cat with sufficient levels of antioxidant vitamins, minerals, enzymes, and cofactors.

The Immune Surveillance Theory

When one of our mentors, Dr. Lawrence Burton (founder of the Immuno-Augmentative Therapy (IAT) cancer clinic), introduced us to the immune system over 20 years ago, we were not aware of some long-held beliefs behind its workings. The immune surveillance theory was elucidated by two distinguished scientists: physician and biologist Lewis Thomas and virologist, physician, and Nobel Laureate Sir Macfarlane Burnet. In the late 1950s, Burnet, being influenced by Thomas' work, proposed that newly forming cancer cells produced a new antigenic substance, which the body would attempt to destroy.

The immune surveillance theory simply holds that while the body continuously produces cancerous cells, a healthy immune system recognizes and destroys these cells. Recent studies have

"There Are No Coincidences in Life"

We were first introduced to the immune system and its link to cancer when we met Dr. Lawrence Burton, one of the early researchers to identify the existence of the immune system. Dr. Burton was treating cancer with injections of an immune serum made from the blood of healthy people mixed with blood from people with cancer. Due to his unorthodox medical philosophies and treatments, political pressure came from the medical establishment and the pharmaceutical industry, forcing Dr. Burton to leave the US in the 1970s. Susan came to know him through her time spent as a volunteer for the Foundation for Alternative Cancer Therapies in New York, while Dr. Burton was a cancer researcher at St. Vincent's Hospital in New York. Eventually we lost track of this maverick scientist when he relocated to the Bahamas. A few years later, an intuitive calling landed us on Grand Bahama Island for a vacation. Reading the local paper one morning, we noticed a reference to Dr. Burton's clinic in the very town we were staying, and at that moment we realized there are no coincidences in life.

We credit so much of our inspiration and earlier work to Dr. Burton, who in our opinion, was the medical equivalent of Albert Einstein. Like many pioneering scientists he had his quirks and faced many challenges. He had a picture of Albert Einstein on the wall of his office which read "Great Spirits Have Always Encountered Violent Opposition From Mediocre Minds."

On a very small scale the two of us, and our brother Dr. Marty Goldstein, encountered the same kind of opposition to our theories and our clinical work—especially during the first few years. We learned quickly that the best way to handle opposition is to turn the other cheek, and luckily for us we had each other to turn to in those pioneering days.

confirmed that the immune system plays a major role in the development and prevention of cancer and other degenerative diseases and that activating and boosting the immune system is really at the heart of "good medicine."

Modern scientific discovery and identification of T- and B-lymphocytes, immunoglobulins, natural killer cells, lymphokines, cytokines, interleukin, etc., can make the simplicity of the immune surveillance theory seem antiquated, but the essential point remains the same—we can't lose sight of the importance of the immune system's function in the healing process.

The Theory of Cellular Autoimmunity

Later in the book, we will present major organ systems and their corresponding diseases. In so doing, we will focus on an important concept relating to chronic degenerative diseases: the tendency for disease to arise as a result of the immune system becoming either overactive (hyper) or underactive (hypo).

As stated above, the central purpose of the immune system is to destroy foreign invaders while simultaneously "sparing" its own healthy cells and tissues. However, when the immune system is out of balance, it sometimes will attack its own healthy tissue. This type of response is called an autoimmune response and is accomplished when the body produces what are called autoantibodies. This response can stem from an underlying genetic weakness or from an insult to the body such as an adverse reaction to a vaccine, a potent drug, exposure to a bacterial or viral infection, toxins, or even an emotional stress. In most animals with a vigorous immune system, the lymphocytes produce a substance called cytokines, which help to control this out-of-balance reaction and not let it proceed to an autoimmune state.

In our opinion, all chronic degenerative diseases can trace their beginnings to a common denominator—either immune suppression or immune over activity—both playing the genetic hand that is dealt and orchestrated by the all-powerful immune system.

Disease at the Cellular Level

Put aside for a moment the classification of a specific autoimmune disease, such as anemia or arthritis. Looking deeper into the body toward the "source," you'll find that it is made up of building blocks of cells, which group together to form tissue and organs. These cells are all susceptible to the same stresses, chemicals, vaccines, bacteria, viruses, and toxins as the body. This simple, logical concept is often overlooked by modern medicine with its focus on the surface organ systems and the associated symptoms.

At this cellular level, cells die daily and are replaced by healthy new cells. However, when the stresses of life weaken the cells and organs of the immune system and pressure it into an unbalanced state, abnormal cell death occurs and eventually alerts the immune mechanism and lymphocytes to act. These dead cells produce cellular debris that is viewed as foreign to the body and should be removed, springing autoantibodies into action. These autoantibodies not only help to remove this debris but can, when directed by an overactive immune mechanism, attack the very organ that produced the debris, leading to a weakening of that organ.

The Cell's Response to Immune Attack

The cells, like the immune system itself, can also overreact or become sluggish and worn out. For example, when attacked by the immune system, the cells that make up the thyroid gland can become tired and overworked or inflamed and excitable. Then this deeper-lying response bubbles up to the surface and produces symptoms of either sluggishness and weight gain (hypothyroidism) or hyperactivity and weight loss (hyperthyroidism).

While these are real diseases that are serious and require immediate medical attention, we believe that the mindset of classifying them by name and organ type covers up the real underlying causes— the common denominator. Hypothyroidism, which is most often seen in dogs, has the same underlying cellular cause as hyperthyroidism, which is almost exclusively confined to cats. In those animals where the immune system is compromised and cannot find a quiet balance, it will often overreact even against its own tissue.

Let's look closer at the thyroid gland. In a weakening thyroid gland, the cells will begin to die. The immune system's reaction against these dying thyroid cells is to produce antibodies. These antibodies can not only attack the dead cells but will also attack the cells of the thyroid, further weakening the gland and setting the stage for an underactive, hypothyroid state. This occurs quite commonly in dogs such as Golden Retrievers.

On the other hand, insults to the thyroid gland can cause an overreactive immune system that inflames the thyroid gland. This inflammation can set the stage for an overworked gland leading to a hyperthyroid condition. This occurs commonly in cats. In fact, if the inflammation in the thyroid gland is not neutralized, this chronic inflammation may lead to a tumor.

The Common Denominator

It is essential to understand this mechanism that we are referring to as the "common denominator" of the disease. Looking past the complex scientific names we give to a particular disease and its symptoms, you see the immune system and its soldiers the T- and B- lymphocytes. At this level, you have a pre-disease mechanism occurring at the cellular level that is common to all diseases.

Something—be it a toxin, vaccine, drug, or chemical—insults and compromises the cell causing weakness and inflammation. Let's look at a cell of the intestines as another example. After constant bombardment by chemical additives and preservatives and indigestible by-products in food, the cell weakens, becomes inflamed, and a chain reaction that inflames surrounding cells begins. This chain reaction at the cellular level leads to an inflamed intestinal tract, resulting in improper absorption and symptoms such as diarrhea and gas.

The lymphocytes of the immune system take notice and produce antibodies that go after these weakening intestinal cells and destroy them. The body sends in lymphocytes to infiltrate the area in response to this chronic irritation. In a normal animal the lymphocyte attack would finally subside, the inflammation reduced, and the diarrhea stopped. However, in an animal with an imbalanced system, the response is an exaggerated attack leading to further inflammation, cell damage, and infiltration with more lymphocytes, resulting in chronic diarrhea mixed with blood.

It is at this point where the conventional medical system steps in and diagnoses the condition as "lymphocytic" inflammatory bowel disease, and prescribes medication such as cortisone to stop the over activity of the immune attack, calm the system, and halt the surface symptoms of the diarrhea. Instead, we approach the disease recognizing the immune system's method of operation, and focus on minimizing and correcting the original insult before it leads to a chronic disease. This is often accomplished through improved diet and the addition of specific nutrients, enzymes, and antioxidants that are used to help the body balance its own immune attack, quiet the inflammation, and finally reach true healing (or prevention).

The "Most Feared Diseases" By System

It is our belief that a disease and its associated signs and symptoms are a manifestation of a deeper underlying process. It is for this reason that we have classified and categorized this chapter on the most feared diseases not by the name of the disease, but rather by the location and organ system of the body that is affected by the disease.

The true holistic approach to disease is focused on strengthening and balancing organ systems in the attempt to support the entire body, thus preventing the disease and maintaining wellness.

Metabolic Therapy

The organ systems of the body are made up of organs and glands, each with specific, individual functions. They do not work individually, but rather together physiologically, biochemically, and metabolically. Focusing upon the specific metabolic and physiological aspects of an organ system means taking into consideration where the system fits into the "overall scheme of things." For example, one of the more common diseases seen and treated by veterinarians is chronic renal failure (kidney disease). In the "overall scheme of things," the kidneys are a receptacle for the elimination of metabolic wastes. The kidneys are not "sick," they are overloaded by wastes resulting from poor quality diets in combination with weakened organs and glands (the pituitary, adrenals, thyroid, and liver) that are not able to do their jobs.

While medical therapy is directed toward a sick kidney, metabolic therapy is directed at improving the function of all organs, thereby "taking the pressure off" the kidneys. Think of the gas tank of a car. What if, each time you filled the tank with gas, sand also was mixed in? The result would be a clogged carburetor. Fixing the carburetor would only solve the problem temporarily. Changing and cleaning the gas and stopping the sand from entering in the first place would solve the problem permanently.

The Cellular Autoimmune Reaction

Cats and dogs seem to be growing old before their time. Diseases normally reserved for old age (like heart disease) are beginning to show in companion animals as early as four to six years old.

What has changed? Many holistic veterinarians believe that underlying causes include poor nutrition; improper breeding, leading to genetic weaknesses; over-vaccination; chronic use of medication such as antibiotics and cortisone; and chronic exposure to environmental pollutants and insecticides.

It is our belief that the continual exposure to toxins leads to an overproduction of free radicals. When this free radical load is coupled with an antioxidant depletion from poor nutrition, local cellular inflammation is ignited. The immune system recognizes this inflammation and takes action by sending in white blood cells and developing antibodies, which further inflames the cells. This process is termed an autoimmune reaction. An imbalanced immune system will overreact and attack the very organ it is trying to heal.

Working Through Illness

In the mid-1970s, we saw a two-year-old English Springer Spaniel with the worst case of skin disease we had ever seen. Brandy had been through dozens of appointments with his family veterinarian and allergy specialists. He had been tested repeatedly for various allergens and received bimonthly cortisone injections. He was given a medicated chemical bath every three weeks, yet he couldn't have been more miserable!

Brandy's eyes were dull and sad. His coat was greasy and clumpy. He had oozing, foul-smelling lesions all over his body. His guardians were at their wit's end. At the time, we were still learning how the body heals. We poured all of our enthusiasm and new learning into Brandy, prescribing vitamins, homeopathics, and a home-cooked diet rich in phytonutrients, and nutraceuticals.

Two weeks later, the couple returned—with a new dog! The oozing was gone, the lesions had healed. Brandy's spirits and energy were restored, and he didn't smell! His family was ecstatic. But three weeks later, Brandy returned to the clinic in a full-blown allergic crisis. This time, we had no choice but to inject him with cortisone.

We were devastated, and even began to question our natural healing approach. A few weeks later, we were sitting in a classroom with the late Dr. Bernard Jensen, one of the pioneers in human natural medicine. Quoting Herring's Law of Cure and the Healing Crisis, Dr. Jensen taught us that "all cures occur in the reverse order in which the symptoms occurred." This intensive period of detoxification is known as a "healing crisis." When an animal in the wild is just not up to par, he or she will simply fast and rest. It is during this period of absolute quiet and rest for the body's organs that true healing can occur.

In modern civilization, when an animal (or person) is given the proper fuel (diet and supplements) as well as rest (sleep and fasting), and plenty of fresh water, the body begins to heal itself by eliminating accumulated layers of wastes. It does so by directing these contaminants to one or more of its natural avenues for releasing toxins—the lungs, kidneys, lower intestine, eyes, ears, skin. Consequently, these organs of elimination may become temporarily inflamed. This inflammation may look just like the disease itself. Common signs of a healing crisis include low-grade fever, runny eyes, foul breath, smelly urine, diarrhea, and just about any skin-related symptoms—oily and oozing as well as itchy skin.

The use of strong medications such as cortisone, which stop the immune system from "doing its thing," actually stops this natural process of eliminating stored toxins and wastes. The result is that the trapped toxins stay in the body, waiting to cause the next episode, weeks or months down the road. When this occurs, your veterinarian may term the condition "chronic," and inform you that your animal may have to stay on medication for the rest of her life.

The majority of healing crises are not as severe as Brandy's, and as you improve the diet and supplement program you may only experience mild flareups that last for two to three days. Be patient and understand that this is normal. Many times true healing requires this "worse before it gets better" process to occur.

Keys to Keeping the Organs Healthy

All of the organ systems we will be discussing need the following:

Nutrition: Glands and organ systems have specific nutritional needs and requirements that must be met in order for their proper and efficient functioning. Organs that are properly nourished will have a positive and beneficial influence on all the glands, thereby improving the overall health.

Natural Remedies and Supplements: Besides the basic food groups of protein, fats, and carbohydrates, there are numerous enzymes, nutrients, cofactors, antioxidants, vitamins, and minerals required for proper function. It is important to make sure that the body has what it needs to stay healthy and free of diseases on a daily basis.

Enhancement of Elimination: The elimination of metabolic wastes and toxins from the body is one of the keys to healing. Toxins, if not eliminated, will cause illness.

Reduction of Inflammation: The cause and reduction of inflammation is similar for all cells, tissues, and organs of the body. Free radicals are reactive oxygen molecules that bond to cells, and evoke an inflammatory response. The goal is to decrease the amount of free radicals by supplementing with sufficient levels of antioxidant vitamins, minerals, enzymes, and cofactors.

This book focuses on the organ systems of the body and how to support their function based upon the deeply rooted belief that if you are able to feed the system the energy it needs, it has the inherent capability of healing itself.

Keep these three principles of healing in mind whenever embarking on an integrative approach to wellness:

1. The body heals by inflammation.
2. The body heals in the opposite way that it gets sick.
3. The body gets sick and degenerates by an autoimmune response.

Adrenal Gland Diseases

The adrenals are a pair of bean-shaped glands located atop the kidneys, known as the "fight or flight" or stress glands. Comprised of two parts—the adrenal cortex and the medulla—the adrenals are central to many metabolic and physiologic processes of the immune system. The adrenals accomplish the "fight or flight" function through the production of the hormone adrenaline.

In addition to the adrenals' reaction to stress, one of their key roles is to produce many of the body's naturally occurring cortisones, such as glucocorticoids, mineralocorticoids, and adrenal androgens. The glucocorticoids help control blood sugar levels. The mineralocorticoids help to regulate the passage of minerals through the body (primarily sodium and potassium). The adrenal androgens, such as dehydroepiandrosterone (DHEA), are believed to help balance the body's hormones by picking up the hormonal slack in the body, for instance when your dog or cat has been neutered or spayed.

The adrenal medulla manufactures the hormones epinephrine (adrenalin) and norepinephrine, which help in the regulation of the nervous system, heart rate, and respiration, in addition to kicking in the "fight or flight" response. The adrenal medulla has a direct attachment to the sympathetic nervous system, which directly controls the secretion of epinephrine and norepinephrine.

In the 1930s and 1940s, adrenal extracts (derived from the adrenal tissue) were widely used to treat human fatigue, diabetes, hypoglycemia, allergies, and to help improve resistance to diseases. Adrenal extracts have been replaced by synthetic versions, such as the ever-popular cortisone (the most commonly used is prednisone). Injections of cortisone are commonly used when immediate action is necessary, such as in the case of severe itching and "hot spots"—when the itch is so bad that your animal is literally chewing through his or her skin to alleviate the discomfort. The chronic administration of cortisone, however, has the direct effect of diminishing adrenal function and weakening the immune system. Stress and repeated use of cortisone can cause the glands to shrink and eventually atrophy.

During periods of chronic inflammation caused by excess free radicals and the depletion of available antioxidants, the adrenal glands will become overworked.

This may lead to inflammation and hyperactivity that may develop into a condition called Cushing's disease (Hyperadrenocorticism). On the other end of the spectrum, the adrenal glands may become underactive, and exhausted, leading to a serious disease called Addison's disease (Hypoadrenocorticism).

Addison's Disease

When adrenal glands say "I quit!" due to exhaustion, the body may go into metabolic crisis. The diagnosis of Addison's disease is confirmed by a physical exam and diagnostic blood work. The hallmark of Addison's disease is low-to-undetectable circulating levels of serum cortisol, which is the body's own naturally produced cortisone. In addition to the low cortisol levels, your veterinarian may also find elevated potassium, alkaline phosphatase (ALP), and liver enzymes (ALT), along with other blood anomalies.

Early Warning Signs

Addison's disease is not one of the more common diseases in dogs and is rare in cats. Symptoms include weakness, depression, vomiting and, in acute cases, shock—certainly not pleasant and potentially life threatening. While Addison's is not the most common disease, it is serious, as the adrenal glands are critical to the immune system.

What Will Your Veterinarian Recommend?

Because of the critical nature of exhausted adrenal glands, your veterinarian will prescribe powerful, cortisone-type drugs, along with synthetic cortisone such as prednisone, to help the body regain its balance and not slip into shock or collapse. While this medical approach is often life saving and necessary, we encourage you to not stop with a wholly conventional approach, as natural support remedies and solutions may help to balance the gland system and regenerate those exhausted adrenal glands.

Another area that your veterinarian will be concerned about is the sudden withdrawal of cortisone, which can bring on an Addison's type of reaction. It is imperative that if your animal is taking corstisone, especially for weeks or months (or in some cases, for years) that you gradually reduce the levels of cortisone weekly or biweekly to allow the normal function of the adrenal glands to return.

Remember from Chapter 7 that the immune system brings about healing through inflammation. For example, if the body is trying to heal the skin, the immune system will inflame the area. Inflamed skin is often itchy and therefore your dog or cat will begin to scratch and self-traumatize his or her skin in an attempt to relieve the inflammation. Cortisone blocks the inflammation and controls the itch. While this sounds like a happy ending, there are adverse affects brewing below the surface.

What's happening is a phenomenon called negative feedback—the steady supply of cortisone injections or pills has tricked the pituitary gland into thinking there is plenty natural cortisone available for the body, so it tells the adrenals to stop internal production. When you abruptly stop giving the steroids, the body cannot cope with the depressed adrenal glands and can actually go into an Addisonian type of crisis, which can lead to shock and other serious complications.

At-Home Support and Prevention

While working on a treatment plan with your veterinarian comes first, you can also support your dog or cat at home. The approach to healing an exhausted gland is to improve the diet and offer a vitamin, mineral, antioxidant, herbal, and glandular program designed to strengthen the adrenal glands, as well as to improve the overall functioning of the entire body.

Diet. If you haven't already, place your animal on Level III of the Goldstein Food Plan (see Chapter 1). This diet contains the highest amount of antioxidants, vitamins, minerals, and phytonutrients that are beneficial not only for the adrenal glands but for support of the entire body.

Tellington TTouch (see Chapter 4) is a massage method that can help your animal release tension, improve behavior, and encourage relaxation, all of which will be beneficial for support of the immune and adrenal systems, and can help lay the groundwork for healing.

Vitamin C. Stressful conditions will often deplete the body's reserves of vitamin C, so it's important to make sure it is part of the daily diet.

Vitamin C (twice daily)	
Cat/Small Dog (up to 14 lb)	100 mg
Medium Dog (15-34 lb)	250 mg
Large Dog (35-84 lb)	500 mg
Giant Dog (85+ lb)	750 mg

Acupuncture. If your animal is chronically ill, under stress, and susceptible to Addison's disease, it would be a good idea to consult with a certified veterinary acupuncturist and get on a regular schedule of preventive treatments. This will help protect the adrenal system by removing energy blockages that result from chronic stress. (See Chapter 4.)

Flower Essences. Because the adrenal gland is the stress gland, all treatment programs should include emotional support. We always recommend as part of any therapy program that you add flower essences (see Chapter 4). The two that we recommend are from Anaflora: Return to Joy for one month (to help clear out the emotions), followed by Special Stress. The dose for both is to add 5 drops of these remedies daily to fresh drinking water. This will start to balance the emotions and help to reduce the stress associated with chronic illness. Stress is a main factor in decreasing adrenal function.

Glandulars. You can use pituitary and adrenal gland supplements (available at health food stores).

Adrenal Gland (daily)	
Cat/Small Dog (up to 14 lb)	100 mg
Medium Dog (15-34 lb)	200 mg
Large Dog (35-84 lb)	300 mg
Giant Dog (85+ lb)	400 mg

Pituitary Gland (daily)	
Cat/Small Dog (up to 14 lb)	30 mg
Medium Dog (15-34 lb)	50 mg
Large Dog (35-84 lb)	75 mg
Giant Dog (85+ lb)	100 mg

Alternative Veterinary Therapies

First and foremost, Addison's disease is serious, and under *all* circumstances has to be monitored and treated by an experienced veterinarian, and in most instances requires medication to control the situation.

Nutritional Blood Test (NBT). Your veterinarian possesses a powerful tool in the Nutritional Blood Analysis (NBT) test, which offers your animal a scientific nutraceutical program based upon the analysis of the blood and clinical history. (See Chapter 4 for more information on the NBT.) The use of the prescribed NBT nutraceutical program and remedies incorporates vitamin, mineral, antioxidant, herbal and glandular therapy, the latter being one of the more effective treatments designed to strengthen and support the adrenal gland.

The more important aspect of this type of therapy for Addison's disease is that it works well in combination with medications, which is critical for preventing a full-blown crisis and collapse. Once stability has been achieved, it may be possible to reduce the medications as the body's immune and gland systems begin to strengthen and rebuild. (Note: Any reduction in medication should only be done under the direct supervision of your veterinarian.) Glandular therapy targets the damaged gland or organ and also supplies badly needed replacement fats and amino acids.

The following NBT supplement program can help your Addison's animal move toward stability and glandular balance. Typically, you should introduce these targeted nutrients over a three-month period, while your animal is on the prescribed medication. During the second of the three months, after giving the glands a chance to work on their own, and through a series of diagnostic blood testing, your veterinarian can determine if the drugs are holding the condition under control for a longer period of time. It usually takes about six months to determine whether the adrenal glands will regain some or all of their function. Many animals will need to stay on some level of medication for the rest of their lives.

Vitamin C (twice daily)	
Cat/Small Dog (up to 14 lb)	100 mg
Medium Dog (15-34 lb)	250 mg
Large Dog (35-84 lb)	500 mg
Giant Dog (85+ lb)	750 mg

Vitamin E (daily)	
Cat/Small Dog (up to 14 lb)	200 iu
Medium Dog (15-34 lb)	400 iu
Large Dog (35-84 lb)	600 iu
Giant Dog (85+ lb)	800 iu

Vitamin A (daily)	
Cat/Small Dog (up to 14 lb)	2,500 iu
Medium Dog (15-34 lb)	5,000 iu
Large Dog (35-84 lb)	7,500 iu
Giant Dog (85+ lb)	7,500 iu

Licorice (daily)	
Cat/Small Dog (up to 14 lb)	30 mg
Medium Dog (15-34 lb)	35 mg
Large Dog (35-84 lb)	50 mg
Giant Dog (85+ lb)	75 mg

Your veterinarian can chose the Adrenal Support and Pituitary Formulas, produced by Animal Nutrition Technologies (ANT), which contain the cellular repair factors required by the adrenal and pituitary glands for optimal function, including adrenal and pituitary gland support, vitamins, minerals, and specific required amino acids. Generally 1 tablet for every 25 pounds of body weight is prescribed.

Chinese Herbal Remedies. Along with your veterinarian's medical therapy and the NBT nutrient therapy, the Chinese herbal remedy called Addison's is recommended. When using this remedy along with the NBT nutrient therapy you will often find that the amount of cortisone required to keep the Addison's under control can be greatly reduced, and under your veterinarian's guidance you may be able to lower the dose. This remedy is available to your veterinarian through ANT and will be dosed according to your animal's weight.

Cushing's Disease

Cushing's disease is a hyperactive adrenal system that is pumping out excessive amounts of adrenal hormones, primarily the glucocorticoids (the body's natural cortisone). Higher than normal amounts of this hormone drive and push the body's metabolism to such an extent that the physical condition is affected. A Cushing's-like disease (called Cushinoid) can be produced when animals are chronically given high levels of synthetic cortisone medications for long periods of time. Since synthetic cortisone is popularly used to control nagging problems such as excessive itching, pain, and limping, there are many animals that experience Cushinoid-type symptoms, such as excessive thirst, urination, and appetite. The good news is that often, if you slowly decrease the synthetic cortisone, the Cushinoid symptoms will disappear.

Early Warning Signs

Early signs of Cushing's disease are an excessive thirst and urination (polydypsia and polyuria) coupled with an unusually ravenous appetite. Other signs include excessive pacing and hyperactiviy, loss of hair, a thin coat and skin, weakened and atrophied muscles, and a potbellied appearance.

What Will Your Veterinarian Recommend?

Your veterinarian will perform a series of blood evaluations to confirm the diagnosis of Cushing's disease, which may include an ACTH stimulation or a dexamethasone depression test. These tests will also help your veterinarian distinguish between a true overactive adrenal gland (Hyperadrenalcorticism or HAC) or an overactive pituitary gland (Pituitary Dependent Hyperadrenocorticism or PDH).

Once diagnosed, your veterinarian will likely recommend a chemotherapy type of drug called Lysodren (chemically similar to the insecticide DDT). Lysodren can physically and permanently destroy the tissue of the adrenal cortex so it can no longer produce the glucocorticoids that are causing the physical and clinical problems. If your animal cannot tolerate Lysodren, your veterinarian may recommend the drug Ketoconazole; while less toxic, this drug is still very potent with its own side effects, such as vomiting, diarrhea, and loss of appetite. If the pituitary gland is the underlying cause (PDH), your veterinarian may recommend the drug Anipryl (Selegiline hydrochloride), which has few side effects and can help diminish the Cushing's symptoms. Another option is surgery, especially if your veterinarian has determined that the Cushing's is being caused by one enlarged (tumerous) adrenal gland. Surgery is potentially quite dangerous so be sure to review this option closely with your veterinarian.

At-Home Support and Prevention

If Cushing's disease is long standing, the physical changes may be permanent, and your animal may require Lysodren to quiet down the adrenals before they permanently burn out the body. If, however, your veterinarian has diagnosed early Cushing's or a Cushinoid condition and is not recommending immediate therapy, there is plenty for you to do to prevent permanent damage.

Glandular Therapy

Add glandular adrenal and pituitary to the daily diet. These will help to neutralize the body's inflammatory attack of these two organs. (See Chapter 4 for more on gland therapy.) These are available at health food stores or through holistic veterinarians.

Adrenal Gland (daily)	
Cat/Small Dog (up to 14 lb)	150 mg
Medium Dog (15-34 lb)	250 mg
Large Dog (35-84 lb)	350 mg
Giant Dog (85+ lb)	500 mg

Pituitary Gland (daily)	
Cat/Small Dog (up to 14 lb)	30 mg
Medium Dog (15-34 lb)	50 mg
Large Dog (35-84 lb)	75 mg
Giant Dog (85+ lb)	100 mg

Nutrients

Vitamin C (ascorbic acid form) helps to offset the response in the blood from the often-high alkaline phosphatase levels that routinely accompany an overactive adrenal gland.

Vitamin C (twice daily)	
Cat/Small Dog (up to 14 lb)	100 mg
Medium Dog (15-34 lb)	250 mg
Large Dog (35-84 lb)	500 mg
Giant Dog (85+ lb)	750 mg

Research has suggested that phosphatidylserine (a phospholipid) can help to lower cortisol levels. Phosphatidylserine is available in most health food stores.

Phosphatidylserine (daily)	
Cat/Small Dog (up to 14 lb)	25 mg
Medium Dog (15-34 lb)	50 mg
Large Dog (35-84 lb)	100 mg
Giant Dog (85+ lb)	150 mg

Flower Essences

Because the adrenals are the stress glands, all treatment programs should include emotional support. We always recommend adding flower essences (see Chapter 4). The two we recommend are available from Anaflora: use **Return to Joy** for one month (to help clear the emotions) followed by **Special Stress**. The dose for both is to add 5 drops of these remedies daily to fresh drinking water.

Alternative Veterinary Therapies

There are other alternative approaches you can take under the guidance of an experienced veterinarian. Specific disease and organ oriented therapies often can be utilized to control the signs, symptoms, and physiological changes associated with Cushing's, often without the need of the potent conventional mentioned above.

Adrenal Support Formula, produced by Animal Nutrition Technologies (ANT), is a nutraceutical formula that contains the cellular repair factors required by the adrenal glands for optimal function, including adrenal and pituitary gland support, vitamins, minerals, and specific-required amino acids.

Oliver's Story

One of our canine patients, Oliver, was suspected of having Cushing's disease. Gloria, Oliver's companion, was determined to do the right thing. Gloria allowed Oliver to go through the proper diagnostic tests, including repeated ultrasounds, ACTH and dexamethasone blood screenings, and consultations between her conventional veterinarian and Dr Bob. Oliver's Cushing's disease was caused by an overactive pituitary gland pushing on the adrenal gland, therefore surgery was out of the question. Oliver was immediately placed on the NBT nutraceutical powder, along with supportive homeopathics and the Chinese Herbal Remedy Adrenasol. Eighteen months later, Oliver was free from all symptoms of Cushing's disease.

Dosage is generally 1 tablet for every 25 pounds of body weight.

Chinese Herbal Remedies. The addition of Adrenasol, a Chinese herbal remedy, will often reduce adrenal function and lower the associated elevation in blood levels of alkaline phosphatase (ALP). This therapy should be under the guidance of an experienced veterinarian. The dose is usually one capsule for each 20 pounds of weight, or as directed by your veterinarian.

The Nutritional Blood Test (NBT) is an individual and specific approach to Cushing's disease. While symptoms are conventionally adrenal related, the disease often affects many organs, and therefore the NBT organ assessment is often beneficial (see Chapter 4 for details on the NBT process). Often the combination homeopathic sarcodes called Adrenal and Hypothalamus drops will be recommended after the NBT analysis. These drops are anti-inflammatory and regenerative for the individual glands.

Adrenal Drops (daily)	
Cat/Small Dog (up to 14 lb)	7 drops
Medium Dog (15-34 lb)	10 drops
Large Dog (35-84 lb)	12 drops
Giant Dog (85+ lb)	15 drops

Hypothalamus Drops (daily)	
Cat/Small Dog (up to 14 lb)	7 drops
Medium Dog (15-34 lb)	10 drops
Large Dog (35-84 lb)	12 drops
Giant Dog (85+ lb)	15 drops

What's the Prognosis?

When dealing with exhausted adrenal glands and Addison's disease, the prognosis for your animal is usually good. However, because of the seriousness of the condition, medications are often required for the rest of your animal's life.

When dealing with Cushing's disease, if you make a concerted effort to not only support the adrenal glands, but also to improve the diet, pay attention to emotional stresses, and give the proper support remedies and supplements, the prognosis for control of this disease is often quite good.

Cardiovascular Diseases

The heart is an organ of immense metabolic importance. While it does not manufacture or secrete hormones, it is responsible for the circulation of the blood, is vital for life, and feeds and fuels the body so it can carry out important metabolic and physiologic functions. Besides its responsibilities of pumping the blood to all the vital organs, it has its own needs that, if not met, will diminish the quality of life and longevity.

Major enemies of the heart include genetic weaknesses, poor circulation related to lack of exercise, and inflammation secondary to excessive free radicals. Dogs and cats are susceptible to a whole range of conditions that can weaken valves and the heart muscle. Although dogs and cats do not suffer from clogged arteries and heart attacks that plague humans, they are prone to fat-clogged blood which slows circulation leading to stasis and disease. This is especially true in the smaller capillaries that feed the vital organs. It is at this level that disease begins.

Valve Disease and Congestive Heart Failure

This is a condition in which the heart valves become inflamed, then thickened, and eventually scarred, preventing the valves from closing properly. This results in leaky valves causing fluid backup either on the right side (leading to lung congestion and coughing) or the left (leading to abdominal fluid buildup).

Nervous System and Hormonal-Stimulation Problems

Like all muscles, the heart is controlled by electrical impulses. Early stimulation of a weakening heart is designed to ensure blood supply to vital organs. But long-term stimulation overworks the heart muscle, leading to changes in the size and shape of the heart muscle and progressive heart failure.

Cardiomyopathies

Cats and dogs are both prone to a disorder in which the heart muscle becomes inflamed, a condition called cardiomyopathy. This condition is particularly common in Doberman Pinschers and can often cause congestive heart failure and shortened lifespan.

In cats, there are two main forms of cardiomyopathy. The most common, hypertrophic cardiomyopathy (HCM), is marked by a thickening of the heart muscle. A ballooned type is known as dilatative cardiomyopathy (DCM). Cardiomyopathy is associated with an inflammatory, degenerative process often linked to taurine deficiency (an essential amino acid) in cats. To forestall its deficiency and potential for heart disease, most commercial cat foods are now supplemented with taurine.

Early Warning Signs

If you are observant early on you will see your animal slow down. He or she will be slow to get up and down, unable to finish a walk, experience lethargy, and spend increased time sleeping. If the inflammaotry process has led to damage to the heart muscle or the valves, you may notice a dry hacking cough, particularly at night when the right side of the heart is struggling, or a potbellied appearance from fluid buildup when the left side is weakening. Other signs of heart trouble include:

- Loss of appetite
- Reluctance to go upstairs
- Depression and lethargy
- Wheezing, shortness of breath
- Swollen limbs (edema)
- Continual sleeping
- Fainting, stumbling, or weakness

Early detection of these symptoms is ideal for successful treatment. This is one reason we always recommend a complete annual physical examination, during which your veterinarian will listen to the heart and lungs and palpate the abdomen to detect fluid. Also, depending on your location, a yearly or twice-yearly heartworm test may be suggested. We also recommend that your veterinarian perform a complete blood analysis for all animals age three and up.

What Will Your Veterinarian Recommend?

Conventional medical therapy is directed toward managing the symptoms and stopping the inflammatory mechanism that will worsen the condition. As the heart weakens, blood flow and oxygen levels progressively diminish. The immune system responds by directing the heart to keep blood flowing to the vital organs.

Medical therapy seeks to regulate the heartbeat and suppress the hormones that affect blood pressure, ensuring that vital tissues continue to get sufficient oxygen and nutrients.

Your veterinarian may prescribe the following medications:

Enalapril (Enacard) to block hormonal control and help reduce blood pressure by relaxing the vessels. It may cause elevated blood toxins that would normally be removed by the kidneys.

Digoxin is recommended to slow the heartbeat and improve heart contractions, and is often used in heart failure. It may cause vomiting, diarrhea and a loss of appetite.

Lasix (Furosemide) is a diuretic that helps to relieve the fluid buildup in the lungs and abdomen and its resultant cough and pot belly, which are secondary to a weakening heart.

Atenolol (Tenormin) and **Propranolol (Inderal)** are beta-adrenergic blockers, which help to minimize nervous stimulation of the heart, thereby decreasing heart rate and lowering blood pressure.

These medications, while lifesaving initially, eventually block the body's natural response to long-term healing. To treat holistically, it is important to expand the focus of attention to include the support, fueling, and balancing of the immune system, its potential overreaction, and the secondary inflammation that can lead to a further weakening of the gland.

At-Home Support and Prevention

Heart disease in companion animals often brings a difficult prognosis, but a combination of conventional and holistic therapies can team up to stabilize the condition and minimize the day-to-day symptoms. More importantly, when you quiet the underlying inflammation and slow degeneration, you can often extend lifespan and improve quality of life. We have often seen animals with potentially terminal heart disease go on to live years comfortably and free of symptoms.

If your animal is battling a degenerative disorder of the heart—whatever the cause—pull out all the stops. Work with your family veterinarian to integrate more natural remedies. Once your dog or cat is stabilized and your veterinarian is comfortable with the clinical response (controlled fluid buildup and the coughing or bloating is under control), and if energy levels are back to normal it is important to address the body's nutritional needs.

Diet

There's no better place to start than with the Goldstein Food Plan (see Chapter 1). We recommend Level III and replacing up to 40 percent of your natural base food with high-quality chicken, turkey or beef, whole grains and finely chopped vegetables. This will go a long way in preserving the heart tissue and function.

You'll also want to monitor your animal's weight. Overweight animals are prone to circulatory problems, which will worsen the clinical signs of heart disease. Regular exercise will improve general circulation to the organ, bringing much-needed nutrients and oxygen. In addition, daily use of garlic will help regulate blood pressure and thin the blood. Remember to talk to your veterinarian before you add garlic, since too much can cause anemia.

Garlic—fresh chopped cloves (with meals)	
Cat/Small Dog (up to 14 lb)	1/2 clove
Medium Dog (15-34 lb)	1 clove
Large/Giant Dog (35+ lb)	2 cloves

Nutrients

Here are some heart-specific nutrients that you can begin supplementing immediately at home. They are readily available in health food stores. Many of the following nutrients are potent antioxidants and function at the cellular level to combat and neutralize free radicals.

Coenzyme Q10 (CoQ10) has been proven to help animals with heart disease by increasing the oxygen available to the cells. The long-term use of this nutrient can help minimize your animal's dependence on potent medications. It also will help increase energy levels of both dogs and cats, thereby encouraging more exercise, improving circulation, and promoting weight loss. CoQ10 is especially valuable for animals suffering from congestive heart failure and works hand in hand with the amino acid L-carnitine to improve cardiac function.

CoQ10 and Heart Disease

Dr. Stephen Sinatra is a board-certified cardiologist with 25 years of experience in helping patients prevent and reverse heart disease. Here is what Dr Sinatra says about Coenzyme Q10. "More than 100 clinical studies at major universities and hospitals have documented the actions of Coenzyme Q10. I have long considered CoQ10 a wonder nutrient because of its ability to support heart health. The heart is one of the few organs in the body to function continuously without resting; therefore, the heart muscle requires the highest level of energetic support. Any condition that causes a decrease in CoQ10 could impair the energetic capacity of the heart, thus leaving the tissues more susceptible to free radical attack."

Coenzyme Q10 (once daily)	
Cat/Small Dog (up to 14 lb)	25 mg
Medium Dog (15-34 lb)	35 mg
Large Dog (35-84 lb)	50 mg
Giant Dog (85+ lb)	75-100 mg

Amino Acids

Amino acids are the building blocks of proteins and are vital to all cells, tissue, and organ systems. If your animal is not getting the proper amino acids from his food, degenerative disease can follow.

Taurine (2-aminoethane sulfonic acid) is an amino acid that is involved in many metabolic and cellular functions. It is abundant in tissues that are active and rich in oxygen, such as the muscles of the heart. Therefore, it is critical that adequate amounts are present in the diet. In the early 1990s, it was discovered that because of poor-quality protein sources used in cat foods, deficiencies in taurine were developing, leading to cardiomyopathy and death.

Taurine (once daily)	
Cat/Small Dog (up to 14 lb)	500 mg
Medium/Large Dog (15-84 lb)	750 mg
Giant Dog (85+ lb)	1000 mg

L-carnitine, an amino acid that works well in concert with CoQ10, can be added to the diet to improve the strength of the heart muscle and give the body general muscular support. It also will help burn fat and help obese animals lose weight.

L-Carnitine (once daily)	
Cat/Small Dog (up to 14 lb)	250 mg
Medium/Large Dog (15-84 lb)	500 mg
Giant Dog (85+ lb)	750 mg

Antioxidants

You can supplement your animal's diet with all of these vitamins. They do not interfere with other remedies or medications.

Vitamin E is not only a potent antioxidant and anti-inflammatory, it also improves circulation and heart output. Improved circulation will help the body clear excessive fluid that has accumulated in the chest or abdominal cavities. Look for mixed tocopherols from natural sources, rather than the synthetic version called vitamin E acetate. Most pet foods, while they contain adequate levels of vitamin E, use the less expensive, more stable synthetic form (acetate), so your supplement should contain the naturally occurring tocopherols.

Vitamin E (once daily)	
Cat/Small Dog (up to 14 lb)	200 iu
Medium Dog (15-34 lb)	400 iu
Large Dog (35-84 lb)	600 iu
Giant Dog (85+ lb)	800 iu

Vitamin C. We once saw a medical presentation by a popular nutritionist focusing on vitamin C. He was using the argument that because dogs manufacture their own vitamin C, they do not get heart disease. While we agree that dogs and cats do not get typical hardening of the arteries (arteriosclerosis) related to cholesterol buildup, dogs and cats do get heart disease!

We want to dispel the myth about the potent antioxidant and cardio-protective vitamin C. While it is true that many animals do manufacture vitamin C, highly processed, nutrient-depleted foods and exposure to environmental pollutants and pesticides quickly deplete the vitamin C reserves. Couple this with other emotional and physical stressors, we find that vitamin C and other nutrients are rapidly left in short supply, leaving your friend vulnerable to disease.

Vitamin C (twice daily)	
Cat/Small Dog (up to 14 lb)	125 mg
Medium Dog (15-34 lb)	250 mg
Large Dog (35-84 lb)	500 mg
Giant Dog (85+ lb)	750 mg

Minerals

You can choose one of the following mineral sources to supplement your animal's diet.

Kelp (Deep Cold Water). The electrical conduction system of the heart is dependent on the proper amount of minerals in the body. Commercial pet foods are often deficient in minerals or contain minerals that are poorly absorbed. Ground kelp is an excellent source of minerals and can be purchased at human health food stores. We recommend a deep, cold-water source.

Kelp (per meal)	
Cat/Small Dog (up to 14 lb)	1/2 tsp
Medium Dogs (15-34 lb)	1 tsp
Large Dogs (35-84 lb)	1 1/2 tsp
Giant Dogs (85+ lb)	2 tsp

Colloidal Minerals are highly absorbable minerals found in liquid form.

Colloidal minerals (per meal)	
Cat/Small Dog (up to 14 lb)	1/4 tsp
Medium Dog (15-34 lb)	1/2 tsp
Large Dog (35-84 lb)	1 tsp
Giant Dog (85+ lb)	2 tsp

Magnesium acts like a calcium channel blocker and can help to stabilize cardiac conduction, heart muscle, and vascular membranes by blocking the absorption of calcium into the cells. Magnesium has been associated with lower urinary tract disease (LUTD) and the formation of bladder stones (especially in cats); however, we do recommend it when the blood levels of magnesium are low. Make sure you check with your veterinarian first.

Magnesium (daily)	
Cat/Small Dog (up to 14 lb)	15 mgs
Medium Dog (15-34 lb)	35 mg
Large Dog (35-84 lb)	50 mg
Giant Dog (85+ lb)	75-100 mg

Essential Fatty Acids

Much research has been done on the importance of essential fatty acids in the clinical management of various degenerative diseases. Although some manufacturers add omega-3 and -6 fatty acids to the food, these fatty acids are often rapidly destroyed by heat and light. Therefore, it is essential to supplement the diet with a good source of omega-3 fatty acids. The best sources are **flaxseed** and **fish oil**. (See Chapter 2 for more information.)

Flaxseed or Fish Oil (with meals)	
Cat/Small Dog (up to 14 lb)	1/2 tsp
Medium Dog (15-34 lb)	1 tsp
Large Dog (35-84 lb)	2 tsp
Giant Dog (85+ lb)	1 Tbsp

Alternative Veterinary Therapies

When dealing with a weakening heart it is always wise to work with your family veterinarian or an alternatively minded and experienced veterinarian. What follows are the therapies you would use under their guidance.

Cardiac Support Formula, produced by Animal Nutrition Technologies (ANT), is a nutraceutical formula that contains amino acids (taurine and L-carnitine), antioxidants (vitamin E, CoQ10), and minerals (magnesium, selenium) required for optimum cardiac health, heartbeat, and rhythm.

Chinese Herbal Therapy. Heart Assist is an herbal blend that is intended to support animals with congestive heart failure, hypertension, arrythmias (irregular heart beats), and cardiomyopathy. Heart-specific Chinese Herbal Therapy should be used under the guidance of an experienced veterinarian.

The Nutritional Blood Test (NBT) assesses and balance levels of serum calcium, magnesium, sodium, potassium, and chloride. Optimal levels of minerals have a direct effect on contractility, electrical conduction and excitability of the cardiac muscle. In addition, heart-friendly nutrients such as CoQ10, L-carintine, taurine, and vitamin E can be added to the NBT nutraceutical therapy. (See Chapter 4 for more on the NBT.) The following are available from veterinarians who use the NBT.

Heart Drops provides homeopathic support for the heart muscle and improves cardiac rhythm.

Heart Drops (twice daily)	
Cat/Small Dog (up to 14 lb)	5 drops
Medium Dog (15-34 lb)	7 drops
Large Dog (35-84 lb)	10 drops
Giant Dog (85+ lb)	12 drops

Heart Formula is a natural remedy that helps the body to normalize heart function while reducing nervous tension and anxiety.

Heart Formula (twice daily)	
Cat/Small Dog (up to 14 lb)	7 drops
Medium Dog (15-34 lb)	10 drops
Large Dog (35-84 lb)	12 drops
Giant Dog (85+ lb)	15 drops

Hawthorn has been shown to increase blood flow to the heart by decreasing resistance in surrounding blood vessels. Hawthorn lowers blood pressure, acting much like an ACE inhibitor. Combining hawthorn with lower doses of prescription medicines is a great way to use traditional and complementary therapies together. Hawthorne is a medicinal herb. If your dog or cat has heart disease, use only under the guidance of your veterinarian.

Hawthorn (daily)	
Cat/Small Dog (up to 14 lb)	15-20 mg
Medium Dog (15-34 lb)	25-35 mg
Large Dog (35-84 lb)	35-50 mg
Giant Dog (85+ lb)	50-65 mg

Acupuncture can be extremely beneficial in dogs and cats with heart problems, as it can help rebalance the body and remove energy blockages. When dealing with critical heart problems, consult a certified veterinary acupuncturist who is experienced with dogs or cats with heart disease. (See Chapter 4 for more information on acupuncture.)

Heartworms

One of the most-feared diseases of dogs and cats is heartworms, caused by a parasite *Dirofilaria immitis*. Heartworms are transmitted only via the bite of an infested mosquito. When a mosquito bites an infested animal, it ingests heartworm larvae. When it bites another animal, it passes on the infestation. Once in the bloodstream, these larvae circulate throughout the body, maturing into adult heartworms in about six months. Mature worms take up residence in the heart and lungs and begin producing their own larvae, perpetuating the deadly cycle. If the cycle is not interrupted, the worms in the heart, which may grow to one foot long, can clump together, impeding blood flow through the heart chambers and valves, leading to secondary heart and lung disease.

Early Warning Signs

The signs and symptoms of heartworm disease and heart and lung disease are very similar.

What Will Your Veterinarian Recommend?

Heartworm is one of those diseases in which every preventive and treatment method has its inherent risks. If your animal is diagnosed positive with heartworms, the treatment has potential side effects. The older method of intravenous arsenic injections (Caparsolate), required strict hospital confinement and had serious potential complications, such as local irritation and systemic reactions. Most veterinarians now opt for a newer drug, Immiticide, which is much less risky in dogs but does have potential serious side effects in cats. If you chose Immiticide, supporting both the heart and liver function is recommended (see heart conditions earlier in this Part, and liver conditions in Part 8).

Treatment aside, the best method for addressing heartworms is with prevention. Most veterinarians opt for monthly preventives such as Ivermectin (Heartgard) or Milbemycine oxime (Interceptor) over the daily diethylcarbamazine preventive. In all instances, most holistic veterinarians recommend avoiding combination medications that not only address heartworms but also intestinal parasites, fleas, and ticks.

At-Home Support and Prevention

Many holistically oriented companions chose the more natural approach to heartworm prevention, such as additional super supplements (see Chapter 2) and the Goldstein Food Plan (see Chapter 1), along with modifying existing medical protocols to limit the potential toxicity and side effects. One method would be to extend the monthly preventive heartworm medication from every 30 days to 45 days, spreading the total medication from one year to over an 18-month period.

Diet

Another approach taken by naturally oriented guardians is to rely on the immune-boosting effects of a natural dietary program to repel mosquitoes and prevent spread of the disease. In this method the animal is tested twice yearly for heartworm antigen using the occult test (good for dogs, less accurate for cats). This approach relies on natural immunity to prevent the disease, and if the animal does get the disease then the guardian would treat with immiticide for dogs or supportive medical therapy for cats. Follow the Goldstein Food Plan (Level II or III), which is designed to fully boost immunity and improve natural resistance. Add freshly chopped garlic to every meal. The recommended dosage is 1 clove for cats or small dogs, 2 cloves for medium, large and giant dogs. One word of caution—research has shown that garlic can thin the blood, so it is recommended *not* to use garlic before surgery or if you animal has anemia.

You must evaluate the risk of heartworm in your locality (if there is a high incidence of mosquitoes, your pets spend lots of time outdoors, or you live near the woods, a lake, or swamp, your pet is at high risk) and your commitment to natural methods before deciding on a prevention program. Your choice should be either a conventional approach alone or in combination with a natural approach—this disease is potentially serious and needs to be caught early.

Homeopathic Remedies

The more natural approach to heartworm prevention involves homeopathic protocols including the use of heartworm nosodes, and the use of natural worming and mosquito prevention type of products, such as Earth Animal's Herbal Internal Powder and No More Worms. (See Resources for a complete list of available remedies.) This mosquito prevention program is similar to the full program recommended for the prevention of fleas (see Chapter 6).

Internal (Yeast) and **Herbal Powders**. A combination of Earth Animal's Internal (Yeast) and Herbal Powders has proven effective in helping to prevent bites from mosquitoes. During the mosquito season, mix 4 ounces of Herbal Internal Powder with 8 ounces of Internal Powder. Follow package dose for Internal Powder. (See Chapter 6 for more information on Internal Powder.)

No More Fleas, from Earth Animal, contains garlic, wormwood, alfalfa, and nettles to help repel biting insects.

No More Fleas (twice daily)	
Cat/Small Dog (up to 14 lb)	5-7 drops
Medium Dog (15-34 lb)	10 drops
Large Dog (35-84 lb)	12-15 drops
Giant Dog (85+ lb)	18-20 drops

No More Worms and Fungi, from Earth Animal, contains black walnut, wormwood, cloves, and quassia proven effective in the prevention of mosquitoes and heartworms

No More Worms and Fungi (twice daily)	
Cat/Small Dog (up to 14 lb)	7 drops
Medium Dog (15-34 lb)	10 drops
Large Dog (35-84 lb)	12-15 drops
Giant Dog (85+ lb)	18-20 drops

Herbal Flea Collars for Dogs and Cats

These types of collars repel fleas with a blend of herbs and safe essential oils without containing potentially dangerous pesticides and nerve gas derivatives.

Topical Remedies

Earth Animal's **Bug Off** is a combination of rue, black walnut, and wormwood that can be sprayed as a preventative directly on the coat.

Alternative Veterinary Therapies

If your animal has been diagnosed with heartworm disease and requires treatment, your veterinarian can also add specific nutraceuticals that can support and protect involved organs, such as the heart, lungs, and liver.

The following formulas are available from veterinarians who utilize the NBT program (see Chapter 5 for more details). Doses are generally 1/2 tablet twice daily for cats, and 1 tablet for each 25 pounds twice daily for dogs.

Cardiac Support Formula supplies the amino acids, vitamins, minerals, and antioxidants required for optimum cardiac health.

Lung Support Formula contains vitamins and amino acids required for proper function of the lungs and bronchus.

Liver/Gallbladder Support Formula contains vitamins, minerals, amino acids, and antioxidants required to support detoxification, repair, and regenerate cells.

What's the Prognosis?

In matters of the heart, you are dealing with the most vital organ of the body; if the heart stops for just a matter of minutes, death from lack of oxygen will immediately occur. Therefore, your animal's prognosis will be directly related to early detection and prompt correction.

The ultimate answer to heart disease lies in prevention. Diet and exercise share space at the top of the list. However, if you are battling existing heart disease, the following will hold true: If the inflammatory process affecting the heart is discovered early and measures are taken to control or minimize the body's physical response, alternative and conventional therapies used in concert can be quite effective. If the measures described above are taken to strengthen the immune system and reduce its exaggerated response, the prognosis becomes excellent for control of the condition, assuring your animal a continuing high-quality of life.

Central Nervous System Diseases

Your animal's brain and nervous system need to not only "think clearly," but perform many automated processes related to the smooth functioning of the body. Besides controlling voluntary movement through the muscles, the nervous system is involved in vital involuntary functions, such as the beating of the heart and breathing by the lungs.

The brain houses many important glands, which control the body's metabolic and physiological functions. The hypothalamus, the anterior and posterior pituitary, and the pineal gland oversee the general nervous and hormonal control systems of the body.

The brain is categorized in sections called lobes, which carry out various functions. The cerebrum is the largest section of the brain and is composed of two hemispheres which house the following four lobes: the frontal lobe (motor control); the temporal lobes (hearing and vocal); the parietal lobe (sensation); and the occipital lobe (sight).

Other areas are the cerebellum, which oversees coordination, and the medulla, which serves as a transfer station for nerve signals from the brain to the spinal cord. The brain and nerve cells are sensitive to various nutrients and compounds. For example, a lack of oxygen for just minutes can cause destruction of nerve cells. The same is true for sugar. Lack of blood sugar as a result of injecting too much insulin (in the treatment of diabetes) can cause coma and death in a very short period of time.

Besides these strict requirements for sugar and oxygen, the brain and the nervous system require specific nutrients for the insulating of the nerve sheaths that surround the electrical conduction pathways. Lecithin, known in human circles as "brain food," is needed by the body to produce the proper insulation required for these electrical impulses to travel to their proper destination.

As sensitive as the brain is to specific chemicals and nutrients, it is also equally sensitive to the same types of insults as other organ systems. Injury to the brain from an accident can cause permanent brain damage or convulsions and a continuous inflammatory process, secondary to excessive free radicals without neutralizing antioxidants. This can lead to degeneration, premature aging, senility, or even a brain tumor. It is for these reasons that a proper diet (void of harsh chemical additives and preservatives) containing the necessary antioxidants, vitamins, minerals, and phytonutrients is so important when it comes to the health of the brain and nervous system.

Cognitive Dysfunction

If you have an animal who is moving into his or her "golden years," you might have wondered whether dogs and cats get Alzheimer's Disease. While canine dementia isn't officially called Alzheimer's, older dogs (and sometimes cats) can get a similar disorder called cognitive dysfunction, or CD.

CD is a disorder of geriatric dogs and cats that manifests as a change in the behavior or cognitive functioning of the animal. These changes are distinct from primary medical problems such as blindness, deafness, or arthritis, which can also result in a behavior change. Your veterinarian may perform a blood screen and other diagnostic tests to rule out such an underlying medical problem.

Early Warning Signs

Depression, lethargy, listlessness, continual barking or meowing, sleeplessness, and staring into walls are typical signs of senility or cognitive dysfunction.

Your dog or cat may be developing CD if he or she displays one or more of the following signs:

- Disoriented, forgetful, doesn't seem to hear you or respond to outside stimuli.
- Does not recognize familiar people.
- Does not interact with family—will not stand to be petted.
- Sleeps more during the day, less at night.
- More restless in general.
- Loss of bladder control.
- Loss of energy and enthusiasm.
- Difficulty climbing stairs.
- Shaking and trembling.

In people, this type of behavior is associated with dementia or Alzheimer's disease. It is easier to recognize these changes in people due to their progressive inability to function in society. With animals, the signs can be more subtle, and CD often manifests concurrently with conditions such as osteoarthritis, in which pain and inflammation can also affect the behavior of the animal.

What Will Your Veterinarian Recommend?

Deprenyl (Anipryl) is often recommended for the treatment of cognitive dysfunction in dogs.

While we have concerns about overuse of medication in general, deprenyl may be different. It belongs to a class of agents nicknamed "smart drugs" for their ability to preserve and protect brain function and delay loss of cognition. In fact, they are considered by many health professionals as antiaging allies in the human field. Deprenyl has been used in Europe for over 20 years, and is commonly prescribed for Parkinson's disease.

As people and animals age, the body begins to produce more of an enzyme called monoamine oxidase B (MOAB). (Patients with Alzheimer's have extremely high levels of MOAB.) MOAB breaks down a key neurotransmitter called dopamine, lessening its concentration in the body. Deprenyl inhibits this enzyme, helping to restore adequate levels of dopamine. But it is considered an "irreversible inhibitor" of MOAB, an action that may have future unknown side effects. That's why we're still cautious about it.

In recent surveys it is estimated that 60 percent of older animals (over 7 and 8 years) have at least one of the symptoms of CD. We are in favor of the use of deprenyl in animals exhibiting signs of classic cognitive dysfunction, yet we remain concerned about its potential for indiscriminate use. A quick scan of the veterinary archives shows that deprenyl is being considered for:

- a Poodle with nighttime aggression
- a grieving Chihuahua
- a Standard Poodle with fear of thunderstorms
- a Doberman that snapped at a baby
- a cat that was meowing too much

You can see the potential to attribute many behavioral conditions to cognitive dysfunction and prescribe deprenyl as a "magic bullet" therapy. Athough the drug is being embraced by many practitioners within the holistic community, it is still a drug and may have side effects, known and unknown. The manufacturer states that "Clinical experience with this drug is limited and the adverse effect profile may change." What works for humans may not work for dogs or cats.

In our view, the real issue that must be asked is: "Why did the brain function go out of balance in the first place?" If you check the available research, the expert veterinarians all focus on the condition itself and the associated symptoms and changes in personality. Research (especially in people) is focused on such causes as the increased MAOB activity, the deposition of a protein by-product called Amyloid, or the side effects of heavy metal exposure. There is not much focus, however, on events such as a local allergic or inflammatory reaction in the brain, secondary to an insult (such as an adverse reaction to a vaccination or continual ingesting of chemical additives and preservatives), leading to this degeneration of the brain and nervous system.

At-Home Support and Prevention

Because cognitive dysfunction is a newly recognized disorder in companion animals, there are few references in the literature regarding holistic approaches. We know that in people with Alzheimer's, there has been a great deal of success utilizing alternative methods, especially nutritional support, to reestablish failing memory and to restore the ability to function in society.

As with other chronic degenerative conditions, aging and CD are fueled by a weakened immune system secondary to nutritional imbalances, emotional stress, and exposure to repeated environmental toxins or medical stresses (such as chronic use of drugs and vaccines). The resulting secondary inflammation in the brain can lead to loss of cognition and the associated symptoms listed above. It is relatively easy to wait for CD to be diagnosed. The real question you should be asking is: What can I do for my dog or cat to help prevent CD and senility from taking hold to begin with?

> **Follow the Goldstein Antiaging Program**
>
> 1. Live-enzyme foods—to provide essential antioxidants and phytonutrients.
> 2. Fresh filtered water—to flush out toxins, thereby reducing inflammation.
> 3. Exercise and play—to improve circulation, simulate the body and challenge the mind.

Holistic veterinarians often observe the positive effects of improved cognition with the addition of proper nutrition and enhancement of the immune system. If your animal is suffering from one of the signs of dementia, before experimenting with drugs with potential side effects, we suggest that you approach the problem by using the following steps.

Nutrients

The following nutrients can be found in your health food store.

Vitamin E is one of the most powerful antiaging vitamins available. It protects cell membranes from free-radical damage, helps stave off a host of age-related disorders, and has shown tremendous promise in halting and even reversing early signs of Alzheimer's.

Vitamin E (once daily)	
Cat/Small Dog (up to 14 lb)	200 iu
Medium Dog (15-34 lb)	400 iu
Large Dog (35-84 lb)	600 iu
Giant Dog (85+ lb)	800 iu

Ginkgo biloba is harvested from one of the oldest living species of trees on the planet and is known as "the memory enhancer." Recent research shows that this herb may be effective in the early stages of Alzheimer's disease.

Ginkgo liquid tincture (twice daily)	
Cat/Small Dog (up to 14 lb)	5 drops
Medium Dog (15-34 lb)	7 drops
Large Dog (35-84 lb)	10 drops
Giant Dog (85+ lb)	12 drops

Phosphatidylserine (PS). Studies in people have shown that PS can help manage and reverse memory loss, even in those with early signs of dementia and Alzheimer's. PS helps nourish the brain's delicate neurological pathways, nurturing and revitalizing brain cells. In humans, there is evidence that this natural supplement also supports sleep, improves hormonal balance, and eases anxiety.

Phosphatidylserine (once daily)	
Cat/Small Dog (up to 14 lb)	50 mg
Medium Dog (15-34 lb)	100 mg
Large/Giant Dog (35+ lb)	150 mg

Coenzyme Q10 is one of the best all-around antioxidants. It boosts energy in the mitochondria, the power plant contained in every cell of the body.

Coenzyme Q10 (daily)	
Cat/Small Dog (up to 14 lb)	25 mg
Medium Dog (15-34 lb)	50 mg
Large Dog (35-84 lb)	75 mg
Giant Dog (85+ lb)	75-125 mg

Herbal Remedies

Calm Down, from Earth Animal, is a combination of the medicinal herbs ginkgo biloba, gota kola, and chamomile, to help soothe the brain and nervous system.

Occupy the Brain

Just as with humans, animals respond to mental challenges to keep learning. You can keep your cat or dog interested in life with play, tricks, learning, and TTEAM. Linda Tellington-Jones, the founder of TTEAM, has developed an entire system of working with animals using simple materials. For example, set up a simple maze of 3-foot poles and then gently guide your dog through the maze, or coax your cat through by dragging a catnip mouse in front of her. For further information on TTEAM, see the Resources section.

Alternative Veterinary Therapies

For early signs of CD, you may want to begin a prevention program with the vitamins and nutraceuticals mentioned above. For more serious or advanced symptoms of CD, it is recommended that you work with an experienced veterinarian. The following remedies are available through veterinarians who utilize the NBT process. Dose according to your veterinarian's recommendation.

Brain Nerve Support Formula, is a fixed nutraceutical formulation that contains a mixture of vitamins, minerals, and specific nutrients all designed to support the functioning and healing of the brain, including lecithin, phosphatidyl serine, carnitine, and tryptophan, as well as antioxidant vitamins.

Brain Drops, a low-potency homeopathic called a liquescence that helps to improve the circulation to the brain and nervous system.

Brain Nerve Formula, a medicinal herbal combination that helps to tonify the brain and nervous system.

Senility. This Chinese herbal formula is designed specifically for CD and is used along with the NBT nutraceutical program.

Acupuncture. Additionally you may want to get the opinion of a certified veterinary acpuncturist (see Chapter 4). Acupuncture, along with a superior nutritional program and specific nutrients can be extremely beneficial in slowing down the process of degeneration and reestablishing better mental functioning.

Degenerative Myelopathy (DM)

Weakness in the hind legs is quite common in dogs, especially large breeds such as German Shepherds. There are numerous causes of hind leg weakness, the most common being hip dysplasia, degenerative joint diseases (DJD), and arthritis (of the legs and the spine). The popularity of certain large dog breeds has led to an increasing incidence of inherited weaknesses, including DM.

Unfortunately, many people choose puppies from litters whose parents have been inbred to the degree that serious genetic problems occur. Some can be corrected or managed, others cannot.

Weaknesses in the hind legs caused by degenerating and painful joints, cartilage, tendons, and connective tissue respond quite well to both conventional and alternative therapies. Not so with degenerative myelopathy. The hallmark of this neuromuscular disorder is a slowly progressive weakness of both hind legs. Although it is not painful, the animals show incoordination (ataxia) and partial paralysis (paresis) with or without urinary and/or fecal incontinence. This disorder resembles multiple sclerosis in humans and occurs most frequently in males of medium and large breeds, particularly German Shepherds. Other susceptible breeds include Old English Sheepdogs, Labrador Retrievers, Boxers, Belgian Sheepdogs, Chesapeake Bay Retrievers, Siberian Huskies, and Kerry Blue Terriers.

What Will Your Veterinarian Recommend?

Previously, dogs with DM received a grim prognosis. According to conventional veterinary wisdom, effective treatment for DM has not been reported, and affected dogs usually progress to a state of severe non-ambulatory paraparesis within a year of the initial diagnosis. But happily, our story does not end there.

New Treatment Options for DM

Research veterinarian Robert Clemmons, DVM, PhD, has released some fascinating aspects of his research into DM from his Department of Neurology and Neurosurgery at the University of Florida Veterinary School at Gainesville. He has found that the immune system is out of balance in DM patients, giving rise to a markedly elaborated inflammatory response, and that this response plays an important role in the progression of this complex spinal disorder.

We have spoken directly to Dr. Clemmons to further discuss the symptoms, diagnosis, and treatment of DM patients. It is refreshing to hear a knowledgeable conventional-trained veterinarain refer to many attributes that our holistic approach offers to an animal. Dr Clemmons' therapeutic protocol centers on providing natural antioxidants to decrease the immune inflammatory response. His research shows that his protocols are up to 80 percent effective. That is extraordinary for a condition that most veterinary textbooks write off with an abrupt, "No treatment or cure known." Furthermore, Dr. Clemmons is attempting to produce a reliable, replicable diagnostic test for DM. This would herald an earlier accurate diagnosis with the possibility of earlier corrective therapy. Here is this dedicated researcher's treatment protocol:

1. Controlled, aerobic exercise. Allowing your dog to run loose in the backyard is not the correct exercise!

2. Oral administration of aminocaproic acid (to reduce a type of neural scarring resulting from the inflammatory process) and N-acetylcysteine (a free-radical scavenger). Both these preparations are available from WestLab Pharmacy in Gainesville, Florida. If clinical improvement occurs, you can reduce the N-acetylcysteine to every other day dosage, alternating with #3 below. It is of the utmost importance that you first take your dog to your veterinarian for an accurate diagnosis, since your veterinarian will have to issue a prescription to obtain these preparations. Both have minimal side effects.

3. Vitamin E in large doses (2,000 iu per day) for any size dog. At this high dose, vitamin E is a nonsteroidal anti-inflammatory agent. It also improves local circulation and thus oxygenation to the affected sites. The use of aspirin-like agents is contraindicated when these high doses are used due to excessive blood thinning.

4. Vitamin C at 1,000 mg twice a day provides antioxidant effects against prostaglandins and other harmful cellular chemicals produced by an inflammatory response.

5. High potency B vitamins every 12 hours completes the nutritional program. It is well established that B1, B6, and B12 are indicated for their beneficial effects on nerve cells.

Dr. Clemmons' says: "We also recommend that flea control products with which the DM patient may come into contact be restricted to

---

Dr. Clemmons' DM Shopping List

Medications:
- Acetylcysteine and Aminocaproic acid under the guidance of a veterinarian

Dietary Supplements:
- Tofu (4-6 ounces) daily with food
- Carrots (2 raw or 4 cooked) daily
- Sardines (2 or 1 Tbs ground Flax seeds) daily
- Garlic (2 raw cloves or 1/2 to 1 tsp powdered) daily with food
- Ginger (dry or fresh 1/2 to 1 tsp) daily with food
- Mustard (1/2 to 1 tsp dry) daily with food
- GLA (500 mg borage, black current or evening primrose oil) 2 times a day
- Coenzyme Q10 (100 mg) once a day
- Ginkgo biloba (1 capsule or 50 mg standardized extract) 2 times a day
- American ginseng or Dong quai (1 capsule) once a day
- Siberian ginseng (1 capsule) 2 times a day
- Green tea (1 capsule or 1 cup) 2 times a day
- Grape seed extract (1-50 mg capsule or 1 cup grape juice) once a day
- Bromelain (250-2000 gdu) twice a day
- Curcumin (500 mg) twice a day
- Vitamin E (2000 IU) once a day
- Vitamin C (build up to 1000 mg) twice a day
- Vitamin B complex (B100s) twice a day
- Selenium (200 mg) once a day

carbamate and pyrethrum products. Heartworm prevention should be limited to daily medication with a diethylcarbamazine product. I do not recommend dogs with DM receiving ivermectin (Heartgard), styrid caracide, or Filaribits Plus, as all may be associated with potential problems."

Alternative Veterinary Therapies

Your veterinarian may also recommend the following remedies.

Acupuncture

Since acupuncture removes energy blocks and can stimulate healing, this modality should also be considered (see Chapter 4 for more details).

Nutritional Blood Analysis Test (NBT)

Having your veterinarian perform an NBT to pick up on nutritional imbalances and correct gland weaknesses and imbalances is essential. In addition to Dr. Clemmons' nutritional recommendations, the NBT will help to identify underlying gland weaknesses that may be causing the exaggerated immune response. Many of the vitamins, minerals, enzymes and foods such as garlic, bromelain, vitamins C, E, B, and selenium can be added to the NBT powder making it easy for you to administer to your animal. Also available from veterinarians who utilize the NBT are:

Nutraceuticals

Brain/Nerve Support Formula, contains nerve-friendly nutrients that can help to feed the nervous stystem and support better functioning of the nerves to the hind legs. It also supports DNA synthesis and provides the repair nutrients for the brain and nervous system.

Spinal Nerve Drops, a combination homeopathic, can help to lessen the inflammation and improve regeneration of the spinal cord and nerves.

Spinal Nerve Drops (twice daily)	
Cat/Small Dog (up to 14 lb)	7 drops
Medium Dog (15-34 lb)	10 drops
Large Dog (35-84 lb)	12 drops
Giant Dog (85+ lb)	15 drops

Chinese Herbal Therapy

The Chinese herbal remedy H99 Myelopathy can be beneficial in working with the above-mentioned nutraceuticals to help slow down the degeneration and reestablish nervous control of the hind legs. Dose one capsule for each 10 to 20 pounds of body weight.

Seizures/Epilepsy

A seizure is often the result of an inflammatory process in the brain. While seizures are most commonly associated with epilepsy, there are other conditions that can cause convulsions: Low blood sugar (hypoglycemia) that can be secondary to overdosing insulin; head trauma (when hit by a car); foods laced with chemical additives and preservatives; an allergic reaction to potent medications or environmental toxins (pesticides or herbicides); a reaction to a vaccination; or a disease such as a brain tumor or a clogged liver.

Seizures are most common in Beagles, Border Collies, Boxers, Collies, German Shepherds, Golden Retrievers, Labrador Retrievers, Keeshonds, Poodles, Saint Bernards, Springer Spaniels, Welsh Corgis, and Wire-haired Fox Terriers. Epilepsy is rare in cats.

Early Warning Signs

Seizures generally offer no early warning signs. As in people, dogs and cats can experience seizures ranging from the barely noticeable petite mal seizures to the serious convulsions of grand mal seizures. Petit mal seizures, lasting 10 to 25 seconds, typically are nothing more than the clicking of teeth or repeated blinking. In a grand mal seizure, animals may fall on their sides, totally loose awareness, experience violent jerking, uncontrollable leg movement, grinding the teeth, and excessive salivation for a few minutes or longer. Usually in 10 to 15 minutes they are back to 100 percent unless there is a more serious underlying cause. Seizures will often occur at night or early in the morning.

What Will Your Veterinarian Recommend?

One of the difficulties of treating epilepsy is that you and your veterinarian may not be able to determine the cause of the seizures. Veterinarians usually arrive at a diagnosis of epilepsy only after eliminating all other possible causes.

When treating a seizuring animal, veterinarians look for the physical conditions that can trigger these episodes. Recording the complete history that has led to the seizures is important. This should include vaccination history. You should be questioned about a possible head trauma, low blood sugar, or other conditions that have been known to cause seizures.

Convulsions are one of the potential side effects of repeated annual vaccinations. The injection of foreign materials into the blood can evoke an allergic or inflammatory response in the brain and nerves, upsetting the body's natural balance and resulting in seizures. As with any inflammatory process, the situation is only worsened when the immune system is weakened.

If the seizures happen infrequently and are quite mild, your veterinarian may simply advise you to observe the condition and report back if the seizures increase in severity or frequency. Frequent seizures (every two to four weeks) often require the use of sedative drugs such as Phenobarbital. More resistant seizures may require combination drugs such as potassium bromide to bring them under control.

Be forewarned: Extended use of Phenobarbital, which is the most common drug prescribed, destroys liver cells and sets the stage for more serious conditions. This precaution being noted, Phenobarbital does offer the most effective method for controlling seizures. Your veterinarian will be aware of the side effects of the drugs. As soon as the seizures are under control, she or he will seek the minimal effective dose of medication. Your veterinarian should perform periodic blood tests to monitor for liver damage and phenobarbital levels.

At-Home Support and Prevention

Epilepsy, while very frightening because of its unpredictability and visual severity, should be viewed like any other inflammatory process. You must feed and nourish the inflamed system—the brain. Mention "feeding the brain" to some conventional doctors and you'll get that familiar look of disbelief. However, not addressing the metabolic needs of the brain or exploring nutritional deficiencies, adverse reactions to drugs or vaccines, or exposure to foreign chemicals, is a real shortcoming of allopathic medical therapy. If you address this inflammation early, you may be able to reduce the amount of medication necessary or eliminate the need for drugs altogether.

Start your home program by addressing prior vaccines with *Thuja occidentalis*. Since some seizures are linked to past vaccinations, you should first clear the body of the potential negative effects of prior vaccinations. This treatment alone may

Peaches' Story

Peaches was a Standard Poodle who suffered from epilepsy for nine years. Over years of treatment, her guardians visited many veterinarians, including both conventional and holistic. Through the use of medication, they were able to keep Peaches comfortable and seizure-free for many years. However, the chronic use of Phenobarbital eventually took its toll, and caused a secondary liver problem (cirrhosis). Dr. Bob worked with Peaches for about a year, using nutrition, combination homeopathy, and Chinese herbs, and during that time she remained totally off the Phenobarbital, seizure free, and stable from the adverse secondary effects of the drugs.

end seizures for some animals. For vaccinated animals give *Thuja* once daily for seven days. (For instructions on administering homeopathic remedies, see Chapter 4.)

The following nutritional program can be used safely in conjuction with drug therapies. If after two to three months there have been no seizures, ask your veterinarian about reducing the dosage of medications. *Do not change your animal's medication without the consent of your veterinarian.*

Diet

Nutrition is the key to controlling seizures. For animals experiencing seizures, feeding at least Level 1 of The Goldstein Food Plan (see Chapter 1) is important. Feeding a naturally preserved commercial food offers a diet that's free of chemical additives and preservatives, which can provoke seizures. Following Levels II or III of the Food Plan would be more beneficial to boost your animal's immune system.

Nutrients

Lecithin. Rebuild the nerves' protective insulation with Lecithin. In an undernourished body, the myelin sheath that surrounds and insulates nerve cells begins to thin as a result of free radical damage and resultant inflammation. A nutritional and antioxidant depleted body doesn't have the necessary nutrients to regenerate this protective, insulating layer. Lecithin is essential as it contains both phosphatidylcholine and phosphatidylserine building blocks required for the proper formation of the insulating sheaths. It is available at heath food stores.

Lecithin (once daily)	
Cat/Small Dog (up to 14 lb)	100 mg
Medium Dog (15-34 lb)	250 mg
Large Dog (35-84 lb)	500 mg
Giant Dog (85+ lb)	500-1000 mg

Phosphatidylserine (PS) is classified as a phospholipid, one of the important components of the cell membranes of the brain and nerves. These cells require a healthy membrane in order to properly transmit nerve impulses throughout the body. Unlike other cells of the body, nerve cells do not rely on fats and protein for their energy; rather, they rely almost entirely on sugar, and Phosphatidylserine is believed to improve the utilization of sugar by the nerve cells. PS is available in most health food stores.

Phosphatidylserine (once daily)	
Cat/Small Dog (up to 14 lb)	50 mg
Medium Dog (15-34 lb)	100 mg
Large Dog (35-84 lb)	100-150 mg
Giant Dog (85+ lb)	150-200 mgs

Vitamin B Complex. When under stress, the body uses more B vitamins in an effort to calm and rebalance itself. B Complex contains B1, B2, B3, B5, B6, B12 and others such as choline and folic acid. The B vitamins are intricately involved in chemical compounds called neurotransmitters that pass the electrical message via the nerve cells.

Vitamin B Complex (once daily)	
Cat/Small Dog (up to 14 lb)	50 mg
Medium Dog (15-34 lb)	75 mg
Large Dog (35-84 lb)	100 mg
Giant Dog (85+ lb)	150 mgs

Essential Fatty Acids (EFAs)

EFAs have been proven to have anti-inflammatory effects on the body. Omega-3 fatty acids that contain EPA and DHA should be part of any dietary program designed to control seizures.

The best sources are **fish (salmon) oil** and **flax oil**. We recommend a combination of both (at a ratio of 50/50) for epileptics.

Flax and Fish oil combination (with meals)	
Cat/Small Dog (up to 14 lb)	1 tsp
Medium Dog (15-34 lb)	2 tsp
Large Dog (35-84 lb)	1 Tbsp
Giant Dog (85+ lb)	1 1/2 Tbsp

Gamma-linoleic acid (GLA) is an anti-inflammatory type fatty acid that is found in abundance in evening primrose oil, which should be added especially in animals that experience grand mal or cluster seizures. Evening primrose oil is available in health food stores.

Evening Primrose Oil (daily)	
Cat/Small Dog (up to 14 lb)	250 mgs
Medium Dog (15-34 lb)	500 mgs
Large Dog (35-84 lb)	750 mgs
Giant Dog (85+ lb)	1000 mgs

Herbal and Homeopathic Remedies

Calm Down, from Earth Animal, is a combination herbal extract that contains ginkgo, gota kola, and chamomile that will help to settle the brain and nervous system.

Calm Down (twice daily)	
Cat/Small Dog (up to 14 lb)	7 drops
Medium Dog (15-34 lb)	10 drops
Large Dog (35-84 lb)	12-15 drops
Giant Dog (85+ lb)	16-20 drops

Flower Essences. Throughout this book we often speak about the relationship between disease and the emotions. Certainly this is true when dealing with a convulsive disorder. In all instances of convulsions we recommend support with flower essences. Our favorites are a pair of flower essences that can help stop seizures before they start and help to prevent seizures from occurring. These powerful flower essences can help your dog or cat recover more quickly from seizures, have fewer seizures and reduce the dependency on medications such as Phenobarbital and potassium bromide.

Two remedies developed for us by Sharon Callahan are **Anti-Seizure Daily Drops** and **Post-Seizure Recovery**. We recommend that the two remedies be used along with the natural program listed above, and they should be used as desired. Dose five drops directly into the mouth as needed.

The rate of success in treatment of epilepsy with flower essences varies widely from complete cessation of seizures to a mild reduction of the number and duration of seizures. Almost all animals experience some positive change.

Veterinary Alternative Therapies

When dealing with convulsions it is always a good idea to consult with an holistic practitioner, one who understands and is experienced with seizures. After a physical examination and evaluation of the medical history, your holistic practitioner may even prescribe a specific homeopathic or herbal preparation that can replace both the Phenobarbital and potassium bromide. *(Note: Never replace your animal's medicine without permission from your veterinarian.)*

NBT. Request that your veterinarian perform a Nutritional Blood Test (NBT) to help determine underlying gland imbalances and weaknesses as well as nutritional imbalances that might be causing the seizures. (See Chapter 4 for more information.)

Besides the custom-blended nutraceutical and antioxidant-rich supplement, your veterinarian may recommend several of the following remedies depending on your animal's blood results and clinical condition.

Brain Nerve Support Formula, a fixed nutraceutical formulation that supplies brain-friendly nutrients such as lecithin, phosphatidylserine, B vitamins, and tryptophan. Dose 1 tablet per 25 pounds of body weight.

Epilepsy Drops, a combination homeopathic remedy, and **Calming Formula**, a medicinal herbal remedy, are two prescription natural remedies that have been proven to prevent seizures.

Epilepsy Drops (twice daily)	
Cat/Small Dog (up to 14 lb)	5 drops
Medium Dog (15-34 lb)	7 drops
Large Dog (35-84 lb)	10-12 drops
Giant Dog (85+ lb)	13-15 drops

Calming Formula (twice daily)	
Cat/Small Dog (up to 14 lb)	7 drops
Medium Dog (15-34 lb)	10 drops
Large Dog (35-84 lb)	15 drops
Giant Dog (85+ lb)	20 drops

Chinese Herbal Therapy. Epitrol is helpful in controlling seizures (either along with or separate from Phenobarbital). Dose as directed by your veterinarian.

Acupuncture (see Chapter 4) has been shown to be effective in helping animals with epilepsy. The insertion of a needle through the skin into a specific acupuncture point sets up a local inflammatory response. The immune system responds with the release of endorphins, which further reduces inflammation. It is essential that this be performed by a certified veterinary acupuncturist, one who is experienced in the treatment of epilepsy.

What's the Prognosis?

These conditions are serious and require working closely with your veterinarian, but don't give up hope. With a high-quality diet, at-home support program, and your veterinarian's help, you can give your animal years of seizure-free, quality living.

Dermatological Diseases

The skin, your animal's largest and most visible organ, is a reflection of the quality of life inside. A shiny coat and clear skin are cardinal signs of good health. Anything short of a lustrous, gleaming coat should spur you to investigate further. Skin (dermatological) problems are the most common reason for visits to veterinary hospitals. In fact, chronic skin conditions are so widespread and varied that they often require the opinion of a board-certified veterinary dermatologist.

Skin Conditions

Skin conditions run the gamut from allergies (contact, airborne, food), external parasites (fleas, ticks, mites, lice), infections (bacterial, viral, fungal), and hormonal imbalances to more serious autoimmune skin diseases, in which the body is attacking its own skin. Animals with contact allergies will often bite their feet, belly, the tip of the tail, and the back of the hind legs.

Early Warning Signs

Skin disorders in animals pack a one-two punch: initial irritation followed by self-trauma as your animal incessantly licks, scratches, and chews the afflicted area. If you spot any of these early warning signs, you can treat your animal at home before more serious problems erupt. Then follow up with our preventive strategies. Common signs are:

- Dry skin
- Thickened, brittle hair coat
- Excessive shedding
- Odors, despite bathing
- Scabby areas
- Loss of hair on the belly, near the head of the tail or on the face
- Oily, greasy skin

If you wake up one morning to find a hairless patch of inflamed skin oozing a sticky, smelly material, and your animal frantically itching and biting, you must see your veterinarian.

What Will My Veterinarian Recommend?

Your family veterinarian may recommend any of the following to help diagnose the skin condition, depending upon the clinical picture of your animal:

- Physical examination for fleas or ticks, bacterial or fungal infection.
- Allergy testing (via skin or blood work) to determine contact, airborne or food allergies.
- Skin scraping to check for parasites such as sarcoptic or demodectic mange.
- Skin biopsy to check for specific types of skin disease.
- Blood test to check for underlying causes such as thyroid or adrenal disease.

Your veterinarian will likely prescribe cortisone or a course of antibiotics. He or she may also recommend antihistamines, medicated baths, or even a tranquilizer to calm the itching and self-trauma.

Within 48 hours, the raw spots should be healing nicely, and all may appear to be forgotten. But soon after, the peaceful interlude is broken by another scratch/itch episode, and the next bout comes right on the heels of the last one—resulting in more veterinary visits and rounds of medication. Soon, it seems, you're dealing with chronic skin problems that escalate, even though your veterinarian has prescribed more potent medications and specialized diets.

At-Home Support and Prevention

Our natural remedies will help to soothe minor irritations and stop the itch without burdening the immune system or interrupting the natural detoxification process. One word of caution: *To use natural remedies, you must catch the problem before there is broken skin.* If your animal has already chewed or scratched open the skin, see your veterinarian first. Use drugs if necessary to get the acute problem under control, then take action for long-term healing.

Natural Skin Soothers

Aloe vera gel, applied directly from a freshly opened leaf or from a store-bought gel, is one of our favorite home healers. You can also place a wet, cool black tea bag on the irritated spot; the tannins in the tea will soothe the irritation. Mineral-rich baking soda made into a paste also works well, as do fresh plantain leaves, a wild plant that grows throughout much of the US (see Chapter 5 for recipe). Stay with your animal for 15 minutes while your remedy of choice penetrates the skin. Treat the area twice daily for three days or until it is resolved. This procedure will often prevent the acute outbreak that requires a visit to your veterinarian.

Now that you've provided short-term relief, you can turn your attention to long-term skin and coat health.

Rest the Digestive System

Skipping one or two of your dog or cat's meals per week works wonders for maintaining beautiful fur, healthy skin, and all-around health. We often do a 24-hour meal-skip with our dog weekly—usually on Sunday, when we can be home to provide water and fresh juices such as carrot or apple. The next morning, feed breakfast as usual.

Meal-skipping frees up energy that would otherwise be used for digestion, enabling the body to cleanse, repair, and regenerate. We like to give our dogs a light meal just prior to the meal-skip. Oatmeal, yogurt, and apples as an "appetizer," or brown rice and carrots with a touch of olive oil work well. These light, low-protein meals are easy to digest.

Fasting Guidelines

Do not skip meals for:
- Puppies in their first year.
- Pregnant or nursing mothers.
- Diabetic animals or those with a chronic degenerative disease, without the supervision of your veterinarian.
- Elderly dogs who are unthrifty or wasting, unless under the guidance of a veterinarian.

Groom Your Dog or Cat Regularly

Brush and comb your animal's coat on a regular basis to loosen debris, loose hair, and dirt. Use a firm brush or special animal grooming mitt to help stimulate the skin and encourage natural oils to surface. Then use a comb to remove the dead hair and debris that have been lifted by the brushing.

Bathe Your Dog Gently and Sensibly

Shampooing your dog about once per month will help unclog the pores without stripping away the skin's natural oils. There are many natural shampoos available, so read labels carefully, and avoid harsh chemicals, insecticides, and synthetic ingredients.

After rinsing your dog thoroughly, mix 1 quart distilled water with 1/4 cup organic apple cider vinegar. Sponge the mixture onto your animal and rinse, being careful to avoid the eye area. Be sure to bathe your dog in a warm, draft-free area, and thoroughly dry the skin and coat before going outside.

If your animal goes to a groomer or your veterinarian's clinic for bathing, bring along your own shampoo and request that it be used. If your dog is a bit wary, tuck one of the "rescue" formulas into your pocket, such as Rescue Remedy, Calming Essence, or Anaflora's Recovery, and administer several drops upon the tongue before traveling and upon arrival at the groomer's.

Diet

- Follow the Goldstein Food Plan Level II or III (see Chapter 1).
- Feed skin-saving foods, such as chopped cabbage, shredded carrots, diced cucumbers, oatmeal, and cooked potato skins.
- Put celery, kale, parsley, carrots, and apples in a juicer for a skin-soothing tonic. Add organic apple cider vinegar to purified drinking water daily. Work up to 1/4–1/2 teaspoon per bowl of water for cats and small dogs, and up to 1–2 tablespoons for medium and large dogs.
- Make sure you feed high-quality protein, like lamb, chicken, or turkey. If you find that your animal is allergic to chicken or turkey there are numerous types of hypoallergenic foods now available. Amino acid-rich protein is required for healthy skin cells and normal hair growth.

Nutrients

Make sure to provide the following nutrients:

Essential Fatty Acids

Flaxseed oil is a rich source of essential omega-3 fatty acids (alpha linolenic acid, or ALA).

Evening primrose oil is a source of the anti-inflammatory fatty acid gamma-linolenic acid (GLA). These oils are fragile—exposed to light or heat, they can become rancid and ineffective. Look in the refrigerated section of your whole foods market for these healthy oils. Purchase an organic, cold-expeller pressed product in a dark bottle, and keep refrigerated or purchase capsules.

Organic Flaxseed or Evening Primrose Oil	(daily with meals)	
	Flax	Primrose
Cat/Small Dog (up to 14 lb)	1 tsp	250 mg
Medium Dog (15-34 lb)	2 tsp	500 mg
Large Dog (35-84 lb)	1 Tbsp	750 mg
Giant Dog (85 lb+)	1 1/2 Tbsp	1000 mg

Salmon oil (for cats) contains the important anti-inflammatory fatty acids DHA and EPA, as well as arachidonic acid, which is required by felines. Add 1 tsp per meal. (See Chapter 2 for more information on fatty acids.)

Vitamins and Minerals

Vitamin B-6, a natural antihistamine, will help quell the inflammatory response.

Vitamin B6 (twice daily)	
Cat/Small Dog (up to 14 lb)	25 mg
Medium Dog (15-34 lb)	50 mg
Large Dog (35-84 lb)	75 mg
Giant Dog (85+ lb)	100 mg

Quercetin (a flavinoid that is a natural anti-inflammatory and antihistamine) helps to relieve the symptoms of allergic reactions particularly of the skin and upper respiratory systems.

Quercetin (twice daily)	
Cat/Small Dog (up to 14 lb)	25-35 mg
Medium Dog (15-34 lb)	50-75 mg
Large Dog (35-84 lb)	75-100 mg
Giant Dog (85+ lb)	100-200 mg

Zinc is an essential mineral required for a healthy skin and coat. It is important for the proper division of new, healthy skin cells as well as the manufacture of essential fatty acids. Zinc has been clinically proven to be beneficial in the overall metabolism of the skin. Its deficiency has been linked to what is called zinc deficient dermatosis. This condition is usually found in growing puppies (especially Great Danes and Dobermans) and responds well to the addition of zinc to the diet. Many pet food manufacturers will use an inexpensive, inorganic source of zinc (such as zinc oxide), which is not well absorbed in the body and may set the stage for deficiencies.

Zinc (daily)	
Cat/Small Dog (up to 14 lb)	15 mg
Medium Dog (15-34 lb)	15-35 mg
Large Dog (35-84 lb)	35-85 mg
Giant Dog (85+ lb)	85-100 mg

Homeopathics

Scratch Free from Dr. Goodpet, and **Skin and Seborrhea** from Homeopet, are combination homeopathics that work quickly, particularly on acute irritations. Pick the one that best describes your animal's condition.

Give the following doses three times daily for 3 to 4 days. When the incessant itching has subsided and your animal is calmer, give the same number of drops per dose, but twice daily for 7 to 10 days, then discontinue. Follow this procedure for any future flare-ups.

Scratch Free or Seborrhea Drops (three times per day for 3-4 days)	
Cat/Small Dog (up to 14 lb)	7 drops
Medium Dog (15-34 lb)	10 drops
Large/Giant Dog (35+ lb)	12 drops

Itchy Skin, available from Earth Animal, is a combination herbal that contains nettles, red clover, and Echinacea.

Itchy Skin (twice daily)	
Cat/Small Dog (up to 14 lb)	7 drops
Medium Dog (15-34 lb)	10-12 drops
Large Dog (35-84 lb)	15 drops
Giant Dog (85+ lb)	20 drops

Use the Chinese herb **kai yeung** for continuous irritation and excess scratching. Available at health food stores, give the herb three times daily for 3 to 4 weeks or until symptoms abate; reduce the dosage by half for the next month, then discontinue.

Kai Yeung (three times daily)	
Cat/Small or Medium Dog (up to 34 lb)	1 caplet
Large/Giant Dog (35+ lb)	2 caplets

For extremely irritated, red, and itchy skin, use the homeopathic remedy **Rhus toxicodendron 6X** twice daily (or as often as every two to three hours) until you observe an improved appearance and less itching, usually by the end of the first day. Continue for one week. (See Chapter 4 for further instructions on administering homeopathic remedies.)

Rhus toxicodendron 6X (twice daily)	
Cat/Small or Medium Dog (up to 34 lb)	1 pellet
Large Dog (35-84 lb)	2 pellets
Giant Dog (85+ lb)	3 pellets

For dry, itchy, and smelly skin, use the homeopathic remedy **Sulfur 6X**. Give daily for three days; stop for a day and then repeat again for three days.

Sulfur 6X (daily for three days)	
Cat/Small or Medium Dog (up to 34 lb)	1 pellet
Large Dog (35-84 lb)	2 pellets
Giant Dog (85+ lb)	3 pellets

Detoxify for Prior Vaccinations

Vaccines are increasingly linked to chronic skin disease. An animal's immune system that has been weakened from a vaccine can become less efficient in eliminating wastes and often will react with an exaggerated inflammatory response. The skin shows the effects of accumulated toxins and over-reactive inflammation because it is the most visible organ. You can detoxify the body using the homeopathic remedy *Thuja occidentalis* (12X or 30C). Give once daily for seven days (see Chapter 3 for more information).

Flower Essences

The skin is a reflection of the inner environment, and if your animal is emotionally out of sorts, then a flower essence may be in order. (See Chapter 4.)

Evaluate the "emotional energy" in your home. If your animal is left home alone more than usual, or conditions are unsettled, your dog or cat may reflect his or her concern by biting, licking, or chewing excessively. The flower essences **Allergy** or **Lick Granuloma**, both available from

Anaflora, can help rebalance the emotions and set the stage for healing. Add 5 drops daily to the drinking water.

Skin Relief Spray

Dermasol skin relief spray can help dogs or cats who have moved beyond scratching into self-trauma. This over-the-counter product contains Retinol, which is proven to have beneficial effects on the skin. It can be used on dogs, cats, horses, and other animals and is effective on hot spots, insect bites, and other skin irritations.

Isabel, a cat belonging to our *Love of Animals* newsletter editor, had been suffering from flea bite dermatitis with much itching and self-trauma. "Izzy" spent her days huddled under a jade tree, frozen in one position. When she moved, she darted quickly as if trying to escape the discomfort. Her appetite dulled, making it difficult to feed her supplements that would support skin healing. Frequent bathing helped somewhat, but the scabs and scratching would quickly return.

Upon our recommendation, our editor purchased a bottle of Dermasol spray at an animal supply store. With the first application, her cat stopped biting herself, and by the second, her skin was healing and her fur was regaining its luster. The best part, she reported, was that the kitty's appetite returned along with her affectionate, loving nature.

While Dermasol is not purely natural, we believe it is an acceptable alternative to steroids and antibiotics, which are standard treatments offered by conventional veterinarians. It comes in spray and gel form.

Alternative Veterinary Therapies

Nutritional Blood Test (NBT). Chronic skin problems will often require the medical expertise of your veterinarian or a board-certified veterinary dermatologist. While medication is often necessary for skin conditions, you should also consider having your veterinarian run an NBT, and use combination nutraceutical formula or Chinese herbal remedy to help control the situation and minimize recurrences. The NBT analysis and recommended custom blended nutraceuticals is particularly beneficial for animals with skin problems that require chronic use of antihistamines, antibiotics, or cortisone.

In addition, your veterinarian may recommend some of the following natural remedies as part of the NBT analysis.

Skin Support Nutraceutical Formula supplies vitamins (such as vitamin C, A, E, and B6), minerals (such as zinc and potassium), and fatty and amino acids (such as flax, EPA, DHA, and glutamine). These nutrients are required to support new, healthy cell growth and metabolic functioning of the skin. Dosage is 1 tablet for every 25 pounds of body weight.

Derm Guard, the Chinese herbal remedy, is designed for animals suffering from inhalant or contact allergy and will often reduce the itching, biting, and scratching. Dosage is 1 tablet for every 20 pounds of body weight.

Combination Homeopathics

In addition, the following combination homeopathics or herbs are available from your veterinarian and can be helpful, depending on the type of allergy or irritation.

Allergy Formula is an anti-inflammatory and anti-itch remedy for the skin.

Flea Formula is used to alkalinize and nourish the blood while assisting the body in its defense against fleas.

Skin Drops helps to improve the functioning of the skin.

Allergy/Flea Formulas and Skin Drops *(twice daily)*	
Cat/Small Dog (up to 14 lb)	7 drops
Medium Dog (15-34 lb)	10 drops
Large Dog (35-84 lb)	15 drops
Giant Dog (85+ lb)	20 drops

Allergy Drops helps to reduce itching, biting, and scratching.

Fungal Drops helps to reduce the symptoms associated with fungal infestation.

Dust and Mold Drops can help to homeopathically desensitize an animal to the effects of dust, molds, and spores.

Flea Drops helps to decrease flea allergies and the self-trauma associated with flea bite dermatitis.

Grass Drops can help to homeopathically desensitize an animal to the effects of grass pollens.

Tree Drops can help to homeopathically desensitize an animal to the effects of tree allergies

Allergy, Fungal, Dust & Mold, Flea, Grass and Tree Drops (twice daily)	
Cat/Small Dog (up to 14 lb)	5 drops
Medium Dog (15-34 lb)	7 drops
Large Dog (35-84 lb)	10 drops
Giant Dog (85+ lb)	15 drops

What's the Prognosis?

Since the skin is the largest organ of detoxification and the effects are most uncomfortable, it is essential to ease the discomfort your animal is suffering. The best remedies are those that do not inhibit detoxification, but rather support your animal's immune system, which will in turn stop the chronic cycle of skin disorders. While medication such as antiobiotics and steriods may be necessary for acute conditions, prevention, using the above program is key to long-term skin health.

Healing Tip

While treating your animal's itchiness with natural remedies, consider fashioning an Elizabethan collar to keep your animal from biting himself, breaking the cycle of self-trauma which propagates the problem.

Gastrointestinal Diseases

The gastrointestinal (GI) tract consists of the mouth, esophagus, stomach, small intestines, large intestines, colon, and anus. You can imagine how important your animal's diet is to the system that takes in food, digests it, extracts nutrients, and then expels the remaining wastes.

There are a wide range of problems that effect the GI tract, including intestinal parasites such as round, hook, or whipworms; protozoan parasites such as coccidia and giardia; infections; inflammation or allergic reactions. Here are some common early signs to look for with gastrointestinal problems:

- A weak stomach or sensitive system
- Frequent vomiting immediately after a meal
- Periodic diarrhea
- Frequent gas
- Loss of appetite or gradual weight loss

Don't ignore these signs, as a serious inflammation of the stomach, intestines, or colon may be brewing. Your animal's GI system could be letting you know that there is continual inflammation that could, if not corrected, be the beginning of impending disaster.

Besides inflammation, the GI tract may be genetically prone to or have weakened muscle control that could lead to serious diseases such as megasophagus or megacolon (a "flabby" esophagus or colon), or weakened stomach muscles that may contribute to a serious condition in dogs called acute gastric dilatation or bloat. We believe that decades of feeding highly processed, fiber-devoid foods have weakened the stomachs and intestines of domesticated dogs, making them more prone to stretching and dilatation.

Bloat

One of the most dreaded conditions that often occurs in large, deep-chested dogs is called acute gastric dilatation and torsion, more commonly referred to as bloat. You need to be aware of this potentially fatal problem, especially if you live with a large or giant dog. Bloat is an enlargement of the stomach due to a combination

---

What Can Go Wrong?

Bloat

Inflammatory Bowel Disease

of excessive fluids and gases, often mixing with large amounts of concentrated food, particularly dry dog food. The size and weight of a full stomach can actually cause it to flip on itself, blocking the inflow (from the esophagus) and outflow (to the small intestine, or duodenum) of its contents. This rotation (torsion) is extremely serious, often leading to shock and requiring emergency surgery.

Bloat is most prevalent in Saint Bernards, German Shepherds, Borzois, and Great Danes. We have also seen it in Golden and Labrador Retrievers, and even some smaller Cocker Spaniels and Schnauzers. Our own Golden Retriever, Leigh, bloated after breaking into a 20-pound bag of dog food, eating it, and then drinking his full water bowl.

While research veterinarians have never been able to conclusively prove its cause, the condition is commonly associated with overeating, overexertion, and exercise immediately after eating, and the combining of fluids and solids. Bloat has also been linked to low-quality foods containing soy and other ingredients, which can lead to gas and cause ballooning of the stomach.

Breeds at Risk for Bloat: Be Aware!

Is your animal a candidate for bloat? We have put together a breed-prone list, which includes most of the deep-chested dogs:

Basset Hound
Bernese Mountain Dog
Bloodhound
Borzoi (Russian Wolfhound)
Bouvier de Flanders
Boxer
Briard
Chow Chow
Doberman Pinscher
English Setter
Great Dane
Gordon Setter
Golden Retriever
Greyhound
Irish Setter
Irish Wolfhound
Labrador Retriever
Mastiff
Rottweiler
Standard Poodle
Saint Bernard
Scottish Deerhound
Vizsla
Weimaraner

Know the Signs of Bloat

Become familiar with the signs of bloat so your awareness of this sudden and potentially fatal disease becomes second nature.

1. Acute restlessness.
2. Swollen abdomen that continues to increase in size.
3. Gaseous stomach that comes on suddenly with continual burping.
4. Drooling, dry heaving, gagging, trying to vomit, and a distended, firm abdomen.

If any of these conditions occur, you need to seek immediate veterinary assistance. Your veterinarian will determine, after a physical examination, whether bloat has occurred. Treatment can be watchful waiting, the passing of a stomach tube to mechanically remove the stomach contents, or surgery to correct the situation. Once again, torsion is serious, and if not addressed immediately, will cause shock and death.

Tuning In Can Save a Life

One night, our dear friends Amanda and Tony called us in a panic. Their cry for help had to do with Carly, their 12-year-old Chow Chow, whose stomach had distended and whose breathing became labored. Amanda is very knowledgeable about health issues, and immediately suspected an emergency. Based on the symptoms conveyed to us, Dr. Bob confirmed that it sounded like Carly had bloat. Amanda confirmed that earlier that evening Carly was acting peculiarly, pacing a lot and trying to regurgitate to no avail. As a result, Amanda decided to pay close attention to her, and made the decision not to go to bed and leave her unattended, a choice that may have saved the dog's life.

Because Amanda "tuned in" and listened to her inner voice, she and Tony were able to observe the swelling of Carly's stomach and the beginning signs of shock, leading to their call to us. We immediately instructed our friends to administer Rescue Remedy, the Bach Flower Essence that can help calm animals and even prevent the onset of shock. Fortunately Amanda has listened to our preachings over the years and had the Rescue Remedy in the glove compartment of Tony's car. (Be sure to keep Rescue Remedy in your car and your kitchen where it's handy!) Tony administered Rescue Remedy on Carly's neck, ears, paws, and spine. Normally you can place the drops directly in the mouth but because Carly was gagging and trying to vomit, Dr. Bob felt it best to administer it topically.

Tony and Amanda stayed in touch with us on their way to the emergency clinic. Thankfully they arrived in time, and the diagnosis was confirmed. Dr. Bob spoke with the attending veterinarian, and fluid therapy was immediately started, and a large needle (trocar) was inserted to remove some of the gas and temporarily alleviate pressure on the internal organs. A board-certified surgeon was called in to operate, tacking the stomach down in a procedure called a gastroplexy. While this type of surgery is standard for bloat, the imminent danger of shock made the procedure much more dangerous. By the next day, Carly was recovering and delighting in frequent visits from Amanda and Tony, who brought her home-cooked meals consisting of fresh chicken and small amounts of well-cooked white rice.

At-Home Support and Prevention

Prevention is the approach you need to take with your best friend, and the best way to avoid gastric dilatation and torsion is to adhere to these precautions:

- Keep all opened and unopened dry dog food bags out of your animal's reach.
- While plenty of exercise is good for your dog's circulation, never mix exercise and food together. Allow at least two hours after meals before aggressive exercise, such as running, speed walking, Frisbee catching, ball playing, hide-and-seek, etc.
- If possible, feed two to three smaller meals per day rather than one main meal, preferably the high-quality diet recommended in the Goldsteins' Food Plan (see Chapter 1).
- Remove water one half-hour before feeding and withhold for one half-hour immediately after.
- Feed fresh whole foods high in soluble and insoluble fiber to "aerobically" strengthen the GI system.
- Provide antioxidant vitamins and minerals and life-force enzymes to improve metabolism and strengthen the immune system.

Add a digestive enzyme to the food, like Prozyme or Digestive Enzymes from Dr Goodpet.

Inflammatory Bowel Disease (IBD)

Most stomach and intestinal inflammatory conditions start with inflammation secondary to a reaction to food, chemicals, toxins, or residues found in the diet and the resultant formation of free radicals. If the daily insult continues, the inflammation elevates and the symptoms worsen.

While certain breeds of dogs and cats are genetically prone (like Boxers, Irish Setters, Rottweilers, Goldens, and Basenjis) the basic underlying cause of IBD is this chronic inflammation and an immune system overreacting to its own abused tissue. Animals suffering from IBD have a low tolerance for chemical additives and preservatives—common ingredients in standard commercial pet foods. In addition, repeated annual vaccinations and the use of immune-suppressing medications and exposure to environmental toxins can set the stage for autoimmune conditions.

Early Warning Signs

Signs will vary depending on the location in the gastrointestinal tract. If it's the upper portion (stomach or esophagus), vomiting will be the primary sign. If it's in the intestines and colon, there is associated loose stool, diarrhea, weight loss, spasms, gas, and bloody stool.

What Will My Veterinarian Recommend?

Your veterinarian will diagnose IBD using x-rays, blood tests, ultrasounds, fecal analysis, and possibly a biopsy of the stomach or intestinal tract. The specific name of the disease often represents the type of cell the immune system has sent into the area in response to the chronic inflammation. For instance, if the cell type is a lymphocyte (a type of white blood cell), then you may be told your animal has lymphocytic gastro-enteritis. (See Chapter 7 for more information on the immune system.)

The goal of conventional therapy is to suppress the cellular inflammatory response and remove the source of irritation, which often means a total dietary change. Cortisone is generally used to suppress the immune system and limit further attacks on its own tissue. If cortisone is not effective in suppressing the immune system, your veterinarian may recommend Azathioprine, a chemotherapeutic, immunosuppressive drug that can often help to reduce the cortisone required to control the autoimmune reaction. In addition, an antibiotic such as Metronidizole (Flagyl) may be prescribed to combat infection. Fluid therapy may be required if diarrhea or vomiting has caused dehydration. Your veterinarian may also recommend a prescription, high-fiber, or hypoallergenic diet low in meat proteins, food additives, artificial coloring, preservatives, milk proteins, gluten (wheat) and corn.

At-Home Support and Prevention

Control of vomiting and diarrhea is necessary to help prevent further wasting and dehydration. **Kaopectate** (from natural clay) or **slippery elm syrup** are both excellent in helping to soothe the stomach and intestines. If you can't locate slippery elm syrup, you can make it mixing 2 tsp of slippery elm powder (available in health food stores) in 1 cup of water and simmer until it thickens. Let cool. Give for 2 to 3 days or until symptoms are controlled.

Kaopectate or Slippery Elm Syrup *(every 2 to 4 hours)*	
Cat/Small Dog (up to 14 lb)	1 tsp
Medium Dog (15-34 lb)	2 tsp
Large/Giant Dog (35+ lb)	1 Tbsp

A homeopathic formula called **Gastroenteritis**, manufactured by Homeopet, will help heal irritated membranes of the stomach and intestines. Homeopathic remedies are absorbed directly through membranes and do not have to first enter the bloodstream to work. Give three times daily apart from food until the symptoms are under control.

Gastroenteritis (three times daily)	
Cat/Small or Medium Dog (up to 34 lb)	5 drops
Large/Giant Dog (35+ lb)	10 drops

The Runs, available from Earth Animal, is a combination herbal remedy that is anti-inflammatory and soothing for the entire GI tract.

The Runs (twice daily)	
Cat/Small Dog (up to 14 lb)	7 drops
Medium Dog (15-34 lb)	10 drops
Large Dog (35-85 lb)	12-15 drops
Giant Dog (85+ lb)	16-20 drops

Glutamine is an amino acid that has been clinically proven to support and improve intestinal function and set the stage for healing. Under conditions of stress, the body's stores of Glutamine can be depleted, so its addition to the diet is important for the maintenance of intestinal health. L-glutamine is often used by body builders, and is available in most health food stores.

Glutamine (daily with food)	
Cat/Small Dog (up to 14 lb)	250 mg
Medium Dog (15-34 lb)	500 mg
Large Dog (35-85 lb)	1000 mg
Giant Dog (85+ lb)	1000-1500 mg

Diet

A flareup of IBD can be serious, so do not be afraid to use drugs to control the symptoms and stop the vomiting, diarrhea, and dehydration. However, you must address the diet, and begin a plan to strengthen and balance the immune system. Frequently, pet food contains chemical additives, preservatives, coloring agents, dyes, and indigestible by-products that can trigger an allergic response. Read the small print on the label for ingredients such as ethoxyquin, by-products, artificial coloring, and flavor enhancers.

Initially you should make a home-prepared diet for dogs and cats such as boiled white rice, beef, chicken, or cottage cheese, along with cooked mashed carrots. Preparation is important as you want to predigest these food ingredients to further relieve the burden on the already compromised intestinal tract. Simply add the rice, water, chicken, or beef together and slowly cook until the rice is totally soft and stew-like. Usually dogs and cats love this mixture. Prepare in the following proportions:

Dogs: 35% meat, 50% rice, and 15% carrots.

Cats: 60% meat, 30% rice, and 10% carrots.

Once stabilized you may want to make a slow transition to our Food Plan (see Chapter 1). You can help your dog or cat make a full recovery by eliminating these unhealthy ingredients. Level III of the Goldstein Food Plan is recommended, since all the foods are free of health-robbing additives, preservatives, and by-products. Decreasing your reliance on commercial pet foods, while strengthening the immune system, will also assist healing. The vegetables and multivitamin/mineral supplements recommended in our Food Plan help replace the depleted enzymes, vitamins, and minerals. (You may want to look at hypoallergenic, minimal ingredient base foods when you construct your food plan.)

You can add minced raw garlic and a dollop of plain, low-fat organic, live culture yogurt (1 tsp to 1 Tbsp). The garlic will help cleanse the intestinal tract of putrid material and the yogurt will replenish beneficial bacteria. Weekly fasting of your animal is extremely important to allow the intestinal tract to rest.

Dose fresh organic garlic as follows. A word of caution: High doses of garlic have been associated with anemia, so don't use garlic if your animal is prone to or has anemia, and refrain from its use before any surgery.

Garlic (once daily)	
Cat/Small Dog (up to 14 lb)	1 clove
Medium Dog (15-34 lb)	2 cloves
Large Dog (35-84 lb)	3 cloves
Giant Dog (85+ lb)	4 cloves

A word of caution when dealing with IBD: Protein can begin leaking from the instestines into the stool (protein loosing enteropathy). This complication can be very dangerous as protein is necessary for proper immune system function. If your veterinarian finds low blood protein, you must provide additional highly digestible protein. Your best choices are raw, organic egg yolks or boiled chicken meat (no skin) added to the usual portion. In addition to the glutamine mentioned above, you may want to add a multiple amino acid supplement (available at health food stores or see the Resources section) to make sure that there are adequate amino acids in the diet. Review this protein or amino acid requirement with your veterinarian.

Egg Yolk (every other day)	
Cat/Small Dog (up to 14 lb)	1 yolk
Medium Dog (15-34 lb)	1 yolk
Large Dog (35-84 lb)	2 yolks
Giant Dog (85+ lb)	2 yolks

Max Amino or Amino Max Beyond (with meals)	
Cat/Small Dog (up to 14 lb)	1/2-1 cap
Medium Dog (15-34 lb)	1-2 caps
Large Dog (35-84 lb)	2- 3 caps
Giant Dog (85+ lb)	3-5 caps

Alternative Veterinary Therapies

Often dogs and cats with IBD are sickly, losing weight, and feeling terrible. It is always better to check the entire body and not just focus on the intestines. We recommend that you discuss with your veterinarian the benefits of specific nutraceuticals and homeopathics as well as Chinese herbal remedies. You may also want to use the following fixed formulations and/or combination homotoxicology, homeopathics, or Chinese herbal combinations, all available through your veterinarian.

The Nutritional Blood Test

Discuss with your veterinarian doing an NBT to help identify underlying weaknesses and help formulate a specific nutritional program to promote healing. The following remedies are available at veterinarians who utilize the NBT process.

Thuja Occidentalis. To alleviate possible allergic affects of prior vaccinations, we recommend the homeopathic remedy *Thuja* or Vaccine Drops as listed in our plan for vaccinations (see Chapter 3).

Acetylator. If you are consulting with a holistic veterinarian, he or she can order an excellent product for protecting the lining of the stomach and intestines. Acetylator (n-acetyl glucosamine) is available through veterinarians from Vetri Science Laboratories (see Resources). Give 1 capsule daily for every 10 pounds of body weight, divided between morning and evening. Use as often as needed.

For Upper GI Support (Common in Cats)

Esophageal/gastric Support Formula has an antacid effect on the stomach and helps to reduce stomach motility and acid production while helping to spare the cells of the stomach lining. For cats, the dosage is half a tablet twice daily. For dogs, 1 tablet for every 25 pounds of body weight twice daily.

Gastritis Drops is a combination homeopathic remedy that provides cellular support for the stomach. Helpful with vomiting, gagging, belching and bad breath related to gastric disturbances.

Gastritis Drops (twice daily)	
Cat/Small Dog (up to 14 lb)	7 drops
Medium Dog (15-34 lb)	10 drops
Large Dog (35-84 lb)	12 drops
Giant Dog (85+ lb)	15 drops

Stomach Drops is a combination homeopathic remedy that provides specific cellular and gland support for the stomach.

Stomach Drops (twice daily)	
Cat/Small Dog (up to 14 lb)	7 drops
Medium Dog (15-34 lb)	10 drops
Large Dog (35-84 lb)	12 drops
Giant Dog (85+ lb)	15 drops

Stomach Formula, a combination Western herbal formula, helps to reduce digestive inflammation and soothe the mucous membranes of the stomach and upper digestive tract. Used for gastritis, gastric ulcers, dyspepsia, lack of appetite, nausea, and vomiting

Stomach Formula (twice daily)	
Cat/Small Dog (up to 14 lb)	7 drops
Medium Dog (15-34 lb)	10 drops
Large Dog (35-84 lb)	12-15 drops
Giant Dog (85+ lb)	16-20 drops

BHI Combinations Homeopathics (see Homotoxicology section in Chapter 4 for more information). A mixture of BHI - Stomach + Inflammation + Enzyme or Stomach + Nausea + Inflammation is beneficial for both dogs and cats with IBD.

BHI Stomach + Inflammation + Stomach	
BHI Stomatch + Nausea + Inflammation	
(twice daily)	
Cat/Small Dog (up to 14 lb)	1/3 dropper
Medium Dog (15-34 lb)	1/2 dropper
Large Dog (35-84 lbs)	1 dropper
Giant Dog (85+ lb)	1 1/2 dropper

For Lower GI Tract Support (Common in Dogs)

Intestinal/IBD Support Formula has an antacid effect on the GI tract and supplies L-Glutamine, acetyl glucosamine, as well as intestinal protective herbs and plants such as aloe and slippery elm. Dosage is 1 tablet for every 25 pounds of body weight twice daily.

ColonGuard, the Chinese herbal remedy, is specifically formulated to support animals with inflammatory bowel disease. Dosage is 1 capsule for every 10 pounds twice daily.

Protein Losing Enteropathy/H50 is another remedy specifically designed for those animals with severe IBD and enteropathy (protein loss). Dosage is 1 capsule for every 10 pounds twice daily.

Diarrhea Drops, a combination homeopathic, can be used for simple and chronic diarrhea.

Intestine Drops, a combination homeopathic that provides cellular and tissue support for the large intestines, is especially useful in chronic colitis and IBD.

Diarrhea or Instestine Drops	
Cat/Small Dog (up to 14 lb)	7 drops
Medium Dog (15-34 lb)	10 drops
Large Dog (35-84 lb)	12-15 drops
Giant Dog (85+ lb)	16-20 drops

Intestinal Formula is a combination Western herbal used for diarrhea, and to reduce inflammation in the GI tract.

Intestinal Formula	
Cat/Small Dog (up to 14 lb)	7 drops
Medium Dog (15-34 lb)	10 drops
Large Dog (35-84 lb)	12-15 drops
Giant Dog (85+ lb)	16-20 drops

BHI Combinations Homeopathics (see Homotoxicology section in Chapter 4 for more information). A mixture of BHI - Intestine + Inflammation + Enzyme or Diarrhea + Intestines + Inflammation is beneficial for both dogs and cats with IBD.

BHI Intestine + Inflammation + Enzyme	
BHI Diarrhea + Intestines + Inflammation	
(twice daily)	
Cat/Small Dog (up to 14 lb)	1/3 dropper
Medium Dog (15-34 lb)	1/2 dropper
Large Dog (35-84 lb)	1 dropper
Giant Dog (85+ lb)	2 droppers

What's the Prognosis?

For bloat, prevention is key! Following our program, and making sure you are intimately aware of the early warning signs of this serious disease are the best ways to help your dog.

IBD can be tricky to diagnose and a challenge to control. If you catch it early, the damage can be minimized; in certain animals you may be faced with long-term medical or nutritional control rather than a cure. Using the whole, natural foods plus the recommended remedies will be your best assurance of avoiding the debilitating effects of IBD.

Infectious Diseases

The serious infectious diseases that affect dogs and cats have different symptoms and require a variety of therapies in order to heal, but they do have one common thread: A healthy immune system is directly related to an animal's ability to resist and heal these dangerous diseases. Although we can't compartmentalize these diseases under a single system, as we have with the other diseases discussed in this chapter, we can think of them as a group linked to the immune system.

Tick-Borne Diseases

In most parts of the country, spring signals the surge of an army of tiny creatures, including many species of ticks. These hardy, eight-legged creatures (technically members of the spider family) often hitch a ride on all sorts of mammals who stroll through wooded areas. When they sense the presence of a warm-blooded animal, they drop onto their unsuspecting subject. Later, a creepy-crawly feeling may prompt you to find a tick marching across your skin. You must be as vigilant about plucking ticks from your four-footed friends as you are the human members of your family. They are clever at hiding in the fur of the head and neck area, in the ears, and between the pads of the feet.

You've undoubtedly heard of Lyme disease, which was discovered in the 1970s near Old Lyme, Connecticut. The disease is transmitted through the bite of tiny deer tick, *Ixodes scapularis*, which passes a Rickettsial organism (*Borrelia burgdorferi*) that causes the disease. Since that time, Lyme disease has become the most common tick disease in humans and dogs (and to a lesser degree, in cats). In dogs and cats the most common sign of Lyme disease is lameness; however, more serious diseases such as heart and kidney failure (glomerular nephritis) are possible.

Other tick-borne diseases in animals and people have been around since the early 1900s. These include Rocky Mountain Spotted Fever (RMSF) and Ehrlichiosis. Both are caused by tiny Rickettsia microorganisms and require multiple hosts (including deer and field mice) to survive. The most common cause of RMSF is *Rickettsia rickettsii*; and of Ehrlichiosis, *Ehrlichia canis* in dogs, and

Ehrlichia risticii in cats. Unlike Lyme disease, both RMSF and Ehrlichia can be transmitted by the common dog tick (*Dermacentor variabilis*) or wood tick (*D. andersoni*).

One of the main problems in diagnosing any tick-borne disease is that the signs and symptoms are often vague and nonspecific, meaning they can be associated with many chronic diseases. Signs might include persistent fever, loss of appetite, weight loss, joint pain, and neurological symptoms. More serious signs such as life-threatening anemia and collapse of the major organs are also seen, especially in instances of Ehrlichiosis.

Pinning down a cause often requires ruling out other diseases first—thereby "backing into" the diagnosis. The most common diagnostic test for tick-borne diseases is a blood (titer) test to check for antibody levels. For example, a positive (high) titer is often the basis for a diagnosis of Lyme disease; however, either natural exposure or the vaccine can also produce a high titer. This results in some controversy about treatment and whether Lyme disease even exists in dogs. Many labs now perform a more specific diagnostic test called the Western Blot. This test can distinguish between antibodies produced from actual exposure and those triggered by the vaccine.

Still, many cases of tick-borne disease go undiagnosed for months or even years. Recently, at our Healing Center for Animals, we have had animals who were suffering for years from periodic flareups of fever, limping, and organ disease or failure. Although undiagnosed, these animals required repeated prescriptions of potent medications such as cortisone and antibiotics. When finally tested for tick-borne diseases, Ehrlichiosis and Lyme disease were found.

In these chronically ill animals, the animal has to first go through three to four weeks of antibiotics to stabilize the progression of the disease. As holistic practitioners, this approach is not normally our first recommendation; however, because of the deep-seated nature of the tick-borne infection, and the fact that the immune system is compromised, we feel the

Remove Ticks the Safe Way

Grasp the tick's body with fine-pointed tweezers close to the animal's skin. Apply steady traction for a few seconds, and then twist the tick with more force, and pull away from the skin. This method has its risks, as the head of the tick may remain under the skin, causing the area to become inflamed. Should this be the case, clean the area where the head remains with soapy water or hydrogen peroxide. Should the area become infected, consult your veterinarian. You can also try a drop of cinnamon or peppermint oil on the tick to get it to release.

Here's what doesn't work: a hot match, petroleum jelly, nail polish, or alcohol. None of these will cause the tick to "back out" of the skin, and these methods may cause further injury.

integrative approach (combination of conventional medicine and supportive nutrition) is best. Stabilizing the system first will help avert a potential crisis, then you can focus on rebuilding and rebalancing the body.

Lyme Disease

Because of the vague symptoms and lack of definitive diagnostic testing, some veterinarians do not believe that Lyme is really a disease in animals. Others believe that the presence of a high titer is responsible for the symptoms and proceed to treat with a four- to five-week course of an antibiotic (such as doxycycline).

From a nutritional support point of view, this debate is irrelevant. What's important is that the immune system is weakened, and the underlying signs must be addressed. If a blood titer is high and clinical signs for Lyme are present, we will recommend four weeks of antibiotics because he or she often cannot recover without outside help.

While there is a Lyme vaccine available, it is not 100 percent effective, and for that matter, may not be safe. There are numerous reports in the literature implicating the vaccine as the cause of Lyme disease and in some instances resulting in permanent disease. For this reason (and because we are cautious about vaccinations), we do not recommend the Lyme vaccine.

Ehrlichiosis

Ehrlichiosis is now considered endemic in many parts of the US. While this disease can also exhibit the vague signs of persistent fever, weakness, lethargy, lack of appetite, and depression, it can be associated with more serious situations such as anemia, hemorrhage, convulsions, arthritis, and kidney disease. As with Lyme disease, when any chronic, nonresponsive condition is present, a blood titer test should be performed and steps taken to strengthen the immune system. Conventional antibiotic treatment will also be required, typically with doxycycline or tetracycline.

Rocky Mountain Spotted Fever

Rocky Mountain Spotted Fever (RMSF) exists worldwide and is most often transmitted by the tick *Dermacentor variablis* or *D. andersoni*. It also shows the vague symptoms as listed above. In certain instances, immune-suppressed animals can be vulnerable to organ collapse and death. The treatment of choice is also doxycycline.

At-Home Support and Prevention

Various reports have shown that 5 to 10 percent of animals bitten by infected ticks develop a tick-borne disease. In other words, 90 to 95 percent of animals that are exposed through the bite of a tick have an immune system that is capable of destroying the bugs before disease occurs. Interestingly, most people think that if their animal is bitten by an infected tick, they will automatically get the disease. This is not so!

In the prevailing medical model, it's the species—the germ, the bug, the invader—that is thought to "cause" the disease. But another model, one that is based on the immune status of the body, holds that disease is literally created by the body because of a run-down immune system. In an animal with a strong immune system, repeated exposure only strengthens immunity; as you can see from the low rates of disease incidence, lots of people and animals are bitten and never develop the disease.

Regardless of what paradigm you align yourself with, your animal's best defense against tick-borne disease is prevention—check your animal for ticks carefully whenever he or she has been outside and remove and discard the tick. If your animal should test positive for one of these diseases, we recommend the following program along with appropriate antibiotic therapy.

Diet

Put your animal on Level III of the Goldstein Food Plan (see Chapter 1). Add the following antioxidants and phytonutrients as part of your home program when you are in an endemic tick area or you believe that your animal is particularly prone to tick-borne diseases.

Tick Prevention Tips

Stay away from tick breeding grounds. Avoid walking your dog in locations that are known to be infested with ticks, especially in the spring and summer when there is much new tick growth and feeding. Stay away from low-lying, moist, shaded, leaf-covered, and low-growing ground cover. The most common carriers are deer and small rodents like rats, so stay clear of areas where these carriers are in abundance.

Check for ticks after your walk. It generally takes upwards of 36 hours for the infection from the tick bite to begin, therefore checking after each walk and removing any moving or attached ticks will prevent infection. Remember, deer ticks are quite small—check first between the toes and legs and especially around the eyes and inside the earflaps.

Vitamin C (twice daily)	
Cat/Small Dog (up to 14 lb)	250 mg
Medium Dog (15-34 lb)	500 mg
Large Dog (35-84 lb)	750 mg
Giant Dog (85+ lb)	1000 mg

Vitamin A (once daily)	
Cat/Small Dog (up to 14 lb)	2500 iu
Medium Dog (15-34 lb)	5000 iu
Large Dog (35-84 lb)	7500 iu
Giant Dog (85+ lb)	7500 iu

Vitamin E (once daily)	
Cat/Small Dog (up to 14 lb)	200 iu
Medium Dog (15-34 lb)	400 iu
Large Dog (35-84 lb)	600 iu
Giant Dog (85+ lb)	800 iu

Vitamin B Complex (once daily)	
Cat/Small Dog (up to 14 lb)	50 mg
Medium Dog (15-34 lb)	75 mg
Large Dog (35-84 lb)	100 mg
Giant Dog (85+ lb)	150 mg

Spirokete (twice daily)	
Cat/Small Dog (up to 14 lb)	1/2 capsule
Medium Dog (15-34 lb)	1 capsule
Large Dog (35=84 lb)	1 1/2 capsules
Giant Dog (85+ lb)	2 capsules

No More Ticks is a natural herbal remedy available from Earth Animal traditionally used to help ward off and address the symptoms associated with tick bites and related tick-borne disease. You also may want to add **aged garlic** and **echinacea**.

No More Ticks (twice daily)	
Cat/Small Dog (up to 14 lb)	7 drops
Medium Dog (15-34 lb)	10 drops
Large Dog (35-84 lb)	15 drops
Giant Dog (85+ lb)	20 drops

Garlinase 4000, or an aged garlic preparation (daily for 2 to 3 weeks)	
Cat	1/4 tablet
Small Dog (up to 14 lb)	1/2 tablet
Medium Dog (15-34 lb)	1/2 tablet
Large Dog (35-84 lb)	1 tablet
Giant Dog (85+ lb)	2 tablets

Echinacea (twice daily) (use for 4 weeks, then stop for 2 weeks, and then again for 4 weeks)	
Cat/Small Dog (up to 14 lb)	200 mg
Medium Dog (15-34 lb)	300 mgs
Large Dog (35-84 lb)	400 mgs
Giant Dog (85+ lb)	600 mgs

Veterinary Alternative Therapies

Support the immune system's weaknesses and imbalances by asking your veterinarian to run a Nutritional Blood Test (NBT) (see Chapter 4). The NBT accomplishes two critical goals. First, it identifies specific tissue and organ imbalances. Second, it supplies the required nutrients needed by the body to heal and strengthen the immune system. Some of these nutrients also have organ- and tissue-protective attributes that will help to offset the long course of antibiotic and other medical therapies. This NBT nutraceutical therapy will also contain the specific gland support that is so important if your animal's immune system is compromised.

Your veterinarian may also choose to support your animal with the following remedies.

Immune/Autoimmune Support Formula, contains the supportive and regenerative nutrients of the humoral and cellular immune system. This formula contains immune-balancing nutrients such as: vitamins C, A, and E, whey, glutathione, bee pollen, alpha lipoic acid, and N-acetyl cysteine.

Tick Drops, a combination homeopathic, helps in resolving and healing tick-borne diseases such as Lyme disease and Rocky Mountain Spotted Fever, and helps to alleviate their symptoms. These drops can be used along with and after a conventional regimen of antibiotics.

Our Simple Program of Prevention

• Examine your animal every day during tick season, and remove ticks before they imbed.

• Groom and bathe your animal frequently during the tick season.

• Make your animal more resistant and less attractive to ticks by boosting and supporting the immune system with the diet and nutrients discussed in this chapter..

• A combination of Internal Powder plus Herbal Internal Powder, available through Earth Animal, can also help boost immune function and is effective at helping to repel ticks. Mix together the daily doses of each natural remedy (listed on the packages), and give the combination during peak tick season in your geographical area.

Tick Drops (twice daily)	
Cat/Small Dog (up to 14 lb)	7 drops
Medium Dog (15-34 lb)	10 drops
Large Dog (35-84 lb)	15 drops
Giant Dog (85 lb +)	20 drops

Tick Formula, a medicinal herbal remedy, helps to repel ticks and addresses the symptoms associated with tick bites and related tick borne diseases.

Tick Formula (twice daily)	
Cat/Small Dog (up to 14 lb)	7 drops
Medium Dog (15-34 lb)	12 drops
Large Dog (35-84 lb)	15 drops
Giant Dog (85+ lb)	20 drops

Immune Drops, a combination homeopathic remedy, helps to stimulate and balance the cellular and humoral immune systems as indicated in chronic degenerative diseases.

Immune Drops (twice daily)	
Cat/Small Dog (up to 14 lb)	5 drops
Medium Dog (15-34 lb)	7 drops
Large Dog (35-84 lb)	12 drops
Giant Dog (85+ lb)	15 drops

Tick Drops, Tick Formula, and Immune Drops are all available through the NBT.

H7 Stimulator, a Chinese herbal remedy available through your veterinarian, is used for immunodeficient conditions and tick borne diseases. The general dose for Chinese herbs is 1 capsule for every 10 to 20 pounds of weight.

Viral Diseases

Canine Viral Diseases

The principal viral diseases of the dog include canine distemper, canine hepatitis, and parvo disease. Veterinarians have been vaccinating for distemper and hepatitis for decades, and these diseases now rarely occur. Parvo disease has developed more recently (in the late 1970s) and is now a bigger threat, especially in puppies and immune-compromised dogs. Transmission can be airborne, by direct contact, or by contact via feces and urine.

Dr. Bob graduated from veterinary school in 1967 and, like his peers and instructors, was trained in the use of annual vaccinations for distemper and hepatitis. Our profession has been vaccinating for these diseases since the early 1950s. That's 40 to 50 years of giving annual distemper and hepatitis vaccines to dogs every year throughout their life.

Two observations: Like whooping cough and smallpox, two diseases that have been eradicated by vaccines in children, new epidemics of more serious disease, such as polio and cancers, can develop in their aftermath. Dr. Fred Klenner, a pioneering researcher in the therapeutic use of vitamin C, boldly stated that the blanket use of the polio vaccine in children directly led to the rapid rise in childhood leukemia.

The second observation has to do with parvovirus. When the initial outbreak occurred in the New York City area in the late 1970s, the demand for parvo vaccine was so great that manufacturers couldn't keep up, so feline distemper vaccine (a similar type of virus) was used to vaccinate dogs until the canine version was available. Is it possible that repeated injections of feline distemper helped to set the stage for the rapid development of the modern canine-specific parvovirus disease, which is much more virulent and fatal than this original disease? (Our thoughts on the use and misuse of vaccinations and their immune-suppressing affects are presented more fully in Chapter 3.)

Warning Signs and Veterinary Recommendations

Signs of distemper, hepatitis, and parvo are directly related to an overwhelmed immune system, which allows the virus to get a foothold.

If clinical signs are already present, your veterinarian may prescribe broad-spectrum antibiotics to fight any secondary infections. Other common support aids include painkillers, decongestants, and fluids (to counter dehydration). Cortisone is not normally used for viral infections because of the dampening effect it has on the immune system.

Canine Distemper Virus (CDV), caused by a morbillivirus, results in serious systemic signs such as fever, loss of appetite, weakness, and debilitation. It usually begins with a serious upper respiratory infection, including sneezing, coughing, a thick yellowish discharge from both the eyes and nose, high fever, lack of appetite, and diarrhea. As the disease progresses, the pad becomes quite hard (distemper is nicknamed "Hard Pad Disease") and finally the virus enters the central nervous system. Left untreated, the disease can progress to the brain (encephalitis), showing up as a head-tilt, circling, paralysis, convulsions and finally, death. Most veterinarians will recommend euthanasia when distemper arrives in the nervous system. Antibiotics are recommended for the secondary infections and Phenobarbital is used to help prevent seizures.

Infectious canine hepatitis, caused by the canine adenovirus (CAV-1), shows similar signs as most liver diseases: High fever, loss of appetite, vomiting, diarrhea, enlarged swollen liver, abdominal pain, belly full of fluid (ascites), swollen lymph nodes, and sometimes convulsions. As the disease progresses, the cornea of the eye may turn blue in color (one of the side effects of the original hepatitis vaccines was a condition called "blue eye"). Since there are no specific medications for this virus, treatment is supportive medical care such as fluid therapy, antibiotics such as cephalexin and amoxicillin, tagamet to help control vomiting, and metronidazole to help control diarrhea. Caution must be exercised when using medications with this disease because of their effect on the liver. Because of the liver's important role in detoxification, when compromised, toxicity can easily occur as a side effect of the drugs.

Parvovirus disease, caused by the virus CPV-2, is a devastating, debilitating disease that afflicts weakened and very young dogs. It causes severe vomiting and diarrhea leading to loss of fluid (dehydration), blood in the stool, rapid weight loss, shock, and death. It is often not responsive to medical treatment and requires time and supportive care for the intense vomiting and diarrhea, including fluid therapy and antibiotics, to counter dehydration and prevent secondary bacterial infection.

Feline Viral Diseases

The viral diseases of cats are among the most feared of all animal diseases because they often are associated with the words "hopeless" and "incurable" and can lead to death.

Warning Signs and Veterinary Recommendations

Signs of these serious viral diseases may include fever, loss of appetite, vomiting, diarrhea, lethargy, depression, skin conditions (rough coat), dehydration, stubborn infections of the gums, upper respiratory tract, sinuses, eyes, stomach, intestines, liver, brain, kidney and urinary tract. One or more of these signs call for prompt, immediate veterinary attention, or they may become progressively more serious and even life threatening.

If clinical signs are already present, your veterinarian may prescribe broad-spectrum antibiotics to fight any secondary infections. Other common support aids include painkillers, decongestants, and fluids (to counter dehydration). Cortisone is not normally used for viral infections because of the dampening effect it has on the immune system.

Feline Immunodeficiency Virus (FIV)

Also known as "feline AIDS," FIV is caused by a retrovirus which is from the same family of viruses that causes HIV in people. This virus often afflicts outdoor cats and may be spread by bite wounds. The virus directly affects both the cellular and humoral immune systems (see Chapter 7). Once the immune system is compromised, secondary effects such as fever, swollen lymph glands and infections are usually seen. As the immune system continues to weaken and the virus strengthens, secondary conditions arise, such as chronic diarrhea, periodontal problems, loss of appetite, weight loss, anxiety, and skin diseases.

Some cats that test positive for FIV show no signs—their immune systems are balanced enough to keep the progression and associated clinical signs under control. Once the cat has developed the clinical signs, antibiotics may help with secondary infections. Drugs such as interferon or immunoregulin may help boost the immune system; however, they do have potential side effects.

Corticosteroids may alleviate pain and inflammation initially, but their long-term immune suppression make them counterproductive.

Feline Leukemia (FeLV)

FeLV is the number-one killer of cats, second only to accidental death. Up to 70 percent of all cats may be exposed to this virus during their lives. The disease is spread by contact with infected cats. This is an immune-suppression disease and symptoms can be chronic diarrhea or vomiting, serious skin disease, and chronically inflamed gums and throat. A non-healing, inflamed mouth with gum disease is a cardinal sign of FeLV. Advanced signs are anemia and fluid accumulation in the chest. (See Chapter 9: Cancer, for more on the treatment of FeLV.)

Feline Panleukopenia (Feline distemper)

This disease is caused by the FPV virus and results in a devastating depression of the body's immune cells (loss of white blood cells), a shriveling of the thymus gland (a prominent gland of the immune system), and a loss of the body's ability to fight infections. Symptoms are acute vomiting and diarrhea with associated dehydration often leading to death. After the initial gastrointestinal effects, the immune system will collapse, allowing the virus to affect any organ system. While the vaccine for feline distemper almost always controls the disease, what is unknown is the potential long range secondary effects of the vaccine (see Chapter 3 for more on vaccines).

The focus of medical therapy is to prevent the dehydration asssociated with the violent vomiting and diarrhea. Often your veterinarian will prescribe antibiotics to help control secondary intestinal infections.

Feline Infectious Peritonitis (FIP)

FIP is caused by a coronavirus that can incubate within the cat for years, until a stressor (such as vaccination) depresses the immune system, resulting in an activation of the virus. You may see few signs until the disease is well advanced. Symptoms may include persistent fevers and infections in various organ systems, such as swollen lymph nodes, vomiting, or diarrhea. The "wet form" of this virus, which results in fluid accumulation in the chest or the belly area can cause secondary complications such as difficulty breathing and bloating and often leads to the decision of euthanasia.

There is no routine accepted therapy for FIP, and once the disease shows itself, the animal usually sickens quickly, and often dies. Antibiotics, corticosteriods, and immune-stimulating drugs (such as interferon) are usually ineffective. The FIP vaccine usually does not offer effective prevention.

Feline Upper Respiratory Virus

This virus is quite common, especially in kittens. It is characterized by serious upper respiratory signs such as sneezing, coughing, and thick discharge from the eyes and nose. Generally there is a loss of appetite, mainly because when cats cannot smell they will often stop eating their food. It can be caused by multiple viruses and bacterial infections such as Feline Herpes Virus (FHV) or *Chlamydia psittacae*. While kittens will often survive from these upper respiratory infections, long-term complications such as chronic sinusitis and conjunctivits may be permanent. These cats can remain as permanent carriers for the disease.

The treatment of choice for upper respiratory infections is antibiotics, such as amoxicillin or baytril. Routine vaccines are often recommended by veterinarians.

Prevention

Let's go back to the very beginning, because with these serious diseases, their prevention is far better than their treatment.

Dogs

Distemper, hepatitis, and parvo most often occur in puppies and stressed animals, such as those kept in crowded kennel conditions. There is a strong genetic component to this viral complex and many puppies are born with a weakened immune system that makes them more susceptible to these diseases. Since many newborn dogs (and cats) are immune-compromised at birth (due to their parents' and grandparents' repeated exposure to vaccinations, excessive use of medications, chemically adulterated food and exposure to environmental toxins), it is important to vaccinate puppies following a modified vaccine program that gives immunity without overwhelming their immature immune systems. (See Chapter 3 for vaccination recommendations.)

Cats

We believe that many cats have inbred immune weaknesses. If you are adopting or purchasing your cat from a reputable breeder, take your time and do your homework; avoid purchasing an inbred cat. Ask about their incidence of these diseases, and insist upon talking with several people who have purchased cats or kittens from that breeder. Starting out life with a competent immune system will go a long way toward preventing these serious diseases. If you're adopting from a shelter it is important to introduce an immune-building and balancing dietary and supplement program as soon as possible (see Chapter 1).

We believe that the immune-suppressing affects of vaccines are linked to not only the development of the disease, but also the spread and virulence of these illnesses. If your cat is going to be vaccinated, follow our instructions for the minimal vaccination program and always "detoxify" your animal after a vaccination is given. (See Chapter 3 for instructions on vaccinations and detoxification.)

Catching these diseases early is the key to successful control. Be sure to bring your cat to your veterinarian for an annual physical and blood work. If weaknesses of the immune system can be picked up early, and the proper diet and supplements used to correct nutrient deficiencies and organ imbalances, you'll have done your best to prevent the disease. Certainly, routine blood testing for FeLV, the most common viral disease, is prudent.

At-Home Support

Many veterinarians offer a pessimistic prognosis for cats and dogs with any one of these diseases. While these are serious diseases, we believe there is much that can be done to enhance the compromised immune system and improve the animal's day-to-day quality of life.

If these viral conditions are diagnosed early, there is a much higher chance of survival. When nutritional and supplemental treatments are started before the development of the serious signs, we have seen these diseases go into remission. So don't give up too early.

Most veterinarians hospitalize animals in isolation with these infectious conditions and immediately start supportive type of therapies: antibiotics, antidiarrheal, and antinausea medications, along with intravenous fluids to help flush the body and prevent dehydration. Cortisone is not normally used for viral infections because of its immune-suppressing effects and potential for worsening the condition.

The following natural therapies can be administered during or after the clinical signs are under control and your animal is released from the hospital. Their choice is dependent on your veterinarian's experience with integrative therapies.

Fasting

Resting the system for 24 to 36 hours with a liquid fast such as potato peeling broth (see recipe in Section 10), is helpful. This assists the body in ridding itself of the toxins that usually underlie the fever and can counter immune suppression. This should only be done after speaking with your veterinarian, as your animal may have been off food while being hospitalized.

Diet and Supplements

Follow the Goldstein Food Plan Level III to help boost your dog or cat's immune system (see Chapter 1). If you live with a young dog or cat, now is the time to acquaint her with living foods. For small finicky dogs and cats, begin by adding the smallest pinch of finely chopped vegetables and cover or mix with plain low-fat yogurt. If it's carrots, zucchini, or watercress, for example, start with 1/2 tsp and increase to 2 to 3 tsp per day over a period of months.

In addition, the following potent antioxidant vitamins are also administered:

Ester C (twice daily)	
Cat	250-500 mg
Small Dog (up to 14 lb)	250 mg
Medium Dog (15-34 lb)	500 mg
Large Dog (35-84 lb)	750 mg
Giant Dog (85+ lb)	1,000 mg

Vitamin E (daily)	
Cat	100-200 iu
Small Dog (up to 14 lb)	200 iu
Medium Dog (15-34 lb)	400 iu
Large Dog (35-84 lb)	600 iu
Giant Dog (85+ lb)	800 iu

Vitamin A (daily)	
Cat	1,000–2,500 iu
Small Dog (up to 14 lb)	2,500 iu
Medium Dog (15-34 lb)	5,000 iu
Large Dog (35-84 lb)	7,500 iu
Giant Dog (85+ lb)	10,000 iu

The herb **Echinacea** is a valuable ally when it comes to fighting any kind of infection. This ancient herbal remedy works directly to boost production of important cells in the immune system. Use an alcohol-free tincture.

Echinacea (twice daily)	
Cat/Small Dogs (up to 14 lb)	5-7 drops
Medium Dogs (15-34 lb)	10 drops
Large Dogs (35-84 lb)	15 drops
Giant Dogs (85+ lb)	20 drops

Viratox is a homeopathic formula that aids in detoxification while fighting the viral infection. Your veterinarian can order it for you from HomeoVetix. Give 1 teaspoon daily for 30 days, stop for two weeks and then give again for one month.

Treating the Symptoms of Infectious Viral Diseases

For Upper Respiratory Symptoms

Cough and Wheeze, an herbal remedy from Earth Animal, soothes and tones the tissue lining of the upper respiratory system.

Cough and Wheeze (twice daily)	
Cat/Small Dog (up to 14 lb)	7 drops
Medium Dog (15-34 lb)	10 drops
Large Dog (35-84 lb)	15 drops
Giant Dog (85+ lb)	20 drops

Earth Animal's **Sinus** is an herbal remedy to help the inflammation of the nasal passages and sinuses.

Sinus (twice daily)	
Cats/Small Dog (up to 14 lb)	7 drops
Medium Dog (15-34 lb)	10 drops
Large Dog (35-84 lb)	15 drops
Giant Dog (85+ lb)	20 drops

For Fever

Aconitum napellus 30C. In the early feverish stages of any viral disease, use the homeopathic remedy *Aconitum napellus 30C*. (For instructions on using homeopathic remedies, see Chapter 4.)

Aconitum napellus 30C (twice daily for one week)	
Cat/Small Dog (up to 14 lb)	1 pellet
Medium Dog (15-34 lb)	2 pellets
Large Dog (35-84 lb)	3 pellets
Giant Dog (85+ lb)	3 pellets

For Vomiting

Ipecacuanha 6C. For vomiting we recommend the homeopathic remedy *Ipecacuanha* 6C every 2 hours until vomiting stops, then give twice daily for 1 week. (For instructions on using homeopathic remedies, see Chapter 4.)

Ipecacuanha 6C (twice daily)	
Cat/Small Dog (up to 14 lb)	1 pellet
Medium Dog (15-34 lb)	2 pellets
Large Dog (35-84 lb)	3 pellets
Giant Dog (85+ lb)	3 pellets

For Diarrhea

Apomorphine 6C is a homeopathic remedy to help stop diarrhea. Give it to your animal every 2 hours until diarrhea stops, then twice daily for one week. (See Chapter 4 for more information on administration of homeopathic remedies.)

Apomorphine 6C (twice daily)	
Cat/Small Dog (up to 14 lb)	1 pellet
Medium Dog (15-34 lb)	2 pellets
Large Dog (35-84 lb)	3 pellets
Giant Dog (85+ lb)	3 pellets

The Runs is an herbal remedy available from Earth Animal, to help stop simple diarrhea.

The Runs (three times daily)	
Cat/Small Dog (up to 14 lb)	5-7 drops
Medium Dog (15-34 lb)	10 drops
Large Dog (35-84 lb)	15 drops
Giant Dog (85+ lb)	20 drops

For Emotional Well Being

Generally all dogs and cats that have these serious viral infections are depressed and lethargic and generally not feeling well. We recommend the flower essences **Return to Joy** and **Recovery**, both available from Anaflora. Add the drops to your animal's fresh drinking water.

Return to Joy (daily, for 4 weeks)	
Cat/Small Dog (up to 14 lb)	5 drops
Medium/Large/Giant Dog (15+ lb)	10 drops

Use Recovery after four weeks of using Return to Joy.

Recovery (daily, for 4 weeks)	
Cat/Small Dog (up to 14 lb)	5 drops
Medium/Large/Giant Dog (15+ lb)	10 drops

Alternative Veterinary Therapies

If signs of viral disease are already present, we strongly recommend that you seek the expertise of a holistically oriented veterinarian who can set up a program of nutritional and homeopathic support. Use this program in conjunction with your family veterinarian's medical support program. Many veterinarians have helped dogs and cats with intravenous fluids containing vitamin C and other nutraceuticals, combination homeopathics, or Chinese Herbal Remedies that are designed to boost the immune system and the important glands such as the adrenal and thymus glands (the main glands of the immune system).

The following remedies are available for use by all veterinarians who utilize NBT testing program and are designed for use under the direction of your veterinarian.

Vitamin C

In treating these diseases in dogs and cats over the years, one of the most potent methods of helping the body fight the virus is to add vitamin C in high doses to the intravenous drip. This would have to be performed by a trained, experienced veterinarian. In any systemic crisis—such as the uncontrollable diarrhea present in parvo or distemper—it is critical that the immune system be nourished and stimulated to help the body survive the crisis. When your dog or cat comes home from the hospital, we recommend continuing the use of increased amounts of vitamin C. This antioxidant has been proven to boost the immune system and help fight off viruses. We recommend the use of powdered Ester C as it is highly absorbable, pH balanced, and easy to give mixed with food.

Treating the Symptoms of Infectious Viral Diseases

For Fever

BHI Combination Homeopathics can help with fevers. (For more information on Homotoxicology, see Chapter 4.)

BHI Inflammation + Infection + Enzyme (twice to four times daily)	
Cat/Small Dog (up to 14 lb)	1/4 dropper
Medium Dog (15-34 lb)	1/2 dropper
Large Dog (35-84 lb)	1 dropper
Giant Dog (85+ lb)	2 droppers

For Vomiting

Esophageal/Gastric Support Formula is available from your veterinarian and has an antacid effect on the stomach, which helps to reduce stomach motility. For cats: 1/2 tablet. For dogs 1 tablet for each 25 pounds of weight twice daily

Bile Reflux Gastritis or **Gastritis/Chronic** are Chinese Herbal Remedies good for any type of gastritis or vomiting. The general dose is 1 capsule for each 10 to 20 pounds of weight or as directed by your veterinarian

BHI Combination Homeopathics can help with vomiting. (For more information, see the section on Homotoxicology in Chapter 4.)

BHI - Stomach + Nausea + Pain (twice daily)	
Cat/Small Dog (up to 14 lb)	1/4 dropper
Medium Dog (15-34 lb)	1/2 dropper
Large Dog (35-84 lb)	1 dropper
Giant Dog (85+ lb)	2 droppers

Gastritis Drops, a combination homeopathic remedy, can help quiet the stomach if given 15 to 20 minutes before feeding.

Gastritis Drops (three times daily)	
Cat/Small Dog (up to 14 lb)	5 drops
Medium Dog (15-34 lb)	7 drops
Large Dog (35-84 lb)	10-12 drops
Giant Dog (85+ lb)	15 drops

Stomach Drops, a combination homeopathic, provides specific cellular and gland support for the stomach.

Stomach Drops (three times daily)	
Cat/Small Dog (up to 14 lb)	5 drops
Medium Dog (15-34 lb)	7 drops
Large Dog (35-84 lb)	10-12 drops
Giant Dog (85+ lb)	15 drops

Stomach Formula is a combination Western herbal remedy that reduces digestive inflammation and soothes the mucous membranes of the stomach and upper digestive tract. It can be useful for lack of appetite, nausea, and vomiting.

Stomach Formula (three times daily)	
Cat/Small Dog (up to 14 lb)	7 drops
Medium Dog (15-34 lb)	10 drops
Large Dog (35-84 lb)	12-15 drops
Giant Dog (85+ lb)	20 drops

For Diarrhea

Intestinal/IBD Support Formula is a nutraceutical remedy. It supports intestinal health. For cats: 1/2 tablet twice daily. For dogs: 1 tablet for each 25 pounds twice daily.

ColonGuard, a Chinese Herbal Remedy available from your veterinarian, is a supplement designed for use in animals with an inflamed GI tract. Dose 1 capsule for each 10 pounds of body weight or as directed by your veterinarian

Diarrhea Drops, a combination homeopathic, is used for simple and chronic diarrhea.

Diarrhea Drops (three times daily)	
Cat/Small Dog (up to 14 lb)	5 drops
Medium Dog (15-34 lb)	7 drops
Large Dog (35-84 lb)	10-12 drops
Giant Dog (85+ lb)	15 drops

Intestine Drops is a combination homeopathic that provides cellular and tissue support for the large bowel.

Intestine Drops (twice daily)	
Cat/Small Dog (up to 14 lb)	5 drops
Medium Dog (15-34 lb)	7 drops
Large Dog (35-84 lb)	10-12 drops
Giant Dog (85+ lb)	15 drops

Intestinal Formula is a combination Western herbal remedy used for diarrhea.

Intestinal Formula (twice daily)	
Cat/Small Dog (up to 14 lb)	7 drops
Medium Dog (15-34 lb)	10 drops
Large Dog (35-84 lb)	12-15 drops
Giant Dog (85+ lb)	20 drops

BHI Combination Homeopathics can be used for diarrhea.

BHI Intestine + Inflammation + Enzyme or BHI Diarrhea + Intestines + Inflammation	
(three times daily)	
Cat/Small Dog (up to 14 lb)	1/4 dropper
Medium Dog (15-34 lb)	1/2 dropper
Large Dog (35-84 lb)	1 dropper
Giant Dog (85+ lb)	2 droppers

For the Respiratory System

Bronchus/Lung/Sinus Support Formula provides repair and healing nutrients for the lungs and membranes. For cats: 1/2 tablet twice daily. For dogs: 1 tablet for each 25 pounds twice daily.

The following Chinese herbal remedies can be used:

Pneumonia - H23 (for viral or bacterial pneumonia) or **Sinusitis/chronic - H57** (for chronic or recurrent bacterial or viral sinusitis). The dosage is 1 capsule for each 10 to 20 pounds of body weight or as directed by your veterinarian.

The following combination homeopathics can be used for respiratory problems.

Cough Drops, a combination homeopathic, helps to relieve cough due to infectious bronchitis.

Cough Drops *(twice daily)*	
Cat/Small Dog (up to 14 lb)	5 drops
Medium Dog (15-34 lb)	7 drops
Large Dog (35-84 lb)	10-12 drops
Giant Dog (85+ lb)	15 drops

Lung Drops provides tissue and gland support for the lungs.

Lung Drops *(twice daily)*	
Cat/Small Dog (up to 14 lb)	5 drops
Medium Dog (15-34 lb)	7 drops
Large Dog (35-84 lb)	10-12 drops
Giant Dog (85+ lb)	15 drops

Sinusitis Drops provides support for sinuses.

Sinusitis Drops (twice daily)	
Cat/Small Dog (up to 14 lb)	5 drops
Medium Dog (15-34 lb)	7 drops
Large Dog (35-84 lb)	10-12 drops
Giant Dog (85+ lb)	15 drops

BHI Combination Homeopathics can help with the symptoms of respiratory infections. Use these BHI remedies as directed by your veterinarian. (For more information see the section on Homotoxicology in Chapter 4.)

BHI – Cough + Sinus + Infection	
BHI – Flu + Infection + Inflammation	
(three times daily)	
Cat/Small Dog (up to 14 lb)	1/4 dropper
Medium Dog (15-34 lb)	1/2 dropper
Large Dog (35-84 lb)	1 dropper
Giant Dog (85+ lb)	2 droppers

Cough Lung Formula is a combination Western herbal is used as an anti-inflammatory for the mucous membranes of the upper respiratory system.

Cough Lung Formula (three times daily)	
Cat/Small Dog (up to 14 lb)	7 drops
Medium Dog (15-34 lb)	10 drops
Large Dog (35-84 lb)	12-15 drops
Giant Dog (85+ lb)	20 drops

For Viral Infections

Viral Immune Drops, a combination homeopathic which supplies homeopathic support to the body's cellular and humoral immune systems against viral infections.

Viral Immune Drops (three times daily)	
Cat/Small Dog (up to 14 lb)	5 drops
Medium Dog (15-34 lb)	7-10 drops
Large Dog (35-84 lb)	12 drops
Giant Dog (85+ lb)	15 drops

For the Brain and Nervous System

Brain Nerve Support Formula supports DNA synthesis and provides repair nutrients for the brain and nervous system. For cats: 1/2 tablet twice daily. For dogs: 1 tablet for each 25 pounds of weight twice daily.

The following Chinese Herbal Remedies are useful: **Chronic Encephalitis H29** (for chronic encephalitis associated with fevers or seizures) and **Epitrol** (designed as a supplement for treating convulsions). Dosage is 1 capsule for each 10 to 20 pounds of weight or as directed by your veterinarian.

Epilepsy Drops, a combination homeopathic that supplies homeopathic support for the control of seizures.

Epilepsy Drops (twice daily)	
Cat/Small Dog (up to 14 lb)	5 drops
Medium Dog (15-34 lb)	7 drops
Large Dog (35-84 lb)	10 drops
Giant Dog (85+ lb)	15 drops

Spinal/Nerve Drops, a combination homeopathic that provides specific cell and tissue support for the cranial and peripheral nervous system.

Spinal/Nerve Drops (twice daily)	
Cat/Small Dog (up to 14 lb)	5 drops
Medium Dog (15-34 lb)	7 drops
Large Dog (35-84 lb)	10 drops
Giant Dog (85+ lb)	15 drops

Brain Drops, a combination homeopathic which is useful for degenerative conditions of the brain.

Brain Drops (twice daily)	
Cat/Small Dog (up to 14 lb)	7 drops
Medium Dog (15-34 lb)	10 drops
Large Dog (35-84 lb)	12-15 drops
Giant Dog (85+ lb)	18-20 drops

Calming Formula is a combination Western herbal that relaxes, calms, and tonifies the brain and nervous system.

Calming Formula (twice daily)	
Cat/Small Dog (up to 14 lb)	7 drops
Medium Dog (15-34 lb)	10 drops
Large Dog (35-84 lb)	12-15 drops
Giant Dog (85+ lb)	18-20 drops

BHI Combination Homeopathics can help with various problems associated with the brain.

Neuralgia + Pain/Spasm + Inflammation	
Recovery + Neuralgia + Inflammation	
Neuralgia + Infection + Recovery	
(three times daily)	
Cat/Small Dog (up to 14 lb)	1/4 dropper
Medium Dog (15-34 lb)	1/2 dropper
Large Dog (35-84 lb)	1 dropper
Giant Dog (85+ lb)	1 dropper

Anti-Seizure Drops and **Post Seizure Drops** are flower essences that help support brain nerves. Give 5 Anti-Seizure drops prior to or at the onset of a seizure. For Post Seizure Drops, add 5 drops to fresh drinking water daily for cats and dogs.

For the Liver

The following Chinese herbal remedies may be recommended: **Cholangiohepatitis/Chronic** - **H77** (used for chronic cholangiohepatitis) and **LiverGuard** (used as a dietary supplement for patients with elevated liver enzymes, elevated bile acids, or total bilirubin. Dosage is 1 capsule for 10 to 20 pounds of body weight or as directed by your veterinarian.

Liver/Gall Bladder Support Formula is a nutraceutical remedy that supplies vitamins, minerals, and amino acids that support metabolic detoxification and cellular regeneration of the liver. For cats: 1/2 tablet twice daily. For dogs: 1 tablet for each 25 pounds of weight twice daily.

Liver/Gallbladder Drops, a combination homeopathic available through veterinarians who use the NBT, improves the metabolic functions of the liver and gallbladder.

Liver/Gallbladder Drops (twice daily)	
Cat/Small Dog (up to 14 lb)	5 drops
Medium Dog (15-34 lb)	7 drops
Large Dog (35-84 lb)	10-12 drops
Giant Dog (85+ lb)	15 drops

Liver Formula, a combination western herbal remedy available through the NBT, helps the liver with detoxification.

Liver Formula (twice daily)	
Cat/Small Dog (up to 14 lb)	7drops
Medium Dog (15-34 lb)	10 drops
Large Dog (35-84 lb)	15 drops
Giant Dog (85+ lb)	20 drops

BHI Combination Homeopathics can help with liver and gall bladder inflammation. (For more information see the section on Homotoxicology in Chapter 4.)

Liver + Inflammation + Infection	
Gall bladder + Inflammation + Infection	
Liver + Gall Bladder + Inflammation	
(three times daily)	
Cat/Small Dog (up to 14 lb)	1/4 dropper
Medium Dog (15–34 lb)	1/2 dropper
Large Dog (35–84 lb)	1 dropper
Giant Dog (85+ lb)	1 dropper

Nosodes

Nosodes are homeopathic remedies. Simply, a nosode is the actual disease-causing agent, such as the bacteria or virus that is homeopathically diluted. (See Chapter 4 for more information.) The theory is that by giving the diluted form of the disease orally—one of the body's natural routes of exposure—the immune system has the opportunity to develop antibodies and natural immunity without the potentially devastating affects of vaccines. Nosodes seem to be most effective if they are given as soon as the animal is exposed to the causative agent such as the virus. Some veterinarians administer the nosode immediately after the diagnosis as part of their treatment for the viral disease. It has been reported by holistic veterinarians that when they administer these nosodes for the viral diseases discussed above (including feline leukemia), they have had a very positive response. While more research and proof needs to be established for the use of nosodes, the truth is that many of these viral disease are incurable, not responsive to medications, and often terminal. Therefore we support the use of nosodes in these conditions.

What's the Prognosis?

Viral diseases of dogs and cats are serious and require a combination of both medical and alternative therapies—a true integrative approach. If caught early and the immune system and the emotions are supported, the symptoms can be controlled, and you can often bring your animal through these diseases. The problem that often arises is that the diagnosis of these viral diseases (especially with FIP or FIV in cats) does not come until the animal is quite sick and has much less chance of survival. Even in these cases, the above program should be administered, because you can never predict an animal's response.

Kidney and Bladder Diseases

As one of the body's main organs of elimination, the kidneys remove wastes from the blood, which are combined with water, and excreted in the urine. The kidneys are biological filters that also maintain bodily fluid, the proper acid/alkaline balance, red blood cells, adequate blood protein level, and the required amounts of mineral levels. These metabolic processes are regulated through the filtration process and overseen by specific hormones.

Kidney disease is the second leading cause of death among cats, and an estimated 25 percent of dogs have some form of this condition. Kidney disease in dogs and cats most commonly results from chronic inflammation of kidney cells, scar tissue formation, and ultimately a reduction in the organ's filtering abilities. As the disease progresses, the kidneys can no longer eliminate wastes, and the animal suffers from internal poisoning (uremia) which can lead to death.

Chronic Renal Failure and Other Kidney Diseases

While the most common kidney disease in dogs and cats is chronic renal failure (CRF) there are many types, with various underlying causes. Acute renal failure is usually secondary to conditions such as heart failure, circulatory disorders, reaction to blood transfusion, adverse effects of medications (such as chemotherapeutics or non steroidal anti-inflammatory drugs (NSAIDS)), antifreeze or heavy metal poisoning, reaction to anesthetics or vaccines, and shock. Other diseases, such as kidney or bladder stones, leptospirosis, and cancer, can also be the cause of kidney disease. There are immune-mediated kidney diseases in dogs such as glomerular nephritis (which can occur secondary to Lyme disease) and amyloidosis. For cats, Feline Infectious Peritonitis (FIP) or diabetes may also be an underlying cause of kidney problems.

It is important to remember that the kidneys are a receptacle for ridding the body of metabolic wastes. The inflammation that precedes kidney disease is generally secondary to other circumstances, such as genetically weak kidneys, exposure to excess toxins, and poor diet. Many animals' kidneys become overwhelmed as they work to filter out chemical preservatives from commercial pet foods, flea and tick insecticides, and chemically treated drinking water. The result of this burden is progressively damaged, inflamed, and eventually nonfunctional kidneys.

Kidney function is a prime example of how all the organs in the body work together, and if any one of them is out of balance, it can wreak havoc on the rest. Protein metabolism and catabolism are under the control of the pituitary, thyroid, adrenals, and the liver. It is these organs that oversee protein breakdown (catabolism). If these organs are working with heat-adulterated, highly indigestible, amino acid-deficient proteins, and they themselves are in a weakened or degenerative state, then the end result will be excessive metabolic wastes that will overload and overburden and eventually lead to kidney burn out. The holistic approach to kidney disease therefore requires viewing the whole body and not focusing on one diseased organ. The key to kidney disease is in prevention, and the strengthening and balancing of the all the organs—in effect taking the pressure off the weakened kidneys.

Susceptible Breeds

While all dogs and cats are susceptible to kidney disease, the following breeds seem to be more prone:

CATS
Abyssinian cats
Persian cats
Siamese cats

DOGS
Beagles
Bull and Cairn Terriers
Chow Chows
Dalmatians
Doberman Pinchers
English Cocker Spaniels
German Shepherds
Miniature Schnauzers
Poodles
Shar-Peis
Samoyeds
Shih Tzu

Early Warning Signs

It is estimated that about 75 percent of the kidney is damaged before the signs of kidney disease are manifested. These signs include:

- Excessive thirst and urination (polyuria and polydypsia or PU/PD)
- High blood levels of nitrogen-rich metabolic wastes (azotemia)
- Loss of appetite (anorexia) and weight loss
- Lethargy and depression
- Vomiting and diarrhea
- Anemia
- Urine smell from breath

- Mouth and tongue ulcers
- Dehydration
- Dull coat, loss of hair, heavy shedding.

We encourage you to take your animal to your veterinarian for an annual physical examination, including bloodwork for those ages three and up. You'll be alerted to a problem long before signs of a disease are apparent. We identified a kidney problem in one of our own dogs through a routine blood test and were able to prevent kidney disease for years.

There are important blood tests related to the physiology of kidney function, such as creatinine and blood urea nitrogen (BUN). While these tests are used for determining kidney function, it is important to understand that creatinine and BUN levels are connected with the function of other organs. Creatinine is the protein by-product of muscle contractions and metabolism. It is an indicator of muscle metabolism, which is related to the functioning of the gonadal hormones, the pituitary, and the adrenal glands.

Blood urea nitrogen, while it ends up in the kidneys, is formed in the liver under processes controlled by the pituitary gland. Therefore, an elevated BUN level indicates less-than-optimal functioning of the pituitary, liver, and thyroid, as well as the kidney.

Creatinine and BUN levels show how the glands of the body all work in concert to metabolize and eliminate nitrogenous wastes. It is a mistake to focus on failing kidneys without taking into account the kidneys' relationship to the other organs of the body.

What Will Your Veterinarian Recommend?

Conventional veterinary medicine offers little hope for animals with advanced kidney disease. The prognosis is guarded and the end result is usually death or euthanasia. Veterinarians are taught that kidney tissue and cells cannot regenerate, and therefore will progressively degenerate. But we've seen evidence to the contrary, so it is important not to get trapped in the diagnosis, but to focus on improving the health of the entire body

Once the diagnosis is made, your veterinarian will likely recommend fluid therapy to correct dehydration and flush the body of wastes. Since dialysis for animals is not readily available, fluid therapy is given either intravenously (in the vein) or subcutaneously (under the skin). The fluids flush the system, thus reducing the risk of internal poisoning. Caution: Do not rely on the excessive thirst of your animal to function as dialysis, because it will not.

Depending on the severity of the disease, fluid therapy may be essential to keep blood poison levels to a minimum, so work closely with your family veterinarian on this approach. Most veterinarians will also prescribe medications such as cortisone to reduce inflammation and pain and increase appetite, sucralfate suspension to quiet the stomach, or stomach acid reducers like Cimetidine

(Tagamet) or Famotidine (Pepsid). Antibiotics are used to prevent infection. Lastly, your veterinarian will probably recommend a prescription diet that's low in protein. A primary function of the kidneys is to remove the waste products left after the body breaks down protein, so a diet lower in protein takes strain and pressure off the kidneys.

At-Home Support and Prevention

Holistic therapies have a lot to offer. Specific natural remedies and proper nutrients nourish the kidneys and strengthen the body's organs, enabling all systems to work more efficiently.

Diet

While formulated prescription diets are chemically correct (low in protein, fat, and sodium), they often contain chemical additives and preservatives as well as by-products and wastes from the human food industry which further tax the kidneys. So, to further ease the burden on your dog or cat's system, we offer the following home-cooked kidney diet. This diet may be served solo or mixed with any natural, low-protein food. This recipe meets all the needs of a kidney patient. You may vary the grains by feeding oatmeal or barley. Parsley and asparagus work as gentle diuretics, helping the kidney flush wastes and impurities. You may occasionally substitute tofu for the chicken. The recipe calls for a multivitamin/mineral—an important part of your animal's daily diet. We recommend multiples such as Daily Health Nuggets (available from Earth Animal) or Maximum Protection Formula (available from Dr. Goodpet).

Watch your animal's appetite closely. This is a good way to gauge when levels of wastes (poisons) are rising in the blood. If the appetite diminishes, even slightly, report to your veterinarian right away. Also, cats who eat dry food exclusively will tend toward dehydration, so it is important that

Sony Whan's Story

Sony Whan, a 15-year-old terrier mix, was brought in to see me by his guardian, Barbara. Sony had been diagnosed with early-stage kidney disease, and even though he was feeling fine, Barbara wanted to do some good before he became seriously ill. Sony's BUN and creatinine levels were elevated (not enough to indicate acute renal disease), but because of the nature of this disease, it was likely Sony would eventually develop symptomatic kidney failure. The NBT analysis of Sony's blood showed an underactive liver with the requirement for B complex vitamins. We addressed the imbalances with a glandular supplement and a B complex formula. Six months later, Sony's BUN and creatinine levels were normal. Instead of waiting for the inevitable crisis, Barbara and Sony stopped the degeneration of the kidneys, and Sony thrived for years.

Alternative Kidney Diet

Dogs	Cats
2 egg yolks (organic and soft boiled)	1 egg yolk (organic and soft boiled)
1/2 cup boneless, skinless chicken, cubed (preferably hormone- and antibiotic-free)	1/2 cup boneless, skinless chicken, cubed (preferably hormone- and antibiotic-free)
1 cup brown rice or millet	1/3 cup brown rice or millet
3 cups filtered or distilled water	2 cups filtered or distilled water
2 Tbsp minced parsley	1/2 tsp minced parsley
2 Tbsp grated asparagus	1/2 tsp finely grated asparagus
1 Tbsp sesame or flax oil (unrefined)	1 tsp salmon oil
3 multivitamin/mineral tablets or nuggets	1 multivitamin/mineral tablets or nuggets

Cook rice (or millet) well with 2/3 of the water, for approximately 45 minutes. In remaining water, cook chicken slightly (5 minutes). Add finely chopped raw vegetables and oil. Crush multi-vitamin/mineral and add to cooled mixture. If your animal's appetite is poor, flavor the mixture with raw, organic liver or organic fat-free yogurt (2 tsp for cats and 1 Tbsp for dogs). Use as a meal or topping over natural base senior-type food (reduce commercial pet food by the amount of "topper" recipe added).

As a Meal	
Cat/Small Dog (up to 14 lb)	1/2 cup
Medium Dog (15-34 lb)	1 cup
Large Dog (35-84 lb)	2 cups
Giant Dog (85+ lb)	2- 3 cups

you add water-containing foods to your cats' daily diet. You can also offer them a mineral-rich soup made from chicken, celery, and potato skins, simmered for 20 minutes to make a tasty broth that cats love. Besides the water, your cats will receive lots of naturally occurring minerals, which can help to alkalinize the system and help set the stage for the reduction of inflammation at the cellular level.

Alternative Veterinary Therapies

Kidney disease is serious and you should always manage your animal's condition under the guidance of your family veterinarian.

The Nutritional Blood Test (NBT). These specific remedies are available from veterinarians who utilize the NBT testing system can help support animals with kidney disease (see Chapter 4 for more information). We've seen good results with these remedies—they can extend and improve the day-to-day quality of your animal's life.

Kidney Support Formula contains repair (RNA/DNA) factors required for improved kidney function while helping to regulate protein metabolism by balancing the metabolic functions of the liver, pituitary and adrenal gland thereby reducing the excretion stress on the kidney. Dose for cats: 1/2 tablet twice daily. Dogs: 1 tablet for each 25 pounds of body weight.

Chinese Herbal Remedies

Kidney Guard, a preparation designed for use in animals with renal disease.

Renal Disease - H79 is a remedy used for chronic renal failure.

Generally these Chinese herbal remedies will be dosed at 1 capsule for every 10 to 20 pounds of body weight, or as directed by your veterinarian.

Combination Homeopathics

Hypothalamus Drops provides specific cellular and glandular support for the hypothalamus and pituitary glands.

Hypothalamus Drops (twice daily)	
Cat/Small Dog (up to 14 lb)	7 drops
Medium Dog (15-34 lb)	10 drops
Large Dog (35-84 lb)	12 drops
Giant Dog (85+ lb)	15 drops

Kidney Drops provides tissue and glandular support for the kidneys. The drops improve circulation, elimination of waste and filtration, and are especially useful in chronic nephritis.

Kidney Drops (twice daily)	
Cat/Small Dog (up to 14 lb)	7 drops
Medium Dog (15-34 lb)	10 drops
Large Dog (35-84 lb)	12 drops
Giant Dog (85+ lb)	15 drops

Kidney, Ovarian, Adrenal Drops provides specific cellular and glandular support for the kidney, ovary, and adrenal glands.

Kidney, Ovarian, Adrenal Drops (twice daily)	
Cats/Small Dogs (up to 14 lb)	7 drops
Medium Dogs (15-34 lb)	10 drops
Large Dogs (35-84 lb)	12 drops
Giant Dogs (85+ lb)	15 drops

Kidney, Prostate, Adrenal Drops provides specific cellular and glandular support for the kidney, prostate, and adrenal glands.

Kideny, Prostate, Adrenal Drops (twice daily)	
Cat/Small Dog (up to 14 lb)	7 drops
Medium Dog (15-34 lb)	10 drops
Large Dog (35-84 lb)	12 drops
Giant Dog (85+ lb)	15 drops

Kidney/Bladder Formula reduces inflammation and strengthens the entire urinary tract in conditions such as lower urinary tract disease (LUTD), nephritis, cystitis, urolithiasis, and urethritis.

Kidney/Bladder Formula (twice daily)	
Cat/Small Dog (up to 14 lb)	7 drops
Medium Dog (15-34 lb)	10 drops
Large Dog (35-84 lb)	15 drops
Giant Dog (85+ lb)	20 drops

BHI Combination Homeopathics. We also recommend a homeopathic combination remedy from BHI Laboratories with three combination homeopathics: Kidney, Inflammation, and Exhaustion. (For more on Homotoxicology, see Chapter 4.)

BHI Kidney/Inflammation/Exhaustion (three times daily)	
Cat/Small Dog (up to 14 lb)	1/3 dropper
Medium Dog (15-35 lb)	1/2 dropper
Large Dog (35-84 lb)	1 dropper
Giant Dog (85+ lb)	1 dropper

What's the Prognosis?

Most of us learn the hard way that kidney disease is a silent killer. If your animal is diagnosed with this disease, enlist the help of both a holistic and conventional veterinarian. The integrative approach of medical fluid therapy combined with natural remedies to strengthen the internal organs usually improves your animal's quality of life. Don't give up on your animal until you've tried the natural remedies and diet discussed in this chapter.

Lower Urinary Tract Disease

Lower Urinary Tract Disease (LUTD) is actually a constellation of conditions affecting the urinary tract, including infections (cystitis) and stones (urolithiasis). Crystal and stone formation (especially in male dogs and cats) can lead to a blockage of urine flow that if not corrected can cause serious complications and can be fatal. Infections and stones occur most often in male cats, ages one to four (regardless of whether or not they have been neutered). Stone formation also occurs in dogs— blockages (particularly in males) can occur, and commonly, surgical removal of the stones from the urinary bladder is required. Both cats and dogs should be put on a preventive dietary and supplementation program, or the condition can become chronic, requiring ongoing treatments such as antibiotics, urinary acidifiers or alkalinizers, or repeated surgeries.

Feline Bladder Stones

The veterinary community and pet food industry have been trying to solve the issue of feline bladder stones for years. While much has been written about this disease, a great deal of confusion still surrounds it. The suspected causes of this perplexing disease began to surface early in Dr. Bob's veterinary career. Back then, it was called Feline Urological Syndrome (FUS), and the ash content of dry cat food was thought to be the culprit. The cat food industry responded by making low-ash foods. Still, blocked cats continued to show up at clinics and emergency hospitals.

Research in the '90s indicated that the magnesium content of the food was the troublemaker, especially in the formation of struvite stones (magnesium ammonium phosphate). At this time it was determined that these stones would not form if the urine was kept acidic (a pH below 7). So, manufacturers soon formulated and began selling cat foods that contained low levels of magnesium and ingredients that helped to keep the urine acidic. While helping to solve this condition, other complications surfaced. It appears that when pet food makers formulate diets designed to "fix" a specific problem, the body responds with another variation of the problem.

Veterinarians now see cats who are eating this low-ash, forced-acidification type of food, and guess what? Different types of stones called calcium oxalate crystals are forming. These calcium oxalate stones form in acidic urine, and it is now being suggested that the low levels of magnesium designed to prevent struvite stones are actually causing the body to eliminate more calcium, setting the stage for this calcium type of stone.

Clearly, our approach to helping prevent stone formation is missing something! Let's consider more carefully what has been left out of the equation:

When your cat eats, food is digested, assimilated, and absorbed. Wastes are eliminated through the bowel, urinary tract, lungs, and skin. Urine is composed of metabolic waste products and minerals that are filtered out of the blood, diluted with water, and excreted. A big part of the problem is that the body cannot use all minerals in the same way. When minerals are in a biologically active or bioavailable form (we call them "nutrient minerals"), they can be used for the body's metabolic processes, such as digestion. When minerals are not biologically active, or inorganic, the body can't use them (we call them "waste minerals"). The body must eliminate waste minerals via the urine. If the amount of inorganic minerals in the diet is too great, the excessive amounts would be eliminated in the urine. If the environment of the urine in the bladder is right, crystal and stone formation would begin. In LUTD, it is these minerals that bind together to form bladder stones.

While veterinarians and pet food manufacturers are focused on these minerals' ability to stay dissolved in the urine, and the acid/base qualities of the food, there is little focus on the type of magnesium and other minerals that are being added to these commercial cat and dog foods. While most commercial pet foods are fortified with minerals required to meet minimal government requirements, some pet food manufacturers use the cheapest inorganic minerals they can buy such as copper sulfate, iron oxide (rust), and magnesium oxide to fortify their foods (see Chapter 1).

Early Warning Signs

Please don't take chances with this disease! Urinary blockages can be life threatening, and the signs of irritation and complete blockage are nearly indistinguishable. Common symptoms are:

- Increased frequency of urination
- Reduced urine volume and production
- Noticeable blood in the urine
- Straining with no urine being produced
- In cats—urinating outside the litter box (such as in the bathtub)
- In dogs—frequent accidents in the house.

It's often difficult to determine whether an animal has a severe irritation or a urinary blockage. If urine is retained, the toxic wastes flow back into the bloodstream, and internal poisoning (uremia) can occur, often leading to coma and death in as short as 24 to 48 hours. If your cat shows signs of urinary trouble, the safest course of action is to promptly have him checked out by your family veterinarian.

What Will Your Veterinarian Recommend?

Cystitis usually responds well to antibiotics, and most animals recover promptly. Your veterinarian will probably select an antibiotic such as enrofloxacin or amoxicillin to combat the infection, and provide other medications designed to acidify or alkalinize the urine and relieve spasm of the bladder and urethra.

More resistant infections require a urine culture to pinpoint the most effective antibiotic. Other testing might include a urinalysis and a radiograph or sonogram to give your veterinarian an image of the contents of the bladder, which will indicate whether or not there are larger stones. Blocked males may require insertion of a catheter to unplug the system. If your cat blocks repeatedly, your veterinarian may recommend surgery to permanently enlarge the opening of the urethra.

Surgery will also be necessary to remove large bladder stones in both dogs and cats. The stones can then be analyzed to identify their chemical makeup and serve as a basis for a dietary prevention program, such as an acidification diet for struvite stones, or an alkalinizing diet for calcium oxalate stones.

There are also prescription diets available from veterinarians designed to dissolve crystals and stones. These are usually low-magnesium, forced acidifying diets. While this may sound like a good solution, there are flaws. First, these dissolving-type of diets are only good for struvite stones. Second, they require ingredients that do not necessarily support long-term health of the body. For example, excessive amounts of inorganic minerals, by-products, and preservatives make them incompatible for long term health and wellness.

At-Home Support and Prevention

Diet and nutrition are the keys to help prevent LUTD.

Diet

Begin by following the steps in The Goldstein Food Plan, Level III, which is high in naturally occurring antioxidants, phytonutrients, protein, and fat and lower in carbohydrates. Most alternative veterinarians agree that feeding a diet that is higher in protein and fat and lower in carbohydrates reduces the incidence and recurrences of both urinary tract infections and stone formation. It is for this reason that we recommend selecting a highly rated canned natural base food (see Chapter 1) for animals prone to LUTD.

In addition, most natural base foods rated high enough to qualify for our Food Plan contain chelated minerals, which the body absorbs and utilizes much more easily and are less likely to cause crystal and stone formation.

Water

For general prevention in healthy animals, properly filtered water is adequate. But for animals chronically plagued with LUTD, steam-distilled water or reverse osmosis, which has inorganic minerals removed, is recommended. This water, along with biologically active minerals found in fresh vegetables, will help prevent LUTD.

Encourage water intake. If your dog or cat doesn't drink much, add water directly into the food: For cats and small dogs add a few teaspoons; for large dogs up to 1 to 2 cups. If he'll accept it, add a little organic apple cider vinegar (another good source of digestible minerals) to his water.

Supplements

You can further boost your animal's system with antioxidants. The following supplements can be added to your animal's dietary program for struvite stones. *Note: For calcium oxalate stones use only vitamin E and B6 and check with your veterinarian.*

Vitamin C (Ascorbic Acid) (twice daily)	
Cat/Small Dog (up to 14 lb)	125-250 mg
Medium Dog (15-35 lb)	500 mg
Large Dog (36-84 lb)	750 mg
Giant Dog (85+ lb)	1,000 mg

Vitamin B6 (daily)	
Cat/Small Dog (up to 14 lb)	25 mg
Medium Dog (15-35 lb)	50 mg
Large Dog (36-84 lb)	75 mg
Giant Dog (85+ lb)	100 mg

Vitamin E (daily)	
Cat/Small Dog (up to 14 lb)	100 iu
Medium Dog (15-35 lb)	200 iu
Large Dog (36-84 lb)	400 iu
Giant Dog (85+ lb)	400 iu

Vitamin A (daily)	
Cat/Small Dog (up to 14 lb)	2,500 iu
Medium Dog (15-35 lb)	2,500 iu
Large Dog (36-84 lb)	5,000 iu
Giant Dog (85+ lb)	5,000 iu

Earth Animal's **Pee Pee Formula** is a Western herbal combination of uva ursi, horsetail, dandelion, yarrow and marshmallow, which is helpful for both infections and stones.

Pee Pee Formula (twice daily)	
Cat/Small Dog (up to 14 lb)	7 drops
Medium Dog (15-35 lb)	10 drops
Large Dog (36-84 lb)	15 drops
Giant Dog (85+ lb)	20 drops

Cranberry Extract can also be used, but not for animals with calcium oxalate crystals.

Cranberry Extract (twice daily)	
(Not to be used for calcium oxalate crystals)	
Cat/Small Dog (up to 14 lb)	100 mg
Medium Dog (15-34 lb)	250 mg
Large Dogs (35-84 lb)	500 mg
Giant Dogs (85+ lb)	750-1,000 mg

Alternative Therapies

Bladder infections and stones can be serious, and you should seek the guidance of your family veterinarian for treatment protocol.

The natural remedies available from veterinarians who utilize the NBT testing system can help support active bladder condition and often prevent a chronic condition (see Chapter 4 for more on the NBT).

Urinary Bladder Support Formula helps reduce bladder inflammation and improves control of the urine. General dose for cats is 1/2 tablet twice daily. For dogs, 1 tablet twice daily for every 25 pounds of body weight.

Chinese Herbal Remedies

Cystitis (Chronic) - H63 is used for chronic urinary bladder infections.

Urinary Stones/Crystals - H27 is used for prevention and helping to dissolve urinary crystals and stones.

Urinary Tract Infection (UTI) - H51 is used for recurrent urinary tract infections.

The general dose of Chinese herbal remedies is 1 capsule for every 10 to 20 pounds or as directed by your veterinarian.

Combination Homeopathics

Urinary Drops are helpful for cystitis and urolithiasis.

Urinary Drops (twice daily)	
Cat/Small Dog (up to 14 lb)	5-7 drops
Medium Dog (15-34 lb)	10 drops
Large Dog (35-84 lb)	12 drops
Giant Dog (85+ lb)	15 drops

BHI Combination Homeopatics can also be used. (For more on Homotoxicology, see Chapter 4.)

BHI Kidney + Bladder + Inflammation	
BHI Kidney + Bladder + Infection	
(twice daily)	
Cat/Small Dog (up to 14 lb)	1/3 dropper
Medium Dog (14-34 lb)	1/2 dropper
Large Dog (35-84 lb)	1 dropper
Giant Dog (85+ lb)	1 1/2 dropper

What's the Prognosis?

The prognosis for recurrent infections and crystal formation is generally good if you address the condition and set up a preventive dietary and supplemental program. Chronic stone formation in dogs and cats also requires early detection and prevention. It is important, however, to realize that stones themselves can mechanically irritate the bladder and urethra, causing ongoing inflammation and cell damage. This will often lead to scarring and narrowing of the urethra, often leading to chronic problems.

Liver Diseases

The liver is known as the "seat of metabolism" because so many physiological and metabolic processes occur in the organ. Next to the skin, the liver is your animal's largest organ. Located between the diaphragm and stomach, it performs hundreds of important functions of your dog or cat's metabolism, including waste removal and detoxification. This all-encompassing organ also acts as a storage and dispensing center for important nutrients.

The liver breaks down hormones and enzymes no longer required by the body. It stores the body's main supply of energy—glycogen, the precursor of sugar that comes from the digestion of carbohydrates. It manufactures hormones required for day-to-day functioning and is the body's main filtering "plant," clearing away toxins, metabolic wastes and poisons on a daily basis. Besides these important functions, liver cells also produce bile salts, which aid in the digestion of fats.

Liver disease is a serious condition common in cats and dogs. Liver disease can result from infections (hepatitis), inflammation, and degeneration, which can develop through continual exposure to chemicals or drugs. This organ can also clog with fats, becoming swollen and inefficient, leading to a disease called hepatic lipidosis. As with any organ or tissue, a continually irritated and inflamed liver can develop into serious degenerative diseases, such as liver cancer.

Liver disease usually begins with an inflammatory process leading to swelling and a decrease in blood flow. If not corrected, this stagnation leads to inflammation and damaged liver cells. Over time, damaged cells can be replaced with scar tissue, a condition called cirrhosis. If the swelling is severe, it can block the flow of bile through the liver, leading to jaundice or icterus.

Manufacturers and government regulatory agencies want you to believe that the levels of chemical additives and preservatives in pet foods are too low to cause liver probelms. They fail to tell you, however, that the effects of daily exposure at the level of the liver cells are cumulative, and daily intake increases the load of free radicals. Common causes of free radical production include exposure to toxins in food and the environment, and the chronic use of medication and repeated annual vaccinations. Removal of the inciting causes, coupled with remedies to reduce inflammation, will help to restore liver health and prevent future disease.

Diseases of the Liver

Liver disease in dogs and cats takes different forms and may have many different causes:

- **Viral hepatitis** is an infection leading to liver cell destruction.
- **Fatty liver disease (hepatic lipidosis)** eventually leads to fat deposits in the liver that clog and inhibit healthy function.
- **Chronic active hepatitis** signals prolonged inflammation of the liver, generally with secondary bacterial or viral infection.
- **Liver cancer** is often the result of a compromised immune system and chronic inflammation of the liver.

Early Warning Signs

The liver is one of the most badly abused parts of your animal's body. It's constantly being challenged by toxins and poisons such as pesticides, insecticides, pollution, drugs, vaccinations and body waste, some of which, like the pesticide DDT, cannot be broken down or excreted. Signs of toxic overload range from fatigue, depression, flatulence, irritability, stomach discomfort, skin eruptions, foul breath, body odor and general aches and pains. If your animal has been overvaccinated or treated for chronic disease with prescription drugs, he is most likely in need of attention to his liver.

The good news about the liver is that, for the most part, it can take a lot of abuse. It has an amazing ability to regenerate provided that it's given sufficient rest and support. The classic sign of a diseased liver is jaundice, a condition in which the whites of the eye or the mucous membranes of the mouth turn yellow from the backup of bile pigment into the bloodstream. Unfortunately, once jaundice occurs, the disease is already advanced—so it's much better to diagnose liver problems early.

Breeds at Risk for Liver Weakness

Australian Shepherd
Bedlington Terrier
Bernese Mountain Dog
Boxer
Cairn Terrier
Chihuahua
Cocker Spaniel
Doberman Pinscher
Golden Retriever
Irish Wolfhound
Labrador Retriever

Miniature Schnauzer
Pomeranian
Pug
Saint Bernard
Samoyed
Shih Tzu
Toy Poodle
West Highland White Terrier
Yorkshire Terrier

If your animal begins showing symptoms such as loss of appetite, depression, vomiting, or weight loss, it's imperative that you visit your veterinarian promptly for a physical examination and complete blood analysis. At this early stage, he or she can confirm early liver disease and set up a prevention program.

What Will Your Veterinarian Recommend?

Your veterinarian will check several blood parameters specific to the liver. They include:

- ALT (alanine aminotransferase) levels. ALT is an enzyme found in liver cells. When elevated amounts of ALT are found in the blood it may indicate a liver problem.
- AST (aspartate aminotransferase) levels. AST is also an enzyme found in liver cells and may indicate liver damage (and can also indicate problems in muscle tissue such as the heart). The AST level needs to be elevated in conjunction with other results to determine liver function.
- Total Bilirubin. Bilirubin is a bile pigment that results from the breakdown of old red blood cells. If the liver cannot filter out bilirubin, it elevates in the blood, causing yellow skin and inside of eyes and ears (jaundice).
- Albumin levels. Albumin is a blood protein manufactured by the liver. With liver disease, not enough albumin is produced, so low levels can indicate disease.
- GGTP (gamma-glutamyltranspeptidase). GGTP is a liver and bile system enzyme which will can indicate a blocked liver.
- If X-rays or an ultrasound confirm an enlarged, swollen liver or a mass, your veterinarian may recommend a guided biopsy. Liver cells will be analyzed to determine whether the problem is inflammatory (mild noninfectious hepatitis), degenerative (lipidosis, or fatty deposits in the liver), infectious (hepatitis) or cancerous. (There is danger of excessive bleeding with this type of procedure, so your veterinarian will recommend a blood clotting test before it is done.)

Toxic Liver Inventory

Be aware if your animal is at risk for liver disease. Check off any that apply to your animal:

- Chronically prescribed drugs of any kind.
- Vaccines given repeatedly and without detoxification.
- Genetic predisposition to liver disease in family medical history.
- Drinks non-purified tap water.
- Use of chemical, nerve gas-derived pesticide, or insecticide in shampoo, flea or tick collars, dips or sprays.
- Household toxins, exposure to vapors from commercial carpets or chemical household cleaners and sprays.
- Poor-quality, highly chemicalized diet.
- Exposure to backyard herbicides, radiation, or other environmental toxins.

Common therapies include drugs such as cortisone to reduce inflammation and slow down the immune response. Your veterinarian will be careful with cortisone as it can cause liver cell death. Broad-spectrum antibiotics may be recommended to fight off or prevent infections. Drugs such as Ursodiol (Actigall) may be recommended to reduce immune system activity and help prevent scarring, as well as improving the flow of bile through the liver.

Other therapies are aimed at relieving symptoms of the disease. For example, using diuretics to remove excess fluids, subcutaneous fluids to treat dehydration, and zinc to help prevent copper toxicity. Interestingly, this is one disease in which conventional veterinarians recommend antioxidants such as vitamins E and C to help reduce free radical-induced inflammation.

At-Home Support and Prevention

It is important that you work closely with your family veterinarian. Liver disease is dangerous, and you need to support your cat or dog during difficult periods with fluid and drug therapies when necessary. Once your animal's condition has stabilized, you can use gentle holistic remedies at home that help cleanse the blood and liver, ease symptoms, and stimulate the true healer—the immune system. Immediately discontinue all topical insecticides, chemical flea collars, dips, sprays, and shampoos, which all place further burden on the liver.

Diet

Conventional veterinarians acknowledge the importance of diet in healing liver disease. In fact, according to the *Book of Dogs*, published by the UC-Davis School of Veterinary Medicine, "The liver is able to heal if the patient is provided with a diet that supports an optimal return to normal function...The diet must be based on protein from milk and/or soybean; healing is impaired when the protein source is meat. No commercially prepared foods are acceptable." Key foods listed in this reference book include cottage cheese and/or tofu as the protein source; boiled rice; and a vitamin/mineral mixture, especially vitamin C and zinc. We'll discuss more about diet and supplements in just a moment.

Good nutrition is the key to managing liver disease. You must pay particular attention to the protein levels in the diet when dealing with any disease of the liver. As mentioned above, the liver is the body's filter, removing impurities that may have adverse affects on the all cells, tissues, and organs. When protein enters the digestive tract and is prepared for absorption, ammonia is one of the by-products of protein digestion. When ammonia is absorbed into the blood stream it immediately goes directly to the liver then to the kidneys for removal.

When the liver is swollen, blood flow may be restricted, causing this ammonia-rich blood from a heavy protein meal to bypass and travel directly to the brain, causing seizures. This is called a hepatic shunt and requires feeding a lower level of high-quality protein.

If you feed the Goldstein Food Plan, you should lower the protein levels to about 20 to 25 percent for dogs, 35 to 45 percent for cats, offer plenty of organic vegetables, fish or flax oil, and about 50 percent complex carbohydrates (found in organic brown rice, oatmeal, or millet). This will reduce the liver's workload by providing limited amounts of protein, highly digestible complex carbohydrates, and quality omega-3 and omega-6 rich fatty acids to help minimize further liver damage and improve function. Other liver-enhancing foods include garlic, celery, beet greens, ginger, tofu, green beans, kale, parsley, dandelions, and vegetable broth (go organic with the vegetables, or scrub well with a veggie wash).

Liquids are important to help detoxify your animal's body. Try the Rejuvenation drink from the box on this page, which is beneficial for liver problems. This drink must be introduced in moderation to promote gentle detoxification.

> **Susan's Rejuvenation Drink**
>
> Use a juice extractor with the following ingredients:
>
> 1 apple
> 1 small beet
> 1 handful of dandelion leaves
> 1 handful of dark green lettuce
> 1 carrot
> 1 Tbsp powdered wheat grass
>
> Start by offering several teaspoons to several tablespoons. Over a two-week period, work up to 1/2 to 1 cup per day for small animals, and 2 to 4 cups per day for large ones. If your animal is on a long-term medication program, you can offer the juice once or twice a day after the introductory period.

Nutritional Remedies

These nutritional remedies will be the cornerstone of your animal's preventive therapy.

Milk Thistle. Prevention can be accomplished with short-term ingestions of liquid milk thistle, an herb and member of the daisy family (available at health food stores). Milk thistle contains a special flavonoid called silymarin, which enhances liver function, promotes cell development and acts as an antioxidant, ridding the liver of harmful toxins. Use for two weeks and then rest for two weeks.

Milk Thistle Elixir (twice daily)	
Cat/Small Dog (up to 14 lb)	7 drops
Medium Dog (15-34 lb)	10 drops
Large Dog (35-84 lb)	15 drops
Giant Dog (85+ lb)	20 drops

Licorice is a natural anti-inflammatory.

Licorice (daily)	
Cat/Small Dog (up to 14 lb)	7 drops
Medium Dog (15-34 lb)	10 drops
Large Dog (35-84 lb)	15 drops
Giant Dog (85+ lb)	20 drops

Here are some other supplements we've found helpful in the prevention of liver disease, available from heath food stores.

Alpha Lipoic Acid (daily)	
Cat/Small Dog (up to 14 lb)	50 mg
Medium Dog (15-34 lb)	100 mg
Large Dog (35-84 lb)	150 mg
Giant Dog (85+ lb)	200 mg

Ester C (twice daily)	
Cat/Small Dog (up to 14 lb)	100 mg
Medium Dog (15-34 lb)	250 mg
Large Dog (35-84 lb)	500 mg
Giant Dog (85+ lb)	750 mg

Vitamin E (daily)	
Cat/Small Dog (up to 14 lb)	100 iu
Medium Dog (15-34 lb)	200 iu
Large/Giant Dog (35+ lb)	400 iu

Zinc (daily)	
Cat/Small Dog (up to 14 lb)	15 mg
Medium Dog (15-34 lb)	25 mg
Large Dog (35-84 lb)	35 mg
Giant Dog (85+ lb)	50 mg

Vitamin B Complex (daily)	
Cat/Small Dog (up to 14 lb)	50 mg
Medium Dog (15-34 lb)	100 mg
Large Dog (35-84 lb)	125 mg
Giant Dog (85+ lb)	175 mg

Alternative Veterinary Therapies

The following is a list of special liver-oriented nutraceutcials and remedies that are available through veterinarians who utilize the NBT process.

Nutritional Blood Test

If your animal has been diagnosed with a liver problem, besides his or her suggested medical therapy (or in place of the recommended therapy if the liver condition is not serious) request that your veterinarian perform a Nutritional Blood Test (NBT) (see Chapter 4). Here's why: Since liver disease often has its beginning elsewhere in the body, the NBT can act like a detective to determine the source of the problem. When an animal's body begins to degenerate, organs such as the adrenal, pituitary, or thyroid glands become overburdened and begin to function inefficiently. These imbalances overload the major elimination organs such as the liver.

If this process is unchecked, the end result may be liver disease—when in reality the real cause is a weakened gland elsewhere in the body. The NBT can pick up these related weaknesses and point to healing agents that address the source. In the process, this will take the burden off the liver so it can heal. Veterinarians throughout the country can now perform the NBT via Antech Laboratories.

The NBT nutraceutical powder containing vitamins, minerals, antioxidants, and gland support nutrients will be custom blended for your animal based upon the weaknesses and imbalances as determined by the analysis of the blood. It will help to strengthen the entire system, not just the liver.

As an alternative to this blood-based therapy, your veterinarian may recommended specific non-drug liquid remedies, Chinese herbs, or fixed-formula nutraceuticals that will further enhance the entire gland system or reduce the inflammation in the liver itself.

Liver/Gall Bladder Support Formula supplies vitamins (C, A, E, K, B2, folic acid), minerals (calcium, zinc), and amino acids (methionine, taurine, cysteine, glutathione) that support metabolic detoxification and cellular regeneration. For cats: 1/2 tablet twice daily. For dogs 1 tablet for each 25 pounds of body weight or as directed by your veterinarian.

Chinese Herbal Remedies

The following Chinese herbal remedies can be added along with the custom-blended NBT Nutraceutical Powder or added to the Liver/Gall Bladder Support Formula based upon your veterinarian's specific diagnosis.

Cholangiohepatitis/Chronic-H77 is a Chinese herbal remedy used for chronic cholangiohepatitis, a condition that affects both the liver (hepatitis) and the bile system (Cholangio).

Gallbladder Disease is Chinese herbal remedy used for gallbladder stones, sludge, or inflammation or infection in the gallbladder.

Hepatic Lipidosis, a Chinese Herbal preparation that is specific for Hepatic Lipidosis (fatty deposits in the liver). It helps fight this disease common in cats.

Cirrhosis is a Chinese herbal used in the treatment of cirrhosis of the liver.

Hepatic Copper Toxicity is a Chinese herbal preparation used for Copper Toxicity (a serious liver disease common in Bedlington Terriers).

LiverGuard is a Chinese herbal combination that is used as a dietary supplement for patients with an enlarged or diseased liver or with elevated liver enzymes.

The general dose for Chinese herbal preparations is 1 capsule for each 10 to 20 pounds of body weight twice daily.

Combination Homeopathics

Combination homeopathics work with the body's own healing systems to minimize inflammation. They will be selected by your veterinarian based upon the diagnosis and your animal's clinical condition.

Liver/Gallbladder Drops is a combination homeopathic remedy that reduces inflammation in the liver cells and helps regenerate healthy tissue.

Liver/Gallbladder Drops (twice daily)	
Cat/Small Dog (up to 14 lb)	7 drops
Medium Dog (15-34 lb)	10 drops
Large Dog (35-84 lb)	12 drops
Giant Dog (85+ lb)	15 drops

Detox or **Chemical Drops** is a combination homeopathic that aids in the detoxification process. Helps the body inactivate toxins and assists the organs of elimination (such as the liver) to gently get rid of the toxins.

Detox or Chemcial Drops (twice daily for 4 weeks then stop for 2 weeks and restart)	
Cat/Small Dog (up to 14 lb)	10 drops
Medium Dog (15-34 lb)	15 drops
Large Dog (35-84 lb)	20 drops
Giant Dog (85+ lb)	25 drops

BHI Combination Homeopathics (Alcohol Free). Your veterinarian might select any of these combination homeopathics. (See Chapter 4 for more information on Homotoxicology.)

BHI Liver + Inflammation + Infection	
BHI Gallbladder + Inflammation + Infection	
BHI Liver + Gallbladder + Inflammation	
(twice daily)	
Cat/Small Dog (up to 14 lb)	1/3 dropper
Medium Dog (15-34 lb)	1/2 dropper
Large Dog (35-84 lb)	1 dropper
Giant Dog (85+ lb)	1 to 2 droppers

Combination Western Herbs

Liver Formula is an herbal extract used for support and reduction of inflammation, and contains herbs such as milk thistle (a liver anti-inflammatory) and licorice.

Liver Formula (twice daily)	
Cat/Small Dog (up to 14 lb)	7 drops
Medium Dog (15-34 lb)	10 drops
Large Dog (35-84 lb)	15 drops
Giant Dog (85+ lb)	20 drops

Liquid Liver extract from Enzymatic Therapy is a concentrated liver supplement produced from a fraction of beef liver from animals raised in Argentina with no exposure to chemical toxins, sprays, or pesticides.

Liquid Liver (daily)	
Cat/Small Dog (up to 14 lb)	1 capsule
Medium Dog (15-34 lb)	2 capsules
Large Dog (35-84 lb)	3 capsules
Giant Dog (85+ lb)	3 to 4 capsules

What's the Prognosis?

Prevention is the key when it comes to the liver. Eliminating chemical additives and preservatives and supplying the appropriate diet and detoxifying liquids will help maintain a healthy liver, one that is not overworked and inflamed. If your animal's liver weakness has progressed to the point of disease, it is important to work with a veterinarian who understands that liver disease often has its beginning elsewhere in the body. Degenerating adrenal, pituitary, or thyroid glands cause imbalances that can overload a major elimination organ like the liver. Also, it's important to vaccinate wisely (see Chapter 3).

Musculoskeletal Diseases

The musculoskeletal system is composed of muscles, bones, ligaments, tendons, joints, cartilage, and the connective tissue that holds the body together, and is responsible for movement. Inflammation of the musculoskeletal system is among the most widely talked about problem for both people and animals. Drugs to help the pain and discomfort of the tendons, joints, and ligaments are responsible for a large part of the pharmaceutical industry.

More research and clinical testing has been conducted on the effects of alternative remedies as they relate to musculoskeletal function than any other system. One of the biggest-selling nutraceuticals is Cosequin, a natural remedy which contains glucosamine and chondroitin, building blocks for healthy joints and cartilage.

Many animals are exposed on an ongoing basis to toxins and other free radical-producing agents such as chemical additives and preservatives in pet foods, insecticides, medications, and vaccines. The organs can become overburdened with foreign substances or free radicals produced during the process of detoxification. Increased free radicals and diminished reserves of antioxidants lead to inflammation in the joints, resulting in a decrease in the production of synovial fluid. This decrease in synovial fluid causes further deterioration of joint function as well as friction and pain. If the proper levels of antioxidants and nutrients (vitamins, minerals, etc.) are not available, the inflammatory process will progress and can result in a painfully crippling degenerative disease.

Arthritis

Arthritis is not a disease of the joints per se—it is a systemic disorder whose main symptoms show up in the joints. Inflammation and degeneration always seek the body's "weak spot," be it the joint, a kidney, the heart, or even a tooth. Arthritis involves a breakdown of the body's glandular and immune components, which can no longer maintain production of synovial fluid in the joints, resulting in swelling, pain, erosion of cartilage, and reluctance to move. Joint fluid acts as a shock absorber to help protect the cartilage and also serves as nourishment to the joint surface. Once joint fluid disappears, a mechanical friction process begins to degrade the cartilage and sets the stage for the mineral deposits and finally the diagnosis of arthritis.

Early Warning Signs

- Your animal spends more time sleeping.
- Your animal seeks warmth.
- Your animal is limping.
- Your animal has difficulty going up or down stairs, or jumping up into or out of your car.
- Your animal seems to be down in spirit.

What Will Your Veterinarian Recommend?

Conventional veterinary medicine has been reluctant to let go of the premise that the only solution is potent steroidal and non-steroidal anti-inflammatory drugs such as cortisone, aspirin, Rimadyl, and Deramaxx. Such beliefs are fed by advertisements for these drugs, perpetuating the myth of seemingly miraculous effects delivered by pharmaceuticals. Yes, you can bring a painful, crippled animal to your veterinarian, and within 24 hours your friend may be acting like a puppy again and eating with gusto. However, it is at best only a temporary reprieve, distracting the guardian from the real issue. While we are not against the use of painkilling medication when absolutely necessary, such drugs fail to address the underlying cause of arthritis and are not without their own side effects.

Rimadyl (carprofen), a nonsteroidal anti-inflammatory drug (NSAID) and Meloxicam (Metacam), claim to have fewer side effects than cortisone. We have seen animals that could barely get up, or go up and down stairs, come back to life and begin to thrive on this drug. However, as with most medications, there is a price to pay with potentially serious side effects. Rimadyl is a potent painkiller and anti-inflammatory metabolized and detoxified by the liver. Adverse reactions can occur within hours of the first dose, or days or weeks later. The drug's label reflects the range of side effects, including decreased appetite, vomiting, diarrhea, jaundice, seizures, and even death. We are especially concerned about the potential for liver and kidney damage with the use of this drug.

Another potential side effect of potent painkillers is one that might not be readily apparent— the symptoms of the disease are a way to instruct the body to rest. By controlling the pain and covering up the symptoms, your animal's body may feel like it is back to normal, but continual exercise of inflamed joints can increase friction, increasing inflammation. In the long run this can cause further breakdown of the joints, leading to a more painful arthritic condition.

At-Home Support and Prevention

While a painkilling drug can bring temporary relief, more effective therapy boosts the body's internal healing mechanisms, reducing inflammation and restarting the rebuilding of lubricating fluid production.

In our view, a better long-term approach to arthritis is to address the problem at its origins—a general weakness in the internal organs along with a specific inflammatory process within the joints and connective tissues. Fortunately, you can turn the tide on joint pain and inflammation without reliance on drugs. Our program is based on a good diet, supplementing with antioxidants, and the combination of glucosamine and chondroitin. These nutraceuticals will allow the gradual elimination of NSAIDS. (*Note: Never reduce any medication without first consulting your veterinarian.*)

Diet

A joint-rebuilding diet is exactly what the doctor ordered. The Goldstein Food Plan (see Chapter 1) is high in phytochemicals found in fresh vegetables. Chopped or juiced carrots, celery, and greens (parsley, broccoli) can help to ease joint pain and inflammation.

When mixed with an eye toward palatability, dogs and cats usually lap them up. The best combination we have found is carrot, celery, parsley, and apple. This juice is loaded with organic, acid-neutralizing minerals such as sodium and potassium as well as phytochemicals that help to fight free radicals and reduce inflammation. And of course, the base is pure water, which enhances the cellular elimination of metabolic, clogging wastes.

Water is essential for keeping the joints working. It may be difficult to get your dog, and especially your cat, to drink lots of water. Here's a tip: add water to the daily food. Use Susan's potato peeling broth (see Part 10 in this chapter), fresh juices, as well as the "juice" from steamed veggies to add precious water to your animal's system. When it comes to arthritis, the best water is that produced by steam distillation or reverse osmosis. Distillation removes the inorganic minerals, which can settle in the joints, causing inflammation, pain, and loss of mobility. Steam-distilled water, being mineral free, will attract metabolic wastes and discarded minerals, flushing them out of the body. We have long used and recommended the Pure Water brand of steam-distilled water (see Resources).

Nutraceuticals

The Arthritis Cure by Jason Theodosakis, MD, exploded many longstanding myths about arthritis. For example, it has long been believed that arthritis is a disease of unknown origin and "incurable," requiring long-term use of anti-inflammatory medication including cortisone. Theodosakis introduced a scientifically validated alternative: chondroitin and glucosamine. Together these compounds form the building blocks of healthy cartilage and can help to slow or even reverse the damaging effects of joint degeneration.

Glucosamine sulfate is required for the formation of glycosaminoglycans (GAGS), building blocks of joint cartilage. In addition to building cartilage, it helps maintain joint fluid thickness and elasticity. Chondroitin sulfate works in tandem with glucosamine to increase mobility in the joints. It acts as a "fluid magnet," helping to attract fluid to the GAGS while blocking the destructive effects of certain enzymes within the joint capsule.

Glucosamine and chondroitin are the twin keys to healing—the building blocks for healthy joint tissue and repair. They come in various forms, such as sulfate and hydrochloride. If your animal is on a potent NSAID such as Rimadyl, and you want to reduce the dependence on the drug, speak with your veterinarian about a reduction schedule. Don't withdraw the drug suddenly, or without advice from your veterinarian.

Start your dog or cat on the glucosamine/chondroitin combination, along with the medication, for the first two weeks; then wean him or her off the medication over a two- to three-week period, under the guidance of your veterinarian.

These combinations are now readily available in most pet stores and human health food stores.

Joint-Juice Elixir

2 medium carrots
3 stalks celery
1 handful parsley
1/2 apple for sweet flavoring

Juice all ingredients, then give once or twice daily. Try a weekly 12-hour meal skip and offer the juice instead of solid foods.

Joint-Juice Elixir	
Cat/Small Dog (up to 14 lb)	1/4 cup
Medium Dog (15-34 lb)	1/2 cup
Large Dog (35-84 lb)	1 cup
Giant Dog (85+ lb)	2 cups

Glucosamine (daily, for one month)	
Cat/Small Dog (up to 14 lb)	500 mg
Medium Dog (15-34 lb)	750 mg
Large Dog (35-84 lb)	1,000 mg
Giant Dog (85+ lb)	1,500 mg

Chondroitin (daily, for one month)	
Cat/Small Dog (up to 14 lb)	250 mg
Medium Dog (15-34 lb)	350 mg
Large Dog (35-84 lb)	500 mg
Giant Dog (85+ lb)	750 mg
After one month, cut dose in half for maintenance.	

There are now numerous companies that are producing glucosamine/chrondroitin combinations for animals. One such combination, Cosequin (manufactured by Nutramax Labs), was proven effective in the management of joint pain in the knee in a randomized, placebo-controlled and peer-reviewed clinical study. In this study, 3,080 veterinarians were asked about Cosequin for over 28,000 joint problems (the most commonly affected joint being the hip, followed by the knee and elbow). These veterinarians rated Cosequin as "good to excellent in reducing pain and improving mobility and improving attitude in over 80 percent of the animals administered Cosequin. Side effects were also recorded with less than 2 percent of the dogs developing a mild gastrointestinal upset." Follow the dosage recommended on the package.

K-9 Liquid Health is a liquid remedy that contains glucosamine and chondroitin sulfate. It is void of sweeteners, starch, salt, wheat, yeast, corn, milk, or derivatives of soy. It's easy to administer—simply mix into wet or moist food. The dose can be adjusted down for maintenance or prevention or increased during cold weather or a flareup of symptoms. K-9 Liquid Health can also be given to our feline friends—just follow label instructions.

We found this product so successful with our animals we had to order the human version for some of our friends and family. We found that the human experience mimics the animal one. Amanda Bennie, Earth Animal store manager, gave some to her Aunt Candy, and her arthritis symptoms lessened overnight. A young 40-year-old customer of ours whose fingers were already curled up from arthritis is very enthusiastically moving her fingers free of pain now that she's tried the remedy.

Antioxidant Support

Specific antioxidant supplements may be helpful for dogs with arthritis or hip dysplasia. We recommend the following home program:

Ester-C® (twice daily)	
Cat/Small Dog (up to 14 lb)	250 mg
Medium Dog (15–34 lb)	500 mg
Large Dog (35–84 lb)	750 mg
Giant Dog (85+ lb)	1,000 mg

Vitamin A (once daily)	
Cat/Small Dog (up to 14 lb)	2,500 iu
Medium Dog (15–34 lb)	5,000 iu
Large Dog (35–84 lb)	7,500 iu
Giant Dog (85+ lb)	7,500-10,000 iu

Manganese (once daily)	
Cat/Small Dog (up to 14 lb)	15 mg
Medium Dog (15–34 lb)	25 mg
Large Dog (35–84 lb)	35 mg
Giant Dog (85+ lb)	45 mg

Vitamin E (once daily)	
Cat/Small Dog (up to 14 lb)	200 iu
Medium Dog (15–34 lb)	400 iu
Large Dog (35–84 lb)	600 iu
Giant Dog (85+ lb)	600-800 iu

(In 6 to 8 weeks, cut the dose of vitamin E in half.)

Superoxide Dismutase (twice daily)	
Cat/Small Dog (up to 14 lb)	50 mg
Medium Dog (15–34 lb)	75 mg
Large Dog (35–84 lb)	100 mg
Giant Dog (85+ lb)	150 mg

No More Pain, available from Earth Animal, is a combination herbal remedy used to relieve the pain and inflammation associated with injuries, fractures, stretched and torn ligaments, and general aches and pains.

No More Pain (twice daily)	
Cat/Small Dog (up to 14 lb)	7 drops
Medium (15-34 lb)	10 drops
Large (35-84 lb)	13 drops
Giant (85 lb +)	20 drops

Earth Animal's **Achy Joints** is a combination of herbal extracts, including white willow bark, meadowsweet, black cohosh, devil's claw, and yucca. It is designed to reduce pain and inflammation in joints, ligaments, and tendons.

Achy Joints (twice daily)	
Cat/Small Dog (up to 14 lb)	7 drops
Medium Dog (15-34 lb)	10 drops
Large Dog (35-84 lb)	15 drops
Giant Dog (85 lb +)	20 drops

Exercise and Fresh Air

Exercise improves the circulation and gets the "juices" flowing, essential for managing arthritis. Remember, there is no blood supply to the cartilage—it gets all of its nourishment through the synovial fluid. Fresh air will perk up your animal's mental attitude, as arthritic animals often become depressed and lethargic.

Caution: If your animal has been maintained on a potent non-steroidal anti-inflammatory drugs (NSAIDs) such as Rimadyl, be careful when introducing more exercise. Keep in mind that the underlying mechanism of arthritis is the drying up of the lubricating fluid (synovial fluid). When a NSAID or cortisone is used, the animal's pain and inflammation are masked, while the joint continues to degenerate. Continual exercise on a "dry" joint will, through friction, make the condition worsen.

Once you've made the transition to our natural program, gradually increase the level of exercise. Strive for gentle, steady exercise on a forgiving surface. This program, along with the other steps we've listed, will encourage the body to again produce lubricating joint fluid.

Consider the Emotions

If your animal is lethargic or withdrawn due to pain, consider flower essences to revive the spirit. We recommend **Return to Joy**, available from Anaflora, given in fresh drinking water daily for four weeks.

Return to Joy (daily)	
Cat/Small Dog (up to 14 lb)	5 drops
Medium Dog (15-34 lb)	5 drops
Large Dog (35-84 lb)	5-10 drops
Giant Dog (85+ lb)	5-10 drops

Veterinary Alternative Therapies

Arthritis is not a disease of the joints but rather a compromised immune system that is unable to keep its own tissue from becoming inflamed. There is generally an excessive free radical load coupled with a deficiency in antioxidants leading to a furtherance of the inflammatory response. In these circumstances, the immune system often overreacts to its own tissue (autoimmune reaction) resulting in increased inflammation. It is for these reasons (especially with severe or crippling arthritis and pain) that you work with your family veterinarian or an experienced alternative veterinarian. The following therapies are available.

Acupuncture

Acupuncture is traditionally the insertion of very fine, filament-like needles in specific areas, which help reduce pain and provide a sense of well-being (see Chapter 4 for more information). The needles stimulate the acupoints to release and redirect blocked energy. A certified veterinary acupuncturist may insert needles alone, inject a homeopathic solution (Aquapuncture) or add warmed herbs (Moxibustion), vitamin B12 or a low electrical current (electro-acupuncture) to enhance the effects. Acupuncture is especially effective in older and aging animals suffering from arthritis and degenerative joint conditions such as hip and elbow dysplasia.

COX-2 Inhibitors

Zyflamend and **Kaprex** are botanical and natural COX-2 inhibitors. Zyflamend is a botanical non-steroidal combination of phytonutrient-rich herbs that help to inhibit the COX-2 enzyme (a contributor to inflammation) and help to promote healthy joint tissue.

Kaprex has been found to inhibit the formation of prostaglandin E2 (PGE2). PGE2 formation is associated with joint discomfort. Kaprex is made with hops, rosemary and oleanolic acid, which are beneficial plant compounds that can support the health of joints by interfering with signals that promote PGE2 synthesis.

Since Zyflamend and Kaprex are botanically derived, they do not have the potential adverse effects of drugs like Pyroxicam and Metacam, COX-2 inhibitors that can cause stomach upsets and even bleeding ulcer.

Zyflamend (daily)	
Cat/Small Dog (up to 14 lb)	1 capsule
Medium Dog (15-34 lb)	2 capsules
Large Dog (35-84 lb)	3 capsules
Giant Dog (85 lb +)	3-4 capsules

Kaprex (twice daily)	
Cat/Small Dog (up to 14 lb)	1/2 tablet
Medium Dog (15-34 lb)	1 tablet
Large Dog (35-84 lb)	1 1/2 tablets
Giant Dog (85 lb +)	2 tablets

Nutritional Blood Test (NBT)

By the time the arthritis, pain and inflammation show themselves, there are often other areas of degeneration lurking below the surface. Remember, arthritis is the superficial symptom of a deeper-lying problem. It is for this reason that we recommend our NBT testing to make sure that the "whole" body is examined. Using the NBT analysis, your veterinarian can find the best therapies for your dog or cat. The-custom blended nutritional powder derived from the NBT analysis will specifically address the nutrient, gland support, and antioxidant needs of your animal.

The following remedies can be recommended by your veterinarian based upon the diagnosis and the area of the body that is inflamed and painful.

Cartilage/Ligament/Muscle/Skeletal Support Formula is a remedy that will help in the regeneration of connective tissue, cartilage, and tendons while reducing inflammation at the cellular level. For cats: 1/2 tablet twice daily. For dogs: 1 tablet for each 25 pounds of body weight twice daily.

Chinese Herbal Remedies

The following Chinese herbal remedies can enhance the basic nutritional and nutraceutical supplements more focused on a specific condition.

Arthritis/Shoulder & Elbow - H3 is used for musculoskeletal disease of the front legs, including tendonitis, osteochondrosis dessicans, and ununited anconeal process.

BackRelief is designed for use in animals with pain from spinal disease or muscle spasms along the back.

HipGuard is designed for animals with hip dysplasia and osteoarthritis of the hips, knees, and hocks.

Joint Guard is designed for animals with pain due to polyarthritis and polyosteoarthritis.

Osteoarthritis - H20 is used for severe degenerative joint conditions with loss of articular cartilage and remodeling of bone.

The general dosage for these Chinese herbal remedies is 1 capsule for every 10 to 20 pounds of weight or as directed by your veterinarian.

Combination Homeopathics

The following combination homeopathics can help with pain and inflammation associated with arthritis.

Arthritis Drops reduces the pain and inflammation associated with osteoarthritis, tendonitis, bursitis, contusions, and associated muscle injury.

Arthritis Drops (twice daily)	
Cat/Small Dog (up to 14 lb)	5 drops
Medium Dog (15-34 lb)	7 drops
Large Dog (35-84 lb)	10 drops
Giant Dog (85+ lb)	15 drops

Ligament Drops provides specific cellular and tissue support for the ligaments, joints, connective tissue, and muscles.

Ligament Drops (twice daily)	
Cat/Small Dog (up to 14 lb)	5 drops
Medium Dog (15-34 lb)	7 drops
Large Dog (35-84 lb)	10 drops
Giant Dog(85+ lb)	15 drops

Pain Drops alleviates and reduces localized and generalized pain.

Pain Drops (twice daily)	
Cat/Small Dog (up to 14 lb)	5 drops
Medium Dog (15-34 lb)	7 drops
Large Dog (35-84 lb)	12 drops
Giant Dog (85+ lb)	15 drops

The following combination Western herbs are also useful as part of an arthritis program. **Arthritis Formula** relieves painful and inflamed joints, ligaments and tendons.

Arthritis Formula (twice daily)	
Cat/Small Dog (up to 14 lb)	7 drops
Medium Dog (15-34 lb)	10 drops
Large Dog (35-84 lb)	15 drops
Giant Dog (85+ lb)	20 drops

Pain Formula relieves the pain and inflammation associated with injuries, fractures, inflamed and torn ligaments, muscles and tendons.

Pain Formula (twice daily)	
Cat/Small Dog (up to 14 lb)	7 drops
Medium Dog (15-34 lb)	10 drops
Large Dog (35-84 lb)	15 drops
Giant Dog (85 lb +)	20 drops

BHI Combination Homeopathics. BHI Traumeel Pain/Spasm Inflammation, BHI Arthritis Traumeel Inflammation, BHI Zeel/Traumeel/Inflammation, BHI Back/Inflammation/Pain, can be mixed together specifically for each animal, and they are alcohol free. (See Chapter 4, section on Homotoxicology for more information).

BHI Combination (twice daily)	
Cat/Small Dog (up to 14 lb)	1/3 dropper
Medium Dog (15-34 lb)	1/2 dropper
Large Dog (35-84 lb)	1 dropper
Giant Dog (85 lb +)	1 dropper

Hip Dysplasia

Dr. Bob, a graduate of the University of Pennsylvania School of Veterinary Medicine, was privileged to study under Dr. Wayne Riser. Dr. Riser was a research pioneer who identified hip dysplasia (HD) as an inherited disease that develops as an animal grows and matures. In hip dysplasia, the ball and socket joint of the hips do not fit correctly and develop into secondary arthritis. It is Dr. Riser's work, as well as many organizations dedicated to eliminating HD, that has led to the incredible awareness about hip dysplasia. Organizations such as the Orthopedic Foundation for Animals (OFA) and the Penn Hip Program identify and issue certificates for dogs whose hips are free of dysplasia.

Dr. Riser's work took place in the 1960s and '70s, and since then there have been tremendous strides in identifying causes and treatments of hip dysplasia, including the ability to identify HD early in an animal's life, genetic awareness to try to eliminate HD from breeding lines, and sophisticated surgical procedures such as the triple pelvic osteotomy and total hip replacement surgery.

While this work has done wonders for early identification and surgical correction of hip dysplasia, as well as associated genetically linked diseases such as elbow dysplasia (an inherited disease of the elbow) and osteochondritis dessicans (an inherited disease characterized by cracks and flaps in articular cartilage), these diseases are still very common. Even with all this sophisticated and comprehensive data, they are often diagnosed just after your animal's first year, burdening you with hard treatment decisions—potent pain killers, steroids, and very expensive corrective surgeries are all possibilities.

The underlying causes for these often painful and even crippling diseases have been linked to genetics (improper breeding), over-exercise in a genetically prone puppy, and diet (poor nutrition, especially mineral imbalances).

Our Golden Retriever, Leigh, developed crippling arthritis and hip dysplasia at the tender age of two. By the time he was seven, none of the standard "solutions"—steroids, painkillers—were helping, and we faced surgery or euthanasia. At that time we were working with a group in New York City that helps people locate alternative cancer therapies. The proverbial light bulb switched on when we realized that all of these therapies for human cancer patients relied on treatments that fueled their internal healing power—the immune system. We immediately switched our strategy. We began feeding Leigh a diet of cooked whole grains, fresh meat, and vegetables along with freshly extracted juices. Our beloved dog made a stunning recovery and lived to the ripe old age of 17.

Prevention

There is really only one sure-fire way to prevent diseases such as hip and elbow dysplasia—by totally eliminating the breeding of animals that are prone to these diseases (which, of course, is next to impossible). Something we can control, however, is the feeding of chemically ladened, heat-sterilized foods loaded with non-nutritious by-products, chemical additives, and preservatives that don't support the control of pain and the body's attempt to heal itself.

For puppies that are prone to these diseases, supplementing vitamin C during growth stages has been proven effective in strengthening the connective tissue that holds the joints in place, thereby helping to prevent the disease from occurring.

For treatment and prevention of hip dysplasia, elbow dysplasia, or osteochondritis dessicans, follow the programs listed for arthritis (above).

What's the Prognosis?

Many folks accept arthritis as an inevitable part of aging. While your buddy may not be as spry as he or she used to be, we believe that it's part of our job as guardians to do everything we can to minimize pain and maintain mobility and health in our companions. And it's not only the humane thing to do—following our plan will also extend the longevity of your pal, giving you many more active years to enjoy together.

If your dog or cat is suffering from the effects of chronic arthritis or hip dysplasia, he or she may already be on medication. While this is fine to temporarily reduce pain and inflammation and restore mobility, we encourage you to go deeper and address the body's core needs with help from the therapies discussed in this chapter.

Pancreatic Diseases

The pancreas is located directly alongside the first section of the small intestines. It is involved in many metabolic processes, and has both exocrine and endocrine functions. The exocrine function involves the production of digestive enzymes—enzymes that cause the breakdown of fats, proteins, and carbohydrates so that they may be properly absorbed and assimilated by the cells of the body. The endocrine function directly oversees the levels of sugar in the blood by producing insulin to control blood glucose levels.

Disease of the pancreas can broadly be categorized as either inflammatory or degenerative. Since the pancreas is involved in the digestion of nutrients, and because many of the foods fed to dogs and cats are loaded with highly indigestible nutrients, this gland is in constant danger of being overloaded, overworked, and compromised.

The most common condition of the pancreas is diabetes mellitus, related to a decrease in the production of or utilization of insulin. An overworked pancreas can also result in exocrine pancreatic insufficiency (EPI), leading to a decrease in the production of the digestive enzymes: lipase (breaks down fat), amylase (breaks down carbohydrates), and protease (breaks down proteins). If the pancreas becomes inflamed it can lead to a painful and serious disease called acute pancreatitis. A long-standing inflammation coupled with a compromised immune system may lead to further degeneration and even cancer.

Diabetes Mellitus

Many people think that diabetes is a human condition, but this chronic degenerative disease commonly affects dogs and cats, as well. Diabetes develops most commonly when the pancreas no longer produces adequate amounts of insulin. Without sufficient insulin, blood sugar cannot be properly regulated, resulting in a variety of symptoms and complications.

Many cats and dogs eat a diet high in simple (refined) carbohydrates. Commercial pet foods contain up to (and in some cases in excess of) 50 percent refined carbohydrates, as contained in white flour and white rice. Processed

Tips for Helping Your Diabetic Animal

- Medical stability is essential
- Diet should be fixed and fed at specific times
- Supplement with the nutrients described on page 294

carbohydrates act like sugar in the body, and are rapidly absorbed into the bloodstream and burn quickly. These spikes in sugar levels followed by a rapid burn can spell trouble for the pancreas. The resulting rapid ups and downs in blood sugar levels send misleading messages to the pancreas, which becomes exhausted trying to meet the demand for insulin. Eventually, the pancreas slows and may even cease production of insulin. Without adequate insulin, glucose becomes trapped in the bloodstream, unable to nourish your animal's tissues. The end result is the diagnosis of diabetes mellitus.

As with people, there are two types of diabetes. Insulin dependent diabetes (type 1) most often affects dogs and can be congenital in origin. Diabetic dogs generally require daily insulin injections to help maintain proper blood sugar levels. This disease is commonly seen in Golden Retrievers, German Shepherds, Keeshonds, and Poodles. Cats are more prone to non-insulin dependent diabetes (type 2). This type of diabetes is often linked to obesity and may be controlled with diet, without the need for insulin injections.

Always keep in mind that diabetes is a disease not solely related to the pancreas. Sugar metabolism is complex and involves many organs, including the pancreas, the stomach, the intestines, the adrenals, liver, thyroid, and the pituitary gland. Since these multiple organs must work together to metabolize sugar, diabetes is a weakness of the entire organ system, which is totally dependent on adequate levels of sugar for survival.

Early Warning Signs

Early signs of both types of diabetes include:
- Dramatic increase in thirst.
- Dramatic increase in appetite.
- Increase in urine production.
- Noticeable weight loss.

What Will Your Veterinarian Recommend?

Diabetes is diagnosed based on physical examination, medical history, blood tests, and urinalysis. In all instances of acute diabetes—especially when there is serious wasting—you must control the medical condition. Work with your veterinarian, who will determine the appropriate dosage and schedule for the insulin injections.

Your veterinarian will stabilize your dog or cat's diet with insulin injections (for type 1 patients). He or she will determine the proper dosage schedule of insulin to control the condition and then train you to give the injections at home. Dietary recommendations often include a diet that is high in fiber. Fiber slows the absorption of glucose and helps maintain more consistent blood sugar levels. More recent research has revealed that higher protein diets (especially in cats) are quite helpful in controlling diabetes.

Cats with insulin-dependent diabetes are more difficult to regulate than dogs, and in general are more nutrient sensitive and prone to deficiency diseases. They may require more than insulin injections to stabilize the condition. Strict adherence to a high-protein diet, which has been shown to help cats maintain a more constant blood sugar level may be required. This may be true because a cat's body can convert protein to sugar, requiring less in the diet necessary to maintain adequate blood levels. It is our opinion that eliminating the need for carbohydrates in the diet can help to reduce the resultant sugar "peaks and valleys," leading to a more controlled blood level, requiring less insulin.

> ## Simple At-Home Method to Monitor Blood Glucose
>
> - Start the insulin injections at your veterinarian's recommended level.
> - Before giving the next injection, check the urine glucose level with a glucose urine test strip (available at drug stores).
> - The goal is to have the urine glucose just at trace (or one positive). If the urine sugar is at 3, 4 or more, you should increase the amount of insulin; conversely, if the urine sugar is negative, the amount of insulin should be reduced. This should always be done under the direction and approval of your veterinarian.

Insulin injections, while essential to manage the medical crisis, indirectly tell the pancreas to stop producing insulin. Consequently, the body becomes dependent on the daily insulin injections as the pancreas becomes less responsive. Natural compounds such as vitamins, minerals, antioxidants, digestive enzymes, herbs, and homeopathics can help stimulate the pancreas into producing adequate amounts of insulin, thus reducing the need for injections.

Diabetics, once stabilized with proper diets and nutritional supplements, often require less insulin to control blood sugar levels. (*Note: Never decrease any medication without consent from your veterinarian.*) Alternative nutritional programs can work along with insulin, strengthening the pancreas and balancing other organs, so the need for these injections is either diminished or in some cases eliminated.

At-Home Support and Prevention

Feed your animal on a strict schedule recommended by your veterinarian. There must be adequate sugar in the blood when the insulin injections kick in, otherwise it will further reduce already low glucose levels, potentially causing incoordination, coma, and even death. Veterinarians will periodically check blood glucose levels to make sure that the insulin dosage is correct.

Diabetic Menu

For Dogs
1 cup senior base food, about 20% protein
1 cup chicken, beef, or turkey (lightly steamed)
1/2 cup finely chopped raw green beans or green pea sprouts
2 tsp chopped parsley
1 clove finely chopped garlic
1 Tbsp flaxseed oil

For Cats
1/2 cup senior base food, about 30% protein
1/2 cup chicken, beef, or turkey (lightly steamed)
1 tsp finely chopped raw green beans or green pea sprouts
1/2 tsp chopped parsley
1 1/2 tsp salmon oil
Mix ingredients together and follow the timed feeding schedule established by your veterinarian.

Diet

Switch to a high-fiber diet. Your veterinarian will most likely prescribe a high-fiber or protein diet that will help to regulate the absorption of carbohydrates from the intestines into the bloodstream. Our Food Plan Level III (see Chapter 1) can also work for a diabetic animal since it is inherently higher in naturally occurring fiber and high-quality protein.

Keep in mind that recent research has shown grain-based diets loaded with wheat and corn may contribute to higher incidences in diabetes. Therefore, diets that are higher in protein and lower in carbohydrates are recommended.

If you are following our Food Plan you should add additional protein (chicken, beef, turkey, lamb) and decrease the carbohydrate contents to below 20 percent. For dogs, protein levels should reach about 40 to 45 percent, and for cats, about 55 to 65 percent. Fat should make up about 15 percent for dogs and 20 percent for cats. The balance of the diet should consist of finely chopped green vegetables. When dealing with diabetes and insulin injections, it is imperative to review your selected diet with your veterinarian.

The box on this page includes menus we created especially for diabetics. The whole grains offer beneficial fiber and complex carbohydrates. The green beans or sprouts contain enzymes that perform insulin-like activity, as does the parsley, which also contains chlorophyll (a good cleanser). Garlic helps purify the intestines, making them more efficient, and flaxseed and salmon oil are highly digestible fats rich in essential fatty acids.

Shattering Five Common Myths of Diabetes

While diabetes can take its toll on your animal's vision, kidneys, and heart, and in some cases can prove fatal, many myths continue to swirl about this much-feared disease. Let's set the record straight, so you are empowered with "clinical wisdom" to prevent diabetes or deal with it effectively should it come your dog or cat's way.

Myth #1. Once the pancreas stops making insulin, it will never start again.
This is just plain untrue. The pancreas can often be rejuvenated and coaxed back into proper function by a nutrient- and antioxidant-rich diet that is high in naturally ocurring fiber, increased exercise, and a correct balance of vitamins, minerals, nutraceuticals and herbs. You can introduce such changes after your veterinarian brings the disease under control with insulin.

Myth #2. Once on insulin, always on insulin.
Good news—often an integrated nutritional program combined with appropriately dosed and monitored insulin (directed by your veterinarian) will help to control the condition and can eventually reduce the amounts of insulin or even totally eliminate any dependency on it. Your animal's program should include a well-balanced whole food, additional fiber, appropriately dosed vitamins, minerals, antioxidants, and herbs, as well as an increased exercise program. Your veterinarian can instruct you on how to closely monitor the blood sugar levels by frequently checking the urine.

Myth #3. Diabetes is hereditary and you cannot prevent it.
Untrue! Nothing exhausts a pancreas more than sugar-ladened food. Yet today, many cats and dogs exist on just that—an overprocessed diet high in refined carbohydrates, which can add up to a serving of straight table sugar, and in some cases more than 50% of the food could be considered sugar. The rapid burning off of these simple carbs results in a speedy elevation and depression of blood sugar levels, which can tire out the pancreas as it tries to meet the insulin needs in a rapidly changing environment. Follow our guidelines for a diet containing low levels of complex carbohydrates (such as oatmeal and brown rice) and high-quality protein and fats.

Myth #4. Sugar "highs" go with the territory and there is nothing that you can do to help control them.
If your animal appears ravenous, serve him a bowl of freshly cooked oatmeal. Oats, along with green beans and sprouts, contain vitamins, minerals, and enzymes that have insulin-like activity. Oats are rich in beneficial fiber.

Myth #5. You will just have to live with frequent "accidents" in the house.
Don't buy into this grim prognosis. The serious side effects of excessive thirst and urination is temporary if the diabetes is controlled medically. Simultaneously, the proper feeding and nourishment (vitamins, minerals, cofactors, and antioxidants) of the pancreas and other important glands of the body will start the process of reestablishing glandular balance and function. This, combined with an increased exercise program, can help to bring the condition under control and diminish all adverse symptoms associated with diabetes.

Nutritional Supplements

It's a good idea to begin using nutritional supplements while you and your veterinarian are working to stabilize your animal.

Vitamin E. High sugar levels thicken the blood, which impedes the transport of nutrients to cells as well as the elimination of toxins and wastes. A daily dose of vitamin E (available in capsule form at health food stores) will help increase circulation and reduce inflammation. You can give the full daily dose of vitamin E at a single meal. Pierce the capsule with the tip of a knife and squeeze the oil onto your animal's food.

Vitamin E (once daily)	
Cat/Small Dog (up to 14 lb)	200 iu
Medium Dog (15-34 lb)	400 iu
Large Dog (35-84 lb)	600 iu
Giant Dog (85+ lb)	800 iu

Chromium and **Goldenseal.** The following nutritional supplements should be used once your animal is stable and diet and medication well established. The mineral chromium has been shown to help regulate blood sugar levels and lessen the secondary effects of diabetes. The herb goldenseal has been shown to reduce the amount of insulin necessary to control blood sugar. Mix the recommended amount of alcohol-free goldenseal tincture with 1 to 2 tsp of water and administer twice daily. Both are readily available in health food stores.

Chromium GTF (once daily)	
Cat/Small Dog (up to 14 lb)	25 mcg
Medium Dog (15-34 lb)	50 mcg
Large Dog (35-84 lb)	100 mcg
Giant Dog (85+ lb)	150 mcg

Goldenseal (twice daily)	
Cat/Small Dog (up to 14 lb)	5 drops
Medium Dog (15-34 lb)	10 drops
Large Dog (35-84 lb)	12 drops
Giant Dog (85+ lb)	15 drops

Alternative Veterinary Therapies

With diabetes, it's essential to support and boost all of the key glands of the body. Your veterinarian has many alternative options to help support and control diabetes. The following remedies can be obtained through veterinarians who use the NBT program.

The Nutritional Blood Test (NBT)

We recommend asking your veterinarian to run a Nutritional Blood Test (NBT) for an individualized approach to control diabetes. Your veterinarian can use this analysis to recommend either a custom-blended powder, or a fixed formulation (in tablet form) to support the organ systems.

The NBT will also help your veterinarian select combination homeopathics, herbal formulations, and homotoxicology remedies that can enhance, support, and help to balance the pancreas and other glands that are involved in sugar metabolism. These remedies can support the pancreas in the production of the proper insulin levels again, thus reducing or even eliminating the need for daily injections.

Pancreas Endocrine/Exocrine Support Formula helps to reduce inflammation by supplying antioxidant vitamins and specific amino acids. It supports pancreatic enzyme levels while helping digestion and assimilation, and supplies chromium that has been proven to help in the regulation of blood glucose levels. For cats: 1/2 tablet twice daily. For dogs: 1 tablet for 25 pounds of body weight twice daily.

You can also use the following combination homeopathics for animals with diabetes.

Diabetes Drops helps relieve symptoms associated with diabetes and hyperglycemia such as polydypsia (excessive thirst), polyuria (excessive urination), and polyphagia (excessive hunger). Take orally, without food.

Diabetes Drops (twice daily)	
Cat/Small Dog (up to 14 lb)	5-7 drops
Medium Dog (15-34 lb)	8-10 drops
Large Dog (35-84 lb)	12 drops
Giant Dog (85+ lb)	15 drops

Hypothalamus Drops is a combination homeopathic product that provides specific cellular and glandular support for the hypothalamus and pituitary glands. Take orally, without food.

Hypothalamus Drops (twice daily)	
Cat/Small Dog (up to 14 lb)	5-7 drops
Medium Dog (15-34 lb)	8-10 drops
Large Dog (35-84 lb)	12 drops
Giant Dog (85+ lb)	15 drops

Pancreas Drops provides tissue and glandular support for the pancreas, and is especially useful in supporting symptoms of pancreatitis and diabetes. Take orally, without food.

Pancreas Drops (twice daily)	
Cat/Small Dog (up to 14 lb)	5-7 drops
Medium Dog (15-34 lb)	8-10 drops
Large Dog (35-84 lb)	12 drops
Giant Dog (85+ lb)	15 drops

BHI Combination Homeopathics. BHI - Pancreas + Inflammation + Pain is a combination homeopathic (see Chapter 4, section on Homotoxicology for more information).

BHI - Pancreas + Inflammation + Pain (twice daily)	
Cat/Small Dog (up to 14 lb)	1/3 dropper
Medium Dog (15-34 lb)	1/2 dropper
Large Dog (35-84 lb)	1 dropper
Giant Dog (85+ lb)	1 dropper

Pancreatitis

When pancreatic cells become overworked and sluggish they begin to break down. This breakdown releases cellular debris into the bloodstream, which signals the immune system to mobilize antibodies against this "foreign" material. A local inflammatory response occurs, and dangerous molecules called free radicals are formed. The body then sends in antioxidants to neutralize the free radicals, which usually stops the process. However, if the pancreas continues to be overworked and pancreatic cells continue to break down, eventually the body will use up its antioxidant reserves, and the inflammatory process begins to overtake the pancreas.

> ## At-Risk Dogs and Cats
>
> Acute pancreatits can occur in both dogs and cats. Most commonly acute pancreatits occurs in middle-aged female dogs and cats of the following breeds:
> Miniature Poodle
> Miniature Schnauzer
> Cocker Spaniel
> Siamese cat

If this inflammatory process is not corrected, acute pancreatitis may result. This painful condition can cause violent vomiting and diarrhea, which can lead to dehydration and even death. If your dog or cat is diagnosed with acute pancreatitis, medical intervention with antibiotics, anti-inflammatory medication, and fluid therapy may be required to save the life of your animal. Recovery takes about two to four weeks before your animal returns to normal.

However, even if the pancreas heals, it will now be susceptible to secondary complications such as pancreatic insufficiency, which is a reduced ability to produce digestive enzymes. The enzyme reduction is caused by scar tissue left from the acute inflammation. Animals with pancreatic insufficiency can no longer digest and absorb nutrients efficiently, and may become very thin and weak. To prevent wasting, afflicted animals will need to be supplemented daily with digestive enzymes.

While your veterinarian may try to pin the cause on an "infection" the overworked, stressed pancreas is the real culprit. But what caused this pancreatic panic in the first place? Many commercial pet foods are made with poorly digestible proteins (tendons, cartilage, hair), highly cooked, saturated fats, and simple carbohydrates (such as white flour and sugar). Flavor enhancers and preservatives create even more work for an animal's GI tract. When these low-quality foods are the main staple of your dog or cat, the pancreas has to work overtime in order to produce the necessary digestive enzymes to process this highly undigestible and preserved food.

Warning Signs

Signs of acute pancreatitis begin with a painful, tense abdomen, along with vomiting, diarrhea, depression, loss of appetite, and loss of weight.

What Will My Veterinarian Recommend?

If your veterinarian makes the diagnosis of acute pancreatitis, hospitalization, intravenous fluids, and medications to control the pain, vomiting, and diarrhea are often essential.

At-Home Support and Prevention

After your veterinarian has stabilized the condition, an at-home prevention program should follow.

Diet

If your animal is on the Goldstein Food Plan (see Chapter 1), you have taken a major step toward prevention of pancreatitis. Our Food Plan is low in saturated fats and high in omega-3 and -6 fatty acids, which are easy to digest and anti-inflammatory in their action. Next, raw or partially cooked fresh meat (preferably free-range or organic) is added to the program along with complex carbohydrates from whole grains. Finally, fresh vegetables such as shredded carrots and broccoli add phytonutrients, antioxidants, vitamins, and minerals.

If you have an overweight animal who has been primarily fed an overprocessed, saturated fat-rich diet and the diagnosis is acute pancreatitis, your first task will be to stabilize your animal with medication prescribed by your veterinarian. When your animal is stable and off medication, start with a meal skip or a 24-hour fast to rest the digestive tract. During the fasting period, offer your animal potato peeling broth (see box). Following this short rest, a good "soft" dietary program for your animal is boiled chicken, mashed carrots, and cooked brown rice with added flaxseed or salmon oil.

Susan's Potato Peeling Broth

This broth is rich in alkalinizing minerals, particularly potassium. Most chronic diseases, such as arthritis and upper respiratory infections, occur in acid conditions. The broth changes the environment of the body toward alkaline and sets the stage for the body to heal.

We always recommend organic produce, especially when a vegetable grows in the ground. Be sure to clean the potatoes before peeling.

   2 quarts filtered water
   8-10 medium potatoes, peeled 1/4-inch thick. (Throw away or use the peeled potato core for your own dish.)
   6 carrots, chopped
   6 stalks of celery, chopped

Combine peelings, carrots, and celery and place in water. Bring to a boil and simmer for about an hour. Makes about a three-day supply. You can feed the broth on its own or add it to your animal's food. Note: We recommend feeding potatoes to your animal provided you cook them first. They may be hard for your animal to otherwise digest.

Dogs

25% cooked organic carrots

35% boiled free-range chicken

40% cooked organic brown rice

1 tsp of flaxseed oil per 25 pounds of body weight

Cats

25% cooked organic carrots

25% cooked organic brown rice

50% boiled free-range chicken

1 tsp of salmon oil per 10 pounds of body weight

Follow this plan for three to four weeks, then over the next two weeks wean your animal off the "soft" diet, mixing it with your natural-base food.

Supplements

Digestive Enzymes. After the acute crisis has passed, you can begin supplementing with digestive enzymes. Digestive Enzymes from Dr. Goodpet is a good choice.

Digestive Enzymes (per meal)	
Cat/Small Dog (up to 14 lb)	1/2–1 tsp
Medium Dog (15-34 lb)	1–2 tsp
Large Dog (35-84 lb)	1 Tbsp
Giant Dog (85+ lb)	1 1/2 Tbsp

Yogurt. Organic, plain, low-fat yogurt can provide live cultures that help with digestion by supplying beneficial probiotics.

Organic Yogurt (per meal)	
Cat/Small Dog (up to 14 lb)	1/2 tsp
Medium Dog (15-34 lb)	1 tsp
Large Dog (35-84 lb)	2 tsp
Giant Dog (85+ lb)	1 Tbsp

Pancreas Gland Extract helps support the pancreas. Enzymatic Therapy is a good brand found in health food stores.

Pancreas Gland Extract (daily)	
Cat/Small Dog (up to 14 lb)	50 mg
Medium Dog (15-34 lb)	75 mg
Large Dog (35-84 lb)	100 mg
Giant Dog (85+ lb)	150 mg

Superoxide Dismutase (SOD) can be used to reduce inflammation. It is available in health food stores.

Superoxide Dismutase (SOD) (daily)	
Cat/Small Dog (up to 14 lb)	50 mg
Medium Dog (15-34 lb)	75 mg
Large Dog (35-84 lb)	100 mg
Giant Dog (85+ lb)	150 mg

Alternative Veterinary Therapies

Veterinary support is essential to help normalize pancreatic function. The following remedies are likely to be recommended—all are available through veterinarians who utilize the NBT program.

Nutritional Blood Test (NBT). We suggest asking your veterinarian to run a Nutritional Blood Test (NBT) for an individual nutritional approach to help the pancreas. Your veterinarian can use this analysis to recommend either a custom-blended nutritional support powder, or a fixed formulation (in tablet form) to support the organ system. The NBT will also help your veterinarian select liquid homeopathics, herbal formulations, Homotoxicology, and Chinese herbals to be used along with the custom powder or fixed formulations, which will help with treatment and symptoms.

Pancreas Endocrine/Exocrine Support Formula helps to reduce inflammation by supplying antioxidant vitamins and specific amino acids. This formula supports pancreatic enzyme levels while helping digestion and assimilation of food. For cats: 1/2 tablet twice daily. For dogs: 1 tablet for each 25 lbs of body weight twice daily.

Pancreatitis, a Chinese herbal remedy, is beneficial in the control of chronic pancreatitis. General dosage is 1 capsule for 10-20 pounds of body weight or as directed by your veterinarian.

Pancreas Drops, a combination homeopathic remedy, is especially useful in treating pancreatitis by providing tissue and glandular support for the pancreas.

Pancreas Drops (twice daily)	
Cat/Small Dog (up to 14 lb)	5 drops
Medium Dog (15-34 lb)	7 drops
Large Dog (35-84 lb)	10-12 drops
Giant Dog (85+ lb)	15 drops

Pain Formula is an herbal combination in liquid form that relieves symptoms of pain and inflammation.

Pain Formula (daily)	
Cat/Small Dog (up to 14 lb)	7 drops
Medium Dog (15-34 lb)	10 drops
Large Dog (35-84 lb)	15 drops
Giant Dog (85+ lb)	20 drops

BHI Combination Homeopathics (see Chapter 4, section on Homotoxicology for more information) can also support the pancreas.

BHI - Pancreas + Inflammation	
BHI - Pancreas + Infection	
BHI - Nausea + Pain + Traumeel	
Cat/Small Dog (up to 14 lb)	1/3 dropper
Medium Dog (15-34 lb)	1/2 dropper
Large Dog (35-84 lb)	1 dropper
Giant Dogs (85+ lb)	1 dropper

What's the Prognosis?

Acute pancreatitis and diabetes are both potentially serious diseases and should be addressed only under the care of your veterinarian. Once the acuteness of these diseases is medically and dietarily controlled, you can continue to support your animal with a natural antioxidant-rich diet and natural remedies that can help keep these diseases under control and prevent recurrences.

Thyroid Diseases

The thyroid gland consists of two butterfly-shaped lobes located in the neck. Its hormones levothyroxine (T4) and triiodothyronine (T3) are essential for the normal functioning of all cells. The thyroid is also the key to the control of your animal's metabolism (the conversion of nutrients to energy). The thyroid is in charge of the body's metabolic rate and therefore directly affects all organs and metabolic processes, including:

- The metabolism of fat, carbohydrate, and protein.
- The levels of enzymes in the body.
- The strength and rhythm of the heartbeats.
- New bone formation.
- Body weight.
- Heart rate, circulation, and blood pressure.
- Increases the rate of respiration as the demand for oxygen increases.
- Increases the rate of absorption of food from the intestines.

The thyroid gland and its relationship with the pituitary gland is an excellent example of how the body's glands work in concert to maintain blood hormone levels. The thyroid gland is under the direct control of the pituitary gland, via the Thyroid Stimulating Hormone (TSH). This hormone instructs the thyroid to produce and maintain adequate levels of thyroid hormone in the blood. As thyroid hormone levels increase, there is a feedback to the pituitary gland which in turn decreases the production of TSH. In a healthy animal, these glands are in perfect balance with each other.

Hypo- and Hyperthyroidism

Both dogs and cats can fall prey to thyroid imbalances and problems, but the two species typically display different manifestations of a gland gone awry. Hypothyroidism (an underactive, sluggish gland) is more common in dogs, while hyperthyroidism (an overactive, racing gland) is more typical in cats.

Like most other chronic degenerative diseases, both hypo- and hyperthyroid conditions usually begin with gland inflammation in combination with an imbalanced immune system. While there may be a genetic predisposition for a weakened or inflamed gland, other triggers may include exposure to environmental toxins, reaction to a vaccination, or an adverse reaction to a drug.

These triggers set the stage for an autoimmune reaction, in which the body launches an inflammatory reaction against its own tissue—in this case the thyroid. One of the most common underlying causes for an autoimmune condition is the use of repeated annual vaccinations (see Chapter 3 for more on vaccines). The subsequent inflammation results in either the destruction of thyroid cells (leading to hypothyroidism) or the irritation and over activity of thyroid cells (leading to hyperthyroidism). In cases of hyperthyroidism, if the inflammation continues and the body's immune system remains compromised, a thyroid tumor may develop, requiring surgical removal or destruction with radioactive iodine. Left unattended, thyroid conditions can require a lifetime dependence on medication.

Early Warning Signs

Although there are few early warning signs, a diseased thyroid can produce a variety of signs, including:

- **Hypothyroidism** (in dogs): Weight gain often with no change in eating habits; quiet, depressed, sluggish, lethargic; excessive dry, itching coat, often with hair loss; poor-quality coat and/or change in color; darkening of skin; personality changes.
- **Hyperthyroidism** (in cats): Weight loss; change in personality: irritable, depressed; lethargy, general malaise; rapid heart rate; greasy look, unkempt fur, normal grooming habits stop.

What Will Your Veterinarian Recommend?

Thyroid problems can be detected in the early stages from a routine blood test that measures the levels of the hormone thyroxine (T4 or Free T4). Your best avenue for early detection and treatment is to visit your veterinarian for an annual physical examination, including blood work, for all animals three years and older.

Diagnosis is made based on your animal's clinical signs, medical history, and blood analysis. Levels of T4 will be below normal in hypothyroidism and above normal in hyperthyroidism. Drug therapy for each condition is noted below. Additional medications may be necessary to treat complications; for example, severe itching may lead to a skin infection that requires antibiotics and antiseptic shampoo.

- **Hypothyroidism** (in dogs): Treatment is straightforward and usually effective. The most commonly prescribed drug, Levothyroxine (L-Thyroxine), replaces deficient thyroid hormone. With the proper dose of L-Thyroxine, most animals' symptoms disappear. While dogs generally respond well to this treatment, we recommend that you test the blood periodically in order to monitor hormone levels. Also, when the thyroid gland weakens it automatically affects the thyroid/pituitary balance and can stress other organs (such as the liver and adrenal glands), which become overworked because the thyroid is not performing well.

- **Hyperthyroidism** (in cats): The treatment, although often effective, can present its own set of problems. To treat a hyperthyroid animal, the goal is to reduce excessive levels of circulating T4 hormone. Veterinarians usually prescribe a drug called Tapazole to curtail production of thyroid hormone. Many cats, however, do not tolerate this drug well, showing symptoms such as loss of appetite, increase in thirst and urination, an unkempt greasy coat, and a listless personality. Because many cats respond poorly to Tapazole, your veterinarian may recommend surgery (especially if a tumor has developed) or the destruction of thyroid cells with radioactive iodine. An overactive thyroid gland can overwork the general metabolism, often leading to secondary complications such as heart and or kidney disease. These secondary complications illustrate the importance of viewing the "whole body's needs"— the systems of the body are intricately interrelated, and true healing stems from this understanding.

At-Home Support and Prevention

Alternative therapies offer many benefits by helping to alleviate symptoms and reestablishing balance among the organs, decreasing the dependence on drugs.

Take your animal in for an annual physical exam with a routine blood test (for animals age three and up; earlier if you see any symptoms). If early thyroid disease is detected, much can be done to reestablish balance in the body. A holistically oriented veterinarian can recommend a program designed to correct nutrient deficiencies and gland imbalances before they have a chance to wreak hormonal havoc. A preventive strategy is preferable to drug therapy because medications such as Tapazole, Soloxine, or Synthroid can make your animal increasingly dependent upon medication instead of healing the thyroid.

Blue's Story

One of our Healing Center clients, Judith, had a cat named Blue suffering from hyperthyroid disease. Judith was pursuing classical homeopathic therapy for Blue. However, Blue's blood thyroid levels crept up, and he was beginning to show classical symptoms of hyperthyroidism. We developed a program that included homeopathy along with nutritional and dietary support, plus low-dose Tapazole therapy. Blue's thyroid stabilized, and he lived to the ripe old age of 17, thanks to his integrative medical/nutritional program.

Diet

Diet makes a big difference. Levels II and III of The Goldstein Food Plan (see Chapter 1) are beneficial for animals with thyroid conditions. Since the metabolism is thrown off with this disease, your animal's body often cannot digest fats and cholesterol properly. Enzyme-rich foods, such as Daily Health Nuggets, aid digestion. The Nuggets offer a rich supply of lecithin, a nutrient that assists in the digestion of fats and cholesterol.

Alternative Veterinary Therapies

Whether your animal has hyper- or hypothyroid disease, the main issue is that the thyroid is out of balance, inflamed, and beginning to degenerate. In our practice, we use the following remedies to encourage true healing. These remedies can be used in conjunction with the veterinary prescribed thyroid hormone replacement or Tapazole, and may enable you to eventually lower the dosage of these synthetic medications. When dealing with a weakening or inflamed thyroid it is always wise to work with your family veterinarian or an alternatively minded and experienced veterinarian. They will be able to order the following products for you.

Glandular Support

Glandular support, besides being a source of enzymes, amino acids, and cell lipids, will help to neutralize the body's attack against the gland itself. Glandulars protect the thyroid, and give it an opportunity to rest and heal. This also enables the thyroid to metabolize more efficiently. In practice, the use of glandular support helps to lessen the reliance on medications such as Tapazole. Depending on which organ has been effected by the thyroid malfunction, your veterinarian may prescribe any of the following.

Thyroid Glandular (twice daily with food)	
Cat/Small Dog (up to 14 lb)	25 mg
Medium Dog (15-34 lb)	45 mg
Large Dog (35-84 lb)	65 mg
Giant Dog (85+ lb)	90 mg

Pituitary Glandular (twice daily with food)	
Cat/Small Dog (up to 14 lb)	15 mg
Medium Dog (15-34 lb)	25 mg
Large Dog (35-84 lb)	35 mg
Giant Dog (85+ lb)	50 mg

Heart Glandular (twice daily with food)	
Cat/Small Dog (up to 14 lb)	50 mg
Medium Dog (15-34 lb)	75 mg
Large Dog (35-84 lb)	125 mg
Giant Dog (85+ lb)	175 mg

Kidney Glandular (twice daily with food)	
Cat/Small Dog (up to 14 lb)	50 mg
Medium Dog (15-34 lb)	75 mg
Large Dog (35-84 lb)	150 mg
Giant Dog (85+ lb)	250 mg

The Nutritional Blood Test (NBT)

We recommend asking your veterinarian to run a Nutritional Blood Test (NBT) for the most individual and specific approach to help with thyroid problems (see Chapter 4 for more information). The NBT will determine how well the other organs of the body are working in face of a weakened or inflamed thyroid gland. Your veterinarian will use this analysis to recommend either a custom-blended nutrient and gland powder, or a fixed formulation (in tablet form) to support the organ system. The NBT will also help your veterinarian recommend the addition of combination homeopathics, herbal formulations, homotoxicology, or Chinese herbal remedies, to make the treatment more specific for the condition while helping control the symptoms.

Thyroid Support Formula is a nutraceutical formula that supports cellular regeneration, helps reduce inflammation and autoimmune reactions. For cats: 1/2 tablet twice daily. For dogs: 1 tablet for each 25 pounds of body weight twice daily.

Chinese Herbal Remedies

Hyperthyroid Formula H55 is a Chinese herbal remedy that can often be used to replace Tapazole therapy (only at the recommendation of your veterinarian). Average dose is 1 capsule for every 10 to 20 pounds or as directed by your veterinarian.

Hypothyroidism Formula H81 supports both dogs and cats with hypothyroidism Average dose is 1 capsule for every 10 to 20 pounds or as directed by your veterinarian

Homeopathic Remedies

Thyro Drops is a remedy containing homeopathically diluted glands and minerals. It is used for both hyper- and hypothyroid conditions. Thyro Drops help rebuild the thyroid and restore its normal function.

Thyro Drops (twice daily)	
Cat/Small Dog (up to 14 lb)	5 drops
Medium Dog (15-34 lb)	7 drops
Large Dog (35-84 lb)	12 drops
Giant Dog (85+ lb)	15 drops

Hypothyroid Drops, a homeopathic remedy, helps to support and regenerate the thyroid gland.

Hypothyroid Drops (twice daily)	
Cat/Small Dog (up to 14 lb)	7 drops
Medium Dog (15-34 lb)	10 drops
Large Dog (35-84 lb)	15 drops
Giant Dog (85+ lb)	20 drops

Hypothalamus Drops provides homeopathic support for the hypothalamus and pituitary glands.

Hypothalamus Drops (twice daily)	
Cat/Small Dog (up to 14 lb)	5 drops
Medium Dog (15-34 lb)	7 drops
Large Dog (35-84 lb)	10 drops
Giant Dog (85+ lb)	12 drops

What's the Prognosis?

The prognosis for hypothyroid disease is generally good if caught early. Often the symptoms of weight gain and itchy, thickened, discolored skin can be reversed. Hyperthyroidism in cats is more complicated because of the potential secondary effects on other organs, such as the kidney or heart. It is essential to catch hyperthyroid conditions early for successful treatment and prevention. This is why routine annual physical examinations and blood work are so important in the early detection and prevention of these diseases.

Chapter 9

Cancer

Cancer is arguably the most dreaded word in all of medicine—human or animal. Yet at its roots there is a common cause: A weakened or imbalanced immune system that has been overwhelmed on the job, and has lost control of healthy cell division. It can no longer effectively manage metabolism, eliminate wastes, and destroy unwanted organisms and cells. Cancerous cells crop up on a daily basis but are routinely neutralized by a healthy immune system. It is the body with the run-down immune system that has lost the ability to destroy unwanted cancerous cells.

Many veterinary clinics and university teaching hospitals are now equipped with sophisticated equipment that can make an early diagnosis of cancer. Sonograms (diagnostic ultrasound) view internal organs noninvasively, determining areas of inflammation or early growth long before the cancer shows itself. In common use are Magnetic Resonance Imaging (MRIs) and Computer-aided Tomography (CAT Scans) that show internal images that detect early diseases. Guided biopsies

Diet Makes a Difference

We've used hundreds of alternative treatments for dogs and cats with cancer, but the one thing that has always struck us is the simple fact that dietary changes make a remarkable difference in the course of the disease, and in the day-to-day quality of life for the animal.

yield tissue samples that assess the status of an organ suspected of harboring cancerous cells.

While these tests are truly advanced, they usually come into play after a problem has developed. Once cancer shows up on the screen, you've gone past the window of wellness—past your best opportunity for maintaining health. Our entire health care industry—animal and human—is based on a disease-screening model rather than true awareness and prevention of chronic diseases. It is our hope that in following our plan, your animals will be protected from the types of stressors (both internal and external) that set the stage for disease, and help to maintain true wellness.

One point that we find fascinating and quite sad in regards to cancer is that while veterinary diagnostic capabilities have advanced by light years, there has been a simultaneous increase in the incidence and mortality rates of cancer, which have accelerated exponentially. The Morris Animal Foundation has confirmed that cancer is indeed the leading cause of disease and death in companion animals. This well-respected research foundation conducted an in-depth study of over 2,000 animal guardians. In dogs, cancer was listed as the condition "most affecting" dogs (39 percent of the time) and as the cause of death in 47 percent of cases. Even in cats, cancer was the number-one cause of disease-related death in 32 percent of respondents.

Many purebred dogs and cats are born with a genetically weakened immune system that predisposes them to cancer. We regularly see in our practice animals as young as three and four years old with cancer—a disturbing trend. In our view, the entire population of companion animals is genetically weaker today than it was 20 years ago. As a result, these animals are more vulnerable to emotional, environmental, and dietary insults that can set the stage for cancer, such as:

- Emotional stressors, including mismanaged breeding in undesirable conditions, abandonment, abuse, and a stressful home life.
- Commercial pet foods containing animal and grain by-products, contaminated protein sources, chemical additives and preservatives, and lack of "living" or "life force" foods due to the high heat of cooking.
- Long-term exposure to vaccinations, antibiotics, corticosteroids, and other systemic medications (such as heartworm and flea-control products) that continually eat away at the strength of the immune system.
- Chronic exposure to environmental toxins, such as chemical insecticides (flea bombs, collars, "spot-ons," spray, etc.) and premise pesticides.

What's Gone Wrong?

Cancer is a group of chronic degenerative diseases that are named for the cell type or tissue where the body allows it to grow. In its broadest sense, cancer is toxin overload in combination with an immune system that can no longer recognize abnormal cells when they arise and can no longer maintain healthy tissue.

One of our mentors, the late Dr. Lawrence Burton, a renowned immune system specialist, firmly believed that 60 percent of the human cancer patients he treated had genetically weak immune systems. This genetic link is quite obvious in dogs. For example, Golden Retrievers and Rottweilers are at high risk for cancer because their popularity resulted in much inbreeding. One of our patients, a Golden Retriever named Teddy, was sent to the veterinary teaching hospital at the University of California at Davis for a medical evaluation. After the exam, Teddy's companion told us that of the 13 animals in the oncology waiting room with cancer, 12 were Golden Retrievers. Golden Retrievers became one of the most popular breeds in the country in the early 1980s. In the wake of that popularity came indiscriminate breeding, resulting years later in multitudes of genetically weak, cancer-prone Golden Retrievers.

Other factors linked to cancer are more directly under your control than genetics, such as eliminating chemical-laden foods, discontinuing pesticides, and vaccinating wisely (see Chapter 3), which we will also discuss briefly in this chapter.

Cancer: A Preventable and Controllable Disease

The good news is that regardless of breed and immune status of your dog or cat, you can help the body control and prevent cancer in animals who are at high risk for this disease. We have become cancer experts not out of choice, but necessity. Cancer is one of the most feared diseases in humans and animals alike; however, there are some important differences, especially when it comes to an animal's metabolism. A cat's or dog's metabolism is much quicker than a human's, therefore the disease can be accelerated, and an animal can sicken quickly. Likewise, animals can respond faster to therapies and achieve stability or remission quicker.

To make decisions on the best cancer therapy for your animal, you should understand both the conventional and alternative options before initiating any therapy. As soon as the diagnosis is made and you receive your veterinarian's recommendations, seek out a holistic opinion so that your decision is made with all of the facts. Second to prevention, early detection and selection of the proper therapy (which should not only attack the cancer but support the body's natural healing systems), give the best chance of long-term remission and quality of life.

There are two important factors we want you to be clear about. The first is that cancer, while a serious disease, is not automatically hopeless or terminal; the second is that suffering and pain are not inevitable or automatic. We've seen the energy of our clients completely change once they realize that there is hope for their companions. When holistic therapies are added, the approach is positive and operates from the point of view that your animal is receiving exactly what he or she needs to maintain wellness.

Our clients are told to take a step back and face each day as a new day. If a problem or complication arises, handle it at the time it surfaces. This way, expectations and long-term prognosis are not part of the equation, and the focus is on the day-to-day well-being of your animal. Likewise, we suggest that there be a shift in focus from "cure" to daily remission and quality of life. This takes away any expectation of success or failure, and focuses people and their companion animal's energy on living a good life on a day-to-day basis.

What Will My Veterinarian Recommend?

Early diagnosis and therapy combined with nutritional support are keys to winning the battle! Conventional treatment choices include those commonly available for humans: chemotherapy, radiation therapy, medical immuno-therapy, and surgery. Some cancers are more deadly and difficult to treat than others. An isolated skin cancer, for instance, is much less dangerous than a systemic cancer of the lymph system or blood. Treatment recommendations differ depending on the type and location of the cancer. A problem such as throat cancer, which could impede eating and swallowing, would probably require surgery, as would tumors of the intestines, liver, urinary tract, and extremities. Systemic cancers such as lymphoma and lymphosarcoma may require chemotherapy. The chemotherapy drugs in this case may be able to buy the time necessary to allow the slower-acting natural therapies to take effect and begin to benefit the immune system and the body. Still others, such as nasal cavity cancers, may get the recommendation of radiation therapy. Exciting research is currently underway in such areas as genetics, anti-angiogenesis, and photo-dynamic (light) therapies.

Conventional Approaches to Cancer

Surgery

Most commonly, surgery is elected to remove a mass, an affected organ, or a diseased limb. This may be necessary when the growth of the cancer begins to block a vital organ or causes serious pain. For example, cancer of the intestines may create a blockage, a condition in itself as serious as the cancer. In this case, surgery would eliminate the threat of the blockage.

Surgery may also be used for debulking, which removes a portion of the mass of cancerous tissue. Debulking frees the body's immune system from fighting the total existing mass, and allows it to spend energy on the prevention of future cancer. We often recommend cryosurgery for debulking, which is essentially a "controlled frostbite" to destroy the cancer. Cryosurgery is used most often for oral tumors, a much less invasive procedure than traditional surgery, which often requires removing functional tissue such as the jawbone. Dr. Bob was a pioneer in the development of cryosurgery for the veterinary profession, and it is a technique now widely used by veterinarians.

Chemotherapy

This is the most common form of medical therapy recommended by veterinarians. The basic premise is that chemotherapeutics kill rapidly growing cancer cells. Unfortunately, this may include normal body tissue.

The good news is that chemotherapy protocols are usually more gentle than human protocols. Dr. Jerry Post, a board certified veterinary oncologist, states, "Chemotherapy in veterinary oncology is handled differently than in human oncology. The primary focus for veterinarians is quality of life, with a secondary focus on trying to "cure" the patient. Veterinarians and pet owners have made the conscious decision not to put their pets through the high level of toxicity that people on chemotherapy experience. Despite the reductions in dose, we can still offer our patients and clients significant life extension with good to excellent quality of life."

We do recommend and support chemotherapy when it is necessary to stabilize an animal that is blocked, or there is imminent danger of the animal being overwhelmed by the cancer. However, whenever possible and allowed by the attending veterinarian, we often recommend a "lower dose" schedule of chemotherapy.

It is important to realize that chemotherapy is directed at the cancer. Yet cancer is a symptom of a deeper problem—typically a suppressed and toxically overwhelmed immune system. Suppressing symptoms is little more than putting on a bandage. Chemotherapy, with its focus on destroying cancer cells, can also bring potential side effects, such as destruction of both red and white blood cells, or affecting the liver, bone marrow, or kidneys.

Radiation Therapy

Radiation therapy works by destroying cancer cells with pointed x-rays. The problem associated with radiation therapy is that it can also destroy healthy adjacent and surrounding tissue. Destroying cells with radioactive waves can also have an immune-suppressing effect on the entire body. In addition, radiation therapy is often recommended daily or weekly and usually requires repeated anesthesia, which in itself has an immune-suppressing effect on the body. Radiotherapy in animals is most commonly recommended in contained tumors such as brain, nasal cavity, and oral tumors. If your animal is being treated with radiation therapy, use the cocktail on page 314 to help with the side effects and detoxification.

Radiation Cocktail

1/4 cup distilled or filtered water
2 organic raw egg yolks
1 Tbsp powdered kelp
1 Tbsp nutritional yeast (unprocessed)
1 tsp organic apple cider vinegar
1/2 tsp ground rosemary
400 iu vitamin E (squeeze from a soft gel capsule)
Fresh juices (prepare just before feeding):
  1 Tbsp parsley juice
  1 Tbsp aloe vera juice
  1/2 cup organic carrot juice

In a blender, gently mix all ingredients on the lowest speed possible. The juices are concentrated, so your animal will benefit from even small amounts; if he or she wants more than this, that's fine.

Cats/Small Dogs (up to 14 lb)	1-2 Tbsp
Medium Dogs (15-34 lb)	3-4 Tbsp
Large/Giant Dogs (35+ lb)	5-10 Tbsp

A controversial theory about radiation therapy and antioxidants also exists. Although it has not been proven, some radiation oncologists believe that if you add potent antioxidants (such as vitamins A, E, and C) to the diet, they may block the cell-destroying effects of the radiation, making them ineffective against cancer. Dr. Rachael St. Vincent, a board certified veterinary radiation oncologist, believes that this is so, and she is cautious about using antioxidants as part of her treatment protocol. Our belief is that if antioxidants are powerful enough to protect the body from the direct assault of radiation, then their benefit to a treatment program for cancer far outweighs the slowing down of the radiation therapy's destruction of cells.

Work With Your Veterinarian

Even though these conventional therapies focus on eliminating the cancer without regard for the immune system, we believe that medical and surgical therapies may be essential and lifesaving in many cases. They frequently buy the time needed to stimulate, balance and strengthen the immune system. If you are interested in pursuing holistic and nutritional therapies, it is still important to get your veterinarian's opinion and support when dealing with any cancer. He or she can help you evaluate the pros and cons about adding (or not) chemotherapy, radiation therapy, and/or surgery to your program.

Ultimately, the choice of therapies—whether conventional, alternative, or complementary—is yours. We recommend that you make this important decision with input from both your family veterinarian and an experienced holistic practitioner. You may find both comfort and wisdom by speaking with other people whose animals have experienced similar cancers.

Your approach should be based upon your animal's current state of health, quality of life, emotional state (both of the patient and the family), medical diagnosis and history. Before any decisions are made about your animal or treatment of the cancer, gather the following information:

- Complete medical history, including vaccination history.
- Confirmed diagnosis (through biopsy, sonogram, x-rays, blood work, etc.).
- Recommended conventional approach (surgery, chemotherapy, etc.), including potential risks and anticipated side effects.
- Expected prognosis.

You should then do the same thing with an alternative veterinarian who is experienced in the treatment of cancer in animals. Once you have all the facts (both alternative and conventional) you are then in a position to make a rational decision, one that is best for your animal and your family. This information is essential in determining not only the therapy but also the prognosis, quality of life, expected success rate, and longevity.

Your choices are going to fall into one of the following categories:

Conventional treatment alone. This would include surgery, chemotherapy, radiation therapy, and so on.

Conventional and alternative therapies together. This approach is often recommended when dealing with an overwhelming cancer such as lymphosarcoma (a systemic cancer of the lymph system). Often the chemotherapy is necessary to "stop the cancer" while the alternative therapy is designed to support the immune system while helping to minimize the side effect of the drugs.

Alternative therapy by itself. While this route is often chosen because of your personal belief system or the potential side effects of conventional methods such as chemotherapy and radiation therapy, it may often be recommended along with surgery.

> ### Raise Your Chances for Success
>
> Successful cancer therapy depends on three forces working hand in hand: your veterinarian's medical support for the management of acute symptoms; the immune-enhancing therapies to strengthen the body's true healing powers; and your emotional support for your animal.

If you decide on a conventional medical protocol without a specifically designed theraputic nutritional program, you should strongly consider our at-home support program for your dog or cat. Our program brings in a broad range of therapeutic nutrients, which will help to strengthen the immune system and detoxify the body.

At-Home Support Program

In addition to the medical therapies that you may choose with your veterinarian, here's an at-home program that provides nutritional, homeopathic, nutraceutical, and herbal support for your animal. If you are working with an holistic practitioner, he or she may want to add other natural remedies to this program after examining your dog or cat.

Step One: Feed a Cancer-Fighting Diet

The proper diet is critical for cancer patients. Cancer patients often have a diminished appetite and therefore whatever you can get your animal to eat is terrific—especially if it's fresh, organic, and free of chemical preservatives. Naturally preserved commercial dog or cat food supplemented with fresh meat, healthy oils, and plenty of vegetables is recommended.

A cancer-fighting diet is higher in fat and protein, and lower in carbohydrates than a normal diet. The more "body friendly" the food—that is, the more bioavailable or digestible—the more energy is derived by the body for its tasks. In general, high-quality protein (beef, chicken, fish, tofu, and eggs), whole grains, and unsaturated fats (fish oil, flaxseed, olive oil, sesame oil), *preferably organic*, provide more energy than by-products, highly processed carbohydrates, chemical additives, preservatives, dyes, coloring agents, and fillers. (See the strict dietary restrictions on page 325 when using Chinese herbal remedies for cancer.)

Your dog or cat may crave protein by instinct. Proteins are necessary for the manufacture of immuno-proteins that fight cancer. Offer all the organic protein your dog or cat wants to eat, especially raw or lightly steamed meat and egg yolks. Protein (amino acids) forms the basic building blocks for tissue repair and integrity. Proteins are used for dozens of vital functions in the body, including a leading role in immunity. Mix your protein with raw organic vegetables such as broccoli, carrots, baked potatoes, whole grains such as brown rice and millet, plain organic yogurt, chopped garlic and parsley, and flaxseed or fish oil.

The Dr. Burton Protein Story

Whenever we talk about the importance of protein, we are reminded of Dr. Burton, a controversial and respected cancer specialist who founded the Immuno Augmentative Therapy Center in the Bahamas. While dealing with a person with cancer who was a staunch vegetarian, Dr. Burton would emphatically say to the patient, "I treat a lot of patients with your type of cancer and let me tell you something, it's the vegetarians that I have the most difficult time stimulating and balancing the immune systems. So forget your doubts and go home and eat a steak."

- Grated organic carrots are rich in vitamin A, beta-carotene, chelated minerals, and life-force enzymes. Remember, cats can't convert beta-carotene and do require vitamin A. A good source of vitamin A for cats is non-preserved, non-processed fish oil. You should also grate up a few sprigs of organic parsley.

- Finely chopped organic garlic is a rich source of allicin, a natural antibiotic. Garlic also contains about 30 sulfur compounds with immune-boosting and anticancer properties, including thioallylamino acids, along with significant levels of vitamins A and C and germanium.

- Flaxseed oil and fish oil are rich sources of beneficial essential fatty acids (EFAs) and alpha-linolenic acid, which have been proven to reduce inflammation and enhance the immune system. In addition to the high level of omega-3 fatty acids, flaxseed oil contains significant amounts of flax lignan, phyto-compounds that have direct anticancer effects. It has been shown that flax seed has over 100 times the amount of lignans than any other plant. Fish oils contain about 40 percent polyunsaturated omega-3 fatty acids and high amounts of both eiscosapentaenoic acid (EPA) and docahexaenoic acid (DHA). (For more information on the benefits of flax and fish oils, see Chapter 2.) Be aware that cancer or chemotherapy may dampen your dog's or cat's appetite. If this is the case, then feed whatever your animal will eat, so long as it's fresh, organic (if possible), and not chemically preserved. If the appetite is severely depressed, or your animal is wasting away or having trouble eating, try the "Radiation Cocktail" described on page 314.

Daily Diet Guide

After you make your selection of organic meats or chicken, fresh organic vegetables and whole grains, use the following diets as your starting points for sound nutrition:

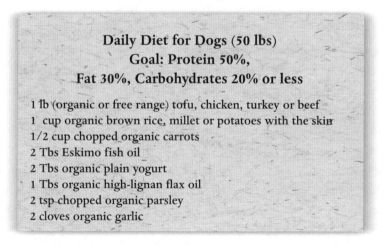

Daily Diet for Dogs (50 lbs)
Goal: Protein 50%,
Fat 30%, Carbohydrates 20% or less

1 lb (organic or free range) tofu, chicken, turkey or beef
1 cup organic brown rice, millet or potatoes with the skin
1/2 cup chopped organic carrots
2 Tbs Eskimo fish oil
2 Tbs organic plain yogurt
1 Tbs organic high-lignan flax oil
2 tsp chopped organic parsley
2 cloves organic garlic

> **Daily Diet for Cats**
> **Goal: Protein 60%,**
> **Fat 30%, Carbohydrates 10% or less**
>
> 1/2 lb organic or free-range chicken, turkey, or beef
> 1/4 cups organic brown rice, millet, or potatoes (with the skin)
> 1/2 chopped organic carrot
> 1 1/2 tps Eskimo fish oil
> 1 tsp organic plain yogurt
> 1/4 tps organic high-lignan flax oil
> 1/2 tsp chopped organic parsley
> 1/2 clove organic garlic

Don't Forget the Water

Water is critical for flushing out toxins while not contributing further to toxic overload. If your animal is not a water drinker, cook with excess water or add additional amounts to the food. Broths such as the Potato Peeling Broth (see page 298) are excellent to keep the body flushing toxins through the kidneys and adding beneficial minerals such as potassium to the diet. Mineral-rich broths help to alkalinize the body, fighting off the acid environment that cancer cells thrive in. Make sure the water you provide your animal is at least filtered, and preferably from a pure souce.

The Convenience of a Commercially Prepared Cancer Diet

Many people referred to us for cancer have been told by their veterinarian to feed Prescription Diet Canine N/D produced by Hills Pet Food. We are bringing this food up at this juncture to make an important point for the benefits of a whole food diet. Hills Pet Food has done 10 years of research on their N/D Diet in over 9 clinical trials using over 250 dogs and have come up with the following data:

- N/D diet increases the survival time of dogs by 56 percent.
- N/D diet reduces the painful side effects of radiation therapy, thereby improving the quality of life for dogs with cancer.
- N/D diet suppresses the clinical signs of cancer for increased periods (longer periods of remission).
- N/D diet counteracts the persistent metabolic changes found in canine cancer patients.

The Hill literature states, "Prescription Diet Canine N/D is a significant adjuvant to antineoplastic therapy, improving quality of life and survival time beyond that afforded by traditional therapy alone. In addition, in clinical studies, 95 percent of dogs undergoing cancer treatment readily accepted Canine N/D."

This research is quite informative and the results sounds quite impressive until you get to the ingredients that Hills selects for their N/D diets. These include meat by-products; white rice; chicken liver flavor; powdered cellulose; beet pulp; iron oxide; zinc oxide; copper sulfate; and thiamine mononitrate.

If the positive results of the clinical trials were achieved with this commercial diet, imagine the results if whole foods such as fresh organic meat, fresh oil rich in omega-3 and -6 fatty acids; and moderate amounts of whole organic grains containing complex carbohydrates are used. The results can be spectacular.

Step Two: Counteract Effects of Vaccines With Homeopathic *Thuja Occidentalis*

Overvaccinations can compromise the immune system, set in motion an autoimmune reaction and set the stage for the development of cancer. (Please review Chapter 3 in this book on vaccination and vaccinosis.) To counteract the adverse effects of vaccinations in animals diagnosed with a malignancy, give a single dose of the homeopathic *Thuja occidentalis* 30C. This remedy will help in the overall process of healing without triggering additional symptoms as a result of detoxification. This should be your first step, especially if your animal has received recent or repeated annual vaccinations. This simple process releases the immune system from any prior adverse effects of vaccines. To administer:

- Fold a 3" x 5" index card lengthwise.
- Drop into the fold one to three pellets of *Thuja occidentalis* (without touching the pellets).
- With your fingers outside the card, crush the pellets into a powder.
- Dump the powder into your animal's mouth (landing on the tongue or inside the lips is fine).

Thuja ocidentalis (daily for 7 days)	
Cat/Small Dog (up to 14 lb)	1 pellet
Medium Dog (15–34 lb)	2 pellets
Large/Giant Dog (35+ lb)	3 pellets

For animals with cancer, give just one dose on one day and then stop. In addition, we strongly recommend that you avoid administering vaccinations when your animal is fighting cancer, as they may counteract positive and immune-enhancing effects of your home-support program. In some states, certain vaccinations are required by law, so speak with your veterinarian before making any decisions. If need be, ask your veterinarian to write to your state officials stating that in his or her opinion, giving your dog or cat a vaccination (i.e., for rabies), may further compromise the health of your animal. Most states will let you off the hook for mandatory rabies vaccines in these instances.

Step 3: Release Negative Emotional Influences

Stress saps vital healing energy. As our holistic knowledge expands, we have become aware that stress and negative emotions have an adverse affect upon the health of our patients. Our companion animals are unconditional in their love and loyalty for us. As a result, they will often absorb negative emotions and stresses that are present because they do not have the "intellectual filter" to reason out the solution. This will drain healing energy. When discussing the medical history, we have often found that in animals with cancer, there is a similar disease diagnosis or some emotional or stressful situation present in the family.

> **Positive Thinking Can Help**
> Please know that you and your animal have the power to push cancer into remission.

Fear and Cancer

Few diseases radiate the "death sentence" like cancer. Human literature is filled with references confirming the connection between actual disease and fear of the disease. It has been definitively proven that survival rates for human cancer patients are far greater when the person's mental attitude about the cancer is positive rather than negative.

If the diagnosis of cancer resonates the "death sentence" for you, it is absolutely essential that you don't immediately assume that your animal will die. Don't buy into the conventional wisdom that there is no hope for cancer patients, and that the available medical therapies will only delay the inevitable.

It is not our intention to minimize the seriousness of this disease. You should always proceed by assessing then choosing the proper alternative and conventional (if necessary) therapy program. Just don't allow fear to drive your assessment and approach. There is new technology along with natural remedies and nutritional approaches that can help slow down and potentially reverse the process. And, as our technology advances, methods and remedies will be available that will help with genetic weaknesses and emotional stresses as well.

We always consider the importance of emotions and the "spirit" of the animal in our cancer therapy plans. An emotionally distraught animal, one who is lethargic, withdrawn, depressed, or sad, will not be able to mobilize internal energy that is necessary to balance and boost the immune system.

This is why it is so important to "tune into" your animal and make sure his or her emotional systems are being supported. Often animals with cancer do not feel well, have lost their appetite, and are in pain and discomfort. It is even more important that you offer emotional support to these animals.

We often include specific flower essences into our treatment protocols when emotional distress and detachment are present to help remove and neutralize negative thought patterns.

The ones we use routinely are Anaflora's Recovery, Return to Joy, and Tranquility. (For more information on flower essences, please see Chapter 4.)

At-Home Nutritional Support for Cancer

After 30 years of treating animals with cancer, we have developed the following home program that includes specific vitamins, minerals, antioxidants, and natural remedies. However, cancer is a serious disease, and it is advisable to consult with your family veterinarian, as well an integrative veterinarian who has experience with the treatment and control of cancer.

If you have a dog or cat whose breed is prone to cancer (such as a Golden Retrievers, Labrador Retrievers, Rottweillers, or Siamese cats) then incorporating some or all of the following nutrients, antioxidants, and vitamins into your daily preventative feeding program along with the Goldstein Food Plan is advisable.

Vitamin A (once daily)	
Cat/Small Dog (up to 14 lb)	2,500 iu
Medium Dog (15-34 lb)	2,500-5,000 iu
Large Dog (35-84 lb)	5,000-7,500 iu
Giant Dog (85+ lb)	7,500 iu

Vitamin C (twice daily)	
Cat/Small Dog (up to 14 lb)	250 mg
Medium Dog (15-34 lb)	500 mg
Large Dog (35-84 lb)	750 mg
Giant Dog (85+ lb)	1,000 mg

Vitamin E (once daily)	
Cat/Small Dog (up to 14 lb)	200 iu
Medium Dog (15-34 lb)	400 iu
Large Dog (35-84 lb)	600 iu
Giant Dog (85+ lb)	800 iu

Selenium (once daily) micrograms (mcg)	
Cat/Small Dog (up to 14 lb)	25 mcg
Medium Dog (15-34 lb)	50 mcg
Large Dog (35-84 lb)	50-75 mcg
Giant Dog (85+ lb)	75 mcg

Coenzyme Q10 (once daily)	
Cat/Small Dog (up to 14 lb)	35-50 mg
Medium Dog (15-34 lb)	50-75 mg
Large Dog (35-84 lb)	75-100 mg
Giant Dog (85+ lb)	100-200 mg

Quercetin (once daily)	
Cat/Small Dog (up to 14 lb)	75 mg
Medium Dog (15-34 lb)	100 mg
Large Dog (35-84 lb)	150 mg
Giant Dog (85+ lb)	250 mg

Treating Cancer

Conventional protocols often include chemotherapeutic "cocktails" given orally, intravenously, or both in an effort to knock out rapidly growing tumor tissues. These protocols are typically targeted toward the cell or organ affected, with the aim of controlling and destroying rapidly growing cancer cells. The downside of this approach is that these potent drugs and radiation may also destroy healthy tissue, and further suppress an already compromised immune system.

Holistically, we direct our efforts more toward the "whole" body and the immune system, giving the body the energy and nutrient support needed to heal itself. While certain types of cancers may require natural therapies that target a specific cancer type, the basis of the natural approach is to support and nourish the body, and enhance the detoxification process. In addition, these natural therapies also have tissue-sparing properties that can offset the toxic side effects and help minimize the potential adverse effects of chemotherapy and radiation therapy (if those therapies are part of your animal's treatment plan).

Here are some natural therapies that can be used either alone or in combination with chemotherapy, radiation therapy, or surgery. These therapies are available through veterinarians, and should only be used as part of an overall cancer treatment protocol as discussed with your family or holistic veterinarian.

Anti-angiogenics

Dr. Judah Folkman, a researcher at Harvard Medical School and Children's Hospital in Boston, discovered in the 1970s that angiogenesis (the growth of new blood vessels) plays a significant role in the development of cancer. At first, Folkman's research was attacked and ridiculed by his colleagues, but it has been proven that the anti-angiogenic drugs (developed based on his research) have been found to help kill cancer cells in both people and in animals. Since his discovery, an entirely new field of cancer research has developed. However, as is the case with most cancer research, the focus is almost entirely on the development of drugs that can be commercially sold, while little attention is paid to natural anti-angiogenics, since they are not as economically viable.

The Anti-Angiogenesis Foundation (www.angio.org), which was established in 1994, states, "Doctors now are testing drugs that stop the growth of the blood vessels that tumors rely upon for nutrients and growth. They're known as anti-angiogenic drugs, and they deprive a tumor of its life source by killing the blood vessels that feed it. Today, more than 50 anti-angiogenic drugs are being used as therapy for cancer patients. At least 10,000 cancer patients have been treated with anti-angiogenic drugs, and four billion dollars have been devoted to angiogenic drug research to date. The drug Avastin (Bevacizumab) becomes the first anti-angiogenic drug proven by clinical trials to inhibit tumor blood vessel growth. Avastin received FDA approval in 2004. This year, the amount of money spent by the federal government and the pharmaceutical industry on cancer research is expected to exceed ten billion dollars."

Natural Anti-angiogenics

Cartilage therapy (bovine or shark). The basic theory behind this therapy is that cartilage, besides having an immune-boosting effect, is anti-angiogenic—it helps the body diminish blood supply to tissue. Since cancer is often rapidly growing, it requires lots of new blood vessels for its survival. Interfere with the blood supply, and you are in effect stopping the growth of cancer. (By the way, many newly developed drugs, such as Angiostatin and Endostatin, work in this fashion.)

Dr. John Prudden, a surgeon at Columbia-Presbyterian Medical Center in New York City, began to study bovine cartilage in 1954. He discovered that it reduced inflammation and speeded wound healing in animals. Dr. Prudden began treating human cancer patients with bovine cartilage, and published a report on over 30 patients in which he records some remarkable remissions of serious malignant cancers such as breast, skin, and brain tumors (some in excess of five years).

Much research has been done in both people and animals on the effectiveness of cartilage—shark and bovine. It is believed that when cartilage is taken orally, it has the effect of decreasing blood supply to the cancer and thereby inhibiting its growth (i.e., it has an anti-angiogenic effect against the tumor). The cartilages (shark and bovine) appear to be more helpful against solitary, solid tumors as opposed to systemic forms such as lymphoma. Shark cartilage (which has lost favor because of the negative ecological impact on the oceans) became popular based upon the books written by William Lane called *Sharks Don't Get Cancer: How Shark Cartilage Could Save Your Life* and *Sharks Still Don't Get Cancer: The Continuing Story of Shark Cartilage Therapy*.

The popularity of these books, plus a segment on *60 Minutes* on using shark cartilage for cancer, brought William Lane to the attention of the FDA, who sued Lane for making unproven claims about its use as a cancer therapy and forced it off the market. It is still sold as a supplement without the cancer-fighting claims.

At one time in our practice we used bovine and shark cartilage, but now we prefer the natural anti-angiogenic VascuStatin, especially for cancers that have an abundant blood supply, such as hemangiosarcoma (a type of tumor). VascuStatin is 100 times more potent then the cartilages.

VascuStatin. VascuStatin PGM is a dietary supplement that is produced by Allergy Research Group. It contains a leaf extract of bindweed (*Convolvulus arvensis*), which is a potent immune stimulator and an anti-angiogenic. Native Americans used plants like bindweed to treat skin ulcers, reducing wound inflammation and swelling.

VascuStatin has been shown to not only enhance the immune system, but also inhibit angiogenesis. Besides helping to maintain a balanced immune system, VascuStatin helps to improve white blood cell activity and stimulate the growth of new lymphocytes. VascuStatin is particularly beneficial in animals that have a high blood supply, such as hemangiosarcomas and tumors of the liver and spleen.

VascuStatin (twice daily)	
Cats/Small Dogs (up to 14 lb)	1/2 capsule
Medium Dogs (15-34 lb)	1 capsule
Large Dogs (35-84 lb)	2 capsules
Giant Dogs (85+ lb)	3-4 capsules

Chinese Herbal Medicine (CHM)

Dr. Bob has been working with Dr. Jay Wen, a veterinary acupuncturist who was trained in Chinese herbal medicine at Beijing Agricultural University. Dr. Wen believes, "The benefits of herbal therapy for cancer are numerous. First off, they can be combined with chemotherapy or surgery to decrease side effects or enhance the action of the chemotherapeutic agent. Often the dose of chemotherapy given can be increased for greater efficacy without increasing the side effects. Many times when using Western agents alone, doses must be decreased or treatment delayed due to the destruction of white blood cells by the chemotherapy drugs, for example."

It is important that we address the diet when using traditional Chinese herbal supplements for treatment of neoplasia. Through years of study it has been shown that Chinese herbs are much more effective when the diet consists of beef or pork, and vegetables. Lamb, poultry, fish, and related products may interfere with the action of the herbs, slowing their effectiveness. In addition to diet, avoid oversupplementing the patient with vitamins, minerals, and herbal supplements, which have strong tonifying (immune stimulating) functions. Therefore, it is important that you are under the guidance of an experienced veterinarian if Chinese herbal medicine is part of your chosen program. When Chinese herbs are selected, your veterinarian will set the program and select the dosage, preventing over-supplementation and duplication, which would weaken the effectiveness of the program. Chinese herbs are available from Dr. Wen (see Resources), or from veterinarians who utilize the NBT program.

COX-2 Inhibitors

COX is an abbreviation for the natural enzyme cyclooxygenase. There are two forms of this enzyme in the body, COX-1 and COX-2. COX-1 is produced throughout the body and helps manage day-to-day cellular and metabolic activities, including maintaining the health of the lining of the stomach, regulating blood flow to the kidneys and balancing platelet function. COX-2 is important in initiating the pain response and is only present in the body on a limited basis; however, dietary factors such as stress and injury can increase COX-2 production.

COX-2 inhibitors have proven to have anticancer properties, but with potent drugs come untoward side effects, such as the heart problems associated with the well-known COX-2 inhibitor Vioxx. There are natural, botanical COX-2 inhibitors available for animals without these unwanted side effects.

Botanical COX-2 Inhibitors

Zyflamend. Inflammation begins with omega-6 fatty acids. These oils are converted into arachidonic acid and then converted by the COX-2 enzyme into prostaglandin E2, causing inflammation and discomfort. Zyflamend contains some 78 known naturally occurring COX-2 inhibitors and direct anti-inflammatory compounds. Together they give Zyflamend the power to inhibit and reduce COX-2 levels while helping to alleviate aches and discomfort from inflammation.

Zyflamend is a natural anti-inflammatory and painkiller without having the serious side effects such as stomach ulcers, intestinal bleeding, and negative effects on the heart.

Zylfamend	
Cat/Small Dog (up to 14 lb)	1 capsule daily
Medium Dog (15-34 lb)	1 capsule twice daily
Large Dog (35-84 lb)	1-2 capsules twice daily
Giant Dog (85+ lb)	2-3 capsules twice daily

Kaprex is a botanically derived supplement produced by Metagenics that helps alleviate pain and inflammation without the typical side effects of potent nonsteroidal anti-inflammatory drugs (NSAIDs). Kaprex and NSAIDs work similarly by reducing the amount of prostaglandin E2 (PGE2), the hormone-like chemical responsible for the majority of the pain and inflammation associated with conditions such as arthritis.

Kaprex (twice daily)	
Cat/Small Dog (up to 14 lb)	1/2 tablet
Medium Dog (15-34 lb)	1 tablet
Large Dog (35-84 lb)	1 1/2-2 tablets
Giant Dog (85+ lb)	2-4 tablets

Both Zyflamend and Kaprex have the ability to not only reduce pain and inflammation common with cancer patients, but also help reduce inflammation at the cellular level (where cancer cells are produced). Several studies have shown that the botanical COX-2 inhibitors can decrease the growth of cancer cells. In addition, clinical evidence shows that these herbal anti-inflammatories can actually bring on apoptosis, which is the selective destruction of cancer cells while preserving healthy cells.

Corydalis PIS from Natura Products is a potent botanical Cox-2 inhibitor. Corydalis PIS (Pain, Inflammation, and Spasm) helps relieve the side effects of chronic disease that you may see not only in cancer, but in other degenerative diseases. This product contains Corydalis and other potent herbs, such as Rabdosia rubescens, Panax notoginseng (Tienchi ginseng), Chinese peony (Paeonia lactiflora), Dong guai, Boswellia serrata (Indian frankincense), white willow, wild turmeric, and Chinese licorice.

In addition to helping relieve pain, it also helps to reduce spasms and swelling particularly secondary to fluid retention (edema). It also assists in healing after surgery or from an injury or trauma. It is believed to help suppress further cancer growth and spread of tumors (metastasis).

Corydalis PIS (daily)	
Cat/Small Dog (up to 14 lb)	1/4 capsule
Medium Dog (15-34 lb)	1/2 capsule
Large Dog (35-84 lb)	3/4 capsule
Giant Dog (85+ lb)	1 capsule

Botanical Treasures. Another Botanical COX-2 Inhibitor, also formulated by Donnie Yance, is Botanical Treasures. This formula is a more potent form of Zyflamed and contains much higher levels of tumeric and green tea. It is formulated to deliver a maximum antioxidant effect, thereby reducing oxidation and the associated inflammation and pain. In addition, it is also anti-angionegic by helping to reduce the blood supply to rapidly growing tissue, such as tumors.

Botanical Treasures (daily)	
Cat/Small Dog (up to 14 lb)	1/4 tsp
Medium Dog (15-34 lb)	1/2 tsp
Large Dog (35-84 lb)	3/4 tsp
Giant Dog (85+ lb)	1 tsp

Enzymes

Metabolically, enzymes are essential for the conversion of foods into the energy, and are often catalysts in various biochemical processes. Enzyme deficiencies result from the lack of production by a specific organ, or from a deficiency of the proper nutrients (such as essential minerals in the diet). Enzymes are important in many aspects of metabolism.

Digestive enzymes include amylase (carbohydrate), protease (proteins), lipase (fats), and cellulose (cellulose). The primary causes of enzyme deficiencies or inadequacy are:

- Mineral deficiency.
- Organ malfunction (i.e., underactive salivary gland or pancreas).
- Excess free radicals—depleted antioxidants.
- Allergies and chronic inflammation.
- Chronic disease.
- Medications (i.e., chronic use of antibiotics upsetting the intestinal environment).

Besides the obvious benefits of helping the digestive process, which in turn improves the general food absorption and metabolism, enzyme supplementation has an indirect effect of helping to restore overall health. Given with meals, enzymes help with digestion. Given away from meals, they can help to replenish the body's normal reserves of enzymes, as well as help to digest undigested and abnormal protein fragments. This allows the organ to rest in its enzyme manufacturing function.

For cancer patients, improving the digestion and assimilation of food will help deliver more nutrients to the cells of the body. These nutrients will be converted to the energy necessary for the immune system to help control and prevent cancer. There is also research that supports the theory that digestive enzymes may have a direct anti-cancer effect on the cancer cells themselves by breaking down proteins and immune complexes that help protect cancer cells from the immune system's attack. Your veterinarian will recommend the appropriate dosages.

Essential Fatty Acids

There has been much research done on the importance of the essential fatty acids in the daily diet, as well as in the clinical management of various degenerative diseases. The importance of the ratio between omega-6 and omega-3 fatty acids has been substantiated (see Chapter 2 for more details).

Marine Fish Oil contains good levels of EPA and DHA that maintain the proper levels of eicosinoids, which can help mediate the body's response to cancer cells. Research has shown that EPA can slow tumor growth, and its presence actually improves the response of the cell to chemotherapeutics.

Marine Fish Oil (per meal)	
Cat/Small Dog (up to 14 lb)	2 tsp
Medium Dog (15-34 lb)	1 Tbsp
Large Dog (35-84 lb)	1 1/2 Tbsp
Giant Dog (85+ lb)	2 Tbsp

Flaxseed Oil contains over 55 percent of linolenic acid (omega-3). It is considered the "Rolls Royce" of fatty acids because it contains more than any other oil. It has antioxidant, anti-inflammatory and anticancer effects on the body.

Flaxseed Oil (per meal)	
Cat/Small Dog (up to 14 lb)	2 tsp
Medium Dog (15-34 lb)	1 Tbsp
Large Dog (35-84 lb)	1 1/2 Tbsp
Giant Dog (85+ lb)	2 Tbsp

Evening Primrose Oil contains about 70 percent gamma linolenic acid (omega-6) which is essential in the formation of eicosinoids, which are anti-inflammatory and anti-cancer as well as being used in the formation of other good fatty acid derivatives.

Evening Primrose Oil (daily)	
Cat/Small Dog (up to 14 lb)	500 mg
Medium Dog (15-34 lb)	750 mg
Large Dog (35-84 lb)	1,000 mg
Giant Dog (85+ lb)	1,500 mg

Siberian Sea Buckthorn and **Siberian Pine Oil**. Siberian Sea Buckthorn (*Hippohae rhamnoides*), also known as Oblepikha, is a shrub that grows in Russia. Siberian Sea Buckthorn has been used for centuries for people for skin care, reducing wrinkles and preventing aging, and has been added to horse feed to improve the shine of the coat. The essential fatty acid content of this oil is (amazingly!) above 80 percent and also contains high levels of phytonutrients and phytosetrols which offer additional medicinal value.

Siberian Pine Oil (Oleum Pini sibiricae) has been used for many medical problems in Russia, including as an antiseptic, a diuretic, and to help prevent scurvy (vitamin C deficiency). The seed is used in Traditional Chinese Medicine (TCM) as an adaptogen to improve health. The fatty acid levels of Siberian Pine Seed oil are mostly polyunsaturated acids, including linoleic acid and gamma linolenic acid (GLA). In fact it contains more than double the amount of GLA then evening primrose oil.

Beyond Essential Fats from Natura Products is a fatty acid mixure of fish oil, Siberian Sea Buckthorn and Siberian Pine Oil.

Beyond Essentials (daily)	
Cat/Small Dog (up to 14 lb)	1/4 tsp
Medium Dog (15-34 lb)	1/2 tsp
Large Dog (35-84 lb)	3/4 tsp
Giant Dog (85+ lb)	1 tsp

Our Modification of Dr. Budwig's Formulation

2 Tbs organic cottage cheese or live culture organic yogurt
1 Tbs high lignan flax seed oil
Optional: 2 tsp fresh ground flax
Give with meals

Cat/Small Dog (up to 14 lb)	1-2 tsp
Medium Dog (15-34 lb)	2-3 tsp
Large Dog (35-84 lb)	1 1/2 Tbs
Giant Dog (85+ lb)	2 Tbs

Most dogs and cats love the taste of yogurt or cottage cheese, even when they are debilitated from the secondary effects of cancer. This mixture also helps cover up the bitter taste of flax seed oil.

Dr. Johanna Budwig, a German biochemist and six-time Nobel Prize nominee, is known for her research on the benefits of flaxseed oil when combined with high sulphur containing proteins. Her book *Flax Oil as a True Aid Against Arthritis, Heart Infarction, Cancer and Other Diseases*, reported that cancer patients were almost always deficient in compounds called lipoproteins and phosphatides, which were always found in healthy patients in adequate amounts. She developed a formulation that when fed to cancer patients was able to act as a "spark plug." The nutrient mixture replaced the missing compounds, and the serious and adverse secondary effects of cancer (such as weakness, anemia, weightloss) were reversed.

We have been using Dr. Budwig's formulation in our patients with cancer for over ten years, and truly do see a difference when this combination is added to the diets of dogs and cats.

Herbs

Adaptogens

In 1948, Dr. Nicholai Lazarev, a pioneer in the field of preventive medicine, began the study of medicinal plants known as "adaptogens." The term was coined when he found that they helped people adapt to their environment and in so doing achieve health and wellness. Prolonged stress, be it emotional (such as an abused animal) or physical (prolonged exposure to chemical insecticides and potent drugs), depresses the immune system. Scientific studies have established that adaptogens not only possess the ability to maintain adequate levels of antioxidants, but can even raise their levels under stress. Adaptogens also shorten the recovery time from surgery or disease.

While the scientific community has researched adaptogens for over 40 years, it was in the 1950s that research conducted in Russia with the herb *Eleutherococcus senticosus* (Siberian ginseng) made these herbs popular. Research on sailors, factory workers, and Russian cosmonauts demonstrated that Siberian ginseng increased energy levels as well as helped to minimize the side effects of all types of stress. The Soviet government realized that this new class of herbs would give Russians an advantage in sporting events, in the military, and in space travel, and this interest led to a tremendous increase into research to support the use of adaptogens. More than 5,000 scientific studies have been carried out on adaptogens.

Adaptogens help the body achieve balance (homeostasis) while improving resistance to external toxins and stressors. They also help to delay the effects of aging of the glands and organ systems. In addition, adaptogens:

- Help to control or prevent obesity.
- Increase muscle mass and help to reduce fat accumulation.
- Support all glands, especially the adrenal and thyroid.
- Boost the immune system and natural killer cell activity.
- Help ease depression and anxiety.
- Help prevent chronic diseases such as heart, liver and kidney disease, diabetes, obesity. and autoimmune conditions.
- Help cells eliminate toxins by activating free-radical enzyme systems.
- Protect the liver and enhance its ability to eliminate drugs and chemicals from the body.
- Help guard against cancers, including breast, stomach, oral cavity, skin melanoma, and ovarian cancer.
- Are tissue-protective and reduce the side effects of chemo and radiation therapies.

We have been working with master herbalist Donald Yance, author of *Herbal Medicine: Healing and Cancer*, to treat animals with chronic diseases with these herbs. Donnie has achieved excellent results using Russian herbs as part of a treatment plan for cancer in people. At the Healing Center for Animals, Dr. Bob has been using these very potent herbs for animals with arthritis, liver and kidney disease, Cushing's disease, and cancer, with excellent results.

Besides learning much about adaptogens from Donnie Yance, one of the most important lessons he taught us is that not all adaptogens and herbs are created equal. The herbs in Donnie's formulas that we use at our Healing Center for Animals grow wild in remote areas of Russia, and are processed using a cold-water extraction technique following standards approved by the Russian Ministry of Health, Department of Pharmacology. In contrast, most of the "Russian" adaptogens available in the US are not even from Russia, are of poor quality, and use improper manufacturing techniques. Many of these products have little or no biological activity and are essentially useless when it comes to therapeutic effects.

We use several combination products that incorporate these Russian herbs.

Vital Adapt is a product developed by Donnie Yance and used in his human cancer protocols. We have been prescribing Vital Adapt at the Healing Center for Animals in similar situations and have found that it helps dogs and cats gain better emotional and physical control when suffering from stressful conditions. Vital Adapt helps to tonify, strengthen, and balance the adrenal glands, heart, liver, lungs, kidneys, and spleen. It is a powerful antioxidant and deep immune system restorative compound that increases energy and harmonizes all organ systems.

Vital Adapt (twice daily)	
Cat/Small Dog (up to 14 lb)	5-7 drops
Medium Dogs (15-34 lb)	10 drops
Large Dog (35-84 lb)	15 drops
Giant Dog (85+ lb)	18-20 drops

Power Adapt, another Donnie Yance product, enhances the body's energy (Chi or Qi) by providing deep nourishment for the blood, spleen, and kidney systems. Power Adapt promotes rapid healing and recovery from injury or fatigue.

Power Adapt (twice daily)	
Cat/Small Dog (up to 14 lb)	5-7 drops
Medium Dog (15–34 lb)	10 drops
Large Dog (35–84 lb)	15 drops
Giant Dog (85+ lb)	18-20 drops

Botanabol supports muscle development and repair of old and damaged tissue. It is anabolic (tissue-building) and helps to prevent tissue breakdown and wasting (catabolism). It is rich in phytoecdisterones, beneficial in insulin production and blood sugar control, and improves overall energy and stress resistance. It also helps boost immunity and speeds up healing.

Botanabol	
Cat/Small Dog (up to 14 lb)	1 capsule daily
Medium Dog (15-34 lb)	1 capsule twice daily
Large Dog (35-84 lb)	1 capsule three times daily
Giant Dog (85+ lb)	2 capsules twice daily

Other Herbs

Artemisinin is an herb that has a proven track record as an anti-malarial agent and also has effectiveness in treating some types of cancer. Artemisinin (or Qinghaosu as it is known in its native China), is the active ingredient of the herb sweet wormwood (*Artemesia annua*).

Artemisinin appears to work because of its relationship to iron. The artemisinin has oxygen molecules attached to its chemical structure. It is believed that the oxygen reacts with the mineral iron to form a highly reactive free radical combination. It seems artemesinin will destroy malarial parasites because they contain high levels of iron.

Rapidly dividing cancer cells may also require iron in order to divide and grow. When these cancer cells with higher levels of iron come in contact with artemesinin, the same free radical combination is formed, which destroys the cancer cells while causing no toxic damage to healthy cells and tissues. This is one time in this book that we "bless" the formation of free radicals (see Chapter 7 for more on free radical formation).

Artemisinin (twice daily)	
Cat/Small Dog (up to 14 lb)	25-50 mg
Medium Dog (15-34 lb)	50 mg
Large Dog (35-84 lb)	75 mg
Giant Dog (85+ lb)	100 mg

Artemis Plus. Donnie Yance has formulated an artemesinin product that he calls Artemis Plus. It contains artemesinin, as well as burdock seed, celandine, and red clover—all helpful in animals with cancer.

Artemis Plus (daily)	
Cat/Small Dog (up to 14 lb)	1 capsule
Medium Dog (15-34 lb)	1-2 capsules
Large Dog (35-84 lb)	2 capsules
Giant Dog (85+ lb)	2-3 capsules

One word of caution with artemesinin: We recommend that it be initiated as part of a comprehensive approach to cancer as described in this chapter. The process of detoxification and breakdown of cancer cells must be monitored closely by an experienced veterinarian so that it does not overwhelm your animal's liver and kidneys. Because artemisinin is also antiparasitic, the associated kill-off of internal "bugs" can be significant in some animals.

Essiac Tea. This potent herbal tonic helps to stimulate and balance the immune system. It helps to promote detoxification and the excretion of metabolic wastes. Essiac (Caisse backward) is named after nurse Rene Caisse, who in the 1920s learned about an old Indian herbal formula that was purported to cure cancer. Rene was put through the ringer by the medical establishment in Canada while simultaneously helping thousands of people who were battling cancer. She operated a cancer clinic for people in Ontario, Canada, where she treated people for no charge.

Essiac is a combination of sheep sorrel, burdock root, slippery elm bark, and rhubarb root. It is claimed that the formula will stimulate and boost the immune system in helping to fight off cancer cells. Certainly as part of an overall cancer treatment protocol, Essiac will be beneficial.

To prepare, follow the directions on the box. Essiac can be purchased at health food stores.

Essiac Tea	
Small animals (up to 25 lbs	1 oz every 12 hours
Medium animals (up to 60 lb)	1.5 oz every 12 hours
Large animals (90 lb)	2 oz every 12 hours
Larger animals (over 100 lb)	3 oz every 12 hours

Homotoxicology

Homotoxicology is the branch of medicine that seeks to identify the toxins in the body, then aid the natural defense mechanisms by mobilizing what are termed "homotoxins"—substances that neutralize and free the cells and tissues of the body from toxic debris. (For more information on homotoxicology, and its differences from classical homeopathy, please see Chapter 4.) Founded by Dr. Hans Heinrich Reckeweg in the 1950s, homotoxicology worked on the principle of biological medicine utilizing the body's own self-regulating processes (autoregulation) to achieve self-healing.

Dr. Reckeweg devised a brilliant concept for the tracking of the flow of disease in his Six Phase Table of Homotoxicology. It is, in effect, a road map of the biological system's response to the presence of toxins in the system, and provides a logical sequence of events for the veterinary practitioner to evaluate therapeutic efficacy.

Six Phase Table of Homotoxicology and Cancer

The following table outlines the progression from health to disease. (Please see the section on Homotoxicology in Chapter 4 for a complete explanation of this Six Phase Table.)

Phases where treatment and prevention of disease are still possible:

Phase 1: The Excretion (Fluid) Phase—characterized by toxin excretion (vomiting, diarrhea, etc.).

Phase 2: The Inflammation Phase—characterized by fever and inflammation.

Phase 3: The Deposition Phase—toxins deposited; cells diseased beyond this point cannot return to health.

Phases where only control of the disease is possible:

Phase 4: The Impregnation Phase—characterized by toxic, diseased cells.

Phase 5: The Degeneration Phase—where the cell's defenses and energy production are gone. This is a severe state of illness.

Phase 6: The Dedifferentiation Phase—the state of cancer. Cell growth control mechanisms are damaged, and out of control cell growth will eventually kill the body.

It is important for you to understand the meaning of these phases, which occur inside the body at the cellular level. If the process of toxin accumulation and excretion in Phase 1, 2, or 3 can be detected, you can initiate measures to assist the body in detoxifying and returning to, or maintaining, health and wellness. After Phase 4, you can only assist the body by helping to improve its function (through diet and natural remedies such as combination homeopathics and herbal remedies). This table illustrates a simple explanation of how disease works that is often missed when the focus is on the disease itself, and its medical treatment.

It is important for both doctors and guardians to understand these phases as the natural progression from health into disease. With this understanding of the body's defense mechanisms, we can then stimulate and motivate them for the benefit of our animals by using homotoxicology remedies (combination homeopathics) to help assist the body in detoxification, regeneration, and healing.

Unlike drugs, which can temporarily stop the healing process, these combination homeopathics actually assist the body in its normal attempt at healing without any side effects. One of the advantages of homotoxicology is that it is simple in its approach, and the veterinarian (or medical doctor) does not require a thorough and deep understanding of the underlying principles to find these therapies successful.

In Chapter 4, we provide a complete explanation of homotoxicology and some of the remedies used in our practice, like those from Biological Homeopathic Inc. (BHI), one of Dr. Reckeweg's companies. BHI makes combination homeopathic remedies for the more common conditions. The Heel company, part of the BHI/Heel family of companies, makes homotoxicology remedies for more specific diseases, and is geared toward medical conditions. The Heel remedies are oriented toward use by the practitioner, while the BHI remedies are geared toward at-home use, and sold over the counter. In this book we speak mostly about the BHI remedies. If you are working with a veterinarian who is trained in homotoxicology, you'll most likely be using the Heel remedies.

Natural Chemotherapuetics

Poly-MVA (Poly-Vet). Poly-MVA is a nontoxic chemotherapy agent. Poly-MVA kills cancer cells by interfering with their energy metabolism—what the cells use to fuel themselves and grow. Four decades ago, Dr. Merrill Garnett, a dentist, became acutely aware of and scientifically curious about toxic problems with chemotherapy. He began looking for a more effective, gentle approach to cancer.

Dr. Garnett focused on the altered energy metabolism of cancer cells. "Cancer cells," he writes, "are embryonic cells that can't make the transition to mature, differentiated tissue. What this means is that cancer cells are young and immature—they do not follow their genetic orders and methodically duplicate to form healthy adult tissue. Rather, they have lost their direction, remain immature and continue to grow uncontrollably. This unbridled growth is what we call cancer." It would take the next 35 years for Garnett to develop Poly-MVA—the compound that could dismantle and destroy cancer cells without affecting healthy cells around them.

Many chemotherapeutics are based on the element platinum, which is known to be highly toxic to cells. Poly-MVA, a patented nutritional supplement, is a complex compound of the metal palladium combined with lipoic acid, vitamins, and minerals. Using palladium instead of platinum eliminates toxicity; Poly-MVA, therefore, is a nontoxic chemotherapy agent.

It is scientifically accepted that cancer cells grow without using oxygen (anaerobically), unlike most healthy cells, which require oxygen. Poly-MVA acts at the level where the genes of the cell actually make the decision whether to grow with or without oxygen.

In addition to blocking the cancer cell's energy source, Poly-MVA serves as a potent antioxidant, as well as a source of vitamins and minerals. This means that it also can protect healthy cells and organs. Besides feeding the genes, it also boosts the body's immune system, directly helping the body's detoxification and healing mechanisms. Because Poly-MVA acts at the cellular level, it has no direct toxic effects on the body, and because of its oxygen mechanism, it actually helps healthy cells to prosper.

In the veterinary field, a number of veterinarians are utilizing Poly-Vet as an alternative to conventional chemotherapy. Initial reports have been favorable in adenocarcinoma, brain tumors, squamous cell carcinoma, fibrosarcomas, and mast cell tumors. Approximate doses for animals are an initial dose of 5 cc per 25 lb twice daily, and after clinical response (4 to 8 weeks) half that dosage. Once stable, the maintenance dose can be reduced in half again.

Nutritional Blood Test (NBT)

When it comes to animals with cancer, the Nutritional Blood Test (NBT) is a valuable tool for veterinarians to assist in focusing the therapy toward the body and the immune system. This test will allow your veterinarian to assess the seriousness of any complicating medical problems, search out which nutrients (vitamins, minerals, nutrients, amino acids, enzymes, and cofactors) are required for optimum organ function, and determine which immune system glands are weakened, sluggish, or out of balance. (For more information on the NBT see Chapter 4.)

The NBT will help your veterinarian assess the following issues:

Nutrient depletion: Commonly with advanced cancers the body is depleted of antioxidants (such as vitamins A, C, and E), minerals (such as selenium) and other powerful antioxidants (such as Coenzyme Q10 and alpha lipoic acid). This depletion occurs as the stressed body reaches into its reserves, exhausting its supply of critical nutrients.

Gland imbalances: The adrenal and thymus glands are critical to the cancer patient, since the health of these glands is required for a balanced immune response. In addition, other glands and systems such as the spleen, lymph, and bone marrow must also be functioning properly. The liver, which has the important task of detoxifying the body, must also function well, especially if you chose chemotherapy as part of the treatment protocol. With the NBT, weakened and inflamed glands are supported with specific nutraceuticals, whose protective effect allows time for the gland to rest and heal.

Symptomatic support: Animals with cancer exhibit signs and symptoms based upon their medical status and the type and location of the cancer. Often patients' day-to-day health is improved with symptom-oriented remedies such as combination homeopathics, homotoxicology remedies, and medicinal or Chinese herbal preparations.

After a physiological analysis of the blood, the NBT process will recommend a specific combination of nutrients, vitamins, minerals, enzymes, and antioxidants blended into a powder that closely meets the individual needs of the animal. In addition to the powder, your veterinarian can get a complete medicine cabinet full of nutraceuticals, Chinese herbs, and therapeutic remedies for your animal with cancer. These fixed formulations have been based on the accumulated data derived from thousands of animals that have had their blood analyzed with the NBT process.

Immune/Autoimmune/Cancer Support Formula. The Immune/Autoimmune/Cancer Support Formula provides supportive and regenerative effects on the glands and cells of the humoral and cellular immune system. In addition it has a tissue sparing effect and supports the normal pattern of cell division.

Chinese Herbal Medicine. These powerful herbs can be added to the nutraceutical and nutritional remedies to make the therapy programs as focused as possible on the specific type of cancer. (See the section in this chapter on Chinese Herbal Medicine for more information.)

Medicinal Mushrooms. One of the primary focuses of medicinal mushrooms is to stimulate the production and effectiveness of the natural killer cells, which are part of the immune system's natural defense cells (see Chapter 7). Traditional healers in China, Japan and other parts of Asia have prized and recognized the health-enhancing potential of mushrooms for centuries and they have been studied extensively. Maitake (*Grifola frondosa*) is a mushroom indigenous to the northeastern part of Japan. For hundreds of years, this rare and tasty mushroom has been prized in traditional Japanese herbology. The health benefits demonstrated by Maitake include immune system support, normal blood pressure support, normal blood sugar metabolism, and normal cholesterol support. Further laboratory studies and extensive clinical studies are underway in collaboration with leading research institutes both in the United States and in Japan.

Maitake PET-fraction. As part of the NBT process, a bioactive compound called "PET-fraction" is used to stimulate the immune system. A study on three different types of canine cancer cells (lymphoma, connective tissue, and mammary gland) showed that PET-fraction inhibits cancer cell growth in all three cases. Another study on dogs, following surgery and/or chemotherapy for

Harley's Story

Harley Keever is one of our patients with a lymph cancer called lymphosarcoma. He is being treated with chemotherapy, along with Chinese herbs and the NBT nutritional program. Harley had a drop in white blood cells after his chemotherapy, and Dr. Bob added PET-fraction to his program. Within one week Harley's white blood cells were back to normal.

different types of cancer, showed that when given PET-fraction in their food these dogs generally displayed improved appetite and improved quality of life, as judged by their companions.

Maitake PET-fraction (twice daily)	
Cat/Small Dog (up to 14 lb)	7 drops
Medium Dog (15-34 lb)	10 drops
Large Dog (35-84 lb)	15 drops
Giant Dog (85+ lb)	20 drops

Combination Homeopathics are specifically formulated liquid remedies available through the NBT. **Immune Drops** will help stimulate and balance the cellular and humoral immune systems as indicated in chronic degenerative conditions.

Immune Drops (twice daily)	
Cat/Small Dog (up to 14 lb)	7 drops
Medium Dog (15-34 lb)	10 drops
Large Dog (35-84 lb)	12 drops
Giant Dog (85+ lb)	15 drops

Viral Immune Drops Formula supplies homeopathic support and strengthens the body's cellular and humoral immune systems against viral infections. It is often used for feline leukemia.

Viral Immune Drops (twice daily)	
Cat/Small Dog (up to 14 lb)	7 drops
Medium Dog (15–34 lb)	10 drops
Large Dog (35–84 lb)	12 drops
Giant Dog (85+ lb)	15 drops

Finding a Holistic Veterinarian

You may wish to consult a holistic veterinary practitioner to further refine your animal's protocol. For referrals in your area, consult the American Holistic Veterinary Medical Association, 2218 Old Emmorton Road, Bel Air, MD 21015; 410/569-0795; www.ahvma.org.

Combination Western Herbs are medicinal herbs formulated through the NBT process.

Cancer Formula helps to detoxify the blood and dissolve mucous and toxins that accumulate in organ tissue, lymph, and glands. It also helps clear the circulatory, respiratory, urinary, digestive, and lymphatic systems. This formula will help to strengthen the immune system and aid in inhibiting and reducing tumor growth.

Immune Formula strengthens, stimulates, and vitalizes the cells and organs of the immune system against chronic infections and degenerative diseases.

Immune/Cancer Formula (twice daily)	
Cat/Small Dog (up to 14 lb)	7 drops
Medium Dog (15-34 lb)	12 drops
Large Dog (35-84 lb)	15 drops
Giant Dog (85+ lb)	20 drops

BHI Combination Homeopathics are low potency homeopathic remedies used as a solution to a single condition. Often Dr. Bob will mix the remedies together to achieve specific end results. (For more information about Homotoxicology, see Chapter 4.)

Vitamins and Antioxidants

Individual vitamins and antioxidants can be added to the dietary program (follow dosages on pages 321-322), or if your veterinarian is using the NBT, they can be included in the NBT powder.

Vitamin A and Beta-Carotene

Vitamin A is a fat-soluble vitamin and potent antioxidant that is required for all cell health. It is also important for the membranes of the body, especially those of the respiratory system and the membranes of the urinary tract. Cats and dogs differ when it comes to converting vitamin A and beta-carotene (pro vitamin A). Dogs can utilize both vitamin A and beta carotene. Cats, however, cannot convert beta-carotene to vitamin A, and therefore require vitamin A in its final form.

Low vitamin A levels have been associated with increased incidence of cancers, usually those affecting areas with mucous membranes (such as lung, mouth, esophagus, stomach, small and large intestine, and bladder cancer). While deficiencies of vitamin A can cause several degenerative diseases, excess can also pose problems. Vitamin A, because it is fat soluble, can accumulate in the tissues and cause adverse effects. Levels above 20,000 IU per day may be toxic. That is why it is very important to work with your veterinarian when adding these vitamins to your dog's or cat's diet.

In numerous clinical trials, vitamin A has been shown to prevent primary tumors, stop recurrences, and prevent the spread of cancer to other areas of the body (metastasis). While the mechanisms of the anticancer properties are still being researched, the antioxidant properties of vitamin A are certainly not in question. Current research shows that vitamin A, because of its very nature in the development of healthy cells and tissues, has a "tissue sparing effect" when it comes to the protection of the body from the potential adverse effects of chemotherapeutic agents.

Vitamin C

Vitamin C is a water-soluble vitamin that works as an antioxidant, a general stimulant of the immune system, and it possesses anticancer properties. Vitamin C is also essential for the proper formation and development of muscles, connective tissue and collagen.

The most noted researcher involved in the development of the reputation of vitamin C was Linus Pauling and his research associates. However, even with his credentials (as a two-time Nobel Laureate), he had tremendous uphill battles against the conventional medical establishment. For those readers who are interested in history, the book *Vitamin C and Cancer: Medicine or Politics* shares Dr. Pauling's rocky road.

Thankfully, it now appears that the clinical evidence has moved in the direction of vitamin C (and all antioxidants) for antiaging and the treatment of cancer.

Vitamin C is reported to:

- Stimulate the production of interferon.
- Enhance natural killer cells (NK) and lymphocyte activity.
- Help to neutralize cancer producing chemicals and free radicals.
- Strengthen connective tissue.
- Improve appetite and day-to-day quality of life in cancer patients.
- Have antiviral and antibacterial properties.
- Enhance antibody levels and immune proteins (IgA, IgG).

There are several important concepts related to the use of vitamin C in veterinary practice. Vitamin C is involved in many of the metabolic and physiological processes of the body. Because dogs and cats manufacture vitamin C on their own, it is automatically assumed that this important vitamin is not necessary in the diet. Not true! Vitamin C is one of the antioxidant vitamins that is almost completely inactivated by heat, and most pet foods (canned and dry) are cooked at inordinately high temperatures. Couple this with the fact that the vitamin and antioxidant reserves in the body are quickly depleted by high free radical production, and you can easily see that deficiencies of this important nutrient are possible.

Dr. Wendell Belfield, a pioneering holistic veterinarian, has written many clinical reports on the use of vitamin C in the management of cancer in dogs and cats. Please note, the therapeutic use of vitamin C either orally at high doses or intravenously should be overseen by an experienced veterinarian.

Ester-C

Ester C is a highly absorbable, pH neutral form of vitamin C. Veterinary studies have shown Ester-C is effective in helping with degenerative joint disease, painful conditions and locomotion, regeneration of cartilage, immune stimulation, and antioxidant properties.

Vitamin E

Vitamin E (tocopherol) is a fat-soluble vitamin important for all cell membranes in the body. It is one of the prime antioxidants, and helps to prevent oxidation (commonly called rancidity), and in the generation of cell energy. It is involved in the healing of tissues, and the formation of scar tissue. Vitamin E is also important for the proper function of the heart and blood flow and is required to maintain proper immune function.

It is believed Vitamin E's anticancer activity comes from its antioxidant action and immune enhancement function. In the area of cancer therapy, it has been proven to reverse the cancer process, and also has the ability to enhance the effectiveness of specific chemotherapeutics. Also, in the area of chemotherapy, vitamin E has been shown to have "organ sparing" properties, protecting tissues and cells against the adverse effects of both chemotherapy and radiation therapy.

Coenzyme Q10 (CoQ10)

Coenzyme Q10 (ubiquinone) is a potent antioxidant found in the mitochondria of cells, and is directly involved in cellular energy production. It is essential in the manufacture of adenosine triphosphate (ATP), the energy source for all the body's cells and tissue. Dr. Karl Folkers of the University of Texas is the leading expert on the benefits of CoQ10. Although much of the research related to CoQ10 is in the treatment of heart disease, there are reports by Dr. Folkers on its benefit in cancer patients. He reports that when treating certain patients for heart disease who also had cancer, some went into (and have stayed in) remission.

Because of its powerful antioxidant properties, we include Coenzyme Q10 as part of cancer treatment protocols. It is effective in reducing free radicals and inflammation, which is often predisposing to the cancer process. It also functions to directly stimulate the cellular immune system by increasing macrophage production.

What's the Prognosis?

While dealing with cancer in a beloved companion can be overwhelming, it's important that you do your research and find a veterinarian who you are comfortable with, one who specializes in treating cancer. Know that there are many alternative therapies available that truly can make a difference in your cat's or dog's daily life. Always get the opinion from both a conventional and alternative veterinarian who are both experienced in cancer treatment. Then take a step back and make your decision and move forward with a positive attitude, knowing that you are doing the best for your animal. As the therapy process proceeds handle the ups and downs as they present themselves, and take each day as a new day. Remember, you have many alternatives and positive treatment modalities to choose from. And, don't forget to remove fear from the equation.

Chapter 10

Understanding the Senior Years

The most remarkable and eye-opening story related to aging comes from our own dog, Leigh. We adopted Leigh from the Guiding Eyes for the Blind in Yorktown, New York, because he was rejected from their training program due to his hip dysplasia.

At seven years of age Leigh was crippled and his entire muzzle, face, and back were gray and white (he was originally a deep golden red color). As a conventional veterinary family we assumed this was part of the aging process. It was only when our epiphany regarding the importance of diet for healing occurred that we began "feeding" Leigh's system with living antioxidants and phytonutrients. Soon after he began to heal and revert back to his original deep red-gold color. More importantly, he began to get up and down, walk, and do things that he hadn't done since he was a puppy. The two important things that we did for Leigh were one, stop the strong painkillers and cortisone he was taking, and two, offer him a "living" diet.

It is a sad fact of life that our dogs and cats become seniors at about seven years of age; half of the animal companions living in the United States are six years or over—on their way to senior status. Smaller dogs and cats generally have a longer life expectancy than medium, large, and giant breeds. The following chart gives some examples of how the size of the animal dictates the age as compared to humans.

Comparison to Human Age				
Chronological Age	"Human Age"			
	Small	Medium	Large	Giant
5	35	38	40	45
7	45	48	50	55
10	55	60	65	75
15	75	80	90	100

In addition to this chronological aging process, dogs and cats are exposed to all sorts of negative factors, making them more susceptible to the onset and progression of chronic disease. Cancer, arthritis, diabetes, kidney and liver failure, and congestive heart failure have become commonplace for our canine and feline companions.

Paying attention to the antiaging and longevity strategies that have been outlined in this book is essential to protect your animal from a premature demise. Our planet is inundated with chemicals polluting our air, homes, water, and soil, and until the new consciousness takes hold, it is up to each individual to create a shield of protection around his or her animal (and self).

It's Never too Late to Start on the Goldstein Food Plan

The Goldstein Food Plan, presented in Chapter 1, offers exactly what your senior animal requires. First, please review the section on raw and living foods in that chapter. Certainly if you have the time and inclination to feed a homemade or raw diet loaded with living nutrients, then you should do so. If not, our simple plan of a balanced senior-type food base, enhanced with the proper amount of food-derived antioxidants, essential amino and fatty acids, phytonutrients, and living enzymes is a great way to protect your senior animal.

Here is a good working example. To a naturally preserved senior base food add the following with every meal:

- Lightly steamed meat, chicken, raw, organic egg yolk, or tofu.
- Finely chopped greens such as parsley, broccoli, or organic carrots.
- Salmon or organic flaxseed oil.
- Cooked organic oatmeal, millet, or brown rice.

You can add the following taste tempters if your animal is addicted to an unhealthy diet:

- Organic plain yogurt.
- Raw or soft-boiled organic egg yolk.
- Grated cheese.

At all costs, always *avoid the following* when feeding your senior animal:

- Foods that contain chemical additives and preservatives.
- Foods that contain high amounts of undigestible protein, such as by product meals.
- Foods that contain high amounts of saturated fats (such as poultry fat).
- Foods that contain refined carbohydrates (white flour, white rice).
- Foods that contain allergy-producing ingredients (wheat, corn, brewer's yeast).

Use the Annual Exam to Your Animal's Advantage

Bringing your animal to your family veterinarian for an annual physical examination is highly recommended. Do not go to your veterinarian solely because you received a post card reminder that your companion is due for his annual shots and then automatically inject and leave.

Change the channel and use the notice to get a health checkup that includes the following:

- A vaccine titer test to check antibody levels against the most common diseases in your geographical area.
- A complete physical examination so that your veterinarian checks all the organ systems.
- A complete blood examination to rule out early medical problems, as well as a Nutritional Blood Test (NBT), which further assesses the status of the immune system as well as potential deficiencies and imbalances (see Chapter 4).
- A urinalysis and fecal analysis to assess how your animal's "exhaust" systems are functioning.
- A heartworm test.

All of these tests are performed to give you information and an early indication of problems. Once you know there is a potential problem, then you can put in place the proper preventive measures before a disease takes hold. This is the time to get guidance from your veterinarian about prevention. And if the solution suggested is the chronic use of drugs, then this is the time to seek guidance from an integrative or holistic veterinarian who understands the link between diet and the prevention of diseases.

While most veterinarians understand that early diagnosis of pending problems is a good preventative, many just do not understand that the solution doesn't lie in chronic use of medication, but rather in improving the diet along with the addition of natural, more gentle remedies that work with the body's healing system to bring about a real cure.

While diet is often emphasized in a conventional practice setting, the recommendations are most often a typical senior or prescription type of diet manufactured by one of the larger pet food companies. And more often than not the recommendations for preventive health care for senior animals will be a medication, such as adding thyroid medication to an animal's daily program at

Senior Wellness Program

Antech Diagnostics, the nation's largest diagnostic laboratory for veterinarians and a partner of ours in the Nutritional Blood Testing system, has put together an entire Senior Wellness Program that is offered to veterinarians throughout the country. Antech developed the program because they believe that while many senior animals appear healthy, there are problems that may be occurring below the surface. If caught early enough these problems can be helped through preventive care. The fact that a conventional diagnostic laboratory is offering this program to all veterinarians nationwide is really a breath of fresh air.

the early indications of a weakening thyroid gland ("early hypothyroidism").

While we are in agreement with the judicious use of medication when there is an existing clinical problem, we are not in favor of the chronic use of medications to control recurrent symptoms without focusing on finding, correcting, and preventing the source. For example, while the following signs and symptoms should be taken seriously and in certain instances treated medically, in all instances, once the underlying cause has been diagnosed, a nutritional support and preventive program should always be instituted. *Starting the chronic cycle of medical treatment, leading to a cover-up of the symptoms, followed by a recurrence of the symptoms, and then another treatment episode is simply not acceptable.*

The following short list of signs and symptoms will often signal the occurrence of a disease process:

- Increased thirst or urination.
- Weight loss or weight gain.
- Change in appetite.
- Listlessness, apathy, depression.
- Diarrhea or constipation.
- Vomiting.
- Dull, greasy, smelly coat.
- Bad breath, drooling, pain in the mouth.
- Excessive panting, increased breathing rate.

Use Your Intuition

We emphasize to guardians that observation of their animal is just as important as any physical examination. Over the years we have had numerous clients bring their animals in saying, "I can't put my finger on it, but I know she is just not right" or "I know he looks fine, but I know something is bothering him." This use of intuition, this connectedness to your animal, especially a senior animal that has spent years with you and your family, is one of the most important aspects of disease prevention and the maintenance of wellness. Animals do have emotions and are exposed to the same emotional stresses as you and your family. However, and this is important—animals do not have a highly developed sense of reason that enables them to justify or accept a stressful condition. More often than not they will absorb the stress and suffer the resulting physical consequences. The very fact that they are "seniors" means that chronologically they have lived longer and therefore have absorbed more stress, which is detrimental to their health. So be sure to pay attention to the impact that aging has on your animal's emotions. Here are some simple things that you can keep a watchful eye upon with your older animal companion to help in the prevention of more serious illnesses from occurring.

Cognitive Ability

What to Look For
- Restlessness
- Pacing
- Difficulty in lying down or sleeping
- Excessive dreaming
- Howling, uncontrolled barking
- Staring
- Confusion

Preventative Tips

Don't permit your animal to slack off: engage his or her brain! Encourage the thought process by maintaining a steady flow of quality communication and play activity along with a minimum of 20 minutes of suitable exercise one to two times daily. The brain is a clear case of "use it or lose it." In doing so, your animal will release endorphins, helping to prevent depression.

Brain Benefit

Gingko biloba, an herbal extract sourced from the world's oldest living species of tree, increases circulation to the brain. Gingko is currently used in Europe for the treatment of Alzheimer's disease, and has proven to be effective in people prone to or recovering from a stroke. In animals suffering from cognitive dysfunction, Gingko can be helpful in improving brain function. Symptoms such as lethargy, listlessness, continual meowing or barking, sleeplessness, and staring into walls can all be broadly categorized as senility or cognitive dysfunction.

Ginkgo Biloba (twice daily)	
Cat/Small Dog (up to 14 lb)	15 mg
Medium Dog (15-34 lb)	25-35 mg
Large Dog (35-84 lb)	50 mg
Giant Dog (85+ lb)	75 mgs

We often will mix together a homotoxicology combination from BHI of **BHI Ginkgo + Alertness + Inflammation** that can help in these conditions.

BHI (twice daily)	
Cat/Small Dog (up to 14 lb)	1/3 dropper
Medium Dog (15-34 lb)	1/2 dropper
Large Dog (35-84 lb)	1 dropper
Giant Dog (85+ lb)	1 dropper

Hearing

What to Look For
- Not responsive to commands
- Not listening or coming when called
- No longer a "watch dog"
- Doesn't hear door bell

Preventative Tips

The most common cause of hearing loss is the result of chronic ear infections. It is important to treat ear infections early (with medication if necessary) and then set up a preventive program that will help reduce recurrent infections.

Once the infection is controlled, you can use Earth Animal's **Clean Ear** or Halo **Herbal Ear Wash** on a weekly basis to help dissolve waxy accumulation and stop the head shaking that eventually leads to irritation and secondary infections.

Joints

What to Look For

- Your animal's movement is slowing down
- He or she is slow to get up and down
- Restless sleep
- Pacing, especially during the early morning hours
- Reluctance to go up and down stairs
- Inactivity and reluctance to play

Preventative Tips

For a healthy spine and limber joints, we recommend a combination of freshly extracted vegetable juice (rich in antioxidant-laden phytochemicals) and physical massage. If the arthritis or tendonitis has already progressed to a state of disease, chiropractic care or acupuncture may be considered. Be sure to implement our daily Food Plan and use it to the fullest along with supplements of **glucosamine**, **chondroitin** and **superoxide dismutase (SOD)**—building blocks for healthy joints.

Therapeutic Limbering Juice

If your animal is getting up in years or is suffering from a spinal disease or arthritis, it is imperative to get fresh juice into his or her system. There is nothing better than juicing equal parts of organic celery with carrots and apples. Celery contains naturally occurring sodium, which will alkalinize the body. (Other alkaline-producing minerals are potassium, calcium, and magnesium.) Acid-producing minerals are phosphorus, sulfur, and chlorine. Arthritis and inflammation of the joints and tendons is an "acid" disease, and naturally occurring sodium will help to offset and neutralize this acid environment. Be sensitive to this longevity feature and do a review of your animal's diet. Limit or avoid entirely white refined flour, sugar, acid-producing foods, and red meat. Add sodium-rich foods such as celery, dandelion greens, cucumbers, sprouts, kale, avocado, lettuce, potato skins.

Glucosamine/Chondroitin combination (twice daily)	
Cat/Small Dog (up to 14 lb)	250 mg
Medium Dog (15-34 lb)	500 mg
Large Dog (35-84 lb)	750 mg
Giant Dog (85+ lb)	1,000 mg

Superoxide Dismutase (SOD) *(once daily)*	
Cat/Small Dog (up to 14 lb)	125 mg
Medium Dog (15-34 lb)	250 mg
Large Dog (35-84 lb)	500 mg
Giant Dog (85+ lb)	750 mg

Skin

What to Look For

- Odor
- Flaking, dandruff
- Thinning hair
- Loss of hair/bald spots
- Greasy coat
- Itching, biting, scratching

Preventative Tips

The skin is an organ of elimination and must be kept clean. Brushing and combing to remove dead hair is essential. Bathing with a natural shampoo about once a month is recommended. For mild irritations, aloe vera gel (applied directly to the irritation from a freshly opened leaf or from a store-bought gel), is one of our favorite home healers. You can also place a wet, cool black tea bag on the irritated spot; the tannins in the tea will soothe the irritation. Mineral-rich baking soda, made into a paste, also works well, as do fresh plantain leaves, a wild herb that grows throughout much of the US. Stay with your animal for 15 minutes while your remedy of choice penetrates the skin. Treat the area twice daily for three days or until it is resolved. This procedure will often prevent the acute outbreak that requires a visit to your veterinarian.

Teeth and Gums

What to Look For

- Bad breath/foul odor
- Redness at the gum line

- Bleeding from gums
- Tartar buildup on teeth
- Reluctance to chew

Preventative Tips

Usually dogs and cats that are not under a nutritional preventive program will have to have their teeth cleaned (usually under anesthesia) about every 12 months. While brushing with some animals is out of the question, there is a simple, effective procedure that can help reduce plaque and tartar buildup. The simple method is to wrap your finger with gauze, apply an enzyme-based toothpaste for dogs and cats, and simply rub your finger up the side of the tooth, making sure you lift the gum slightly, and then run your finger down the tooth. This procedure will help to reduce plaque and tartar buildup. Don't tackle the entire mouth at one time. Select a small portion such as the left upper molars, and concentrate on them two to three times in one week. The following week, select another area.

Vision

What to Look For

- Trouble navigating
- Bumping into things
- Inability to focus
- Staring

Preventative Tips

Eyebright, abundant in the Pacific Northwest, will work wonders to strengthen your animal's eyes, decrease inflammation, and improve vision. Your local health food store should carry Eyebright in capsule or elixir form. Earth Animal has a product called Vision that contains eyebright and other beneficial herbs. This herbal combination has proven to be beneficial in animals losing their sight due to cataracts or degeneration of the cornea.

Eye Strengthener Juice

Juice together the following:
1/2 carrot & 1/2 apple for small animals
1 carrot & 1 apple for medium animals
2 carrots and 1 large or 2 small apples for large animals
Mix in drinking water or offer straight. If juicing is not an option, be sure to grate fresh carrots and mix with food daily and offer fresh chunks of apples daily as a snack.

Weight Gain

What to Look For
- Loss of the waist (looking at your animal from the back toward the head, the waist should not be larger than the chest)
- Sagging skin below the abdomen
- Tiredness
- Exercise intolerant
- Excessive sleeping

Preventative Tips

Many animals are addicted to their current foods (because of the chemical flavor enhancers) not to mention that many commercially prepared foods for dogs and cats are simply overloaded with carbohydrates in the form of simple sugars and cooked saturated fats. Simply improving the diet (with the Goldstein Food Plan) and adding nutritious fiber such as chopped vegetables, begins the process of reversing obesity. Along with regular walks and exercise, weight issues become manageable.

Weight Loss

What to Look For
- The bones of the head, shoulders, hips, and spine begin to protrude
- Loss of muscle mass

Preventative Tips

Weight loss and wasting are often secondary to a chronic disease. If your animal has lost his or her appetite and is wasting away, it is important that you visit your veterinarian and get the proper diagnosis or cause for the weight loss. Once established, you can address the real cause.

Don't Forget the Emotions

Any of the conditions associated with senior dogs and cats can lead to emotional upset, including sadness, grief, depression, and apathy. Some great ideas for counteracting these negative emotions include playing beautiful music, spending at least 20 minutes twice daily in the silence together, and treating specific emotions with flower essences, such as Anaflora's Senior formula. (For more information on flower essences see Chapter 4.)

Slow the Aging Process in Your Animal

- Follow the Goldstein Food Plan. Assess your current food, and add healthy, immune-boosting extras such as grated carrots, fresh garlic, plain organic low-fat yogurt, flaxseed oil, and Daily Health Nuggets. (Learn about our food plan and how to rate pet foods in Chapter 1.)
- Give your friend only fresh, pure water—filtered, distilled, or spring water.
- Reduce your animal's exposure to pesticides, heavy metals, and other forms of "environmental pollution."
- Consider an air purifier for your mutual good health.
- Exercise! Daily exercise is possibly the single most important health-enhancing activity that you and your friend can do. (Bonus: Your health will benefit as well.)
- Minimize stress in your animal's world, and be aware that stressful situations in family relationships affect your dog and cat as well. Use flower essences to counteract the effects of stress.
- Carefully review your vaccination schedule, and minimize the number and frequency of vaccines that your animal receives following the initial puppy or kitten series.
- Should your animal become ill, look to natural solutions such as fresh juices, supplements, and nutraceuticals to minimize your reliance on medications.
- Keep your schedule of an annual physical examination with your family veterinarian. When the annual blood examination is done ask your veterinarian to perform a Nutritional Blood Test (NBT) (see Chapter 4). This will pinpoint early underlying weakness in organs and tissues so that your nutritional therapy is targeted at the source, not the symptoms.

Chapter 11

Understanding and Treating Emotions, and Letting Go When It's Time

Susan Goldstein has spent the better part of her 25 years of animal healing dealing with the emotional issues of both guardians and companions. In this very personal and honest interview with TFH Publications, Susan talks about our animals' emotional lives, our own emotional wellness, and how guardians can plan for and cope with the grief of losing a beloved companion.

Q: *How are our animals' emotions tied into their health?*

Susan: As with humans, emotions and how we both express and supress them are linked to disease, so by acknowledging an animal's emotional well-being, we are taking a step forward in wellness and disease awareness. A great example is animals with chronic allergies. Over the years, as we treated these animals, we started asking questions about their earlier experiences. What we found that they had in common was early experiences of abuse and rejection. When we made that link, we started to understand that without addressing the earlier emotional imbalances, we could not get a full healing. All of us, whether we're a professional or whether we're the animal's guardian, need to make sure that as we address the physical issues we're also zeroing in on the animal's emotions. Then we can take it a step further and understand the home culture, family issues, and all of the other things we bring into the animal's environment, including our own stresses. All of these things will contribute to disease. Our animals are emulating us, and constantly taking on our own feelings, and emotional stresses, so we must be aware of what I call their "emotional hygiene." We have to do our best to detach from our own negative emotions, not just for our own well-being, but also for that of our animals.

Q: So it's possible to unintentionally bring stress to our animals by not being aware of our own emotional state?

Susan: I think it's very important for us to take responsibility for what we bring to our animals. Unchecked stress is deadly for all of us if we're not dealing with our own emotional needs. My mom is an example. Her first love was a man who died as a result of the war. The grief that she had as a result was stuck inside throughout her whole life and was never dealt with, because it wasn't appropriate. She was afraid that talking about it might hurt someone, like the man she eventually married (my dad). Louise Hay, a human healer, writes brilliantly about linking parts of the body to emotional imbalances, which then get linked to disease. Grief is associated with the lungs, and my mother died of lung cancer. When I made the connection between her illness and her supressed grief many years later, it really was an eye opener for me. We have to be much more enlightened about our own emotional health, if we really want to have our animals in tiptop shape.

Q: You've seen this same link between emotional imbalance and disease in the animals that you treat?

Susan: We all hold memories; we all have memories on the cellular level—and those memories manifest into our emotions. So an animal who experienced a nonloving, dysfunctional, or abusive household, will have a link to disease. Now that doesn't mean that all animals who have diseases have early similar experiences, but I do believe that an animal who has a chronic disorder of any kind has some sort of emotional imbalance. It's interesting because the emotional imbalance doesn't necessarily start with abuse or neglect. For example, I was speaking with one of my clients about her dog's chronic allergies, and she was telling me that everything was "perfect"—the breeder was perfect, the homecoming was perfect, the adjustment period was perfect. She was essentially challenging my interrogation about what was going on emotionally, and I said, "Okay. I agree, it sounds like you're one in a billion, and you've led the perfect life. But I want to tell you something, I still think that we need to treat your little dog's emotions." When she asked why I said, "Have you ever been stung by a bee or stung by a mosquito? Think about what it feels like when you're itching for a period of 24 hours or 48 hours or even 2 weeks, however long your body is allergically reacting. Think about what it does to your nerves. Think about how it feels." I helped my client realize that it didn't matter what came first, whether some kind of trauma created an emotional imbalance, which then manifested into an allergy; or the immune system was compromised, creating allergies in the animal, and the constant itching and discomfort created an emotional imbalance. Either way there's an emotional component to it. It doesn't matter where it came from. We need to treat it.

Q: *What is the best way to recognize and treat emotional imbalances?*

Susan: Believe it or not, the most important treatment initially is awareness—acknowledging the animal's emotions. Most guardians understand this intuitively, but don't let it surface: Until we draw it out, really look at it and give it some energy and creative thought, we can't begin to heal. Just to be aware and acknowledge that your animal has feelings and emotions, that is the number one step. I must mention that initially there is a disadvantage to acknowledging an animal's emotions, because the animal communicates in a silent language. He or she is not able to say, "I hurt. You hurt my feelings. I'm worried about what's going on in this household." Everything is basically stuck inside, and unless you're a very enlightened guardian you will experience some frustration. Guardians need to learn to take some time to be in the silence, learn how to tap into and interpret their animal's silent language. Working with a healer or communicator can facilitate this.

The next step is to go after the symptom. You look at the symptom, face it, and make the link to understanding the emotional issue. Once you are there, I recommend flower essences as one of the healing modalities. We have worked over the years with the Bach Rescue Remedy, which is a generic flower essence, and we have also worked with the Anaflora, Sharon Callahan's line of organic flower essences, including one called Return to Joy, which is a generic healer. These go after the animal's emotional imbalance in a very broad way, like a broad-spectrum antibiotic. We treat the animal generally in this broad-spectrum way for a period of one month, and then we go after the symptoms. Symptoms may include aggression, anxiety, fears, loneliness, depression, or grief. So I would follow up Return to Joy with a specific flower essence targeting the symptom, such as Aggression, Tranquility, Bereavement, or Loneliness.

It is so important for guardians to know that we actually have remedies that work, and the beautiful thing is that these remedies are alternatives to drugs, which always have side effects. Remember, a pharmacological drug is only going to treat the symptom, it will not actually heal the animal. It won't go to the source. These healing herbs will get to the source, and that is what's so magnificent about having these modalities. I can tell you, as a healer, I wasn't effective before I started to address the emotions and use modalities such as flower essences. This work, in conjunction with all Dr. Bob and I have learned about proper diet, exercise, vaccination wisdom, and other methods of adequate care, has made all the difference.

Q: *How has the general perception of these kinds of modalities and emotional issues changed over the years?*

Susan: I used to be very cautious when I started doing this work. In the beginning of my career, I had many opportunities to address the emotions and I didn't open my "gift." I just thought that people were not ready back in the 1980s, and I think I made a big mistake—people *were* ready. It's an intuitive thing for many of us; we're aware of our animal's emotions and feelings, but maybe we don't verbalize it or intellectualize it. The minute I had the courage to make the link between emotions and wellness for my own animals, I knew I had made a breakthrough. And I was thrilled that here at the Healing Center for Animals, which is a nutritional telephone consultation line, people accepted it right away. I think guardians were really grateful to be able to talk about it; to be able to know what to do.

Finding an Animal Communicator

Use the following tips when looking for a good communicator:

- Does the communicator have references? Speak with at least three clients who have used the communicator.
- Are any of the references veterinarians?
- How many years of experience does the communicator have?
- What is the educational background of the communicator (if any)?
- Has the communicator published any materials, lectured or held workshops? (If so, where and to whom?)
- How is your own intuition resonating with the communicator?
- Ask the communicator what his or her personal mission is. Is he or she coming from a positive place?
- Most important, on the initial visit observe your animal during and after the session to see how he or she is responding.

Q: *How can newcomers find their way through the sometimes confusing maze of holistic or alternative remedies?*

Susan: I had some wishy-washy experiences prior to working with Rescue Remedy and Sharon Callahan's full line. I dabbled back in the 1980s, when products were constantly being introduced. I've been in this field for a long time, and I really feel that Sharon Callahan has written the bible on flower essence therapy and treating the emotions. Her books will ground people, so I recommend them as a great way to get acquainted with these modalities. I also recommend working with a healer and animal communicator when you're first getting started. I'm not at all suggesting that you just call up your local animal communicator in the yellow pages— they're a dime a dozen today, much like psychics. You have to be very, very selective, and my goal with the recommendations in the back of this book is to help people avoid skinning their knees. I've skinned my knees; I've had everybody thrown at me, and believe me, at the Healing Center we are selective. A qualified communicator can be a very special part of the guardians' and the animals' world, and it's such an important part of our work at the Healing Center for Animals.

The novice should read books on both flower essence therapy and how to treat the emotions, and then find a really good healer or communicator, and find out how your animal is feeling. But the truth is that you'll see it for yourself. Once you start working with these modalities, the end result is obvious, you'll know there's a healing. At first it will be very subtle, and when you're working with the right remedy all of a sudden you won't see the issues anymore. The proof is in the pudding. For example, I was dealing with a client who was very frustrated because her little dog would nip at guests. She would have to isolate the dog, and the dog would bark and be unhappy, but she couldn't let him out because of the nipping. She was incredibly frustrated. While our client was working with a trainer, we were also treating the little dog for aggression using flower essences, and it was so easy to understand his imbalance, and so wonderful to be able to treat and heal it.

I've found that at the root of behavioral problems is emotional imbalance. I think that essentially animals want to please us, so if there's antisocial behavior going on, we need to look to the emotions. The end result is you give the remedy, the symptom disappears, and you know you're on to something—you know it works. The neat thing about these remedies also is that they're very economical. They're affordable for everyone, and I just love that.

Q: Is there a chance of harming our animals by misunderstanding their emotional issues or misusing these types of modalities?

Susan: It could lead to a misdiagnosis, but here's the good thing about all this: If you use the wrong remedy, there's no harm—there won't be any side effects. It does take a little while to get the hang of it. I didn't always match the remedy to the right symptom in the beginning, but I was never worried that I would harm an animal in any way. The best way to attempt to heal is through personal observation, listening to your inner voice, and tapping into your own intuition. And as I said before, find an appropriate healer, intuitive communicator, and work with them if it's affordable and if one is accessible. I think that helps a lot. Also, read Sharon Callahan's book, *Healing Animals Naturally with Flower Essences and Intuitive Listening*.

I believe there is no such thing as a bad dog or a bad cat! Rather, many behavioral problems are a symptom of an emotional problem.

Q: *What effects can animals have on our own well-being?*

Susan: The very first day I opened up the Healing Center for Animals, I got a call from a woman on the West Coast who said "I have had lupus for several years, and recently I went into remission. And the doctors are scratching their heads…how did I go into remission? They told me it makes no sense, makes zero scientific medical sense." But the thing is her dog got it. And as she was reading my newsletter, she made this interesting connection, and the burning question she had for me was, "Did her dog take on her lupus?" There is no way of proving certain things, but for me it was valid intuitively. And because that question came from deep within her soul, I believe it was the truth. I've dealt with more than one client who knows that his or her animal took on their disease.

I've also dealt with clients who have shared that their animals have been their healers. They have been at death's door and the animal didn't want to let go, wouldn't let them go, filled them up with purpose and renewed them spiritually. Many years ago, during Christmas week at Earth Animal (which is the retail arm of the Healing Center for Animals), a particular gentleman wanted to talk to me about his experience with his Standard Poodle. This dog never left his side as he declined due to a very serious illness. Everybody had given up—the doctors, his wife, his kids, even him. But his dog wouldn't let him go. He gave such powerful love and unconditional support, and he just wouldn't quit. And somehow, that powerful love by his side literally raised him up out of his deathbed. There have been so many stories of animals who understand their role to heal us, not just emotionally but also physically.

Q: *Guilt is a feeling that many guardians experience, especially with long work hours, time spent away from an animal, not paying enough attention. How does this affect wellness?*

Susan: We do harbor a lot of guilt, and there are many issues that can provoke guilt that we have to deal with. I think, as animal guardians, we're up against some very big decisions from time to time that have the potential for guilt and second-guessing. The issue of euthanasia forces us to do a lot of soul searching—we don't always think we're right when we have to take such a step.

The guilt of living with a latchkey animal is another one. You come home and you know your animal has had an awful day, you know your animal has been lonely, you see the sad eyes, and there's nothing you can do about it. The whole latchkey animal syndrome is something that we need to deal with as a society. If you do have to leave your animal alone all day, what are you doing to minimize the pain? We have flower essence formulas specifically made for the latchkey animal—Loneliness, Missing You. You can play beautiful music, healing music, play a quality video or DVD. There's a lot more that we can be doing.

Treatment decisions are associated with guilt as well. I hear from clients all the time: "I did this horrible treatment to my cat. My cat had cancer and I did this allopathic thing, and now my cat is suffering. Why didn't I do the holistic thing to begin with?" And they are guilty about it. I think it's one of the most unhealthy emotions that we can harbor, and I think that we have to really understand that we're just human, and most of us do the best we can at the time with the information that we have.

I also believe that animals harbor guilt. If we reprimand an animal, the animal doesn't necessarily understand why they are being reprimanded. The animal feels guilty, even if he or she doesn't necessarily comprehend what the reprimand is about. We have to be really careful about how we communicate with our animals, how we reprimand. That, I think, is the real provoker of guilt.

You have to understand that guilt will block feelings 100 percent. It's an emotion that's connected to fear. In a spiritual sense, I think fear and guilt and all these negative emotions basically disconnect you from a much healthier emotion, which is the experience of love. And the thing that you need to do is to look at your animals and understand forgiveness, because they live in the moment. Every one of my patients I nickname "baby Buddhas." And my clients will giggle, but I say, "Look at them, they live in the moment, they don't carry the baggage around that we humans do." And that's one of the major lessons that I think these animals come to teach us.

Q: *Even guilt over the very treatment of illnesses can have a negative effect on our animals?*

Susan: Of course. If we're not experiencing love and joy in the moment, we're expressing something negative. Our animals will pick up on our discomfort, our guilt, our anxiety, all of that. And it's difficult when you're dealing with those kinds of emotions to really create healing. But what I have come to understand is that animals deal with pain and discomfort better than we do. We seem to add a lot of our perceptions to them. We make a big deal out of ear cleanings, dental cleanings, surgical procedures. We make a bigger deal out of them than animals do. I think animals can go with the flow better, I think they can tolerate more than we can.

They are just so brilliant at taking on our stuff. They're really good at it. I find that really frightening. Dr. Bob and I lost an animal to grief, and I truly believe that she passed to make sure that I understand how deep our animals' emotions run, and that I bring it forward to my work. Her death rocked my world, and taught me that I cannot be sloppy. With each client, I never forget to make sure that we check in on the emotions. That's my commitment. That's been near and dear to me at all times.

Q: *How did you come to be a grief therapist?*

Susan: Essentially, I had a personal experience. My mom was diagnosed with cancer when I was a child, and she spent the majority of my childhood fighting it. So I lived it, it was in my pablum so to speak. I had to be her grief counselor…I had to be her transition person. I was one of the people closest to her. So I learned the importance of being able to help a person to express the experience during transition, and also how to really be there. When my mom was dying, there were several requests that she made. One was, "You're marrying a brilliant doctor, can't you do something about this thing called cancer?" (Not that we are curing cancer, but I said, "Sure.") Then she wanted me to know that I had been her strength, which was a gift, and I needed to promise her that it was a gift that would be shared. It took years before I understood, before I could acknowledge or keep that promise. It took a long time to get past the unresolved grief of my mother's passing, and realize that the pain and loss that I felt were necessary for me to be able to feel for others. I wanted to see if I could bring some light to others who were going through the same experience. I started studying with Dr. Elisabeth Kübler-Ross, who was such a genius at sharing her gift. And I began working with children in a cancer clinic in the Bahamas. And then I made the transfer to animals. The death and dying part for the animals is something that is really sacred for me, and it's a sacred experience whenever anyone has to go through it. It's a very spiritually intimate time when you are dealing with a person or an animal (or both)—during transition and after.

Q: *How does animal grief counseling work?*

Susan: When I get such a call from a client, the first thing I do is a great deal of prayer work and deep breathing. I ask that I personally, Susan, be removed, because I'm really not tapping into a science, I'm going to a higher place. For me it's a place of prayer. Then I ask God to bring the healing in and to help me find the appropriate compassionate words. Once reached, the higher place that is, the comforting expressions flow and the healing begins. We all have the ability, if we understand where to go for healing and how to tap into it.

I had a personal experience with our Welsh Corgi, Annie, when she was dying. It took two weeks for her to make her transition and during those fourteen days, I was really clear that we were losing her. Dr. Bob was not. He never gives up. He has to work on the body and find the cure. Bob kept on working until hours before her death, even though I knew we had lost her already.

It was such a hard thing, as the three of us could not let go. Annie especially needed to, and none of us could do so. I began to sense that she was beginning to lose her quality of life. It was at 9:30 p.m. the night before Annie's death that Sharon Callahan made a random act of kindness call, and said, "Hi, I'm Sharon Callahan. I understand that you and Dr. Bob are having a really rough time. I just want you to know that I'm going to be overnighting a remedy that will help you all let go." At that point I wasn't able to understand how to grief counsel my own dying dog or my husband—I didn't know what to do. So we all took the remedy, which was custom blended, and it helped us get emotionally grounded. As a result we were able to face the fact that it was Annie's time to go. And after that, I was able to sing her to heaven.

I think that counseling should take on the appropriate form. It should not be structured. We should meet the person, the animal, or the family at their level. Using your intuition and your spiritual connection is the way to discover what their needs are, and the form the counseling should take. As an example, when most animals are about ready to go to heaven, they will let you know if they want company or they want to be alone. Some animals will stay near you, some animals will go and hide to die because it's too painful to say good-bye. Often animals go into hiding, and you should respect that. You can stay in close contact through mediation, prayer, or a communicator.

> "Were it not for the windstorms in life, one could not see the canyons."
> —Dr. Elisabeth Kübler-Ross

But if the animal should choose to have you around, then it's my opinion that you should sing him or her to heaven. Even if you have a wretched voice, it will be beautiful.

When I'm on the phone with people, and they're having a hard time facing the animal's pain, their own pain, I have to make them understand how important it is not to dodge it. It has to be faced head on. And the best way to face it head on is to bring tools of comfort. You've got to be able to say everything that you need to say. You've got to be able to say it all—the good, the bad, and the ugly. One way to communicate with your animal is to close your eyes, do deep breathing, and then ask for spiritual guidance to find the right images which will be interpreted by your animal. Continue the breathing for approximately 15 minutes and then allow your thoughts to present themselves to your animal (imagine a big screen presenting your heartfelt messages to your animal). Ask that these thoughts be transmitted into a form that your animal can interpret for his or her greater good. Communication is really important during this transition. The most sacred thing we can do is to accompany the dying. I think we all need to become death and dying counselors, and deep inside most of us are.

Q: Death and dying are subjects we don't talk much about in this country. Why do you think that is?

Susan: I think the biggest problem is we're so afraid of it. We're so afraid of death. It amazes me that we're very immature when it comes to one of the most important issues in our mutual lives.

You do get experience with it, like it or not. Sometimes we don't even want to talk about the experiences, but I encourage everybody to talk about them. Another thing, we don't allow ourselves to properly grieve as a society. Grief is a very individual thing, and its longevity is also individual—to the degree that we loved, it may also take longer. To the degree that we didn't have a healthy relationship, to the degree that we have guilt, it may take longer. We have to somehow help everybody understand this. I have clients who call me and say, "You know, it's been over a year. I'm still crying. No one understands. Everybody tells me to get over it. But I'm still crying." And that pains me for clients who don't have a place to go. Is grief supposed to be a two-week thing, or a month-long thing? The depth of our pain and our loss cannot be measured in neat increments. We need to understand that. I cried over Annie for five years. It didn't block me from loving others, nevertheless. She was my dog daughter. She was my best friend. And it's just the way it was.

Q: *Why do you think the pain of losing an animal is sometimes more intense than the pain of even losing other family members?*

Susan: Because people don't know how to love like animals do. Period. A healthy animal is an unconditional being. They're here to teach us how to love unconditionally. They're forgiving. They absolutely live a sacred spiritual life. They exemplify everything that we humans need to be. We should be emulating them. It's a love that we don't get from many humans. Some people never have experienced the kind of love they get from an animal—ever. That's the kind of love we all crave, it's the most nurturing form, and a lot of us don't know how to give it. A lot of us don't know how to receive it from humans, and a lot of us aren't in relationships that are anything quite like it.

Q: *How can a guardian cope during the transition period?*

Susan: First of all, the beautiful thing about the death experience is that you will go into shock. Whether it's Nature's way or God's way, there is a physiological reaction to the body. Most of my clients are afraid. They'll say, "How am I going to get through it? What's it going to be like? I won't be able to do this. I can't. I'm so scared. I'm so afraid of what this pain will be like." And I tell them, "Thank God for shock. You're going to be numb." And both your mind and body will be numb until you can begin to deal with it. That helps everybody have the courage to continue to breathe during such a terrible time. It's really important that people understand this—they will get through it.

The next thing that I recommend is to make sure that while the animal is dying, you are taking a remedy (I prefer Sharon Callahan's Transition over any other remedies). Even a basic Rescue Remedy will help you get a grip on your emotions. You and your animal should both take the remedy, to help take the edge off, and to help keep you both grounded so that you can make it a beautiful, meaningful experience. If you're too worked up emotionally, you're not going to be able to bring quality of life to the last few minutes. Our goal, our common goal as guardians, is always to offer quality of life up until the end. And when the animal is taking his or her last breath, you want to make sure that it's beautiful and loving. That is your greatest opportunity to give back. To be there, to be a companion, to make it physically comfortable, to make it beautiful. To put the candle on, to put the harp music on, to sing your friend to heaven.

Afterward, I recommend that you spend time with the body. It is a good idea to spend as much time as you need. And don't let anyone whisk it away. You let go of the body when you are ready. I feel that that is a time when you can do all sorts of beautiful things for yourself and your loved one as he or she is passing over. You can put little flowers out, you can drape the body in a beautiful flannel shirt or a favorite blanket. You can also place a favorite toy with it, or simply reflect, sit, and cry. Just spend time with the body. It's so important.

After which, you make some decisions. Is it cremation, or burial in the backyard, or a pet cemetery? We need to think that through, and for some reason, a lot of people rush it because it's just an animal. And it isn't just an animal. It's the love of your life that just left you.

It's so important to think it through, because even if you're taking the remedies, and even if you're doing deep breathing, and even if you can get a grip in such a difficult time, it's better to have your plan. Think it through. Don't be afraid of it…it's coming anyway. It's a freight train—you can't get away from it. Our animals are not second-class citizens; they are the loves of our lives, and very deserving of just as much funeral and burial consideration as any humans in our lives.

Q: Is there a way that guardians can get themselves to a place where they have a more beautiful transition experience, rather than the more common clinical one?

Susan: Deal with it now. Plan for it, and know that you can make it beautiful. You can make it special—it can be magnificent. Don't wait until you're vulnerable. Don't wait until some well-intentioned doctor, who probably doesn't know how to deal with death himself or herself says, "You know what? The prognosis is really grave so I'm going to give your animal a shot." And you're sitting in a waiting room in a deep shock because you just got some bad news, and the next thing you know, five minutes later you had no choices, because you were too vulnerable, you didn't think it through, and bam, you walk out without an animal.

Therefore it's a good idea to have a plan in advance. Guardians should let their own spiritual and philosophical feeling dictate what's right for their animal's passage. I've a sense that most animals would rather die at home. If circumstances prevent this, at least they'd like the companionship of their guardian should their death take place in a veterinary hospital. We humans generally have an advanced, detailed plan for ourselves and loved ones, such as instructions for what to do with the body and where to hold funeral and burial services. I suggest strongly that we match those detailed plans we have for ourselves for our animals, and go so far as to record them somewhere. If they have the luxury of time, guardians need to come to terms with the specifics, such as where the animal should die, who should be present, and what are the most loving and supportive materials needed to make their beloved animal's transition as beautiful and pain free as possible. Then, after the death, there needs to be a plan to support the guardian.

Get some help if you're living in fear of death. Get some help before your animal is at death's door. You can be healed from your fear if you can get in touch with what death is actually all about. I always say take a step back when dealing with death. Get out of death's grip. Walk out of it, walk away from it, which is one of the reasons why I use the Rescue Remedy and the Transition. While you are in shock, it can help you get an emotional grip. Then you can think it through and know what is right for your animal and what is right for you.

We must get over our fear of death. We have to understand that by living in the moment, by loving to our maximum, by forgiving, by being in joy, we can do so. We have nothing else. All we have is this very moment. There's nothing else out there in reality right now. I'm here until my work is done or my message has been received. That's it. So what are we worried about? It's done anyway. It's one of those things we can't control. We're such control freaks, we try to control everything…I think we should just give it up.

Q: Do you think a funeral or some kind of memorial is a good way to cope with the loss?

Susan: I'm a great supporter of funerals; I feel they help a great deal. And it can be a small funeral, it can be you and your beloved, or your immediate family, or it can be opened up to friends. It's what's appropriate, who's important during your animal's life. And that's okay—it's okay to say you'd like everybody there. It might not be necessary, but if it is, don't be embarrassed. Don't be embarrassed to say, "I'm going to the beach where Jack liked to chase his ball so I can remember and say good-bye to him. This is where I'm going to be, will you join me?"

About 25 years ago, I got invited to my first animal funeral, and I remember the client saying, "You'll be the only one there. And I need to have a funeral." And I acknowledged her. It was just spectacular. She wasn't embarrassed to say, "I loved that much, and I need to measure up." So I think that helps with the grief.

Plan if you have other animals. When we lost our Boxer, Jack, we laid him out in the driveway where he used to sunbathe all the time, then we put him in the Jeep on a beautiful blanket and gave our Boxer, Vivi, the opportunity to be with him for as long as she wanted to. So she sat with her Jack, and the four of us stayed together for a long time. Our children came and they visited Vivi and Jack and us, and that was our funeral. We didn't do anything more formal—it wasn't necessary. I think it's important to make sure we understand that our animals are grieving, too. Give them an opportunity to have closure. And of course, to little children as well this is very, very important.

Don't be afraid to set up a special spot in your home, whether it's for a day or a week or a month, or someplace you want to come back to visit regularly. I was very proud of how my daughter, Abbey, said good-bye to Sadie, her chocolate Lab. Sadie's favorite spot was her little TV room by a window, and during Sadie's last day, Abbey invited those closest to Sadie to drop by. Abbey had candles going. She also had beautiful flowers all over the room. There was harp music playing, and Sadie's best friends, which included a little puppy from next door, the next door neighbors, myself, my children, my sister, Dr. Bob…we all came by. And the immediate family stayed on the floor with Sadie. And we just kissed and hugged her and loved her and sang to her. And when she made her passing, it was a very holy experience. But it didn't stop there. That part of the room is still a sanctuary. It's Sadie's place. My daughter always remembers to light a candle there. And the room is filled with Sadie's spirit—it's a room of joy. I think people need to create a sanctuary. I think it helps with the loss, but I think it is also a way of giving back, a way of honoring their spirit. And when you can honor long after the physical body is shed, it absolutely will keep the spirit and essence close to home.

You have to find your place in your animal's heaven. You really do. It's there. Also, there's an opportunity to keep on keeping on. This is really important. One of the things I learned through the Kübler-Ross training is that the body is gone and the soul moves on. So life goes on through the soul. And it's important to keep dialoguing with your animal after the transition. Death is nothing more than a veil away from us. It's like a bridal veil—you can almost see through it. If we see death as a final thing, and if we really just say good-bye to the body and then think it's over, that's the most harmful thing that we can do to the essence of the animal that's crossing over, because they're really still with us. If we hide from that, or if we neglect that, or if we don't find that, it must be awfully terrifying for them, because they're not disconnected from us. The physical body is gone but everything else just stays. The most important part stays, anyway. It's a really upbeat thing. It's not the way I thought it was when I was younger. It's not as terrible as we think it is.

Q: *Why do you think we all feel like it's so terrible, then?*

Susan: Because it's something we don't talk about. And because in America we see death as final, it's over, there's nothing left. We don't face it; we hide from it. We don't challenge it. We don't ask the right questions. When we shut down, all the light is gone, and we lose the truth about death. Because that's what fear does: Fear creates walls. And the more we fear something, the further we get away from the reality of it.

When Can I Love Again?

People often ask us how to know when it's okay to get another animal, which is another way of asking "When can I love again?" The grieving and healing process is different for everyone—for some it takes weeks or months, and for others, much longer. Whatever you do, don't push yourself or allow others to do so. One thing we know for sure is that nature has a way of signaling you when the time is right to select a new animal companion. Sometimes nature will take things into its own hands by providing you with someone to love. Maybe you'll discover a scrawny kitten scratching at your screen door one night. Or one day, your car will have a mind of its own and you'll find yourself at the steps of your local animal shelter, wondering how you got there. By being aware of the signs of recovery, no matter how subtle, you'll know when the time has come to parent again. These signs may include changes in your body language, behavior, picking up an animal-related magazine, or doing breed research.

If you find that you need a little help—that the grieving is hanging on for too long—don't be embarrassed to reach out and get some counseling or take a flower essence formula specifically made for grief. After all, we don't want you to waste your love. And please remember to be sensitive to all those around you, especially animals and children—for they are grieving too.

We have to understand that the whole death and dying thing is about love. That's what we're really feeling—huge crescendos of love. It's not terror that we're feeling. When we're saying good-bye, we're feeling love. We think it's darkness, but it's not— it's love. And why are we afraid of that? That's what happens when we say good-bye. We're experiencing all of the love that we had, that we could muster up from the day we looked into that kitten's or that puppy's eyes. Love is what it is. It's nothing more than that.

Product and Services Guide

Many of the products listed in this book are available at your local health food store. Others are available through the following:

Chapter 1: Diet

Food Companies

Blue Buffalo Company
444 Danbury Rd.
Wilton, CT 06897
Telephone: (800) 919-2833
www.bluebuff.com
Products: Blue Buffalo dog and cat food

Breeder's Choice Pet Foods, Inc.
P.O. Box 2005
Irwindale, CA 91706
Telphone: (800) 255-4286
www.breeders-choice.com
Product: AvoDerm

Halo, Purely for Pets
3438 East Lake Road, #14
Palm Harbor, FL 34685
Telephone: (727) 937-3376
Fax: (727) 937-3955
www.halopets.com
Product: Spot's Stew

Natura Pet Products
P.O. Box 271
Santa Clara, CA 95052-0271
Telephone: (408) 261-0770
E-mail: custserv@naturapet.com
www.naturapet.com
Products: Innova, California Natural, Karma Organic, Evo

Newmans' Own Organics
Premium Pet Food
7010 Soquel Drive
Aptos, CA 95003
Telephone: (831) 685-2866
www.newmansownorganics.com

One Earth Pet Food
Eight In One Pet Products
2100 Pacific Street
Hauppauge, NY 11788
Telephone: (800) 8-EARTHY
www.eightinonepet.com

PetGuard
Telephone: (877) PETGUARD
E-mail: petcard@petguard.com
www.petguard.com

Precise
Telephone: (888) 4 PRECISE
www.precisepet.com

Solid Gold Health Products for Pets, Inc.
900 Vernon Way, #101
El Cajon, CA 92020
Telephone: (800) 364 4863
Fax: (619) 258 3907
E-mail: dane@solidgoldhealth.com
www.solidgoldhealth.com

Wellness Pet Food
2005 Old Mother Hubbard
P.O. Box 1719
Lowell, MA 01853-1719
Telephone: (800) 225-0904
Fax: (978) 441-0275
www.oldmotherhubbard.com

Wysong Corporation
1880 N. Eastman Road
Midland Michigan 48462
Telephone: (989) 631-0009
Fax: (989) 631-8801
www.wysong.net

Food Companies (Raw & Premixes)

Amoré Pet Foods
Unit 21
12200 Vulcan Way
Richmond, BC
Canada V6V 1J8
Telephone: (604) 273-8577
Fax: (604) 273-8549
www.amorepetfoods.com

Bravo Raw Diet
c/o Manchester Packing Company, Inc.
1084 Hartford Turnpike
Vernon, CT 06066
Telephone: (866) 922-9222
Fax: (860) 896-1256
E-mail: info@bravorawdiets.com
www.bravorawdiet.com

Dr. Harvey's Dog and Cat Premix
180 Main Street
Keanesburg, NJ 07734
Telephone: (866) DocH123

FarMore Manufacturing Ltd.
5900 Trietsch
Sanger, TX 76266
Telephone: (866) 507-8255
E-mail: info@farmoredogfood.com
www.farmoredogfood.com

The Honest Kitchen
1804 Garnet Avenue, #201
San Diego, CA 92100
Telephone: (858) 483-5995
Fax: (858) 483-5998
E-mail: info@thehonestkitchen.com
www.thehonestkitchen.com

Oma's Pride
Miller Foods, Inc.
308 Arch Rd.
Avon, CT 06001
Telephone: (800) 678-6627
Fax: (860) 673-6454
miller.food@snet.net
www.omaspride.com

Nature's Variety
6200 North 56th Street
Lincoln, NE, 68504
E-mail: info@naturesvariety.com
www.naturesvariety.com

Spring Hills Farm
P.O. Box 1023
Glasgow, KY 42142
Telephone: (270) 646-2838
E-mail: allnatural@springhillsfarm.com
www.springhillsfarm.com

Sojourner Farms
1723 Adams St. NE
Minneapolis, MN 55413
Telephone: (612) 343-7262
Fax: (612) 343-7263
E-mail: mail@sojos.com
www.sojos.com

Steve's Real Food For Pets
1848 Pearl Street
Eugene, Oregon 97401
Telephone: (888) 526-1900
E-mail: info@stevesrealfood.com
www.stevesrealfood.com

Multiple Vitamin and Mineral Supplements (Food Derived)

Merritt Naturals, Animal Essentials
P.O. Box 131388
Carlsbad, CA 92013
Telephone: (888) 463-7748
Fax: (888) 273-9233
E-mail: info@animalessentials.com
www.animalessentials.com
Products: essential fatty acids, multi-vitamin herbal supplements, organic calcium

Designing Health
Telephone: (800) 774-7387
E-mail:
Customer_Service@designinghealth.com
www.designinghealth.com
Product: The Missing Link

Dr. Goodpet
P.O. Box 4547
Inglewood, CA 90309
Telephone: (800) 222-9932
E-mail: info@goodpet.com
www.goodpet.com
Product: Maximum Protection Formula

Earth Animal
606 Post Road East
Westport, CT 06880
Mail Order: (800) 622-0260
Telephone: (203) 222-7173
Fax: (203) 227-8094
www.earthanimal.com
Product: Daily Health Nuggets (Dogs and Cats)

The Wholistic Pet
P.O. Box 1107
Merrimack, NH 03054
Telephone: (888) 452-7263
Fax: (603) 472-3093
E-mail: info@thewholisticpet.com
www.thewholisticpet.com
Product: Canine Complete

Wysong Corporation
1880 N. Eastman Road
Midland Michigan 48462
Telephone: (989) 631-0009
Fax: (989) 631-8801
www.wysong.net
Products: C- Biotic, F-Biotic

Water

Pure & Secure, LLC
P.O. Box 83226
Lincoln, NE 68501
Telephone: (800) 875-5915
customerservice@purewaterinc.com
Product: steam-distilled water

Chapter 2: Nutritional Supplements

Enzymes

Dr. Goodpet
P.O. Box 4547
Inglewood, CA 90309
Telephone: (800) 222-9932
E-mail: info@goodpet.com
www.goodpet.com
Products: K9 and F9 Enzymes

Prozyme Products Ltd.
Telephone: (800) 522-5537
Fax: (510) 638-6919
E-mail: info@prozyme.com
www.prozyme.com
Product: Prozyme

Fatty Acid Supplements

Merritt Naturals, Animal Essentials
P.O. Box 131388
Carlsbad, CA 92013
Telephone: (888) 463-7748
Fax: (888) 273-9233
E-mail: info@animalessentials.com
www.animalessentials.com
Product: Essential Fatty Acids supplement

Barlean's Organic Oils
4936 Lake Terrell Road
Ferndale, WA 98248
Telephone: (800) 445-3529
E-mail: questions@barleans.com
www.barleans.com
Product: organic flaxseed oil

Dr. Harveys
180 Main Street
Keanesburg, NJ 07734
Telephone: (866) DocH123
Product: Health and Shine

Integrative Therapeutics, Inc.
9 Monroe Parkway, Suite 250
Lake Oswego, OR 97035
Telephone: (800) 931-1709
Fax: (800) 380-8189
www.eskimo3.com
Product: Eskimo-3 fish oil

Natura Health Products
249 "A" Street, Suite A
Ashland, Oregon 97520
Telephone: (888) 628-8720
Fax: (541) 482-3844
E-mail: info@naturahealthproducts.com
www.naturahealthproducts.com
Products: Beyond Essential Fats

Spectrum Organics, Inc.
5341 Old Redwood Hwy., Suite 400
Petaluma, CA 94954
Telephone: (800) 995-2705
www.spectrumorganics.com
Product: organic flaxseed oil

Vetri-Science Laboratories
Phone (800) 882-9993
Fax: (802) 878-0549
E-mail: info@vetriscience.com
www.vetriscience.com
Products: Omega-3, -6, -9

Probiotics

Progressive Laboratories, Inc.
1701 W. Walnut Hill La.
Irving, TX 75038
Telephone: 800-527-9512
Product: Acidophilus A.C.

The Wholistic Pet
P.O. Box 1107
Merrimack, NH 03054
Telephone: (888) 452-7263
www.thewholisticpet.com
Product: Acidophilus concentrate

Chapter 3: Cultivate Vaccination Wisdom

Veterinary Laboratories (Blood Tests, Titer Testing)

Animal Nutrition Technologies
606 Post Road East
Westport, CT 06880
Telephone: (203) 341-8875
Fax: (203) 227-8094
E-mail: antnutrition@yahoo.com
www.animalnutritiontechnologies.com
Service: Nutritional Blood Test (NBT)

Antech Diagnostics
Telephone: East Coast (800) 872-1001
West Coast (800) 745-4725
Test Express (888) 397-8378
www.antechdiagnostics.com

Cornell Animal Health Diagnostic Laboratory
College of Veterinary Medicine
Cornell University
P.O. Box 5786
Ithaca, NY 14853-5786
Telephone: (607) 253-3900
E-mail: diaglab@cornell.edu
www.diaglab.vet.cornell.edu

Hemopet
11330 Markon Drive
Garden Grove, CA 92841
Telephone: (714) 891-2022
Fax: (714) 891-2123
www.hemopet.com
Service: blood bank

IDEXX Veterinary Services:
Telephone: Eastern Region (888) 433-9987
Western Region (800) 444-4210
www.idexx.com

Kansas Veterinary Diagnostic Laboratory
1800 Denison
Kansas State University
Manhattan, KS 66506
Telephone: (785) 532-5650
Fax: (785) 532-4481
www.vet.ksu.edu

Michigan State University Clinical Pathology Lab
College of Veterinary Medicine
Telephone: (517) 355-1774
Fax: (517) 432-2598
E-mail: clinpath@dcpah.msu.edu
cvm.mus.edu/clinpath/new.htm

Chapter 4: Natural Healing Modalities

Flower Essences

Earth Animal
606 Post Road East
Westport, CT 06880
Mail Order: (800) 622-0260
Telephone: (203) 222-7173
Fax: (203) 227-8094
www.earthanimal.com
Products: Anaflora flower essences

Nelson Bach USA Ltd.
100 Research Drive
Wilmington, MA 01887
100 Research Drive
Wilmington MA
Telephone: (800) 334-0843
Fax: (978) 988-0233
E-mail: education@nelsonbach.com
www.bachfloweressences.co.uk
Products: Bach flower remedies

Glandular Therapy

Enzymatic Therapy
825 Challenger Drive
Green Bay, WI 54311
Telephone: (800) 783-2286
www.enzy.com
Product: Glandulars

Professional Complementary Health Formulas, Inc.
P.O. Box 80085
Portland, OR. 97280-1085
Telephone: (800) 952-2219
Fax: (503) 479-3149
E-mail: pchf@professionalformulas.com
New Zealand Glandulars, Combination Homeopathics

Progressive Laboratories, Inc.
1701 W. Walnut Hill La.
Irving, TX 75038
Telephone: (800) 527-9512
E-mail: information@progressivelabs.com
Products: Glandulars, Combination Homeopathics

Hair Analysis

PetTest
441 N. Louisiana Plaza, Suite Q
Asheville, N.C. 28806
Telephone: (877) 252.2637
Fax: (877) 252.2629
E-mail: info@pettest.net
www.pettest.net

Harp Therapy

Pet Pause
P.O. Box 1242
Pine Valley, CA 91962
E-mail: petpause2000@yahoo.com
Telephone/Fax: (800) 971-1044

Herbs

Crystal Gardens
504 Masterson Rd
Bethel, VT 05032
Telephone/Fax: (802) 234-5947
E-mail: kristy@CrystalGardenHerbs.com
www.crystalgardenherbs.com
Products: combination herbal remedies

Ecomax Nutrition
116 W. Service Rd. #177
Champlain, NY 12919
Product: Essiac Tea

Herbal Educational Services
P.O. Box 3427
Ashland, OR 97520
Telephone: (800) 252-0688
E-mail: Info@botanicalmedicine.org
www.botanicalmedicine.org
Product: high-quality information on herbal medicine.

Kroeger Herbs
805 Walnut St.
Boulder, CO 80302
Telephone: (800) 516-0690
E-mail: khp@kroegerherb.com
www.krogerherb.com
Products: herbs

Natura Health Products
249 "A" Street, Suite A
Ashland, Oregon 97520
Telephone: (888) 628-8720
Fax: (541) 482-3844
E-mail: info@naturahealthproducts.com
www.naturahealthproducts.com
*Products: Vital adapt, Power Adapt, Botanibol,
Artemesia Plus, Herbs and Adaptogens*

Quantum Herbal Products
20 DeWitt Drive
Saugerties, NY 12477
Telephone: (845) 246-1344
E-mail: info@quantumherbalproducts.com
www.quantumherbalproducts.com
Products: herbal tinctures, shampoos and salves

Homeopathics/Homotoxicology Remedies

Arrowroot Standard Homeopathies
83 East Lancaster Ave
Paoli, PA 19301 USA
Telephone: (800) 234-8998
E-mail: customerservice@arrowroot.com
www.arrowroot.com
Products: homeopathic remedies

BHI/Heel
P.O. Box 11280
Albuquerque, NM 87192-0280
Telephone: (800) 621-7644
Fax: (505) 275-1672
E-mail: info@heelusa.com
www.heelbhi.com
Products: homotoxicology remedies

Boiron Borneman, Inc.
Thierry Boiron
6 Campus Boulevard
Building A
Newtown Square, PA 19073
Telephone: (610) 325-7464
Fax: (610) 325-7480
E-mail: info@boiron.com
www.boiron.com
Products: homeopathic remedies

Dr. Goodpet
P.O. Box 4547
Inglewood, CA 90309
Telephone: (800) 222-9932
E-mail: info@goodpet.com
www.goodpet.com
Products: Combination homeopathics

Earth Animal
606 Post Road East
Westport, CT 06880
Mail Order: (800) 622-0260
Telephone: (203) 222-7173
Fax: (203) 227-8094
www.earthanimal.com
Products: combination homeopathic remedies

Hahnemann Laboratories, Inc.
1940 Fourth Street,
San Rafael, CA 94901
Telephone: (888) 427-6422
Fax: (415) 451-6981
www.hahnemannlabs.com
Products: homeopathic remedies

Homeopet
P.O. Box 147
Westhampton Beach, NY 11978
Telephone: (800) 555-4461
Fax: (631) 288-6711
www.homeopet.com
Products: combination homeopathic remedies

HomeoVetix
Telephone: (800) 521-7722
Fax: (941) 643-7370
Products: Viratox, Chemotox, Detoxisode

Hyland's
Telephone: (800) 624-9659
E-mail: info@hylands.com
www.hylands.com
Products: homeopathic formulas

Newton Laboratories
2360 Rockaway Industrial Blvd.
Conyers, GA 30012
Telephone: (800) 448-7256
Fax: (800) 760-5550
E-mail: info@newtonlabs.net
www.newtonlabs.net
Products: homeopathic formulas

Traditional Chinese Medicine— Chinese Herbs

Kai Yeung A Healing Place
800 Cottage Grove Road, Blg #5
Bloomfield, CT 06002
Telephone: 800-733-4325
Fax: 860-242-0126
E-mail: mk@healingplace.com
Product: Chinese herbs

Institute for Traditional Medicine (ITM)
2017 SE Hawthorne Blvd.
Portland, OR 97214
Telephone: (503) 233-4907
Fax: (503) 233-1017
www.itmonline.net
Products: Seven Forests Herbal Formulas

Natural Solutions, Inc.
176 Montauk Highway
Speonk, NY 11972
Telephone: (631) 325-2047
Fax: (631) 325-1743
E-mail: info@naturalsolutionsvet.com
www.naturalsolustionsvet.com
Products: White Crane Chinese herbs

Chapter 5: Treating Common Conditions

Acne

Dr. Bronner's Magic Soaps
P.O. Box 28
Escondido, CA 92033
Telephone: (760) 743-2211
Fax: (760) 745-6675
www.drbronner.com
Product: Castile soap

Bladder Problems

Earth Animal
606 Post Road East
Westport, CT 06880
Mail Order: (800) 622-0260
Telephone: (203) 222-7173
Fax: (203) 227-8094
www.earthanimal.com
Product: Pee Pee Drops

Eye Problems/Cataracts

Earth Animal
606 Post Road East
Westport, CT 06880
Mail Order: (800) 622-0260
Telephone: (203) 222-7173
Fax: (203) 227-8094
www.earthanimal.com
Products: Clean Eyes, Vision

Halo, Purely for Pets
3438 East Lake Road, #14
Palm Harbor, FL 34685
Telephone: (727) 937-3376
Fax: (727) 937-3955
www.halopets.com
Product: Anitra's Herbal Eyewash

Source Naturals
23 Janis Way
Scotts Valley, CA 95066
Telephone: (800) 815-2333
Fax: (831) 438-7410
www.sourcenaturals.com
Product: Quercetin

Ear Infections/Mites

Earth Animal
606 Post Road East
Westport, CT 06880
Mail Order: (800) 622-0260
Telephone: (203) 222-7173
Fax: (203) 227-8094
www.earthanimal.com
Product: Clean Ears

Halo, Purely for Pets
3438 East Lake Road, #14
Palm Harbor, FL 34685
Telephone: (727) 937-3376
Fax: (727) 937-3955
www.halopets.com
Product: Natural Herbal Ear Wash

Fatty Tumors

Best For Your Pet
Doctors Mutual Service Corp.
18722 Santee La.
Valley Center, CA 92082
Telephone: (800) 952-9568
Fax: (949) 723-5246
Product: Mega LipoTropic

Gingivitis

Earth Animal
606 Post Road East
Westport, CT 06880
Mail Order: (800) 622-0260
Telephone: (203) 222-7173
Fax: (203) 227-8094
www.earthanimal.com
Product: Sore gums

SmilePet

Telephone: (866) 628-9745

E-mail: Kathy@SmilePet.net

www.smilepet.net

Service: anesthesia-free teeth cleaning

Itchy Skin/Hot Spots

Dr. Goodpet

P.O. Box 4547

Inglewood, CA 90309

Telephone: (800) 222-9932

E-mail: info@goodpet.com

www.goodpet.com

Product: Scratch Free

Earth Animal

606 Post Road East

Westport, CT 06880

Mail Order: (800) 622-0260

Telephone: (203) 222-7173

Fax: (203) 227-8094

www.earthanimal.com

Products: Daily Health Nuggets, Itchy Skin, Leciderm shampoo

Veterinarian's Best, Inc.

P.O. Box 4459

Santa Barbara, CA 93140

Telephone: (800) 866-PETS

www.vetsbest.com

Product: Hot Spot shampoo

Kennel Cough

Earth Animal

606 Post Road East

Westport, CT 06880

Mail Order: (800) 622-0260

Telephone: (203) 222-7173

Fax: (203) 227-8094

www.earthanimal.com

Product: Cough and Wheeze

Homeopet

P.O. Box 147

Westhampton Beach, NY 11978

Telephone: (800) 555-4461

Fax: (631) 288-6711

www.homeopet.com

Product: Cough

HomeoVetix

Telephone: (800) 521-7722

Fax: (941) 643-7370

Product: Viratox

Lick Sores

Earth Animal

606 Post Road East

Westport, CT 06880

Mail Order: (800) 622-0260

Telephone: (203) 222-7173

Fax: (203) 227-8094

www.earthanimal.com

Product: Itchy Skin, Anaflora Lick Granuloma

Mange, Demodectic

Animal Nutrition Technologies
606 Post Road East
Westport, CT 06880
Telephone: 203-341-8875
Fax: 203-227-8094
E-mail: antnutrition@yahoo.com
www.animalnutritiontechnologies.com
Products: Chemical Drops, H7 Immune Stimulator

Earth Animal
606 Post Road East
Westport, CT 06880
Mail Order: (800) 622-0260
Telephone: (203) 222-7173
Fax: (203) 227-8094
www.earthanimal.com
Product: Immune Boost, Leciderm shampoo, Neem Shampoo

Institute for Traditional Medicine (ITM)
2017 SE Hawthorne Blvd.
Portland, OR 97214
Telephone: (503) 233-4907
Fax: (503) 233-1017
www.itmonline.net
Product: Seven Forests Viola 13

Tropiclean
Telephone: (314) 281-9445
E-mail: sales@tropiclean.net
www.tropiclean.net
Product: Opti-Neem Citrus shampoo

Veterinarian's Best, Inc.
P.O. Box 4459
Santa Barbara, CA 93140
Telephone: (800) 866-PETS
www.vetsbest.com
Product: Hot Spot shampoo

Motion Sickness

Dr. Goodpet
P.O. Box 4547
Inglewood, CA 90309
Telephone: (800) 222-9932
E-mail: info@goodpet.com
www.goodpet.com
Product: Calm Stress

Earth Animal
606 Post Road East
Westport, CT 06880
Mail Order: (800) 622-0260
Telephone: (203) 222-7173
Fax: (203) 227-8094
www.earthanimal.com
Product: Calm Down, Anaflora Recovery

Parasites/Ringworm

Earth Animal
606 Post Road East
Westport, CT 06880
Mail Order: (800) 622-0260
Telephone: (203) 222-7173
Fax: (203) 227-8094
www.earthanimal.com
Products: Daily Health Nuggets, Leciderm shampoo, No More Worms and Fungi

Sexual Problems

Earth Animal
606 Post Road East
Westport, CT 06880
Mail Order: (800) 622-0260
Telephone: (203) 222-7173
Fax: (203) 227-8094
www.earthanimal.com
Products: Calm Kitty, Good Dog, Special Stress, Spraying Cat

Farnam Companies, Inc.
Pet Products Division
P.O. Box 34820
Phoenix, AZ 85067-4820
Telephone: (602) 285-1660
www.farnampet.com
Product: Feliway Feline Behavior Modification Spray

Stool Eating

Dr. Goodpet
P.O. Box 4547
Inglewood, CA 90309
Telephone: (800) 222-9932
E-mail: info@goodpet.com
www.goodpet.com
Product: Enzymes

PetGuard
Telephone: (877) PETGUARD
E-mail: petcard@petguard.com
www.petguard.com
Product: Enzymes

Solid Gold Health Products for Pets, Inc.
900 Vernon Way, #101
El Cajon, Ca 92020
CA 92020 USA
Product: Solid Gold Sea Meal

Urinary Incontinence

Earth Animal
606 Post Road East
Westport, CT 06880
Mail Order: (800) 622-0260
Telephone: (203) 222-7173
Fax: (203) 227-8094
www.earthanimal.com
Product: Pee Pee Drops, Anaflora Spay and Neuter

Homeopet
P.O. Box 147
Westhampton Beach, NY 11978
Telephone: (800) 555-4461
Fax: (631) 288-6711
www.homeopet.com
Product: Urinary Incontinence

Chapter 6: Flea-Free Forever Naturally

Flea and Tick Products

Animal Nutrition Technologies

606 Post Road East
Westport, CT 06880
Telephone 203-341-8875
Veterinary Information Line 888-533-5162
Fax: 203-227-8094
E-mail: antnutrition@yahoo.com
www.animalnutritiontechnologies.com
Product: DermGuard

Dr. Goodpet

P.O. Box 4547
Inglewood, CA 90309
Telephone: (800) 222-9932
E-mail: info@goodpet.com
www.goodpet.com
Products: Inside Flea Relief, Outside Flea Relief

Earth Animal

606 Post Road East
Westport, CT 06880
Mail Order: (800) 622-0260
Telephone: (203) 222-7173
Fax: (203) 227-8094
www.earthanimal.com
Products: Internal and Herbal Internal Powder, Leciderm Shampoo, No More Fleas, No More Ticks, Solid Gold Shampoo

Halo, Purely for Pets

3438 East Lake Road, #14
Palm Harbor, FL 34685
Telephone: (727) 937-3376
Fax: (727) 937-3955
www.halopets.com
Product: Cloud-nine herbal dip

Natural Animal Health Products, Inc.

7000 U.S. 1 North St.
Augustine, FL 32095
Telephone: (800)-274-7387
Fax: (904)-824-5100
www.naturalanimal.com
Product: Diatom Dust Insect Powder

One Earth

8 in 1 Pet Products
Telephone: (800) 8-EARTHY
E-mail: info@eightinonepet.com
www.eightinonepet.com
Products: Herbal Collars

PetGuard

Telephone: (877) PETGUARD
E-mail: petcard@petguard.com
www.petguard.com
Product: Yeast and Garlic Wafers

Quantum Herbal Products

20 DeWitt Drive
Saugerties, NY 12477
Telephone: (800) 348-0398
E-mail: info@quantumherbalproducts.com
www.quantumherbalproducts.com
Product: 100% Natural Coat Conditioning Spray

Tropiclean
Telephone: (314) 281-9445
E-mail: sales@tropiclean.net
www.tropiclean.net
Product: Natural Dip, Opti-Neem Citrus Shampoo

Veterinarian's Best, Inc.
P.O. Box 4459
Santa Barbara, CA 93140
Telephone: (800) 866-PETS
www.vetsbest.com
Product: All-in-1 Flea Shampoo

Chapter 8: The "Most Feared Diseases" By System

Adrenal Gland Diseases

Animal Nutrition Technologies
606 Post Road East
Westport, CT 06880
Telephone 203-341-8875
Veterinary Information Line 888-533-5162
Fax: 203-227-8094
E-mail: antnutrition@yahoo.com
www.animalnutritiontechnologies.com
Products: Addison's, Adrenal Drops, Adrenal Support and Pituitary Formulas, Adrenasol, Hypothalamus Drops, Nutritional Blood Test (NBT)

Earth Animal
606 Post Road East
Westport, CT 06880
Mail Order: (800) 622-0260
Telephone: (203) 222-7173
Fax: (203) 227-8094
www.earthanimal.com
Products: Anaflora's Return to Joy, Anaflora's Special Stress

Emerson Ecologics
7 Commerce Drive
Bedford, NH 03110
Telephone: (800) 654-4432
www.emersonecologics.com
Product: Phosphatidyl Serine

Cardiovascular Diseases

Animal Nutrition Technologies
606 Post Road East
Westport, CT 06880
Telephone 203-341-8875
Veterinary Information Line 888-533-5162
Fax: 203-227-8094
E-mail: antnutrition@yahoo.com
www.animalnutritiontechnologies.com
Products: Cardiac Support Formula, Heart Assist, Heart Drops, Heart Formula, Liver/Gallbladder Support Formula, Lung Support Formula, Nutritional Blood Test (NBT)

Earth Animal
606 Post Road East
Westport, CT 06880
Mail Order: (800) 622-0260
Telephone: (203) 222-7173
Fax: (203) 227-8094
www.earthanimal.com
*Products: Bug Off, Internal and Herbal Powders,
No More Fleas, No More Worms and Fungi
(prevent mosquito bites)*

Central Nervous System Diseases

Animal Nutrition Technologies

606 Post Road East
Westport, CT 06880
Telephone: 203-341-8875
Veterinary Information Line: 888-533-5162
Fax: 203-227-8094
E-mail: antnutrition@yahoo.com
www.animalnutritiontechnologies.com
*Products: Anti-Seizure Drops, Brain/Nerve
Support Formula, Epilepsy Drops, Epitrol, H99
Myelopathy, Nutritional Blood Test (NBT), Post-
Seizure Recovery,
Spinal Nerve Drops*

Dr. Roger Clemmons

University of Florida College of Veterinary
 Medicine
Campus Box 100125
2015 SW 16th Ave.
Gainesville, FL 32610
Telephone: 352-392-4700
www.vetmed.ufl.edu
Service: Protocol for Degenerative Myelopathy

Earth Animal
606 Post Road East
Westport, CT 06880
Mail Order: (800) 622-0260
Telephone: (203) 222-7173
Fax: (203) 227-8094
www.earthanimal.com
*Products: Anaflora's Anti-Seizure Drops,
Anaflora's Post-Seizure Recovery Calm Down*

Ecological Formulas

1061-B Shary Circle
Concord, CA 94518
Telephone: (800) 888-4585
Product: Sphingolyn

Westlab Pharmacy

4410 W. Newberry Road Suite A5
Gainesville, Florida   32607
Telephone: (352) 373-8111
Toll Free: (800) 493-7852
Fax: (352) 373-8009
E-mail: Info@WestLabPharmacy.com
www.westlabpharmacy.com
Product: aminocaproic acid, N-acetylcysteine

The Epi Guardian Angels

www.canine-epilepsy-guardian-angels.com
*Service: Provides information on canine epilepsy
and other diseases that cause seizures in dogs
including canine hypothyroidism*

Dermatological Diseases

Animal Nutrition Technologies
606 Post Road East
Westport, CT 06880
Telephone: 203-341-8875
Veterinary Information Line: 888-533-5162
Fax: 203-227-8094
E-mail: antnutrition@yahoo.com
www.animalnutritiontechnologies.com
Products: Allergy Drops, Allergy Formula, Derm Guard, Dust and Mold Drops, Flea Drops, Flea Formula, Fungal Drops, Grass Drops, Nutritional Blood Test (NBT), Skin Drops, Skin Support Nutraceutical Formula, Tree Drops

Dr. Goodpet
P.O. Box 4547
Inglewood, CA 90309
Telephone: (800) 222-9932
Email: info@goodpet.com
www.goodpet.com
Product: Scratch Free

Earth Animal
606 Post Road East
Westport, CT 06880
Mail Order: (800) 622-0260
Telephone: (203) 222-7173
Fax: (203) 227-8094
www.earthanimal.com
Products: Anaflora's Allergy, Anaflora's Lick Granuloma Itchy Skin

Homeopet
P.O. Box 147
Westhampton Beach, NY 11978
Telephone: (800) 555-4461
Fax: (631) 288-6711
www.homeopet.com
Product: Skin and Seborrhea

Kai Yeung A Healing Place
800 Cottage Grove Road, Blg #5
Bloomfield, CT 06002
Toll Free: (800) 733-4325
Telephone: (860) 242-0105
Fax: (860) 242-0126
E-mail: mk@healingplace.com

Pet Pharmacy
13925 W. Meeker Blvd., Suite 15
Sun City West, AZ 85375
Telephone: (800) 742-0516
Product: natural cortisone

Gastrointestinal Diseases

Animal Nutrition Technologies

606 Post Road East
Westport, CT 06880
Telephone: 203-341-8875
Veterinary Information Line: 888-533-5162
Fax: 203-227-8094
E-mail: antnutrition@yahoo.com
www.animalnutritiontechnologies.com
Products: ColonGuard, Diarrhea Drops, Esophageal/Gastric Support Formula, Gastritis Drops, Intestine Drops, Intestinal Formula, Intestinal/IBD Support Formula, Nutritional Blood Test (NBT), Protein Losing Enteropathy/H50, Stomach Drops, Stomach Formula

Earth Animal

606 Post Road East
Westport, CT 06880
Mail Order: (800) 622-0260
Telephone: (203) 222-7173
Fax: (203) 227-8094
www.earthanimal.com
Product: The Runs

Homeopet

P.O. Box 147
Westhampton Beach, NY 11978
Telephone: (800) 555-4461
Fax: (631) 288-6711
www.homeopet.com
Product: Gastroenteritis

Vetri-Science Laboratories

Telephone: (800) 882-9993
Fax: (802) 878-0549
E-mail: info@vetriscience.com
www.vetriscience.com
Product: Acetylator

Infectious Diseases

Animal Nutrition Technologies

606 Post Road East
Westport, CT 06880
Telephone 203-341-8875
Veterinary Information Line 888-533-5162
Fax: 203-227-8094
E-mail: antnutrition@yahoo.com
www.animalnutritiontechnologies.com
Products: Anti seizure and Post Seizure drops, Bile Relflux Gastritis, Brain Drops, Brain Nerve Support Formula, Bronchus/Lung/Sinus Support Formula, Calming Formula, Cholangiohepatitis/Chronic-H77, Chronic Encephalitis-H29, ColonGuard, Cough Drops, Cough Lung Formula, Diarrhea Drops, Epilepsy Drops, Esophageal/Gastric Support Formula, Gastritis/Chronic, Gastritis Drops, H7 Stimulator, Immune Drops, Immune/Autoimmune Support Formula, Intestine Drops, Intestinal Formula, Intestinal/IBD Support Formula, Liver Formula, LiverGuard, Liver/Gallbladder Drops, Liver/Gallbladder Support Formula, Lung Drops, Nutritional Blood Test (NBT), Pneumonia-H23, Sinusitis/Chronic-H57, Sinusitis Drops, Spinal/Nerve Drops, Stomach Drops, Stomach Formula, Tick Drops, Tick Formula, Viral Immune Drops,

Earth Animal

606 Post Road East
Westport, CT 06880
Mail Order: (800) 622-0260
Telephone: (203) 222-7173
Fax: (203) 227-8094
www.earthanimal.com
Products: Anaflora's Recovery, Cough and Wheeze, No More Ticks, Sinus, The Runs

HomeoVetix

Telephone: (800) 521-7722
Fax: (941) 643-7370
Product: Viratox

Kidney and Bladder Diseases

Animal Nutrition Technologies

606 Post Road East
Westport, CT 06880
Telephone: (203) 341-8875
Veterinary Information Line: (888) 533-5162
Fax: 203-227-8094
E-mail: antnutrition@yahoo.com
www.animalnutritiontechnologies.com
Products: Cystitis (Chronic)-H63, Hypothalamus Drops, Kidney Drops, Kidney, Ovarian, Adrenal Drops, Kidney, Prostate, Adrenal Drops, Kidney/Bladder Formula, Kidney Guard, Kidney Support Formula, Nutritional Blood Test (NBT), Renal Disease-H79, Urinary Bladder Support Formula, Urinary Drops, Urinary Stones/Crystals – H27, Urinary Tract Infection – H51

Earth Animal

606 Post Road East
Westport, CT 06880
Mail Order: (800) 622-0260
Telephone: (203) 222-7173
Fax: (203) 227-8094
www.earthanimal.com
Product: Pee Pee Formula

Liver Disease

Animal Nutrition Technologies

606 Post Road East
Westport, CT 06880
Telephone: (203) 341-8875
Veterinary Information Line: (888) 533-5162
Fax: 203-227-8094
E-mail: antnutrition@yahoo.com
www.animalnutritiontechnologies.com
Products: Chemical Drops, Cholangiohepatitis/Chronic-H77, Cirrhosis, Detox Drops, Gallbladder Disease, Hepatic Copper Toxicity, Hepatic Lipidosis, Liver Formula, Liver/Gallbladder Support Formula, Liver/Gallbladder Drops, LiverGuard, Nutritional Blood Test (NBT)

Enzymatic Therapy

825 Challenger Drive
Green Bay, WI 54311
Telephone: (800) 783-2286
www.enzy.com
Product: Liquid Liver

Musculoskeletal Diseases

Animal Nutrition Technologies
606 Post Road East
Westport, CT 06880
Telephone: (203) 341-8875
Veterinary Information Line: (888) 533-5162
Fax: 203-227-8094
E-mail: antnutrition@yahoo.com
www.animalnutritiontechnologies.com
Products: Arthritis Drops, Arthritis Formula,
Arthritis/Shoulder & Elbow-H3, BackRelief,
Cartilage/Ligament/Muscle/Skeletal Support
Formula, HipGuard, Joint Guard, Ligament
Drops, Nutritional Blood Test (NBT),
Osteoarthritis-H20, Pain Drops, Pain Formula

Earth Animal
606 Post Road East
Westport, CT 06880
Mail Order: (800) 622-0260
Telephone: (203) 222-7173
Fax: (203) 227-8094
www.earthanimal.com
Product: Achy Joints, K-9 Liquid Health, No
More Pain, Anaflora Return to Joy

Nutramax Laboratories, Inc.
2208 Lakeside Boulevard
Edgewood, MD 21040
Telephone: (410) 776-4000
Fax: (410) 776-4009
www.cosamin.com
Product: Cosequin

Vetri-Science Laboratories
Telephone (800) 882-9993
Fax: (802) 878-0549
E-mail: info@vetriscience.com
www.vetriscience.com
Product: Glycoflex

Pancreatic Diseases

Animal Nutrition Technologies
606 Post Road East
Westport, CT 06880
Telephone: (203) 341-8875
Veterinary Information Line: (888) 533-5162
Fax: 203-227-8094
E-mail: antnutrition@yahoo.com
www.animalnutritiontechnologies.com
Products: Diabetes Drops, Hypothalamus Drops,
Nutritional Blood Test (NBT), Pain Formula,
Pancreas Drops, Pancreas Endocrine/Exocrine
Support Formula, Pancreatitis

Dr. Goodpet
P.O. Box 4547
Inglewood, CA 90309
Telephone: (800) 222-9932
Email: info@goodpet.com
www.goodpet.com
Product: Digestive Enzymes

Enzymatic Therapy
825 Challenger Drive
Green Bay, WI 54311
Telephone: (800) 783-2286
www.enzy.com
Product: Pancreas Gland extract

Thyroid Diseases

Animal Nutrition Technologies
606 Post Road East
Westport, CT 06880
Telephone: (203) 341-8875
Veterinary Information Line: (888) 533-5162
Fax: 203-227-8094
E-mail: antnutrition@yahoo.com
www.animalnutritiontechnologies.com
Products: Hyperthyroid Formula H55,
Hypothalamus Drops, Hypothyroid Drops,
Hypothyroidism Formula H81, Nutritional Blood
Test (NBT), Thyroid Support Formula, Thyro
Drops

Chapter 9: Cancer

Anti-angiogenics

Allergy Research Group
30806 Santana Street
Hayward, CA 94544
Telephone: (800) 545-9960
Fax: (800) 688-7426
Product: VascuStatin

Antioxidant Supplement

Biovet International
3434 North Tamiami Trail, Suite 805
Sarasota, FL 34234
Telephone: 800-488-3899
Email: info@biovetinternational.com
Product: AOX-PLX

Chinese Herbal Medicine

Animal Nutrition Technologies
606 Post Road East
Westport, CT 06880
Telephone: (203) 341-8875
Veterinary Information Line: (888) 533-5162
Fax: 203-227-8094
E-mail: antnutrition@yahoo.com
www.animalnutritiontechnologies.com
Products: Chinese Herbal Formulas for Cancer

Solstice Medicine Co.
Los Angeles, CA 90033
Telephone: (888) 221-3496
www.sosusaco.com
Product: Yunnan Paiyao

COX-2 Inhibitors

Metagenics San Clemente
100 Ave La Pata
San Clemente, CA 92673
Telephone: (800) 692-9400
Product: Kaprex

Natura Health Products
249 "A" Street, Suite A
Ashland, Oregon 97520
Telephone: (888) 628-8720
Fax: (541) 482-3844
Email: info@naturahealthproducts.com
www.naturahealthproducts.com
Products: Corydalis PIS, Botanical Treasures

New Chapter

22 High Street
Brattleboro, VT 05301
Telephone: (800) 543-7279
Fax: (800) 470-0247
info@new-chapter.com
Product: Zyflamend

Essential Fatty Acids

Natura Health Products

249 "A" Street, Suite A
Ashland, Oregon 97520
Telephone: (888) 628-8720
Fax: (541) 482-3844
Email: info@naturahealthproducts.com
www.naturahealthproducts.com
Product: Beyond Essential Fats

Herbs

Natura Health Products

249 "A" Street, Suite A
Ashland, Oregon 97520
Telephone: (888) 628-8720
Fax: (541) 482-3844
Email: info@naturahealthproducts.com
www.naturahealthproducts.com
Product: Artemis Plus, Power Adapt, Vital Adapt

Homotoxicology

BHI/Heel

P.O. Box 11280
Albuquerque, NM 87192-0280
Telephone: (800) 621-7644
Fax: (505) 275-1672
Email: info@heelusa.com
www.heelbhi.com
Products: homotoxicology remedies

Natural Chemotherapeutics

AMARC Enterprises, Inc.

2778-J Sweetwater Springs Blvd #309
Spring Valley, CA 91977
Telephone: (866) POLY-MVA
www.poly-mva.com
Product: Poly-MVA

Nutritional Blood Test

Animal Nutrition Technologies

606 Post Road East
Westport, CT 06880
Telephone: (203) 341-8875
Veterinary Information Line: (888) 533-5162
Fax: 203-227-8094
E-mail: antnutrition@yahoo.com
www.animalnutritiontechnologies.com
*Products: Cancer Formula,
Immune/Autoimmune/Cancer Support Formula,
Immune Drops, Immune Formula, Pet Fraction,
Viral Immune Drops Formula*

Maitake Products Inc.
222 Bergen Tnpk
Ridgefiled Park, NJ 07660
Telephone: (201) 229-0101
www.maitake.com
Product: PET Fraction

Chapter 10: Understanding the Senior Years

Antech Diagnostics
Telephone: East Coast (800) 872-1001
West Coast (800) 745-4725
Test Express (888) 397-8378
www.antechdiagnostics.com
Service: Senior Wellness Program

BHI/Heel
P.O. Box 11280
Albuquerque, NM 87192-0280
Telephone: (800) 621-7644
Fax: (505) 275-1672
Email: info@heelusa.com
www.heelbhi.com
Products: homotoxicology remedies

Earth Animal
606 Post Road East
Westport, CT 06880
Mail Order: (800) 622-0260
Telephone: (203) 222-7173
Fax: (203) 227-8094
www.earthanimal.com
Products: Anaflora's Senior Formula, Clean Ear, Vision

Halo, Purely for Pets
3438 East Lake Road, #14
Palm Harbor, FL 34685
Telephone: (727) 937-3376
Fax: (727) 937-3955
www.halopets.com
Product: Natural Herbal Ear Wash

Chapter 11: Understanding and Treating Emotions, and Letting Go When It's Time

Animal Communicators

Laura Rowley
12090 NW 100th Street
Ocala, FL 34482
Telephone: (352) 369-5993

Sharon Callahan
Anaflora
P.O. Box 1056
Mt. Shasta, CA 96067
Telephone: (530) 926-6424
Fax: (530) 926-1245
E-mail: info@anaflora.com
www.anaflora.com

Flower Essences

Earth Animal
606 Post Road East
Westport, CT 06880
Mail Order: (800) 622-0260
Telephone: (203) 222-7173
Fax: (203) 227-8094
www.earthanimal.com
Products: Anaflora's flower essences

Where To Reach Dr. Bob and Susan

Healing Center for Animals
606 Post Road East
Westport, CT 06880
Telephone: (203) 227-4943
Fax: (203) 227-8094
E-mail: healingcenterforanimals@yahoo.com
www.healingcenterforanimals.com

References

Chapter 1

Animal Protection Institute, *Pet Food Investigative Report*, May 1996.

Association of Animal Feed Control Officials (AAFCO), Official Publication of the Association of American Feed Control Officials, Charles Frank, Dept of Agriculture, Capitol Square, Atlanta, GA.

Billinghurst, I. *Give Your Dog a Bone*. Ian Billinghurst Publishing, Lithgrow, N.S.W., Australia, 1993.

Billinghurst, I. "The Barf Diet." *Barfworld*, 2001.

Carque, O. *Vital Facts About Foods*. Keats Publishing, New Canaan, CT, 1975.

Cusick, W.D. *Canine Nutrition*. Doral Publishing, Wilsonville, OR, 1997.

Goldstein, R., VMD, Goldstein, S. "Super Foods." *Love of Animals*, Phillips Publishing, 1997.

Martin, A.N. *Foods Pets Die For.* New Sage Press, Troutdale, OR, 1997.

McKay, Pat. *Reigning Dogs and Cats*. Pat McKay Publishers, 1992.

Pottenger, FM, MD. "Pottenger's Cats—A Study in Nutrition." The Price Pottenger Nutrition Foundation, Inc., PO Box 2614, La Mesa, CA 92041.

Schultz, Kymythy. *Natural Nutrition for Dogs and Cats*. Hay House, Carlsbad, CA, 1998.

Strombeck, D., DVM, PhD. *Home-Prepared Diets for Dogs and Cats*. Iowa State University Press, Ames, Iowa, 1999.

Chapter 2

Brown, L.P., DVM. "Vitamin C (Ascorbic Acid)—New Forms and Uses in Dogs." In the Proceeding of the North American Veterinary Conference, Orlando, FL, 1994.

Budwig, Johanna. *Flax Oil as a True Aid Against Arthritis, Heart Infarction, Cancer and Other Diseases*. Apple Publishing, Washington, 1994.

Erasmus, U. *Fats and Oils*. Alive Books, Vancouver, BC, Canada, 1986.

Holub, B. "The Role of Omega-3 Fatty Acids in Health and Disease." Proceeding of the 13th Annual American College of Veterinary Medicine, 1995.

Kendall, R.V. "Basic and Preventative Nutrition in the Cat, Dog and Horse." *Complementary and Alternative Medicine*, eds. Allen Schoen, Susan Wynn, Mosby, 1998, p.23.

Kendall, R. PhD. "Therapeutic Nutrition for the Cat, Dog and Horse." *Complementary and Alternative Veterinary Medicine*, eds. Allen Schoen, Susan Wynn, Mosby, St. Louis, MO, 1998, pp 53-74.

Chapter 3

American Animal Hospital Association. Position Statement on Vaccine Issues. The Report of the AAHA Canine Vaccine Task Force, 2003 (www.aahanet.org).

AVMA, Council on Biologic and Therapeutic Agents (COBTA), April 2001 (www.avma.org).

Coulter, Harris L., Fisher, Barbara Loe. *A Shot in the Dark*. Avery Publishers, Garden City, 1991.

"Current Concepts–Are We Vaccinating Too Much?" *Journal of American Veterinary Medical Association*, 4:207, p 421, 1995.

Compton Burnett. *Vaccinosis and its Cure by Thuga*. New Delhi: B. Jain, 1990, p 16-17.

Day, C. *The Homeopathic Treatment of Small Animals*. Saffron Walden, CW Daniels, 1990.

Day, C. "Clinical Trials in Bovine Mastitis Using Nosodes for Prevention." *Journal of International Association of Veterinary Homeopathy*, 1:15, 1986.

Day, C. "Isopathic Prevention of Kennel Cough—Is Vaccination Justified?" *Journal of International Association of Veterinary Homeopathy*, 2:1, 1987.

Dodds, W.J. "Vaccine-Related Issues," Complementary and Alternative Veterinary Medicine, Principles and Practice, by Allen Schoen, DVM, and Susan G. Wynn. Mosby, St. Louis, MO, 1998, p.701.

Dodds, W.J. "Vaccine associated disease in young Weimaraners," Proceedings of the American Holistic Veterinary Medical Association, 1995.

Dodds, W.J. "Immune-mediated Disease of the Blood." *Adv. Vet. Sci. Comp. Med.*, 27:163, 1983.

Dodds, W.J. "Vaccine, Drug and Chemical-mediated Immune Reactions in Purebreds Challenging Researchers," *DVM Magazine*, 21:41, 1990.

Duval, D., and U. Geiger. "Vaccine-associated, Immune-mediated Hemolytic Anemia in the Dog." *Vet. Int. Med.*,10:290, 1996.

DVM Round Table Discussion, "Measles Vaccine: A Different Perspective." *DVM Newsmagazine*, 20(1): 33, 1989.

Esplin, D.G., and R. Campbell. "Widespread Metastasis of a Fibrosarcoma Associated with a Vaccination Site in a Cat." *Feline Practice* 23:1 p 13, 1995.

Goldstein, Martin, DVM. *The Nature of Animal Healing*. Knopf Publishing, New York, 1999.

Halliwell, Richard, and Neil Gorman. *Veterinary Clinical Immunology*. WB Saunders, Philadelphia, 1989.

Kalokerinos, A. and G. Dettman. "Second Thoughts About Disease: A Controversy and Bechamp Revisited." *The Journal of the International Academy of Preventive Medicine*, July 1977.

Macy, D.W. and J. Bergman. "Vaccine Associated Sarcomas in Cats." *Feline Practice*, 23:4, 1995.

McCluggage, D.M., "Vaccinations in Veterinary Medicine–A New Perspective." *J. of Amer. Hol. Vet. Med. Assoc.*, 14:2, p 7, 1995.

McMillen, G.L., Briggs, D.J., McVey, D.S., Phillips, R.M., Jordan, F.R., "Vaccination of Racing Greyhounds: Effects on Humoral and Cellular Immunity." *Veterinary Immunology an Immunology*. Elsevier Science B.V., 1995.

Mockett, A., Stahl, M., "Comparing How Puppies With Passive Immunity Respond to Three Canine Parvovirus Vaccines." *Vet. Med.*, p 430, May 1995.

Olson, P., et al, "Serum antibody response to canine parvovirus, canine adenovirus-1 and canine distemper in dogs with known states of immunization: study of dogs in Sweden," *American Journal of Veterinary Research*, pp 1460-66, 1988.

Ibid, *Journal of Veterinary Internal Medicine*, 11:148, 1997.

Phillips, T, Shultz, R., "Canine and Feline Vaccines," *Kirk's Veterinary Therapy XI: Small Animal Practice*, p. 205, 1990.

Pitcairn, Richard. "Homeopathic Alternatives to Vaccines." *Proc. Amer. Hol. Vet. Med Assoc.*, p 39, 1993.

Tizard, J., "Risks Associated With the Use of Live Vaccines." *J. of the Amer. Med. Assoc.*, 196:1851, 1990.

Vaccine Adverse Event Reporting System (VAERS) – 7-90 through 6-98, National Vaccine Information Center, 512 W. Maple Ave., #206, Vienna, VA, 22180 (800-909-7468).

Wynn S.G. and W.J. Dodds. "Vaccine associated disease in a family of young Akitas." Proceedings of the American Holistic Veterinary Medical Association, 1995.

Chapter 4

Bach, E. *Bach Flower Remedies, Heal Thyself, The Twelve Healers*, Bach Remedy Repertory. Keats Publishing., New Canaan, CT, 1952.

Brockman, K., *The Brockman Work, The Use of Serum Venous Analysis to Establish Individual Nutritional Profiles*, Undated.

Callahan, Sharon. *Healing Animals Naturally with Flower Essences and Intuitive Listening.* Sacred Spirit Publishing. Mt. Shasta, CA, 2001.

Callahan, Sharon. *Flower Essences For Animals.* Sacred Spirit Publishing, Mt. Shasta, CA, 1997.

Cima, J. Biochemical Bloodwork Evaluation, North Palm Beach, FL., 1981.

Day, C. *The Homeopathic Treatment of Small Animals.* Saffron, Walden, CW Daniels, 1990.

Day, C. "Veterinary Homeopathy Principles and Practice." *Complementary and Alternative Medicine.* Eds. Allen Schoen, Susan Wynn, Mosby, 1998.

DeGuzman, E. "Western Herbal Medicine: Clinical Applications." *Complementary and Alternative Medicine*, Allen Scoen, Susan Wynn, Mosby, p 337-378, 1998.

Duke, J., duCellier, J., Beckstrom-Sternberg, S. "Western Herbal Medicine: Traditional Materia Medica." *Complementary and Alternative Medicine*, Allen Schoen, Susan Wynn, Mosby, p 299-236, 1998.

Dharmananda, S., *Bag of Pearls.* Institute for Traditional Medicine and Preventive Health Care, Portland, OR, 1989.

Grosjean, Nelly, *Veterinary Aromatherapy*. C.W. Daniels Company, 2004.

Hamilton, D., DVM. *Homeopathic Care for Cats and Dogs*. North Atlantic Books, Berkeley CA, 1999.

Heinerman, J. *Natural Pet Cures*. Prentice Hall, Paramus, NJ, 1998.

Higley, Connie and Alan. *Reference Guide for Essential Oils*. Abundant Health, 1998.

Hutchens, A., *Indian Herbology of North America*. Merco, Ontario, Canada, 1969.

Kroeger, H., Instant Herb Locator, Boulder, CO (800-206-6722).

Lin, J.H., Rogers, P., Yamada, H. "Botanical Medicine." *Complementary and Alternative Medicine*. Allen Schoen, Susan Wynn, Mosby, p 379-404, 1998.

Lust, J. *The Herb Book*. Bantam Press, New York, 1987.

Mabey, R. *The New Age Herbalist*. MacMillan, New York, 1988.

Mills, S. *The Essential Book of Herbal Medicine*. Arkana, London, 1991.

Mowry, D. *The Scientific Validation of Herbal Medicine*. Keats Publishing, New Canaan, CT, 1986.

Murray, M. *The Healing Power of Herbs*. Prima Press, Rocklin, CA, 1995.

Null, G., Herbs for the Seventies. Robert Speller and Sons, New York, 1972.

Pert, Candace. *Molecules of Emotion: Why You Feel the Way You Feel*. Scribner, New York, 1999.

Reckeweg, H. *Homotoxicology*. Menaco Publishing, Albuquerque, NM, 1989.

Reilly, D. et al. "Is evidence for homeopathy reproducible?" *The Lancet*, December 10, 1994.

Schwartz, C. *Four Paws, Five Directions*. Berkeley: Celestial Arts, 1996.

Tellington-Jones, Linda. *Getting in TTouch With Your Dog*. Trafalgar Square Publishing, London, 2002.

Tellington-Jones, Linda. *Getting In TTouch with Your Cat*. Trafalgar Square Publishing, London, 2003.

Tellington-Jones, Linda. *The Tellington TTouch: A Breakthrough Technique to Train and Care for Your Favorite Animal*. Penguin, New York, 1995.

Tierra, M. *American Herbalism: Essays on Herbs and Herbalism by Members of the American Herbalist Guild*. The Crossing Press, Freedom, CA, 1992.

Tilford, M.L., Tilford, G.L., ed. *Herbs for Pets*. Bow Tie Press, Irvine, CA, 1999.

Chapter 6

Dudley, K. "Eliminate Fleas without Poisons: Integrative Pest Management is a Non-Toxic Way to Effectively Control Fleas." *Whole Dog Journal* 5, March 2002.

Goldstein, R., VMD Goldstein, S. "Flea Free Forever." *Love of Animals*, Phillips Publishing, 1997.

Chapter 8

Broek, A., Thoday, K. "Skin Disease in the Dog Associated with Zinc Deficiency: A Report of Five Cases." *J. of Small Animal Pract.*, 27: 313, 1986.

Brown, L.P., "Ester-C for Joint Discomfort – A Study," *Natural Pet*, Nov/Dec., 1994.

Cenacchi, T., et al., "Cognitive Decline in the Elderly: A Double-Blind, Placebo-controlled Study on the Efficacy of Phosphatidylserine Administration." *Aging Clin. Exp. Res.*, 5:123-133, 1993.

Dodd, W.J. "Auto Immune Thyroid Disease." *Dog World* 77(5), 1992.

Folkers, K., et al. "Biochemical Rationale and Mitochondrial Tissue Data on the Effective Therapy of Cardiomyopathy with Coenzyme Q10." *Proc. Nat'l. Acad. Sci.*, 82: 901, 1985.

Folkers, K., and Y. Yamancria, eds. "Biomedical and Clinical Aspect of Coenzyme Q10." Fifth Edition. Elsevier, N.Y., 1986.

Goldstein, R., VMD Goldstein, S. "Treating the 14 Most feared Diseases." *Love of Animals*, Phillips Publishing, 1997.

Levin, C.D. *Dogs, Diet and Disease: An Owners Guide to Diabetes Mellitus, Pancreatitis, Cushings Disease and More*. Lantern Publications, 2001.

Levine, Caroline. Canine *Epilepsy: An Owners Guide to Living With and Without Seizures*, Lantern Publications, 2002.

Logas, G., Kunkle, G.A., "Double-blind Crossover Study with Marine Oil Supplementation Containing High-dose Eicosapentaenoic Acid for the Treatment of Canine Prurutic Skin Disease." *Vet. Derm.* 5: 99, 1994.

Messonier, S., DVM. *The Allergy Solution for Dogs*, Prima Publications, 2000.

Morris, J.G., Q.R. Rogers, and L.M. Pacioretty. "Taurine: An Essential Nutrient for Cats." *J. Sm. Anim . Practice*, 1989.

Nerozzi, D., et al. "Early Cortisol Escape Phenomenon Reversed by Phosphatidylserine in Elderly Normal Subjects."

Pion, P.D., M.D. Kittleson, M.L. Skiles, and J.G. Morris. "Dilated Cardiomyopathy Associated with Taurine Deficiencies in the Domestic Cat: Relationship of Diet and Myocardial Taurine Content." *Advances in Experimental Medicine and Biology*, 315:63-73, 1992.

Reinhart, G.A., "A Controlled Dietary Omega-6: Omega-3 Ratio Reduces Pruritus in Nonfood Allergic Atopic Dogs," Recent Advances in Canine and Feline Nutritional Research: Iams Proceedings, p 277, 1996.

Theodosakis, J., Adderly, B., Fox, B. *The Arthritis Cure*. St. Martins Press, NY, 1997.

Tilley, L., Smith, F.W.K. *The 5-Minute Veterinary Consult*, Lippincott, Williams and Wilkins, 2001.

Vaz, A.L. "Double-blind Clinical Evaluation of the Relative Efficacy of Ibuprofen and Glucosamine Sulfate in the Management of Osteoarthrosis of the Knee in Outpatients." *Curr. Med. Res. Opin.*, 8:145- 149, 1982.

Chapter 9

Belfield, W.O. "Megascorbic Prophylaxis and Megascorbic Therapy: A New Orthomolecular Modality in Veterinary Medicine," *J. of Int. Acad. of Prev. Med.*, 11(25), 1975.

Belfield, W.O. "An Orthomolecular Approach to Feline Leukemia Prevention and Control," *J. of Int Acad. of Prev. Med.*, 8(3): 40, 1983.

Budwig, J. *Flax Oil as a True Aid Against Arthritis, Heart Infarction, Cancer and Other Diseases*. Apple Publ., Vancouver, 1992.

Cameron, E., Pauling, L. "Vitamin C and Cancer." *Int'l. J. of Environmental Studies*, 75: 4538, 1977.

Diamond, J.W., MD, Cowder, L.C., MD, Goldberg, B. *An Alternative Medicine Definitive Guide to Cancer*, Future Medicine Publishing, Tiburon, CA 1997.

Folkman, J. "Tumor Antiogenesis: Therapeutic Implication." *N. England J. of Med.*, 285: 1182, 1971.

Garnett, M., MD. *First Pulse – A Personal Journey in Cancer Research*. First Pulse Projects, NY, 1998.

Goldstein, R., Goldstein, S. "Cancer – Three Part Series," *Love of Animals*, Earth Animal, 2000.

Kurth, Neumann, and Reinhart. "Homeopathic Remedies Prolong the Lives of Dogs That Have Undergone Cancer Surgery." *Der praktische Tierarzt* 2000; 81 (4) 276-291.

Lane, W., Comac, L. *Sharks Don't Get Cancer*. Avery Publ., Group, 1992.

Larocca, L.M., et al. "Growth-Inhibitory Effect of Quercitin and Presence of Type II Binding Sites in Primary Human Transitional Cell Carcinoma." *J. of Urology*, 152, 3:1029, 1994.

Meyskens, F.L., "Prevention and Treatment of Cancer with Vitamin A and the Retinoids, Vitamins," *Nutrition and Cancer*, Prosad, K.N., Karger, Basil, Switz., eds., 1984.

"Effect of Maitake D-fraction on Cancer Prevention." *Annals of the New York Academy of Science*, Vol.833, Dec.29, 1997, p.204-207.

"The Chemical Structure of an Antitumor Polysaccharide in Fruit Bodies of *Grifola frondosa* (maitake) Chem. Pharm." Bull.35(3):P.1162-1168 (1987).

"Antitumor activity of orally administered D-fraction from Maitake mushroom (Grifola frondosa)" *Journal of Naturopathic Medicine*, 1993, Vol. 4, No. 1, p.10-15.

"Activity of Maitake D-fraction to Inhibit Carcinogenesis and Metastasis." *Annals of the New York Academy of Sciences*, Volume 768, September 30, 1995, p.243-245.

"Maitake D-fraction: Healing and Preventive Potential for Cancer." *Journal of Orthomolecular Medicine*, vol. 12, No. 1, First Quarter, 1997, P.43-49.

Morrison, W.B. DVM, MS. *Cancer in the Dog and Cat*, Lippincot, Williams and Wilkins, 1998.

Moss, R.W. *Questioning Chemotherapy*. Equinox Press, Brooklyn, NY, 1995.

Ogilvie, G. "Nutritional Therapy for the Cancer Patient." College of Veterinary Medicine, Colorado State University, Ft. Collins, CO.

Ogilvie, G. "Nutritional Approaches to Cancer Therapy." *Complementary and Alternative Medicine*, eds. Allen Schoen, Susan Wynn, p 93, Mosby, 1998.

Prudden, J.L. Balassa, L.L., "The Biological Activity of Bovine Cartilage Preparations." Seminars in Arthritis and Rheumatism, 4: 287-321, 1974.

Prudden, J.L. "The Treatment of Human Cancer with Agents Prepared from Bovine Cartilage"

J. of Biological Response Modifiers, 4: 583, 1985.

Riordan N, Meng X, Riordan H. "Anti-angiogenic, anti-tumor and immunostimulatory effects of a non-toxic plant extract (PGM)." *Comprehensive Cancer Care* 2000.

Ranelletti, F.O., et al. "Growth Inhibitory Effect of Quercitin and Presence of Type II Estrogen Binding Sites in Human Colon Cancer Cell Lines and Primary Colorectal Tumors." *Int'l J. of Cancer*, 50: 3 486-492, 1992.

Richard, Eveleen. Vitamin C *and Cancer: Medicine or Politics*. Palgrave: Macmillan, 1991.

Scambia, G., et al. "Quercitin Potentiates the Effect of Adriamycin in a Multi-drug Resistant MCF-7 Human Breast Cancer Line." *Cancer Chemotherapy and Pharmacology* 6: 459-64, 1994.

Shklar, G., et al. "Regression by Vitamin E or Experimental Oral Cancer." *J. of the Nat'l. Cancer Inst.*, 78:5 987-992, 1987.

Sun, T. "The Role of Traditional Chinese Medicine in the Supportive Care of Cancer Patients." *Recent Results in Cancer Research*, 108:327-344, 1988.

Thomas, R. "The Essiac Report," Alternative Treatment, Information Network. Los Angeles, CA, 1993.

Yance, D., *Herbal Medicine and Cancer*. Keats Publishing, New Canaan, CT, 1999.

Suggested Reading

Anderson, N., Peiper, H. *Are You Poisoning You Pets?* Safe Goods, E. Canaan, CT, 1995.

Anderson, N., Peiper, H. *Super Nutrition for Animals*. Safe Goods, E. Canaan, CT, 1996.

Brennan, M. *The Natural Dog*. Plume Publishing, NY, 1994.

Flaim, Denise. *The Holistic Dog Book: Canine Care for the 21st Century*, Howell Book House, NY, 2003.

Frazier, A., Eckroate, N. *The Natural Cat*. Kampmann and Co., 1983.

Goldstein, M. *The Nature of Animal Healing, The Definitive Holistic Medicine Guide to Caring for your Dog and Cat*, Ballantine, NY, 1999.

Heinerman, J. *Natural Pet Cures*. Prentice Hall, Paramus, NJ, 1998.

Howell, E. *Enzyme Nutrition: The Food Enzyme Concept*. Avery Publishing, Garden City, NY, 1985.

Kubler Ross, E., MD. *Death and Dying*, Ross

Medical Associates, Touchstone, NY, 1974.

Lazarus, P. *Keep Your Cat Healthy The Natural Way*. Fawcett Books, NY, 1999.

Lazarus, P. *Keep Your Dog Healthy The Natural Way*. Fawcett Books, NY, 1999.

Kroeger, H. *Instant Herb Locator*. Boulder, CO (800-206-6722).

Messonnier, S. *8 Weeks to a Healthy Dog, An Easy to Follow Program for the Life of you Dog*, Rodale, 2003.

Messonnier, S. *Natural Health Bible for Dogs and Cats*, Prima Publications, Roseville, CA., 2001.

Mindell, E.R. *Earl Mindell's Nutrition for a Healthy Dog*. Prima Publishing, Rocklin CA, 1998.

Null, G. *Natural Pet Care*, Seven Stories Press, NY 2000.

Pitcairn, R., Pitcairn, S. *Natural Health for Dogs and Cats*. Rodale Press, Emmaus, PA, 1995.

Puotinen, C.J. *The Encyclopedia of Natural Pet Care*. Keats Publishing, 1998.

Selye, H. *Stress in Health and Disease*. Buttersworth, London, England, 1976.

Schoen, A. *Love, Miracles, and Animal Healing*, Simon & Shuster, NY, 1995.

Schwartz, C. *Four Paws, Five Directions*. Celestial Arts, Berkeley, CA. 1996.

Siegal, B. *Love, Medicine and Miracles*. Harper, Row, NY, 1986.

Stein, D. *Natural Healing for Dogs and Cats*. The Crossing Press, Freedom, CA, 1993.

Stein, D. *The Natural Remedy Book for Dogs and Cats*. The Crossing Press, Freedom, CA, 1994.

Volhard, W., Brown, K., DVM. *Holistic Guide for a Healthy Dog*, Howell Book House, Forest City, CA, 2000.

Werbach, M. MD. *The Nutritional Influences on Illness*, 2nd Edition, Third Line Press, Tarzana, CA, 1996.

Wright, J.R. *Diagnosis: Cancer Prognosis: ~~Death~~ LIFE, The Story of Dr. Lawrence Burton*. Albright and Co., Huntsville, Alabama.

Zucker, M. *Veterinarians Guide to Natural Remedies for Cats*. Three River Press, NY, 1999.

Zucker, M. *Veterinarians Guide to Natural Remedies for Dogs*. Three River Press, NY, 1999.

Alternative Veterinary Newsletters

Love of Animals
606 Post Road East
Westport, CT 06880
Telephone: (800) 622-0260
www.earthanimal.com

The Whole Dog Journal
Belvoir Media Group
800 Connecticut Avenue
Norwalk, CT 06854
Telephone: (203) 857-3100
www.whole-dog-journal.com

Resources and Organizations

Academy of Veterinary Homeopathy
P.O. Box 9280
Wilmington, Delaware 19809
Telephone/Fax: (866) 652-1590
www.theavh.org

American Academy of Veterinary Acupuncture (AAVA)
100 Roscommon Drive, Suite 320
Middletown, CT 06457
Telephone: (860) 635-6300
Fax: (860) 635-6400
E-mail: office@aava.org
www.aava.org

American Animal Hospital Association (AAHA)
12575 W. Bayaud Ave.
Lakewood, CO 80228
Telephone: (303) 986-2800
Fax: (303) 986-1700
E-mail: info@aahanet.org
www.aahanet.org

American Holistic Veterinary Medical Association
2218 Old Emmorton Road
Bel Air, MD 21015
Telephone: (410) 569-0795
www.ahvma.org

American Veterinary Chiropractic Association (AVCA)
442154 E 140 Road
Bluejacket, OK 74333
Telephone: (918) 784-2231
Fax: (918) 784-2643
www.animalchiropractic.org

American Veterinary Medical Association (AVMA)
1931 North Meacham Road, Suite 100
Schaumburg, IL 60173
Telephone: (847) 925-8070
Fax: (847) 925-1329
E-mail: avmainfo@avma.org
www.avma.org

British Institute of Homeopathy (BIH)

580 Zion Road
Egg Harbor Township, NJ 08234-9606
Telephone: (609) 927-5660
Email: info@bihusa.com
www.bihusa.com

Institute for Traditional Medicine (ITM)

Seven Forests 2017 S.E. Hawthorne
Portland, OR 97214
Telephone: (503) 233-4907
Fax: (503) 233-1017
www.itmonline.org

International Veterinary Acupuncture Society (IVAS)

P.O. Box 271395
Ft. Collins, CO 80527
Phone: (970) 266-0666
Fax: (970) 266-0777
E-mail: office@ivas.org
www.ivas.org

Morris Animal Foundation

45 Inverness Drive East
Englewood, CO 80112
Telephone: (800) 243-2345
Fax: (303) 790-4066
www.morrisanimalfoundation.org

National Center for Homeopathy (NCH)

801 N Fairfax #301
Alexandria, VA 22314
Telephone: (703) 548-7790
Fax: (703) 548-7792
Email: info@homeopathic.org
www.homeopathic.org

National Vaccine Information Center

421-E Church Street
Vienna, VA 22180
Telephone: (703) 938-0342
Fax: (703) 938-5768
www.909shot.com

Index

Photos courtesy of Robert Pearcy